Duane
♡ W9-CUC-193

from

Mother + Dad

" Merry Christmas -1968

To Suzanne.
With lots of love.
The Collinwood residents and staff

23 July, 2016

Pictorial Checklist
of
Colorado Birds

with brief notes on the status of each species in neighboring
states of Nebraska, Kansas, New Mexico, Utah, and Wyoming

by

Alfred M. Bailey

and

Robert J. Niedrach

Published by the
DENVER MUSEUM OF NATURAL HISTORY
1967

Four color letterpress engravings by Mueller-Krus Corporation of Milwaukee, Wisconsin.
Typesetting, printing, cover, and binding by NAPCO, Inc. of Milwaukee, Wisconsin.
Color plates printed on 80# Lustro Gloss, and the rest of the book on 60# Napcopaque.
Type used for records and other data 9 pt. Caledonia, and the narrative 11 pt. Caledonia.

TABLE OF CONTENTS

DR. PERSIFOR M. COOKE, A TRUSTEE OF THE DENVER MUSEUM OF NATURAL HISTORY
FOR NEARLY HALF A CENTURY, SAW THREE WINGS AND BEAUTIFUL PHIPPS AUDITORIUM
ADDED TO THE ORIGINAL BUILDING (1908) SHOWN IN THE MONTAGE ABOVE.

BRISTLECONE PINE
Typical timberline tree of the Colorado High Country

PREFACE

This *Pictorial Checklist of Colorado Birds* is a condensation of the Museum's two-volume *Birds of Colorado* by Alfred M. Bailey and Robert J. Niedrach, off the press in late December 1965. Illustrated with 124 beautiful color plates, the data in *Birds of Colorado* cover the records and life histories of the many species of birds occurring in the varied habitats of the state.

The authors worked together for more than forty years; they roamed from the plains to the tops of high mountains in all months of the year and as a consequence had personal experiences with the resident forms of birds in their natural environments. In *Birds of Colorado* Doctors Bailey and Niedrach discuss at length many interesting phases of natural history under the following chapters: Nomenclature, Geographic Distribution, Migration, Orientation, Hazards of Migration, and Pesticides.

Chapters referring specifically to Colorado include Historical Ornithological Work with brief notes on the activities of naturalists and collectors through the years, starting with Silvestre Velez de Escalante who reported upon Blue Grouse under date of August 26, 1776. Other chapters are: Topography, Colorado Rivers, Climate, Life Zones, Typical Plant Associations in Colorado, Days Afield (narrative of field work), Bird Migration in Colorado, and Spring and Christmas Counts. Following this comprehensive information are the data covering records, observations, and life history notes of the 439 species listed.

Because of the beauty of the color illustrations and the great interest of thousands of amateur naturalists in field work, the Trustees of the Museum requested the authors to prepare a book with all color plates in one volume, using (with necessary changes) accompanying data from *Birds of Colorado* which would include accepted common and scientific names, descriptions of the birds and their ranges, and a brief account of the status of each species in Colorado and neighboring states.

The Trustees of the Denver Museum of Natural History wish to express their appreciation to the authors for their fine contributions to the literature covering Colorado birds.

HUDSON MOORE, JR.
President of the Board of Trustees

SKYLINE SHOWING MOUNT EVANS FROM DENVER MUSEUM

FOREWORD

The *Pictorial Checklist of Colorado Birds*—with brief notes on the status of each species and subspecies in the neighboring states of Nebraska, Kansas, New Mexico, Utah, and Wyoming—is a verbatim condensation, except for necessary changes and additions, of portions of the two-volume *Birds of Colorado*. Published by the Denver Museum of Natural History in 1965, *Birds of Colorado* is illustrated profusely with more than 400 black and white photographs and with 124 plates showing in color 420 species of Colorado birds—by 23 artists, among them outstanding bird artists of the world. The two volumes contain 895 pages of copy and photographs plus color plates with accompanying data for a total of 1175 pages. Four hundred and thirty-nine species and 64 subspecies are discussed under the following headings:

RECOGNITION.—A brief description of each species or subspecies is given, and characters serving to separate one form from another have been italicized. No attempt has been made at thorough coverage of plumages, for such information is readily available elsewhere, and the majority of birds mentioned are shown in spring dress in the 124 color plates made from original water color paintings by some of the foremost artists of Canada, Great Britain, and this country. The average person is eye-minded, and the illustrations in color should do more to aid in the identification of adult birds than any word description. Many field naturalists are so familiar with the songs of birds that they are able to recognize species by sounds alone; but in the present work, no detailed description of songs or calls has been attempted.

RANGE.— A brief statement is given of breeding and wintering areas of each species, as condensed from the 1957 edition of the A.O.U. Check-list, and, in addition, occurrences in neighboring states have been briefly noted, for the majority of species listed in the following pages have been recorded from Nebraska, Kansas, New Mexico, Utah, and Wyoming. Nebraska records have been taken from the *Revised Check-list of Nebraska Birds* (Rapp, Rapp, Baumgarten, and Moser, 1958), with additional notes supplied by Doris Gates; Kansas data have been summarized from the *Check-list of the Birds of Kansas* (H. B. Tordoff, 1956), and the *Directory to the Bird-life of Kansas* (R. F. Johnston, 1960), with added information from L. B. Carson, D. F. Parmelee, Max C. Thompson, and Mrs. A. R. Challans; New Mexico records have been gleaned from the two state books, the first by Florence Merriam Bailey (1928), and the other by J. S. Ligon (1961); the Utah records are from the *Check-list of the Birds of Utah* (W. H. Behle, 1944), with supplemental information received from him and others in personal communications; and the data from Wyoming, except as noted, were supplied by Dr. Oliver K. Scott.

COLORADO.—Under this heading is indicated the relative abundance in the state of each species in its preferred habitat at the proper time of year, with dates of observations and records listed in the literature.

The above format has been used in this Pictorial Checklist, but Colorado records have been summarized only, except for birds uncommon in the state. Specific data are available for each species in the notes under COLORADO or in the life history narratives published in the two-volume *Birds of Colorado* (1965).

Where new data have been added or there has been a change of copy, the sources of information are given. The bibliography is a selective one, condensed from the 33 pages in *Birds of Colorado* which cite 400 authors and list 1120 publications. An extensive Gazetteer of Colorado place names will be found in the latter publication, as well as the many references mentioned in this book but not included in the bibliography.

During recent years there has been an expanding popular interest in field observations of birds, due in large part to the influence and encouragement of the National Audubon Society, the various state ornithological organizations, the garden clubs, the field activities of bird-banding associations, and local natural history groups. The Colorado Field Ornithologists, the Denver Field Ornithologists, the Aiken Ornithological Society, the Boulder, Fort Collins and Longmont Bird Clubs, with many trained naturalists, enthusiastic amateurs, and individuals who merely enjoy a day afield —all have contributed greatly in assembling state records. Many of these "birders" are skilled in recognizing the characteristic identification marks as listed in the popular guides, and they also are ear-conscious, being able to identify birds by their voices. As a result, thousands of reports of Colorado birds have been made, based upon sight or sound. In times past, *sight records* have been considered unreliable, and relegated to hypothetical lists, or ignored. No longer is this desirable, it seems to us, for the day of intensive general collecting of specimens in this country is over; there are large series of bird skins available for study in various museums and in private hands, and, as a consequence, collecting in the future will be the exception rather than the rule. Scientific investigations in ornithology will be based not only upon the study of skins already secured, and future *selective* collecting, but on information derived from banding, photography, the recording of bird sounds, and through the reports of many skilled field ornithologists.

Consequently, instead of arbitrarily demanding a specimen as proof of an occurrence, we have adopted the policy of accepting sight records, made by competent observers, of well-marked and easily recognized species, even though the birds may be far from their normal ranges—but we have required specimens of *races* for which field identifications would be difficult.

In regard to identifications, a paragraph from "Wake Robin" by John Burroughs is of interest. He had been discussing the thrills of observing birds in the field and then added:

> But let me say, in the same breath, that the books can by no manner of means be dispensed with. A copy of Wilson or Audubon, for reference and to compare notes with, is invaluable. In lieu of these, access to some large museum or collection would be a great help. In the beginning, one finds it very difficult to identify a bird from any verbal description. Reference to a colored plate, or to a stuffed specimen, at once settles the matter. This is the chief value of the books; they are charts to sail by; the route is mapped out, and much time and labor thereby saved. *First find your bird; observe its ways, its songs, its calls, its flight, its haunts; then shoot it (not ogle it with a glass), and compare with Audubon. In this way the feathered kingdom may soon be conquered* (italics ours).

SCOPE OF WORK

This *Pictorial Checklist* records briefly the status in Colorado and neighboring states of 441 bird species and 64 additional races, all the latter based on specimens examined by the authors, a total for Colorado of 505 species and subspecies. Of the 441 species, 109 are present the year around and 138 are summer residents for a total of 247 breeding species within the state; 54 are migratory with only occasional individuals occurring in summer or winter; 30 are winter residents; 110 are stragglers which have been reported a few times only. Forty species have been marked with asterisks to indicate the records are based upon observations, or that we have been unable to locate the specimens.

The nomenclature used in this book is based upon the fifth edition of the A.O.U. *Check-list of North American Birds*, published in 1957 by a committee for the American Ornithologists' Union. In the previous edition, which appeared more than a quarter of a century earlier, in 1931, English names were given to all species and subspecies, but in the latest Check-list, common names for races were dropped. The use of English designations for *species only* is in line with general practice of recent years, since differences between subspecies often are minute and are not readily discernible, even when specimens are available for study.

ACKNOWLEDGMENTS

The authors wish to express their appreciation to the Trustees of the Denver Museum of Natural History who sponsored the publication of *Birds of Colorado* and have underwritten the costs of this condensation, and to the many naturalists of Colorado who have provided recent records. Special recognition should be given to field ornithologists Allegra Collister, Sam Gadd, Harold Holt, Nancy Hurley, Thompson G. Marsh, Mr. and Mrs. George R. Shier, Charles and Mildred Snyder, Donald M. Thatcher, Lois Webster and to Patricia Bailey Witherspoon, daughter of AMB, who spent many hours in photographic blinds to secure pictures and record life history notes.

Several members of the Museum staff contributed to the completion of this Pictorial Checklist, and the authors are indebted to Administrative Assistant Julia Smead Rose and to Margaret Denny and Norma Lovelace for their painstaking editorial work, to Curator of Photography Robert R. Wright, and to staff member Donald L. Malick who painted many of the beautiful plates.

ALFRED M. BAILEY

ROBERT J. NIEDRACH

COLORADO

TOPOGRAPHY

Colorado is considered a western state, although it is barely two-thirds of the way across the continent. The 40th North parallel and the 105th meridian West cross near Denver; the state is approximately three hundred and seventy-five miles wide from east to west, two hundred and seventy-five miles north and south, and, except for Wyoming, is the only state bounded by four straight lines. The one spot in the country where four states have a common meeting place is in the southwest, where Colorado, Arizona, New Mexico, and Utah join—at the "Four Corners."

The eastern Great Plains gradually slope upward toward the west from an altitude of less than 3500 feet along the Kansas line to 5500 feet or more near the foothills. The prairies, treeless except along watercourses, merge with the scrub oak and ponderosa pine-clad slopes in the middle and northern sections of the state, and with pinyon and juniper country in the south and west. The easternmost Front Range of the Rockies is dominated by three fourteen thousand-foot mountains—Long's Peak in Rocky Mountain National Park, Mount Evans west of Denver, and Pikes Peak near Colorado Springs. Mount Blanca, to the southward in the Sangre de Cristo Range, is equally spectacular. North, Middle, and South Parks, and the San Luis Valley separate the Front Range from the rugged Park Range to the north and west, and the Sawatch Range to the south. In the latter are some of the well-known mountains, including Mt. Massive, the Mount of the Holy Cross, and Mount Elbert —the highest peak in the state (14,421 feet). In southwestern Colorado are the jagged San Juan Mountains. The Continental Divide from Wyoming follows down the Park Range, cuts eastward along the Rabbit Ears Range to the Front Range in Rocky Mountain National Park, and south where it is crossed by Berthoud, Loveland, and Hoosier Passes. The Divide turns west again to the Mosquito Range and along the Sawatch and Collegiate Ranges, Cochetopa Pass and southward along the crests of the San Juan Mountains.

The western third of the state is an elevated plateau, with flat-topped mesas crowned with pinyon, juniper, and ponderosa pine, cut with deep canyons which have eroded through the centuries. Many areas of great scenic interest are in this part of Colorado—the Black Canyon of the Gunnison, Grand Mesa, the Colorado National Monument with its worn sandstone cliffs, the Uncompahgre Plateau, and, to the southward, Mesa Verde, former home of the Cliff Dwellers who, nearly a thousand years ago, erected great apartment houses along precipitous walls.

COLORADO RIVERS

Although Colorado is a comparatively dry state, with an average of 16.5 inches of precipitation annually, and an occasional low of less than eight inches in the Denver area and on the eastern plains, heavy snows in the mountains usually result in great quantities of water cascading down the stream-beds in the spring runoff. Colorado has been known as the Mother of Rivers, for more major streams rise in its mountains than in any other state, except possibly in Alaska. On the western slope are the Colorado, the Yampa, the White, and the Dolores Rivers, while in the southwest is the San Juan. East of the Continental Divide are the North and South Platte Rivers, the Arkansas, the Republican, and the Arikaree Rivers—and the Rio Grande, rising on the eastern slope of the San Juan Mountains, tumbling into the San Luis Valley, eventually to make its way across New Mexico and along the Texas border into the Gulf of Mexico.

LIFE ZONES

Because of the diversified terrain of Colorado, with great changes in elevation from the rolling eastern prairie counties at an altitude of approximately 3500 feet to the tips of high peaks ranging above 14,000 feet, and the park, canyon, and mesa country west of the Continental Divide, conditions in the state are ideal for a varied plant life, and, consequently, of animals associated with each habitat. The virgin plains were grown with buffalo and grama grass, yucca, cactus, and many flowering plants, and the normally dry stream beds were lined with broad-leaved cottonwoods, willows, and associated shrubs. Today, where the lands have been unbroken by the plow, and not overgrazed, the vegetation is much the same. Rising gradually to 5500 feet, the prairies blend with scrub oak-covered foothills in northern and central counties, and in the south with pinyons and junipers.

Any naturalist traveling in Colorado from the plains into the mountains would be conscious of the change in plant life, and a corresponding difference in animals. It was Dr. C. H. Merriam (1890), working in the San Francisco Mountains of northern Arizona, who first suggested that plants and associated animals are distributed zonally according to *temperature*. He noted that as he ascended from the low deserts into the mountains, the forms of life differed from one elevation to another, and he reasoned that the height to which species of animals and plants thrived was dependent upon temperature. If this were true, these associations should range higher on warm, exposed southern slopes than on the shaded northern ones.

Merriam postulated that each species of life has certain requirements, and if conditions in one area should be duplicated elsewhere, related forms of life could be expected in both regions. He observed that there were plants, birds, mammals, reptiles, and insects in the hot canyons of Arizona that were much like species which occurred in similar environments in Mexico, and that climatic conditions on the tops of high mountains, due to altitude, were the same as those of arctic areas at sea level—altitude in the south being responsible for temperature conditions caused by latitude in northern regions. As a result, plants and associated animals on the mountain summits seemed generally similar to species which lived in the far north. Naturalists who have used Merriam's Life Zone concept as a basis for work have divided their study areas to meet their own requirements. North America, for instance, has been separated into three major faunal regions, Boreal (northern), Austral (southern), and Tropical. The latter, represented in the United States only in southern Florida and Texas, does not concern Colorado, and consequently has been eliminated in the following discussion. The Boreal, subdivided into three major zones—Alpine, Hudsonian, and Canadian—and the Austral into the Transition and Sonoran Zones are all well represented in this state. The zones vary greatly

YUCCA DOTTED PRAIRIE OF THE UPPER SONORAN ZONE

ASPEN AND PONDEROSA PINE IN THE TRANSITION ZONE

ECHO LAKE (10,600 FEET) IN THE CANADIAN ZONE

BRISTLECONE PINE (11,000 FEET) IN HUDSONIAN ZONE

in elevation, according to latitude and slope exposure, and those in Colorado range in altitude as follows:

Region	Zone	Altitude
	Arctic-Alpine	above 11,500 feet
Boreal	Hudsonian	11,000 to 11,500 feet
	Canadian	8000 to 11,000 feet
Austral	Transition	5500 to 8000 feet
	Upper Sonoran	3500 to 5500 feet

The plains and the warm canyons of the southern part of Colorado, grown with cactus, yucca, pinyon, and juniper, are in the Upper Sonoran, the Lower Sonoran of the southern deserts not occurring in the state. The plains rise gradually toward the west, merging with the foothills near Denver, at an elevation of around 5500 feet, where scrub oak, mountain mahogany, red squaw currant, three-leafed sumac, antelope brush, serviceberry, and thimbleberry are characteristic plants. Between the plains and the upper coniferous forests is the Transition Zone, consisting of a broad belt of ponderosa pine, Douglas fir, and aspen on the hillsides, and blue spruce, alder, and willow along the streams. It is a true transition area from the plains to the high mountains, poorly marked, with an intermingling of species of animals and plants which range down to the prairies and upward into the Canadian Zone.

Above the Transition Zone is the true Boreal Region with the lodgepole pines, characteristic trees of the lower part of the Canadian Zone, merging with broad stands of Engelmann spruce and subalpine fir which are dominant in the upper Canadian. The white fir is common from central Colorado to the southern part of the state at altitudes between 7000 and 10,000 feet. Stretches of beautiful aspens surrounded by dense evergreen forests are typical of the mountain slopes, and along the streams are willows, alders, and birches.

The Hudsonian Zone is not well-defined. It is the timberline area, a transition from the Canadian to the Arctic-Alpine Zone of the mountaintops—a region of stunted and wind-twisted trees, among them being the limber pines, age-old bristlecone pines, gnarled and stunted Engelmann spruce, and subalpine fir, oftentimes in little isolated islands surrounded with sprawling willows—all having been matted by the heavy winter snows.

Above the Hudsonian is the treeless alpine tundra, and in this Arctic-Alpine Zone many of the forms of life are related to those found in the far north, the three characteristic breeding birds of Colorado being ptarmigan, rosy finches, and pipits. As soon as the snows begin to melt in spring, rivulets pour down the mountainsides, and a tinge of green comes to the willows and other sprawling alpine vegetation. Then, as if by magic, the flowering plants follow the retreating snow fields—the alpine buttercup, marsh marigold, globe flower, Parry primrose, wand lily, mat plants with their tiny blossoms, and the fields of paintbrush, to name just a few. Late in the season the columbines grow among boulders of the rock slides where they are protected from the ever-blowing winds. In moist seasons there are many flowers on the mountaintops, each species in its preferred ecological niche, depending upon the soil, moisture, slope exposure, and altitude. Some species are widespread and others are so dependent upon certain conditions for their welfare that they are restricted to their own little havens.

Although Merriam's life zones are no longer generally used in discussing the distribution of animals and plants in this country, we have found the terminology a convenience in our work within the state, especially when referring to habitats and associations of animals at varying elevations. Consequently, the majority of bird species mentioned in the following pages are allocated to a specific life zone, or zones, or the zone is inferred by mentioning the favored habitats. It should be emphasized, however, that the type of *environment* preferred by each species is all-important, and not the *life zone*. Grasslands, for instance, are found on the prairies in the Upper Sonoran Zone at elevations

ALPINE ZONE NEAR SUMMIT LAKE (MOUNT EVANS

of 3500 to 5000 feet, in our mountain parks in the Upper Transition Zone into the Canadian between 8000 and 9000 feet, and in the Arctic-Alpine Zone above 11,500 feet. Although there is a difference in elevation of 8000 feet between the extremes, Horned Larks nest in all three zones. Other species breed regularly in one, two, or more zones, but each bird, generally speaking, has a certain habitat, or type of environment, within one zone, where it may be expected to be more numerous than elsewhere at a given season of the year.

Biologists have criticized Merriam's transcontinental concept of life zones on numerous grounds —especially that distribution of plants depends upon temperature; ecologists (students of the relationship between organisms and their environment) have substituted another nomenclature, and they call plant communities and the associated animal life *biomes*. Biomes, to quote Roger Tory Peterson (1942), "are the major landscape units, such as grasslands, deciduous forest, coniferous forest, tundra, etc. Between each is a broad transition band where biomes blend. These are called *ecotones*. . . . Thus an open parkland of our western foothills becomes the ecotone between the coniferous forest biome and the grassland biome, and the mixed or sub-Canadian woodland becomes the ecotone between the coniferous forest biome and that of the deciduous forest."

MIGRATION IN COLORADO

While the migration flights of North American birds are generally north and south, this is oversimplification, for many go "across country." Four north and south migration routes—the Atlantic, the Mississippi, the Central, and Pacific Flyways—are recognized by Federal agencies dealing primarily with the handling of migratory waterfowl problems. The areas are rather indefinite but they make convenient boundaries for the establishing of hunting regulations and bag limits for ducks and geese—based on the anticipated fall movement of the migratory hordes from Canada into the United States.

There is no great migratory movement of small birds through Colorado. It is likely that many of the northward-bound breeding birds of the eastern part of the state use the Mississippi Flyway, turning left up the valleys into Colorado, and following the various easterly flowing streams, particularly

15

the Platte, the Republican, and Arkansas Rivers. Many, however, undoubtedly parallel the foothills of the Rockies on both sides of the Continental Divide in spring, making more or less straight northward journeys to their summer homes.

Anyone expecting the enormous flights of passerines in Colorado, which are so evident in eastern states, is certain to be disappointed. While occasionally arrivals occur in numbers, this is the exception rather than the rule. Migration waves of small birds pass around Colorado, for the most part, and there is merely a filtering in of the summer residents, with comparatively few travelers in spring en route north, or in the fall on their southern trek. A person accustomed to migration elsewhere would expect in Colorado on warm days in early May—when leaves are breaking green among the cottonwoods of the eastern prairies—to see flocks of busy little creatures working through the greening treetops, but often there is a surprising dearth of bird life.

There are seasonal movements upward in the mountains of New Mexico, Colorado, and Wyoming. Many species arriving on the eastern plains in early spring remain until conditions are suitable for nesting at higher altitudes, and then make a vertical migration from a few hundred to several thousand feet upward—which could be done in a short time, but probably is a leisurely process. As noted previously, birds ascending into the Colorado mountains to the edge of timberline, or upward to the Alpine slopes, find temperature conditions and types of habitat, due to *altitude*, similar to those encountered by other migrants flying to the northern part of the continent. Climatic conditions and plant growth of the tundras of the Northern Hemisphere beyond timberline, due to latitude, correspond to those of Colorado mountains above 12,000 feet. It has been estimated that a one thousand-foot ascent into the mountains is roughly the same, temperature-wise, as a northward journey of over three hundred miles. Thus when visitors climb upward seven thousand feet from Denver's one-mile elevation to the shores of Summit Lake, at the base of the beautiful glacial cirque on the eastern slope of Mount Evans, they have traversed the types of habitat to be encountered on a trip through the Canadian forests to the Arctic Circle.

The migration period near the eastern foothills reaches its peak the third week of May, and the Spring Count of birds is made at that time. With members of bird clubs covering all five zones on a statewide basis, from the prairies to mountaintops, a surprisingly large number of species, for an inland state, has been observed in a single day. The Count on May 18, 1963, with 100 observers in thirty-five groups, recorded 221 species and a Composite Count from 1954 to 1963 totalled 269 species.

Christmas Counts are confined to areas of fifteen miles in diameter, but there is no limitation on distances or life zones covered on the May field trips. As a consequence, some naturalists travel from the plains to above timberline, making journeys the equivalent, so far as plant and animal life is concerned, from Denver northward through the Canadian forests to the tundras of the Arctic slope.

ARTISTS

Twenty-three bird artists, some with international reputations, have painted the one hundred and twenty-four original water color plates illustrating this Pictorial Checklist. Included are four Canadian artists, two from Great Britain, and the remainder from the United States. Four hundred and twenty species and over 700 individual birds are shown on the plates. With few exceptions, birds are in spring plumage, and when only one of a species is depicted, the sexes are colored much alike.

The artists, listed alphabetically, are: Walter J. Breckenridge, John A. Crosby, William C. Dilger, Don R. Eckelberry, Owen J. Gromme, D. M. Henry, H. Albert Hochbaum, F. L. Jaques, Edwin R. Kalmbach, Al Kreml, Dexter F. Landau, Donald L. Malick, Robert M. Mengel, Richard A. Parks, Roger Tory Peterson, Earl L. Poole, Orville O. Rice, Charles L. Ripper, Peter Scott, Angus H. Shortt, Terence M. Shortt, Arthur Singer, and Wayne Trimm.

COLOR PLATES

1	Common Loon, Arctic Loon, Red-throated Loon, and Yellow-billed Loon	John A. Crosby
2	Eared Grebe, Horned Grebe, and Pied-billed Grebe	John A. Crosby
3	Red-necked Grebe and Western Grebe	John A. Crosby
4	Brown Pelican, White Pelican, Olivaceous Cormorant, and Reddish Egret	Donald L. Malick
5	Anhinga and Double-crested Cormorant	John A. Crosby
6	Common Egret, Snowy Egret, and Great Blue Heron	John A. Crosby
7	Green Heron, Little Blue Heron, Black-crowned Night Heron and Yellow-crowned Night Heron	John A. Crosby
8	American Bittern and Least Bittern	John A. Crosby
9	Roseate Spoonbill, White-faced Ibis, Glossy Ibis, White Ibis and Wood Ibis	John A. Crosby
10	Trumpeter Swan and Whistling Swan	F. L. Jaques
11	Canada Goose (two races) and White-fronted Goose	T. M. Shortt
12	Blue Goose, Snow Goose, and Ross' Goose	Owen J. Gromme
13	Black Duck, Mallard, Mexican Duck, and Mottled Duck	T. M. Shortt
14	Gadwall and Pintail	T. M. Shortt
15	Cinnamon Teal, Blue-winged Teal, and Green-winged Teal	Peter Scott
16	American Widgeon, Shoveler, and Wood Duck	Peter Scott
17	Canvasback, Redhead, and Ruddy Duck	H. Albert Hochbaum
18	Downy young waterfowl	H. Albert Hochbaum
19	Downy young waterfowl	H. Albert Hochbaum
20	Greater Scaup, Lesser Scaup, and Ring-necked Duck	Angus H. Shortt
21	Barrow's Goldeneye, Common Goldeneye, Bufflehead, and Oldsquaw	Dexter F. Landau
22	Common Eider, White-winged Scoter, Common Scoter, Surf Scoter and Harlequin Duck	Dexter F. Landau
23	Common Merganser, Hooded Merganser, and Red-breasted Merganser	Angus H. Shortt
24	Black Vulture, Turkey Vulture, and Caracara	Earl L. Poole
25	Mississippi Kite and Swallow-tailed Kite	Earl L. Poole
26	Cooper's Hawk, Goshawk, and Sharp-shinned Hawk	Earl L. Poole
27	Harlan's Hawk and Red-tailed Hawk (two races)	Earl L. Poole
28	Broad-winged Hawk, Red-shouldered Hawk, and Swainson's Hawk	Earl L. Poole
29	Ferruginous Hawk and Rough-legged Hawk	Earl L. Poole
30	Bald Eagle and Golden Eagle	Earl L. Poole
31	Marsh Hawk and Osprey	Earl L. Poole
32	Peregrine Falcon and Prairie Falcon	Earl L. Poole
33	Pigeon Hawk (three races) and Sparrow Hawk	Earl L. Poole
34	Blue Grouse	Owen J. Gromme
35	Ruffed Grouse and Spruce Grouse	Dexter F. Landau
36	White-tailed Ptarmigan (seasonal plumages)	Dexter F. Landau
37	Greater Prairie Chicken, Lesser Prairie Chicken, and Sharp-tailed Grouse	Owen J. Gromme
38	Sage Grouse	Dexter F. Landau
39	Bobwhite, Gambel's Quail, and Scaled Quail	Owen J. Gromme
40	Chukar, California Quail, Gray Partridge, Red-legged Partridge, and Ring-necked Pheasant	Dexter F. Landau
41	Wild Turkey	Owen J. Gromme
42	Sandhill Crane (two races) and Whooping Crane	Roger Tory Peterson
43	Black Rail, Sora, Yellow Rail, and Virginia Rail	Donald L. Malick

PIED-BILLED GREBE

Order GAVIIFORMES: Loons

Family GAVIIDAE: Loons

COMMON LOON   *Gavia immer* (Brunnich). [7]

RECOGNITION.—Length 30–36 inches; large, long-billed divers. *Summer:* bill black; head, neck and back greenish black, the back and wings with prominent white spots, and the sides of the neck having patches of parallel white lines; under parts mainly white; iris red. *Winter:* mainly dark brown above, with back faintly spotted; chin, throat and under parts white; iris brown. *Young:* dark brown above, the feathers edged with light gray; throat and breast sometimes mottled; bill brownish; iris brown. (Plate 1)

RANGE.—Greenland, Iceland, Canada, and northern United States including Alaska in summer, and southward in North America to the Gulf of Mexico in winter.

Nebraska: a rare migrant; Kansas: uncommon transient; New Mexico: casual migrant and winter resident; Utah: uncommon transient and winter visitor; Wyoming: uncommon migrant, and breeder in northwestern counties.

COLORADO.—Occurs regularly, singly, or in pairs, in spring and fall upon reservoirs of the eastern prairies, and more rarely west of the Continental Divide; uncommon in winter.

YELLOW-BILLED LOON   *Gavia adamsii* (Gray). [8]

RECOGNITION.—Length 34–38 inches, the largest of the loons. Similar in color to *G. immer* but the adult head and neck purplish black; bill yellow with slight up-tilt, and pronounced angle to lower mandible. (Plate 1)

RANGE.—Breeds along the Arctic coasts of Siberia, Alaska, and Canada, and winters along Asiatic and southeastern Alaskan coasts.

COLORADO.—There is only one record for the Yellow-billed Loon, an unsexed specimen (no. 7808) in immature plumage taken in Adams Co. Nov. 7, 1922 by F. S. Smith.

ARCTIC LOON   *Gavia arctica pacifica* (Lawrence). [10]

RECOGNITION.—Length 24–28 inches, small loon with *thin, straight bill. Summer:* back of head and neck fuscous; throat and lower neck black with white stripes on sides. *Winter:* dark brown above, with white marks on back absent or faint; throat and sides of head white, throat lined with brown. (Plate 1)

RANGE.—Breeds on the Arctic coast of North America, and winters mainly along the Pacific coast of Baja California. Straggler farther east.

New Mexico: one Nov. 1899 near Clayton (F.M. Bailey, 1928); Utah: one near Beaver Oct. 18, 1940 (Behle, 1944).

COLORADO.—Straggler only. A female (no. 7003) was taken at Breckenridge, Summit Co. Nov. 15, 1887 by Edwin Carter, and there are three reports from near Colorado Springs—one shot in the fall of 1882, one of three killed in Nov. 1898, and one observed on Prospect Lake Nov. 3, 1955.

RED-THROATED LOON   *Gavia stellata* (Pontoppidan). [11]

RECOGNITION.—Length 24–27 inches; small, *bill thin and turned upward. Summer:* head and neck light gray spotted faintly with white and grayish brown; throat patch bright chestnut; iris red; back grayish brown; under parts white. *Winter:* adults and young with back dark, finely marked with small white spots; head gray, and throat and forehead white; iris brown. (Plate 1)

RANGE.—Breeds in northern Alaska, Canada, and Greenland. Winters in southern Canada and along both coasts of the United States.

Nebraska: rare migrant; Kansas: straggler, female collected Franklin Co. Oct. 20, 1925 (Tordoff, 1956); New Mexico: one observed on Bitter Lake Nov. 23, 1957 (Ligon, 1961).

COLORADO.—Straggler. Recorded casually from the Mississippi Valley, but only one bird has been taken in Colorado. The specimen, a mounted immature (no. 5584) in the C.C. Museum, was shot on Antero Reservoir in South Park (date not given). An immature, or one in winter plumage, was noted on Marston Res. in southwest Denver Dec. 23, 1956 (C.B.N. 4:37).

Order PODICIPEDIFORMES: Grebes

Family PODICIPEDIDAE: Grebes

RED-NECKED GREBE   *Podiceps grisegena holbollii* Reinhardt. [2]

RECOGNITION.—Length 19–22 inches; large diver with small head crests; dark gray above and silvery white below. *Summer:* top of head and crests bronzy greenish black; chin, throat, and cheeks grayish white; iris brown; beak yellowish; neck rufous; wings with two white patches. *Winter:* crests not evident; general color much paler and iris brownish. (Plate 3)

RANGE.—Breeding range includes northeastern Asia, northwestern Alaska and northern Canada, south to Washington, South Dakota, North Dakota, Wisconsin, and Minnesota. Winters in Asia south to China and Japan and in North America from the Pribilof and Aleutian Islands to southeastern Alaska and California; and from Newfoundland to Florida; and in the interior from Canada to the Gulf coast.

Nebraska: rare migrant; Kansas: straggler, female collected Douglas Co. Oct. 29, 1910; New Mexico: one observed Bitter Lake Dec. 19, 1952 and one Feb 12, 1955 (Ligon, 1961).

COLORADO.—Only one specimen has been taken, a male in winter plumage (no. 20563) collected by Robert B. Rockwell Nov. 8, 1939, at the Mile High Duck Club in Adams County (N. & R. 1939). Six were seen by members of the Colorado Bird Club on a lake near Longmont Apr. 16, 1955 (C.B.N. 2: no. 8, 5); one on Lake Loveland Nov. 25, 1955 by John and Margaret Douglass (3:27) and one Oct. 12, 1956, at Marston Res. west of Littleton (4:28).

HORNED GREBE   *Podiceps auritus cornutus* (Gmelin). [3]

RECOGNITION.—Length 12–15 inches; a small, stout-bodied diver, with slender bill. *Summer:* head bronzy black with tufted ruff and yellow ochre crests back of eyes; neck and sides rufous; back dusky gray; breast and belly white. *Winter:* adults and young with gray and white of neck and throat sharply defined, in contrast to the Eared Grebe; crest lacking. (Plate 2)

RANGE.—Species breeds from Siberia, northern Europe, and Iceland, and this race from northern North America south through Alaska and Canada to northern states. Winters along the Pacific coast south to Guatemala, and locally in many sections of the United States.

Nebraska: an uncommon migrant and rare breeder in Cherry Co.; Kansas: rare transient, two specimens from Riley and Douglas Counties; New Mexico: uncommon fall migrant; Utah: rare transient; Wyoming: uncommon migrant.

COLORADO.—A regular migrant in spring and fall upon the reservoirs of the eastern part of the state.

Early spring Mar. 13 Marston Res.; summer Aug. 26 Longmont; winter Dec. 29 Loveland.

EARED GREBE   *Podiceps caspicus californicus* Heermann. [4]

RECOGNITION.—Length 12–15 inches; a small, stout-bodied diver; similar in general appearance to the preceding species, though bill longer and narrower; *Summer:* head, neck and back black; sides and flanks rufous; breast and belly white; head with *single central crest* and two drooping golden reddish brown ear tufts; iris red. *Winter:* adult and young similar in color to the Horned Grebe, but neck and throat with less white and not sharply separated; light patch behind ear. (Plate 2)

RANGE.—The Old World race breeds from the British Isles, Denmark, Sweden, Russia, and Manchuria south to southern Angola and Cape Province, and this subspecies from British Columbia across southern Canada to Manitoba and south locally through central and western states. Winters from British Columbia to Colombia, and uncommonly from Nevada to Texas; east in migration to Wisconsin.

Nebraska: uncommon migrant, and a breeder in the Sand Hill Lakes region; Kansas: regular transient; New Mexico: summer resident, nesting on Burford Lake, Rio Arriba Co.; Utah: fairly common transient and summer resident; Wyoming: abundant migrant and breeder.

COLORADO.—Common migrant and uncommon resident on the lakes of the Upper Sonoran Zone and occasionally in mountain parks to 10,500 feet.

Early spring Mar. 13 Marston Lake (C.B.N., 2, no. 7); winter Dec. 2 Denver.

WESTERN GREBE   *Aechmophorus occidentalis* (Lawrence). [1]

RECOGNITION.—Length 24–29 inches; a large, long-necked diver. Back dark gray; crown and hind neck blackish; cheeks, throat, foreneck, and under parts white; a single white wing patch; beak yellow, iris red. (Plate 3)

RANGE.—Breeds from south-central British Columbia, Alberta, Saskatchewan, and Manitoba to California, Nevada, northern Utah, west-central Wyoming to North and South Dakota and Minnesota. Winters south to Central Mexico. Casual east to Michigan, Illinois, and Iowa.

Nebraska: migrant throughout the state, more common in west; Kansas: rather rare transient, and one recorded nesting in Cheyenne Bottoms near Great Bend by L. O. Nossaman (L. B. Carson, pers. comm.); New Mexico: rather rare migrant; Utah: common migrant and summer resident; Wyoming: common migrant, breeds in several localities.

COLORADO.—Spring and fall migrant and summer resident on lake areas of the Upper Sonoran Zone; and a few winter as long as the reservoirs are open.

PIED-BILLED GREBE   *Podilymbus podiceps podiceps* (Linnaeus). [6]

RECOGNITION.—Length 12–15 inches; a small, stout-bodied, heavy-billed diver. *Summer:* adults with upper parts dark grayish-brown; chin and throat black; bill whitish with a black band. *Winter:* chin, throat, and breast whitish; bill brownish. *Young:* plumage browner, with head and neck streaked with white and black. (Plate 2)

RANGE.—Breeds from Vancouver Island and central British Columbia eastward across Canada to Nova Scotia and south locally through much of the United States to the Gulf coast and Baja California. Winters casually in areas of open water in northern states south to Cuba and Baja California.

Nebraska: common migrant and uncommon breeder; Kansas: common transient, irregular in summer and rare in winter; New Mexico: migrant, and summer resident in north; Utah: common summer resident and a few winter; Wyoming: common migrant and breeder.

COLORADO.—Regular migrant, summer and occasional winter resident; ranges in small numbers on the eastern plains and into the mountains; uncommon on the western slope.

Order PELECANIFORMES: Pelicans, Cormorants, and Darters

Family PELECANIDAE: Pelicans

WHITE PELICAN   *Pelecanus erythrorhynchos* Gmelin. [125]

RECOGNITION.—Length 52–65 inches; large, conspicuous white birds, wing coverts, primaries, and most of secondaries black; throat pouch and bill yellow; upper mandible with short, rounded horn, which is lost after the breeding season. (Plate 4)

RANGE.—Breeds from central British Columbia, southern Mackenzie, Alberta, Saskatchewan, Manitoba, and southwestern Ontario south locally to California, Nevada, Utah, Montana, North Dakota, and the Gulf coast. Winters from northern California and the Gulf states to Panama.

Nebraska: migrant and nonbreeding summer resident; Kansas: common transient; New Mexico: migrant and summer visitor on larger lakes; Utah: common breeding bird on Hat and Gunnison Islands in Great Salt Lake; Wyoming: common migrant, breeding on island in Yellowstone Lake.

COLORADO.—Regular summer resident in small numbers upon the reservoirs of the state with a breeding colony discovered in 1962 on Riverside Res., Weld Co.; 130 young in June 1966 and 102 in 1967 (A. Collister, pers. comm.). Winter record: one observed by H. Holt circling over Stapleton Airport Jan. 28, 1967 was grounded in Aurora (*Denver Post*, Jan. 29).

BROWN PELICAN   *Pelecanus occidentalis carolinensis* Gmelin. [126]

RECOGNITION.—Length 48–56 inches. *Summer:* silvery-gray above and grayish-brown below; head white, neck chestnut. *Winter:* plumage similar, but neck entirely white. *Young:* grayish-brown above, darker on back; under parts white, with sides brownish. (Plate 4)

RANGE.—The species breeds on islands along both the Atlantic and Pacific coasts south, often in great concentrations, along the islands of South America to Chile. This race nests along the south Atlantic and Gulf coasts of the United States, Cuba, and Panama. Wanders up the Mississippi Valley, and there are records from many northern states from Wyoming eastward to New York. Winters from breeding range southward.

Nebraska: accidental in east; Kansas: observed in Sedgwick Co. in 1910, and one specimen from Linn Co. in 1916; Utah: sight record from Great Salt Lake in 1934, and one observed in Uintah Co. May 18, 1963 (Condor, 68:305); Wyoming: straggler, one taken July 12, 1899 near Cheyenne.

COLORADO.—Straggler. There is one record for the state (H. G. Smith, 1910), a specimen (no. 16280) taken at Wood's Lake, Pitkin Co., in July 1908 by P. J. Engelbrecht. It is a second-year bird, probably, the white head having a scattering of dark feathers.

Family PHALACROCORACIDAE: Cormorants

DOUBLE-CRESTED CORMORANT   *Phalacrocorax auritus auritus* (Lesson). [120]

RECOGNITION.—Length 30–34 inches; a dark, stout-bodied bird with slender head and neck and hooked beak. Adults glossy greenish-black, a small tuft of black feathers with a sprinkling of white back of each eye; throat pouch orange; iris green. *Young:* plumage brownish, more grayish on head and neck; throat and breast lighter. (Plate 5)

RANGE.—The species breeds from the Aleutian Islands and southeastern Alaska south to Baja California, across southern Canadian Provinces to Labrador and south through northern states from Idaho to Massachusetts, Tennessee, northern Texas, Florida, and the Bahamas. This race nests from central Alberta across southern Canada to Newfoundland, south locally in northern states. Winters in the Mississippi Valley from New York and Tennessee south to the Gulf coast, Cuba, and Bermuda. Casual to the northward.

Nebraska: common migrant, summer resident and local breeder; Kansas: regular transient, with one breeding record from Barton Co. in 1961; New Mexico: common migrant, nesting locally; Utah: common summer resident in central north, breeding in colonies on islands of Great Salt Lake, Bear River Refuge, and elsewhere; Wyoming: common migrant and breeder.

COLORADO.—Summer resident on the large reservoirs from the Upper Sonoran into the Transition Zones. A few remain in winter as long as waterways are free of ice. Nests in trees or on ground adjacent to reservoirs. Three ground nests found on island of Riverside Res., Weld Co., Apr. 28, 1963 by Donald G. Davis (not 1962 as recorded in *Birds of Colorado*), and 17 young banded on same island in the summer of 1966 (A. Collister, pers. comm.).

OLIVACEOUS CORMORANT   *Phalacrocorax olivaceus mexicanus* (Brandt). [121]

RECOGNITION.—Length 23–28 inches; like the Double-crested Cormorant, but much smaller, and face and pouch bordered with white. *Summer*: adults entirely black, except for slender white filamentous feathers on head, neck, and belly. *Winter*: plumes lacking and the face partly white. *Young*: dark brown, with throat and under parts nearly white. (Plate 4)

RANGE.—The species has a wide range from the Gulf coast south to Tierra del Fuego, and this race breeds and winters from southeastern Louisiana and southern Texas south to Nicaragua. Accidental farther north.

Kansas: straggler, a specimen taken in Douglas Co. Apr. 2, 1872; New Mexico: several records listed by F. M. Bailey (1928, 84).

COLORADO.—The only specimen recorded from the state, an adult male, was taken at Smith Lake fourteen miles north of Denver Oct. 15, 1899 (Felger, 1901). The skin (no. 26859) is in the collection of the Denver Museum.

Family ANHINGIDAE: Darters

ANHINGA   *Anhinga anhinga leucogaster* (Vieillot). [118]

RECOGNITION.—Length 32–36 inches; a slender, dark, cormorant-like bird with long, snaky neck. *Male*: dark glossy green, with wing coverts marked with silver-gray; tail long, broad, fan-shaped, and tipped with pale brown. *Female*: neck and breast brownish. (Plate 5)

RANGE.—Breeds locally in southern Texas and along the Gulf coast to North Carolina, Arkansas, Oklahoma, and Tennessee, south to Panama. Winters in the breeding range and wanders casually into northern states.

Nebraska: one record from Buffalo Co.; Kansas: straggler, several early records prior to 1900 and other observations, and one specimen from Barton Co. since 1928; New Mexico: two were collected in September 1854 at Fort Thorn and sent to U.S.N.M. (F. M. Bailey, 1928).

COLORADO.—There are two specimens from Adams Co.: an immature female (no. 12296) was taken near Aurora in Sept. 1927; and the other, a male (no. 12247), was shot along Coal Creek Sept. 24, 1931 (B. & N., 1937).

Order CICONIIFORMES: Herons and Allies
Family ARDEIDAE: Herons and Bitterns

GREAT BLUE HERON   *Ardea herodias treganzai* Court. [194c]

RECOGNITION.—Length 42–50 inches; largest of our waders; slate-blue with long neck and legs. *Adult*: bluish-gray above with white crown and black occipital crest; under parts streaked with black and white. *Young*: crown black; wing coverts without brown or white patches. Herons fly with necks folded and heads close to shoulders. (Plate 6)

RANGE.—The species breeds from Alaska across southern Canada south through Mexico, and in the Galapagos Islands. This race nests locally from eastern Washington, southern Idaho, and Wyoming, south through the Great Basin and Rocky Mountain region. Winters uncommonly in the northern part of the breeding range south into northern and central Mexico.

Nebraska: species common throughout the state (three races listed); Kansas: common transient and breeder, with three races reported; New Mexico: common throughout the state in summer, and a few in winter; Utah: fairly common summer resident and transient, wintering in small numbers; Wyoming: common migrant and breeder, and a few in winter.

COLORADO.—A common summer resident about the marshes, reservoirs, and streams of the Upper Sonoran and Transition Zones, with a few present in mild winters. There are records from all parts of the state.

* GREEN HERON   *Butorides virescens virescens* (Linnaeus). [201]

RECOGNITION.—Length 17–20 inches. *Adult:* crown greenish-black, throat buffy-white; rest of head and neck rufous and vinaceous; back and wings greenish; belly gray washed with buff. *Young:* neck and under parts streaked with blackish and wing coverts marked with buff. (Plate 7)

RANGE.—The species breeds from Washington, southern Ontario, and Quebec southward into Mexico, Central America, and northern South America, and this race has an eastern distribution from Colorado, Minnesota, Wisconsin, Ontario, and Quebec southward to the Gulf coast. Winters from the Gulf coast southward to northern South America.

Nebraska: migrant, summer resident, and breeder in eastern half of state; Kansas: common summer resident and migrant; New Mexico: summer resident in southern half of state, nesting in the Pecos Valley; Utah: race *B.v. anthonyi* rare summer resident in southwest; Wyoming: rare migrant.

COLORADO.—There are numerous sight records for this small heron from eastern counties, and one was observed at Grand Junction Nov. 21, 1966 (A.F.N. 21:63).

Early spring May 9, 1964 Barr Lake (Harold Holt); late fall Nov. 30 (C.B.N., 4:42).

* LITTLE BLUE HERON   *Florida caerulea caerulea* (Linnaeus). [200]

RECOGNITION.—Length 22–28 inches. *Adult:* dark bluish, with head and neck purplish; legs and feet black. *Immatures:* white, often washed or mottled with bluish, *primaries* tipped with *slate*, and *legs* and *feet greenish*; young Little Blues have bluish beaks with blackish tips, while the Snowy Egrets have black beaks and legs, with golden-yellow feet. Young of the latter could be confused with immature Little Blues, however, for some have yellowish on the back of the legs. (Plate 7)

RANGE.—Breeds from Massachusetts to Gulf coast, and from Arkansas and Texas southward. Migrates in late summer northward to southern Canada and Labrador and up the Mississippi Valley as far as Michigan. Winters from the Gulf coast south to northern South America.

Nebraska: rare late summer migrant; Kansas: regular summer visitor, and one breeding record in 1952 in Finney Co.; New Mexico: several recent reports including observations at Bosque Refuge May 6, 1962 and May 24, 1963 (A.F.N. 17:423); Utah: a male, captured in the Bear River Refuge Sept. 4, 1957 (Auk, 75, 214), and one found dead near Salt Lake City May 25, 1963 (A.F.N. 17:423).

COLORADO.—Rare summer visitor. Five immatures noted near Boulder June 28, 1955; an adult west of Platteville Aug. 20, 1956; an adult near Julesburg in June 1956; an adult at Berthoud Apr. 17, 1959; and an immature at Boulder (B. & N., 1965).

* CATTLE EGRET   *Bubulcus ibis ibis* (Linnaeus). [200.1]

RECOGNITION.—Length 20–24 inches. Small white heron, stockier than Snowy Egret. Head feathers with elongate crest feathers tawny in spring plumage, bill reddish with yellow tip. Iris reddish, bill yellow and iris straw and head feathers less tawny in late summer and fall. Legs and feet blackish.

RANGE.—Old World species ranging in both hemispheres, this race breeds from southern Portugal and Spain along the north African coast and south of the Sahara to Cape Town; in eastern Turkey, Iraq, Syria, northern Iran, and southwestern Arabia.

Kansas: One shot in Pottawatomi Co. April 26, 1964 (Zimmerman, 1964).

COLORADO.—The first reported from the state was observed at Cherry Creek Reservoir September 12, 1964, and the second along the "settling ponds" west of Nucla, Montrose Co., a single bird, May 27–28, 1967 (Wm. T. Garrett, pers. comm.).

REDDISH EGRET   *Dichromanassa rufescens rufescens* (Gmelin). [198]

RECOGNITION.—Length 27–32 inches. *Summer:* slate-blue, with head and neck dark rufous. In the light phase the plumage is entirely white, with bluish legs, and both phases have characteristic *light-colored* beaks tipped with *black*. *Young:* plumage plain gray, tinged with rusty. (Plate 4)

RANGE.—Breeds in colonies along the Gulf coast of Texas, in the Florida Keys, and in the Bahamas, Cuba, and Isle of Pines. Winters from southern Florida, Louisiana, and Texas south to Venezuela. Straggler to southern Illinois and South Carolina.

COLORADO.—An immature, formerly in the Aiken collection (C.C. no. 106) but now in the Denver Museum (no. 26971), was taken near Colorado Springs about August 1875; and Cooke (1898) listed a second specimen said to have been shot by E. L. Berthoud in 1890, but there has been no verification of this record.

COMMON EGRET   *Casmerodius albus egretta* (Gmelin). [196]

RECOGNITION.—Length 38–42 inches; a large white heron. *Summer*: plumage entirely white; *bill yellow* and *legs* and *feet black*; scapulars plumed with *straight* filamentous feathers which reach beyond tail; iris yellow. Plumes lost after nesting season. (Plate 6)

RANGE.—The species has a very wide cosmopolitan range from southern Europe, Russia, southern Siberia, China, and Japan, south locally to South Africa, southern Asia, Australia, and New Zealand; and in the Americas this race breeds locally from southeastern Oregon, Idaho, north central states, and New Jersey, south to South America. Wanders north after the breeding season. Winters from California, Texas, and South Carolina southward.

Nebraska: a common summer visitor after the breeding season; Kansas: local summer resident, nesting Cowley Co.; New Mexico: summer resident, nesting at the Bosque del Apache Refuge and elsewhere; Utah: uncommon straggler throughout the state.

COLORADO.—Uncommon along the shallow lakes of the eastern prairies. There have been numerous observations, however, and a specimen was collected at Barr Lake in June 1905, and a female (no. 12368) at Dan Lake Apr. 29, 1933.

Early spring Apr. 19 Saguache; late fall Oct. 5 Longmont.

SNOWY EGRET   *Leucophoyx thula brewsteri* (Thayer and Bangs). [197a]

RECOGNITION.—Length 22–27 inches. *Summer:* a small white heron with curved back plumes reaching beyond tail; head crested; legs black, feet yellow; bill black with yellow base, iris yellow. The plumes are lacking in the post-breeding plumage and in the young. (Plate 6)

RANGE.—The species breeds from New Jersey, Oklahoma, Nevada, and California south into South America. This race is western in distribution from California, Utah, and Colorado south to Baja California. Wanders casually to southwestern Canada. Winters from California, southern Arizona, and Texas south into Mexico.

Nebraska: race *L.t thula* uncommon visitor, with breeding records from Lincoln and Scotts Bluff Counties; Kansas: *L.t. thula* post-breeding visitor, and two nests found in Finney Co. in 1952; New Mexico: summer resident, nesting in cattail and tulegrown marshes; Utah: common summer resident in northern Utah; Wyoming: uncommon migrant, and nesting locally in several areas.

COLORADO.—Summer resident along the marshes and reservoirs; well distributed throughout the state in Upper Sonoran Zone and nesting regularly. Mention of 11 nests on Riverside Res. on Apr. 28 (p. 87 *Birds of Colorado*) should read June 28. Forty-seven young banded in 1966 (A. Collister, pers. comm.).

Early spring Mar. 29 Barr Lake; late fall Oct. 12 Timnath Res.

* LOUISIANA HERON   *Hydranassa tricolor ruficollis* (Gosse). [199]

RECOGNITION.—Length 23–28 inches. Very slim, medium-sized dark blue and brown heron with conspicuous *white under parts*. Has slender white plumes back of head and lanceolate plumes on neck and back. Sexes colored much alike, with males slightly larger (not illustrated in color).

RANGE.—Resident and breeding from coastal Maryland to Florida and west along the Gulf coast to Texas, south along Mexico and Central American coasts to Venezuela, Colombia, and Ecuador.

Nebraska: straggler, one record from Kearney, Buffalo Co.; Kansas: a specimen taken at Lake Inman, McPherson Co., Aug. 9, 1934, and one observed in Atchison Co. Sept. 12, 1948; New Mexico: one at Bosque Refuge Apr. 1955, and observed at Bitter Lake June and Sept. 1955 (Ligon, 1961).

COLORADO.—One observed at Barr Lake May 18, 1963.

BLACK-CROWNED NIGHT HERON   *Nycticorax nycticorax hoactli* (Gmelin). [202]

RECOGNITION.—Length 23–26 inches. *Adult:* back and crown black; wings and tail dark gray; forehead, neck, and breast white; belly and sides gray; bill black, legs and feet yellowish; iris red. Two long white plumes extend from crown in breeding plumage. *Young:* generally brown, streaked with brown and white on under parts; throat white, iris yellow or pale orange. (Plate 7)

RANGE.—The species is nearly world-wide in distribution, and this race breeds from southern Canada south to Paraguay, Argentina, Chile, and the Hawaiian Islands; winters casually in northern states.

Nebraska: common migrant, breeding locally; Kansas: transient and summer resident, nesting in localized colonies; New Mexico: common summer resident, nesting in both tree and marsh communities; Utah: common summer resident, and winters in small numbers; Wyoming: uncommon migrant, with a few breeding communities.

COLORADO.—Common summer resident of the water areas in eastern Colorado; less common on western slope. Observed occasionally in winter.

YELLOW-CROWNED NIGHT HERON   *Nyctanassa violacea violacea* (Linnaeus). [203]

RECOGNITION.—Length 22–28 inches. *Adult:* head black, with crown and patch below eye creamy white; rest of plumage blue-gray, heavily striped with black on back and wings; legs and feet yellow; bill black. *Young:* generally brown above with fine white spots on wings; throat and under parts whitish, lined with brown; legs and feet black. (Plate 7)

RANGE.—Breeds locally in eastern United States from Massachusetts, west to Kansas, and south to the Gulf coast, eastern Mexico, and eastern Central America. Wanders irregularly to northern states and southern Canada. Winters from southern Florida southward.

Nebraska: rare spring and summer straggler, and one nesting record near Omaha in 1963; Kansas: summer resident, with breeding records; New Mexico: one observed near Clayton Aug. 10, 1953 (Ligon, 1961), and one at Bosque del Apache Refuge July 19, 1957 (A.F.N. 11:423). One collected in Eddy Co. Aug. 27, 1962, one in Lea Co. Aug. 28, and one in Grant Co. Aug. 24, 1964 (Auk, 82:649).

COLORADO.—An adult female (no. 26972), one of five, was collected in Chaffee Co. May 1, 1908; one (no. 6987) was shot near Byers, Arapahoe Co. May 3, 1914; one found dead near Fort Morgan in 1942; two were seen at Prewitt Res. July 11, 1948; one near Barr Lake May 16, 1964, and one at Barr Lake Mar. 20, 1965 and May 29 (C.B.N. 13:16).

LEAST BITTERN   *Ixobrychus exilis exilis* (Gmelin). [191]

RECOGNITION.—Length 12–14 inches. *Adult male:* upper parts greenish-black; hind neck and large wing patch chestnut; sides of chest dark brown, throat white and under parts buffy; iris yellow, bill largely yellow; legs yellowish-green. *Adult female:* back brown and under parts lined with dusky. *Young:* like female, but back feathers edged with buffy. (Plate 8)

RANGE.—Breeds from Montana, South Dakota, Minnesota, Wisconsin, Ontario, and southern Canada, southern Maine and northern New York south to Texas, southern Mexico, and Central America. Winters from Georgia and southern Texas to Panama.

Nebraska: uncommon migrant, breeding locally; Kansas: transient and irregular summer resident with two nests from Johnson Co. June 1949; New Mexico: summer resident in Rio Grande Valley and nesting on the Bosque del Apache Refuge; Utah: straggler, one specimen from St. George May 30, 1938, listed as *I.e. hesperis*; Wyoming: straggler.

COLORADO.—Uncommon summer resident in the marsh areas of the Upper Sonoran Zone.

Early spring May 1 M.H.D.C.; late summer Sept. 10 M.H.D.C.

AMERICAN BITTER   *Botaurus lentiginosus* (Rackett). [190]

RECOGNITION.—Length 24–34 inches. *Adult:* brown above, broadly streaked with dusky and buff; under parts yellowish, widely striped with white; velvety black patch on side of neck, wing quills black; iris yellow, legs and feet greenish. (Plate 8)

RANGE.—Breeds from central British Columbia across southern Canada and Newfoundland to southern California, Arizona, Missouri, Tennessee, Ohio, Pennsylvania, Virginia, Maryland, and locally in Texas, Louisiana, and Florida. Winters from southern Canada to Guatemala and Panama.

Nebraska: common migrant and local summer resident; Kansas: common transient, and three nesting records, Anderson Co. June 1951, Finney Co. summer of 1952, and Barton Co. 1963; New Mexico: uncommon summer resident, nesting in rushes bordering Wade Lake on the McMillan Res. delta and along the Rio Grande; Utah: fairly common summer resident in north, transient in south; Wyoming: uncommon migrant and breeder.

COLORADO.—Common summer resident in marsh areas in the Upper Sonoran and Transition Zones, rare in winter.

Family CICONIIDAE: Storks and Wood Ibises

WOOD IBIS   *Mycteria americana* Linnaeus. [188]

RECOGNITION.—Length 35-46 inches. *Adult:* plumage white, with wing primaries, secondaries, and tail black; bare head and neck dark bluish; bill long and decurved at tip; legs and feet bluish-black; webs yellowish. *Young:* similar to adults except head and neck thinly covered with grayish-brown, hair-like feathers. (Plate 9)

RANGE.—Breeds and winters on the Pacific coast of North America from Sonora south to Costa Rica, and along the Gulf and Atlantic coasts from Texas, (formerly Louisiana), Florida and South Carolina, south through eastern Mexico locally to Argentina. Has wandered irregularly to many northern states, Ontario, and New Brunswick.

Nebraska: straggler, one record from Hamilton Co.; Kansas: several sight reports and a male collected Oct. 4, 1913 in Sherman Co.; New Mexico: several records including one on the Bosque del Apache Refuge June 24, 1952, three July 14 and four July 26, and other observations; Utah: several sight records since 1930; Wyoming: straggler.

COLORADO.—Rare straggler. There was a specimen in the Maxwell collection, three were shot near Colo. Spgs. in about 1890, and there are two in the Museum from near Denver Aug. 30, 1902, and one July 25, 1934.

Family THRESKIORNITHIDAE: Ibises and Spoonbills

WHITE-FACED IBIS   *Plegadis chihi* (Vieillot). [187]

RECOGNITION.—Length 20–26 inches. *Adult:* bill slender and decurved; head, neck, and under parts chestnut-red; wings, rump, and tail iridescent bronze-green and purple; face bordered with white; iris red; legs and feet dull red. *Young:* heads gray speckled with white and body plumage shiny green, iris brown, legs and beak black. (Plate 9)

RANGE.—Breeds from California, Oregon, Utah, and Minnesota locally to Texas, Louisiana, Florida, and southern Mexico, and in South America from Peru and Brazil southward to Chile and Argentina. Winters from southern states to South America.

Nebraska: irregular migrant, with a nesting record in Clay Co. June 1904; Kansas: irregular transient and summer visitor, with young observed in Barton Co. in summer of 1951 and nesting again in 1962; New Mexico: fairly common summer resident in small flocks; Utah: transient, and common breeding bird of the Bear River Marshes; Wyoming: uncommon migrant.

COLORADO.—A regular summer visitor to the eastern plains and breeder in San Luis Valley. Small flocks occur along the plains reservoirs each summer, and birds were observed in Gunnison Co. in 1950, 1951, and 1954. (A. S. Hyde, pers. comm.). This New World form is considered as a race of the Old World species *P. falcinellus* (Palmer, 1962).

Early spring Apr. 4 Ft. Collins; late fall Oct. 15 Jackson Co.

GLOSSY IBIS   *Plegadis falcinellus falcinellus* (Linnaeus). [186]

RECOGNITION.—Length 20–26 inches. *Adult:* resembles the common Glossy Ibis of the Western Hemisphere, but the lores are blackish and there are no white feathers about the base of the bill. (Plate 9)

RANGE.—Breeds locally from Maryland and New Jersey south to Florida, Texas, and Mexico, and in southern Europe, tropical Africa, Caucasia, India, Burma, and Ceylon.

COLORADO.—There are several published accounts of the occurrence of this wide-ranging bird from the state. A specimen, a high-plumaged bird (C.C. no. 4943) identified by H. C. Oberholser, was taken in northeastern El Paso Co. May 22, 1916.

* WHITE IBIS   *Eudocimus albus* (Linnaeus). [184]

RECOGNITION.—Length 21–27 inches. *Adult:* plumage entirely white except black-tipped primaries; naked face, chin, legs and feet red. *Young:* mainly dark brownish with head and neck speckled with dusky; belly, rump, and tail coverts white. (Plate 9)

RANGE.—Breeds in southern United States from South Carolina and the Gulf coast through Mexico and Central America to Venezuela and Peru. Winters from the coasts of Louisiana and Florida and from Mexico southward, and casually northward in autumn to California, South Dakota, Missouri, Illinois, North Carolina, Virginia, New Jersey, and Quebec.

Nebraska: one record near Bassett, Rock Co., in 1963 (Doris Gates, pers. comm.).

COLORADO.—Although Bergtold (1928) mentions "two records" for Colorado, the only reference we find is of a bird observed in the Todenworth Taxidermy Shop in Denver, which was taken in 1890, supposedly at Barr Lake, but this location is uncertain (H. G. Smith, 1896). The record is included in the 1957 A.O.U. Check-list.

ROSEATE SPOONBILL   *Ajaia ajaja* (Linnaeus). [183]

RECOGNITION.—Length 30–35 inches. *Adult:* plumage generally pink, with lesser wing coverts and tail coverts carmine; bald head and bill greenish-yellow, iris carmine; bill flattened, greatly widened at tip; neck white, legs red, and tail yellowish. *Young:* like adults; but without carmine on wings. (Plate 9)

RANGE.—Breeds locally along the Gulf coast from Texas to Florida and southward to Argentina and Chile. Wanders casually north of breeding range and winters from southern Texas and Florida southward.

Nebraska: one collected at Odessa June 5, 1932, and one seen near Hastings in 1963. Kansas: one, a male taken in Butler Co. Mar. 20, 1899; Utah: flock of five reported from Wendover July 2, 1919, and one collected.

COLORADO.—Straggler. Morrison (1888) reported the capture of an adult at Silverton about June 15, 1888, a specimen which died in captivity and the skin not saved; H. G. Smith (1896) saw one in a taxidermy shop in Denver, said to have been taken near Pueblo; and there is a specimen in the Museum (no. 7388), an immature in typical pink plumage, which was shot on Riverside Res. Sept. 1, 1913 by L. L. Remer. Don Watson (letter) reported an interesting occurrence in the southwestern part of the state, seven spoonbills which he observed on Upper Cahone Res. May 24, 1938. The reservoir is near the Hovenweep National Monument, about one-half mile from the Utah line, in Montezuma County.

Order ANSERIFORMES: Screamers, Swans, Geese, and Ducks
Family ANATIDAE: Swans, Geese, and Ducks

WHISTLING SWAN   *Olor columbianus* (Ord). [180]

RECOGNITION.—Length 48–56 inches. *Adult:* plumage pure white, head and neck sometimes rusty vinaceous, a small yellow spot on lores; eye brown; bill, legs, and feet black; the nostril closer to tip of bill than to the eye. *Young:* plumage washed with gray; bill purplish; legs and feet flesh-colored. (Plate 10)

RANGE.—Breeds mainly in the far north from Cape Prince of Wales and Point Barrow east across northern Canada. Winters along the Atlantic and Pacific coasts, and rarely on the Gulf coast and to Baja California. Migrates through the interior.

Nebraska: uncommon migrant; Kansas: rare transient and winter resident; New Mexico: uncommon migrant; Utah: transient, and regular visitor to Bear River marshes; Wyoming: uncommon migrant.

COLORADO.—An uncommon but rather regular migrant upon the lakes and reservoirs of the Upper Sonoran and Transition Zones.

TRUMPETER SWAN   *Olor buccinator* (Richardson). [181]

RECOGNITION.—Length 60–65 inches. Similar to Whistling Swan, but slightly larger and without yellow spot before the eye; nostril closer to eye than in Whistling Swan. (Plate 10)

RANGE.—Former breeding range extensive over northwestern North America east to Indiana but now limited to Wyoming, Montana, Idaho, British Columbia, and southern Alaska. Winters in southeastern Alaska, British Columbia, Montana, and Wyoming.

Nebraska: irregular migrant, formerly bred in Sandhill Lakes area; Kansas: formerly uncommon migrant; New Mexico: one reported from Mesilla Park in Nov. 1931 (Ligon, 1961); Utah: former rare migrant; Wyoming: resident in northwest, breeding in Yellowstone National and Teton Parks.

COLORADO.—The only record for Colorado appears to be an adult male (C. S. U. no. 4560) found dead near Fort Collins Nov. 25, 1915 by J. L. Gray (Burnett, 1916). The mounted specimen was donated to the Denver Museum of Natural History (no. 25547).

MUTE SWAN   *Cygnus olor* (Gmelin). [178.2]

RECOGNITION.—Length 56–58 inches. Generally similar in appearance to the Whistling and Trumpeter Swans, but has a tubercle or black knob at base of bill. (Not illustrated in color)

RANGE.—Extensive breeding range from the British Isles, Scandinavia, southern Russia to eastern Siberia, and south to Iran; introduced locally in the United States.

COLORADO.—Introduced species: casual breeding pairs near Denver.

CANADA GOOSE   *Branta canadensis maxima* Delacour. [172h]

RECOGNITION.—Length 38–46 inches. Largest of the races of the Canada Goose. Body more elongate, and considerably larger neck, bill, and tarsus than the other subspecies; upper parts buffy-brown and under parts light; sometimes a white ring at base of neck and white spot on front of head. Wing: 426–551 mm.; tail: 147–170 mm.; culmen: 55–68 mm.; tarsus 90–106 mm.; weight of adults 12–18 lbs.

RANGE.—Formerly bred from Manitoba, North Dakota, and Minnesota south to Kansas, northern Arkansas, Tennessee, and western Kentucky. Eliminated over much of its ancestral range but local breeding communities still exist.

Nebraska and Kansas: probably breeding bird of early days, but status at present (1964) undetermined; New Mexico: breeding geese observed in 1853–54 (Henry, 1855) at Fort Thorn, along the Rio Grande near the present town of Hatch, Dona Ana Co., not far north of the New Mexico-Mexico line, were 500 miles farther south than their nearest known breeding neighbors (F. M. Bailey, 1928). They could have been members of this race, or an undescribed form.

COLORADO.—No early day state specimens exist, so far as we know, and the only references of nesting on the eastern slope are those of Dr. Coues who "found them breeding in large numbers" in North Park—on the drainage of the North Platte, and a nest at Niwot, Boulder Co., at 5500 feet in 1897. Approximately 1500–2000 non-migrating birds, derived from captive stock, now nest regularly in Denver and Fort Collins areas.

Branta canadensis moffitti Aldrich. [172f]

RECOGNITION.—Length 35–43 inches. *Adult:* similar to *maxima* but smaller; plumage mainly pale gray, the upper parts buffy brown and the under parts very light to grayish; eye brown, head, neck, rump, and tail black; white cheek patch extending beneath throat; tail coverts white. *Young:* like the adult, but with some blackish on cheeks;

adult: wing: 420–520 mm.; culmen: 48–59; tarsus: 82–101 mm.; weight 6–13 pounds; downy young Plate 18; adults Plate 11. (Length given on color plate should read as above.)

RANGE.—Breeds in the Great Basin from western Colorado to the eastern part of the Pacific states, northward to British Columbia, and Alberta to southwestern Manitoba. Winters from southern British Columbia, Wyoming, and Colorado southward.

Nebraska: species common migrant, five races recognized, but not this form; Kansas: species common transient, possibly six races; New Mexico: common migrant and winter resident as a species; Utah: common breeding bird of Bear River Refuge, and probably winter resident; Wyoming: common resident.

COLORADO.—Formerly bred commonly in the proper habitat west of the Continental Divide. Breeds locally at present in northwestern Colorado. Winters along reservoirs of the eastern prairies and on the western slope—the Colorado nesting population probably migrating to southern California.

Branta canadensis parvipes (Cassin). [172g]

RECOGNITION.—Length 25–30 inches. Medium-sized goose similar to *B.c. moffitti* in shape and color; under parts light. Wing: 406–442 mm.; culmen: 36–49 mm.; tarsus: 72–88 mm.; weight 5–8 pounds. (Plate 11)

RANGE.—Nests in the interior of Canada and west to Fairbanks, Alaska, probably intergrading with the smaller *taverneri* of the north, and larger *moffitti* to the south. Summer range not definitely determined, but center of abundance probably in the Mackenzie basin. Migrates through central states with individuals reaching both coasts.

Nebraska and Kansas: migrant and winter visitor; New Mexico: probably winter resident; Wyoming: common migrant.

COLORADO.—Very common in winter upon some reservoirs of eastern Colorado. Generally reaches the state a short time before the migrant *B.c. moffitti* arrives from Canadian areas.

Branta canadensis interior Todd. [172e]

RECOGNITION.—Length 25–30 inches. Medium-sized bird, darker and browner below than *B.c. parvipes,* and averaging larger. Wing: 410–549 mm.; culmen: 43–64 mm.; tarsus: 75–93 mm. Weight: 6–8 pounds.

RANGE.—Breeds in the northeastern part of Canada adjacent to Hudson and James Bays, south to Minnesota and Michigan; winters from Ontario, Minnesota, and Michigan to the Gulf coast, and migrates down the Mississippi Valley, ranging west to Colorado prairies.

COLORADO.—Casual winter visitor. A male (no. 25406) and a female (no. 33805) were collected in Adams Co. Feb. 26, 1947, and Dec. 20, 1963.

Branta canadensis taverneri Delacour. [172j]

RECOGNITION.—Length 25–28 inches. Similar to *B.c. parvipes,* but smaller and browner below. Larger and much lighter below than *minima,* and browner below and averaging larger than *hutchinsii.* Wing: 362–424 mm.; culmen: 32–40 mm.; tarsus: 64–82 mm. Weight 3–6 pounds.

RANGE.—Breeds along the coastal areas and inland in Arctic Alaska and Canada from Wainwright and Barrow eastward to the Mackenzie, probably intergrading with *B.c. minima* to the west and with *B.c. parvipes* to the south.

COLORADO.—A few small geese occur regularly in the mixed flocks of Canada Geese wintering on the eastern prairies. They arrive from their Arctic breeding ground the latter part of October and remain throughout the winter on the large reservoirs, in company with the other migrating forms. There are twelve specimens in the Museum collection, seven of which we believe originated along the Arctic slope west of the Mackenzie delta, for they seem to agree in color and size with fifteen specimens listed by Bailey (1948) from Arctic Alaska, a new race which Dr. Jean Delacour named *B.c. taverneri* (Am. Mus. Novitates, N. Y. 1537, 1951).

Branta canadensis hutchinsii (Richardson). [172a]

RECOGNITION.—Length 23–26 inches. Slightly larger than the very dark-breasted *minima,* and smaller and paler below than *taverneri.* Wing: 340–408 mm.; culmen: 31–39 mm.; tarsus: 65–75 mm.; weight 3–5 pounds.

RANGE.—According to A.O.U. Check-list this subspecies breeds near the Arctic coast of Northwest Territory from Queen Maud Gulf east to the shores of Melville Peninsula, Southampton and Baffin Islands, and possibly Ellesmere Island. This race, known as Hutchins' Goose to sportsmen, winters along the Gulf coast south into Mexico, and a few wander westward from the Mississippi Valley to the eastern plains of Colorado.

Nebraska and Kansas: uncommon winter visitor.

COLORADO.—Uncommon straggler. There are two specimens from Larimer Co. and three from Baca Co. in the Museum collection.

Branta canadensis minima Ridgway. [172c]

RECOGNITION.—Length 23–25 inches. The smallest race of the Canada Goose; dark cinnamon-brown below; tiny bill. Wing: 330–375 mm.; culmen: 26–32 mm.; tarsus: 60–70 mm. Weight 3–4 pounds.

RANGE.—Breeds along the northwestern coast of Alaska to Wainwright, where it may intergrade with *B.c. taverneri.* Winters from British Columbia to southern California and interior valleys.

Kansas: three on Sherwood Lake near Topeka Mar. 24, 1967 (L. B. Carson, pers. comm.).

COLORADO.—There is one record from the state, a male (no. 26118) collected three miles northwest of Colorado Springs by Robert Stabler April 15, 1949.

BRANT   *Branta bernicla hrota* (Muller). [173a]

RECOGNITION.—Length 23–30 inches. Small dark goose with black head and neck with white crescent on sides of upper neck; chest black, back and scapulars brown, tail black, and upper and lower tail feathers conspicuously white; flanks, breast, and belly light grayish to gray-brown (not illustrated in color).

RANGE.—Nests in Arctic maritime regions of western Europe, Greenland, and west in North America to about 100° W. longitude, Baffin Island, and on Southampton Island. Winters on the northwestern coast of Europe from the North Sea to France, and in North America along the Atlantic Ocean south to North Carolina, and less commonly on the Pacific coast to California. Casual in many interior states.

Nebraska: reported as a straggler; Kansas: one specimen collected Leavenworth Co. Nov. 15, 1879, and some sight records.

COLORADO.—Cooke (1897) lists one shot at Fort Lyon Apr. 11, 1883, and one was live trapped at Two Buttes Res. Jan. 16, 1964 (A.F.N. 18:367).

BLACK BRANT   *Branta nigricans* (Lawrence). [174]

RECOGNITION.—Length 23–30 inches. Similar to *B.b. hrota,* but under parts darker and white on neck more extensive (not illustrated in color).

RANGE.—Nests in Arctic maritime regions of eastern Asia and western North America east to long. 110° W., and south to Nelson Island, Alaska.

Kansas: sight record *B. nigricans* from Coffey Co. in 1955; Utah and Wyoming: *B. nigricans* recorded as a straggler.

COLORADO.—Sclater (1912) lists one shot at Fort Lyon Apr. 11, 1883; AMB and RJN record a bird killed near Loveland, Weld Co., in Nov. or Dec. 1954; and AMB photographed an adult which stayed with Canada Geese in City Park, Denver, from Feb. 5 to Feb. 22, 1966. This species probably will be considered as a race of *B. bernicla* in future editions of the A.O.U.

WHITE-FRONTED GOOSE   *Anser albifrons frontalis* Baird. [171]

RECOGNITION.—Length 27–30 inches. *Adult:* plumage mainly gray-brown, front of face and upper tail coverts white; under parts whitish variably blotched with black; bill pinkish or orange; legs and feet orange-yellow. *Young:* lacks the white on face, and the under parts are brownish. (Plate 11)

RANGE.—The species breeds in high latitudes, and the Old World birds migrate in winter to northern Africa, southern Asia, China, and Japan. This race nests in western Arctic Alaska and Canada. Winters in the western United States and south to central Mexico.

Nebraska: a common migrant and abundant in the central Platte Valley; Kansas: regular transient but more numerous in central and western parts; New Mexico: uncommon winter visitor; Utah: uncommon transient but several specimen records; Wyoming: uncommon straggler.

COLORADO.—Uncommon migrant and winter resident.

Late spring Apr. 28 Middle Park; early fall Oct. 1 Adams Co.

SNOW GOOSE   *Chen hyperborea hyperborea* (Pallas). [169]

RECOGNITION.—Length 24–30 inches. *Adult:* plumage white, except for rusty wash on head, and black primaries; bill, legs, and feet pinkish-red. *Young:* mainly grayish brown, more rusty on head; primaries black; rump, tail coverts, and belly white; bill, legs, and feet dull vinaceous. (Plate 12)

RANGE—Breeds along the Arctic coast of eastern Siberia and Alaska from Point Barrow, eastward to Baffin Island and Greenland, south to Ontario; winters in two disconnected areas, from British Columbia, Washington, and California, and from the Florida Gulf coast to Texas, south into Mexico.

Nebraska: common migrant in east, uncommon in west; Kansas: common transient and less common in winter; New Mexico: fairly common migrant and occasional winter visitor; Utah: common transient and less common in winter; Wyoming: uncommon migrant.

COLORADO.—Regular transient and uncommon winter resident on both sides of the Continental Divide.

Early fall Oct. 10 Denver; late spring May 23 Denver and Durango.

BLUE GOOSE   *Chen caerulescens* (Linnaeus). [169.1]

RECOGNITION.—Length 24–30 inches. *Adult*: head and neck white, eyes brown; mantle and under parts dark bluish-gray. Some are white below—probably crosses between Snow and Blue Geese; tail coverts white. Immatures duller and browner, with brownish-gray heads and white chin patch. (Plate 12)

RANGE.—Breeds on Southampton and Baffin Islands and west coast of Hudson Bay. Winters on the Louisiana Gulf coast from the Mississippi delta along the coast to near Brownsville, Texas and south into Veracruz.

Nebraska: a common migrant; Kansas: common transient in east, less so in west; New Mexico: winter resident; Utah: one record, Bear River marshes, Oct. 13, 1936.

COLORADO.—An adult (no. 28624) was shot on the Ordway City Res. Nov. 22, 1953; one was seen on the Deer Trail Res., Arapahoe Co., in Apr. 1938; an adult observed on Lake Henry Oct. 10, 1954; one photographed on Prewitt Res. Oct. 20, 1961; two were recorded on Sheridan Lake along the Colorado-Kansas line Mar. 18, 1962; and one on Union Res., Weld Co., Sept. 13, 1965 (C.B.N. 13:21).

ROSS' GOOSE   *Chen rossii* (Cassin). [170]

RECOGNITION.—Length 20–26 inches. *Adult*: similar to the Snow Goose but smaller; lacks the black stripe along the bill, and seldom has a rusty head. (Plate 12)

RANGE.—Breeds in vicinity of the Perry River, northeastern Mackenzie, on the coast of Queen Maud Gulf, and on Boas River, Southampton Island. Winters chiefly in California and has been recorded casually in many western states south to Louisiana and Mexico.

Nebraska: one collected in Nov. 1922 south of Hooper, now in Nebr. State Museum, and several observed in 1964 (Nebr. Bird Review, 34:46); Kansas: one sight record at Wyandotte County Lake, Nov. 22, 1951; New Mexico: rare transient, specimen collected in Socorro Co. Dec. 30, 1956 (Condor, 65:166); Utah: rare transient.

COLORADO.—Four specimens of this rare goose from Colorado include: an adult male (no. 416) collected near Longmont Dec. 23, 1906; an immature (no. 28300) from Two Buttes Res. Nov. 7, 1954; another (no. 28625) from near Fort Collins Jan. 21, 1955, and a female in the U.C. Museum obtained in Boulder Co. Nov. 15, 1955. One was shot near Crook in Nov. 1956; one observed at M.H.D.C. May 12, 1956; two banded at Bonny Res. in Apr. 1957; an immature at the City Park duck pond (Denver) from Feb. 7, 1959 into early March; and two were caught at Two Buttes Res. Jan. 16, 1964.

MALLARD   *Anas platyrhynchos platyrhynchos* Linnaeus. [132]

RECOGNITION.—Length 21–27 inches. *Adult male*: head and neck brilliant green; eye brown; breast dark chestnut; wings with purplish-blue speculum bordered by black and white stripes; recurved tail feathers black; sides and belly gray; bill yellowish; legs and feet reddish-orange; the green of the head lost in eclipse plumage. *Adult female*: plumage brown, variously mottled with buffy and black. *Young*: like female, but darker brown; adults Plate 13; downy young Plate 18.

RANGE.—Breeds from Alaska, Canada, and southward except the Atlantic coast and the southeastern states, to northern Baja California; also in Iceland, Norway, Finland, Russia, Siberia to 65°N. south to the Mediterranean, Iran, Tibet, China, Korea, and Japan. Winters from Alaska, Canada, and northern states south to Panama; and in the Old World from northern Europe south to Ethiopia, India, China, and Borneo.

Nebraska, Kansas, New Mexico, Utah, and Wyoming: common migrant, summer resident, and winter visitor.

COLORADO.—Resident; common in summer and winter, and abundant in migration. Upper Sonoran, Transition, and Canadian Zones. Recorded from all parts of the state.

MEXICAN DUCK   *Anas diazi novimexicana* Huber. [133.1]   —

RECOGNITION.—Length 21–22 inches. Similar to female Mallard, but darker, with greenish-yellow bill; wing speculum bordered above and below with white bands as in Mallard, the *two bands* distinguishing this species from Black Duck and Mottled Duck, which have only one; sexes alike, except that males average darker than females. (Plate 13)

RANGE.—Breeds from northern New Mexico south in the Gila watershed and in the Rio Grande Valley to northern Chihuahua; winters from breeding range into Mexico.

Nebraska: one specimen from Cherry Co. Oct. 21, 1921; New Mexico: uncommon summer resident, breeding principally along the Rio Grande drainage.

COLORADO.—Three specimens have been taken in the state, a female (no. 20557) on October 29, 1939 near Henderson; a male (no. 24392) in full plumage at M.H.D.C. Nov. 19, 1944; and a female (no. 25374) on Jumbo Reservoir in Sedgwick Co. Mar. 4, 1947. Ryder saw a pair in Rio Grande County May 16, 1950, and Bailey observed a high-plumaged male at M.H.D.C. June 20, 1957.

BLACK DUCK   *Anas rubripes* Brewster. [133a]

RECOGNITION.—Length 21–25 inches. Similar to common Mallard, but dusky-brown or black, and has *one white wing bar* (below speculum); head streaked with buffy; legs reddish. (Plate 13)

RANGE.—Breeds from northern Manitoba, Ontario, Quebec, and Labrador south to North Dakota, Minnesota, and Wisconsin and east to West Virginia. Winters from the breeding area south to the Gulf coast.

Nebraska: a rare migrant; Kansas: regular but uncommon transient and winter resident in the east; Utah: sight record for Rush Lake, Iron Co., in Nov. 1872, and specimen collected in Bear River marshes Dec. 8, 1942; Wyoming: straggler.

COLORADO.—There have been various sight observations and reported killings of Black Ducks. Bailey and Niedrach (1965) list twelve reports from the eastern prairies, including three specimens in the Museum.

MOTTLED DUCK   *Anas fulvigula maculosa* Sennett. [134a]

RECOGNITION.—Length 20–21 inches. Much like the Mexican Duck, but the wing speculum bordered by only one white band *below* as in the Black Duck, instead of two, above and below, as in the Mallard and the Mexican Duck. Streaked with black on head and under parts; back black, striped with buff; streaks lacking on throat. (Plate 13)

RANGE.—Breeds along the Louisiana and Texas coasts; ranges casually to bordering states.

Kansas: one specimen from Woodson Co. Mar. 11, 1876, and nesting in Barton Co. during the summer of 1963.

COLORADO.—Only two specimens of this duck have been taken in the state, an adult (no. 353) collected near Loveland Nov. 6, 1907 by W. N. W. Blaney, and another adult male (no. 33794) secured by Ronald A. Ryder on Timnath Res., eight miles east of Ft. Collins, on September 18, 1962 (Ryder, 1963).

GADWALL   *Anas strepera* Linnaeus. [135]

RECOGNITION.—Length 19–21 inches. *Adult male*: head and neck streaked with brown and black; eye reddish-brown; breast, back, and sides bluish-gray with a scaled effect; wing coverts edged with chestnut and patch on wing *white*; belly white, tail coverts black; legs and feet yellowish. *Female and young*: plumage mainly brown streaked with black; throat and under parts white; bill, legs and feet dull yellow; adults Plate 14; downy young Plate 18.

RANGE.—Breeds from southern Alaska, British Columbia, Alberta, Manitoba, and Quebec south through California and Nevada, and east to Minnesota and northeastern states; in the Old World from Iceland, British Isles, Sweden, Poland, Russia, Mongolia, south to Spain, Algeria, Iran, Afghanistan, and China. New World birds winter from their breeding range south to the Gulf coast and to southern Baja California and Mexico.

Nebraska: common migrant, and breeder in the Sandhill region; Kansas: transient and recorded breeding near Great Bend in 1962 by L. O. Nossaman (L. B. Carson, pers. comm.); New Mexico: common migrant and less numerous summer resident; Utah: fairly common summer resident, and a few in winter; Wyoming: common migrant and breeder, and occasionally winters.

COLORADO.—Common spring and fall migrant with many remaining locally in summer and winter throughout the state. There are references in the literature of nesting in San Luis Valley, North Park, Brown's Park, the Yampa Valley, and in Boulder, Larimer, Grand, and Alamosa Counties.

PINTAIL   *Anas acuta* Linnaeus. [143]

RECOGNITION.—Length 25–30 inches. *Adult male*: head uniform dull brown sometimes glossed with purplish or green, eye dark brown; neck stripe, breast and belly white; back and sides pearl gray, marked with fine black lines; tail black and pointed. *Adult female*: head and neck dull rusty, finely streaked with black; throat white; rest of plumage brownish, mottled with black and darker above; speculum dark brown; adults Plate 14; downy young Plate 18.

RANGE.—Breeds in Old World in western Greenland, Iceland, Scandinavia south to Netherlands, France, and Spain; from northern Russia east across northern Siberia, Kamchatka; and in the New World from Alaska to Hudson Bay, across northern states from Pennsylvania to Nevada, south to southern California. Winters from southern British Columbia to Central America, Hawaii, and from northwestern Colorado and Chesapeake Bay to Panama. In Old World from southern part of breeding area south to Tanganyika, Kenya, Arabia, Thailand, and the Philippines.

Nebraska and Kansas: abundant migrant and local breeder; New Mexico: abundant migrant, winter resident, and uncommon nesting bird; Utah: common migrant, wintering in small numbers, and nesting in northern areas; Wyoming: common migrant and breeder, occasionally winters.

COLORADO.—One of the most common species of ducks in migration in all parts of the state with many remaining locally to nest.

GREEN-WINGED TEAL   *Anas carolinensis* Gmelin. [139]

RECOGNITION.—Length 12.5–15 inches. Smallest of our fresh water ducks. *Adult male*: head rich chestnut with an iridescent green patch extending from the brown eye to the short black crest; breast brownish, white stripe across body near bend of wing; speculum green. *Adult female*: dark brown above mottled with buffy and dusky; speculum green; yellowish under tail coverts in both sexes; adults Plate 15; downy young Plate 18.

RANGE.—Breeds from north-central Alaska, Manitoba, James Bay, Quebec, and Newfoundland south to California, Arizona, Nebraska, Ohio, Pennsylvania and New York. Winters from southern British Columbia to Nebraska and Chesapeake Bay, south to southern Mexico, and islands of Caribbean.

Nebraska: common transient and winter resident, and occasional breeder; Kansas: common migrant and uncommon in winter; New Mexico: widely distributed migrant and breeding bird of northern lakes; Utah: common in migration, summer resident, and wintering in south; Wyoming: common migrant and breeder, occasionally winters.

COLORADO.—Common spring and fall migrant with a few in summer and winter. Recorded nesting in Adams, Alamosa, Boulder, Jackson, Larimer, Saguache, and Routt Counties.

BLUE-WINGED TEAL   *Anas discors discors* Linnaeus. [140]

RECOGNITION.—Length 14.5–16 inches. *Adult male*: head and neck gray; white crescent patch before eye; eye brown; large pale blue wing patch anterior to green speculum. In eclipse plumage the male resembles the female. *Adult female*: dark brown above mottled with buffy; breast and sides grayish-brown mottled with dusky; belly whitish; blue wing patches; adult Plate 15; downy young Plate 18.

RANGE.—Breeds from British Columbia, Saskatchewan, Manitoba, Ontario, Quebec, and Nova Scotia, south to California, Arizona, Texas, and Louisiana. Winters casually north to Illinois and from southern states to Brazil.

Nebraska and Kansas: common transient and summer resident; New Mexico: common in migration and nests throughout the state; Utah: transient and uncommon summer resident; Wyoming: common migrant and breeder.

COLORADO.—Common migrant and summer resident, ranging from the prairies to mountain lakes of the Transition Zone. The species has been recorded nesting commonly in Adams and Larimer Counties, in North Park, in San Luis Valley and elsewhere.

Early spring Feb. 12, 1959 Platteville and Mar. 18 Boulder (C.B.N. 6:33); late fall Oct. 30 M.H.D.C.; winter Dec. 29 Colo. Spgs. (above).

CINNAMON TEAL   *Anas cyanoptera septentrionalium* Snyder and Lumsden. [141]

RECOGNITION.—Length 15–17 inches. *Adult male:* head, neck, and under parts cinnamon red, with crown blackish; large pale blue wing patch; eye orange. In eclipse plumage the male resembles the female. *Adult female:* resembles the female Blue-winged Teal; adults Plate 15; downy young Plate 18.

RANGE.—Breeds in British Columbia, Alberta, Saskatchewan, Montana, and Nebraska south to central California into northern Mexico. Winters from southwestern United States to Panama and in South America.

Nebraska: rare migrant, and one breeding record from Garden County; Kansas: uncommon transient; New Mexico: transient, and nesting in western half of the state; Utah: migrant and common summer resident; Wyoming: common breeder and migrant.

COLORADO.—Summer resident throughout the state in Upper Sonoran and Transition Zones.

Early spring Mar. 2 San Luis Valley (Sam Gadd); late fall Nov. 15 Weld Co.; winter two Dec. 20, 1962 Longmont.

AMERICAN WIDGEON   *Mareca americana* (Gmelin). [137]

RECOGNITION.—Length 18–22 inches. *Adult male:* back, breast, and sides vinaceous; head greenish with forehead and crown white, with eye yellow-brown; large white patch on *front* of wing helps distinguish this species from the Gadwall; belly and small flank patch white; bill bluish tipped with black; legs and feet yellow-brown. *Female and young:* grayish-brown above mottled with buffy and black; wing patch largely brown; speculum mainly blackish; sides and flanks rusty brown; adults Plate 16; downy young Plate 18.

RANGE.—Breeds from northwestern and interior Alaska to Hudson Bay, and south through British Columbia, northeastern California, and eastward uncommonly across northern United States. Winters along the Pacific coast from southeastern Alaska to Panama, and from Chesapeake Bay and southern Nevada southward to Central America.

Nebraska: common transient, and a nesting record from Cherry Co.; Kansas: common migrant, nested in Barton Co. in 1963, and rare in winter; New Mexico: common migrant and breeds rather commonly; Utah: common in migration, uncommon summer resident; Wyoming: common breeder and migrant, occasional in winter.

COLORADO.—Common in migration throughout the state, breeding in San Luis Valley and North Park, with a few occurring in winter.

* EUROPEAN WIDGEON   *Mareca penelope* (Linnaeus). [136]

RECOGNITION.—Length 17.75–20 inches; *Adult male*: head and neck bright *chestnut*; forehead and crown buffy; body gray, breast vinaceous; wings grayish-brown with conspicuous white areas shown in flight; belly white; bill gray-blue with tip black; iris brown. *Adult female*: grayish-brown above; head and throat buffy, streaked and barred with black; wing coverts brownish, white below (not illustrated in color).

RANGE.—Old World species breeding from Iceland, British Isles, Scandinavia, and northern Finland across northern Russia and Siberia, south to Poland, Turkestan to northwestern Mongolia. Winters from British Isles, southern Scandinavia, and Russia to India, Arabia, and northern Africa. Recorded regularly, but rarely, in North America from Alaska and Newfoundland to southern states.

Nebraska: specimen collected at West Point, Cuming Co.; Kansas: pair reported from Lake Shawnee, Shawnee Co. April 16, 1954; New Mexico: observed near Clayton Apr. 16, 1954 by A. J. Krehbiel and W. W. Cook (Ligon, 1961); Utah: male in full plumage collected at Bear River Refuge on Oct. 19, 1955 (Condor, 58: 390).

COLORADO.—Observed in Park County on South Platte River Apr. 18, 1964 and Antero Reservoir the following day by Robert and Nancy Gustafson.

SHOVELER   *Spatula clypeata* (Linnaeus). [142]

RECOGNITION.—Length 17–20 inches; bill long and broader at tip than in other ducks. *Adult male*: head and upper neck glossy green, eye bright yellow; breast white, under parts chestnut-red; wing shoulders pale blue, speculum green; flank patch white. In eclipse plumage the male resembles the female. *Adult female*: plumage mainly brownish; wing colors less brilliant than males; adults Plate 16; downy young Plate 18.

RANGE.—Breeds from western Alaska irregularly across Canada, south to New York and Pennsylvania, west to Oregon and south to California, Arizona, and Texas, with records from many of the Mississippi Valley states. In the Old World, in British Isles, Scandinavia, Russia, and Siberia, south to Spain and southern Russia. Winters occasionally in northern part of breeding range, but more commonly in southern states and south into Mexico and West Indies; and in the Old World in Ceylon, the Malay States, Africa, and the Philippines.

Nebraska: common transient, breeding locally; Kansas: common migrant, and female with young noted in Barton Co. about 1930, and nest with eggs in Finney County in 1952; New Mexico: common summer and winter resident; Utah: common transient and summer resident; Wyoming: common breeder and migrant.

COLORADO.—Common in migration mid-April into early June, but not numerous in summer; fall migration starts in late September. An uncommon nester in eastern counties, but there are reports of breeding in North Park and San Luis Valley.

WOOD DUCK   *Aix sponsa* (Linnaeus). [144]

RECOGNITION.—Length 17–20 inches. *Adult male*: head and crest glossy-green and purple, crest streaked with white; eye orange-red; white on throat extends on cheeks and side of neck; back and tail glossy-green; breast brownish-purple spotted with white; sides grayish-buff, belly white. *Adult female*: head and neck gray, with crown glossed with purple; breast, sides and back brownish; throat, belly, and eyering white; wing glossy-green and blue; adults Plate 16; downy young Plate 18.

RANGE.—Breeds from British Columbia across southern Canada and south locally over much of the United States. Winters from southern British Columbia, central Missouri, and southern Virginia to Jamaica and central Mexico.

Nebraska: uncommon migrant, and occasional summer resident around Omaha; Kansas: rare transient in west, locally common in east; New Mexico and Utah: uncommon transient; Wyoming rare migrant in northwest.

COLORADO.—Uncommon with the majority of records from eastern counties. Noted nesting along Willow Creek, a tributary of the Dolores River, Dolores Co., in June 1950 (Ferd Kleinschnitz, pers. comm.).

REDHEAD   *Aythya americana* (Eyton). [146]

RECOGNITION.—Length 17–22 inches. *Adult male*: rounded head and neck chestnut-red; eye yellow; breast black; sides and back dark gray. In eclipse plumage the male shows mottled under parts, brownish back, and dull reddish-brown head. *Adult female*: plumage mainly dark brown, with throat, belly, and faint line around tip of bill white; wings gray; eye brown; adults Plate 17, downy young Plate 19.

RANGE.—Breeds from British Columbia, Alberta, Mackenzie, Saskatchewan, and Manitoba, Pennsylvania, Wisconsin, and Iowa to Washington and California, and from Colorado to central Arizona. Winters from British Columbia east to Massachusetts and south into Mexico.

Nebraska: a common migrant, summer resident and breeder; Kansas: migrant, occasional winter resident, and nested in Barton Co. in 1928; New Mexico: fairly common migrant and winter resident, and nesting on high lakes; Utah: transient and common summer resident; Wyoming: common breeder and migrant, with a few in winter.

COLORADO.—Summer resident, fairly common in migration throughout the state in the Upper Sonoran and Transition Zones; a few remain through the winter. Nests regularly in the Barr Lake drainage, and probably elsewhere along eastern reservoirs, in San Luis Valley, North Park, and Brown's Park.

RING-NECKED DUCK   *Aythya collaris* (Donovan). [150]

RECOGNITION.—Length 15–18 inches. *Adult male*: somewhat similar to scaup ducks, but has black back and a chestnut collar; chin and belly white; bill blue-gray with black tip bordered by white band; eye yellow. *Adult female*: plumage mainly grayish-brown with face, chin, and belly white; eyering white; bill as in male, but duller; downy young Plate 19; adults Plate 20.

RANGE.—Breeds from southern Alaska east across southern Canada and south into Maine, Pennsylvania, Iowa, Nebraska, Oregon, California, and Arizona. Winters from southern British Columbia, southern Illinois, northern Arkansas, and Chesapeake Bay to Guatemala.

Nebraska: uncommon migrant and rare breeder; Kansas: fairly common in migration and rare in winter; New Mexico: uncommon migrant, and winter visitor; Utah: uncommon transient; Wyoming: uncommon migrant, and breeds in northwestern part of state.

COLORADO.—Regular transient and uncommon summer resident in marsh and reservoir areas throughout the state. Several broods of downy young observed in Mineral Co. July 18, 1949, and in North Park in the summers of 1952 and 1955.

CANVASBACK   *Aythya valisineria* (Wilson). [147]

RECOGNITION.—Length 20–24 inches. *Adult male*: elongated head and neck reddish-brown and eye red; crown, chin, breast, and tail coverts black; back grayish-white finely crosslined with dusky; belly, sides, and axillars white. *Adult female*: head, neck, and breast dark brown; throat whitish, eye brown; adults Plate 17; downy young Plate 19.

RANGE.—Breeds in central Alaska, northern Mackenzie, Great Slave Lake and Manitoba, Minnesota to Nevada and California. Winters from British Columbia, Montana, Tennessee, Lake Erie, Lake Ontario to Quebec, Massachusetts and south to Mexico.

Nebraska: uncommon transient, and a summer resident in Sandhill region. Kansas: occasional winter resident, common migrant, and recorded breeding near Great Bend by L. O. Nossaman (L. B. Carson, pers. comm.); New Mexico: migrant, winter resident and uncommon breeder; Utah: fairly common migrant, and possible breeder in Bear River Marshes; Wyoming: common migrant and uncommon nesting bird.

COLORADO.—Summer resident in small numbers; a few occasionally in winter. Nests and eggs were found at Barr Lake June 20, 1900 and July 4, and on June 8, 1907. Seven downy young observed in same locality June 25, 1938, and broods of young in North Park in the summers of 1951, 1954, and 1955.

GREATER SCAUP   *Aythya marila nearctica* Stejneger. [148]

RECOGNITION.—Length 16–21 inches. *Adult male*: black head with greenish gloss (in some lights); neck, breast, and upper back black; back light gray with under parts and sides conspicuously white; bill bluish. *Adult female*: plumage mainly brown, with face, speculum, and belly white; long white stripe on extended wing; eye yellow. (Plate 20)

RANGE.—The species ranges throughout much of the Northern Hemisphere, breeding in high latitudes, and migrating in winter in the Old World to the British Isles and south to northern Africa, and through Asia east to China and Japan. The North American race breeds on the Arctic coast of Alaska and Canada and southward, rarely to British Columbia and North Dakota and Michigan. Winters on the Pacific, Atlantic, and Gulf coasts and occasionally around the Great Lakes, and in Nevada and Arizona.

Nebraska and Kansas: rare migrant; New Mexico: rare transient; Utah: uncommon migrant and possibly a winter visitor; Wyoming: rare migrant.

COLORADO.—Rare migrant and winter visitor in the Upper Sonoran and Transition Zones. Reported from Adams, Boulder, La Plata, Montrose, Morgan, San Juan, Summit, and Weld Counties.

Early fall Oct. 30 Longmont (no. 12535); late spring Apr. 5 Longmont.

LESSER SCAUP   *Aythya affinis* (Eyton). [149]

RECOGNITION.—Length 15–18 inches. *Adult male*: similar to the Greater Scaup, but slightly smaller and white stripe on extended wing *shorter* (see color plate for comparison); head purplish in some lights. Majority of "Bluebills" in Colorado are this species. *Adult female and young*: plumage mainly brown, with face, speculum, axillars, and belly white; downy young Plate 19; adults Plate 20.

RANGE.—Breeds from central Alaska across Canada, south into North Dakota to British Columbia and casually in Nebraska, Iowa, Missouri, and Ohio. Winters from British Columbia to Panama, and from Chesapeake Bay southward along the Gulf of Mexico to the West Indies, Central America, and northern South America.

Nebraska: common transient, occasionally breeding in Cherry Co.; Kansas: common migrant with few in winter and summer; New Mexico: common in migration and a few in winter; Utah: uncommon transient, and casual in summer; Wyoming: common breeder and migrant, occasionally winters.

COLORADO.—Common migrant and uncommon in winter and summer throughout the Upper Sonoran Zone. Forty-one broods of young recorded in 1951 in North Park, and sixty-seven broods in 1952.

COMMON GOLDENEYE   *Bucephala clangula americana* (Bonaparte). [151]

RECOGNITION.—Length 16–20 inches. *Adult male*: conspicuous white bird with black back and black head glossed with green; round white spot between eye and bill; eye golden-yellow; large white wing patch evident in flight; neck and under parts white; wings make whistling sound in flight. *Female and young*: head buffy-brown, eye yellowish; rest of plumage dark gray, except white belly and wing patch, and black rump; downy young Plate 19 listed under old name American Goldeneye; adults Plate 21.

RANGE.—The species occurs throughout much of the Northern Hemisphere. The American race breeds from Alaska across Canada and southward through Montana, North Dakota, Minnesota, Michigan, New York, Vermont, and Maine. Winters from Alaska to Baja California and from southern Canada through the central states to the Gulf coast, wherever there is open water.

Nebraska, Kansas, New Mexico, and Utah: uncommon migrant and winter visitor; Wyoming: common migrant and winter resident.

COLORADO.—Common migrant in late fall, and winter resident along the waterways throughout the state. A juvenile female collected Aug. 30, 1874 by Aiken in Conejos Co. at 9000 feet elevation, listed by B. & N. (1965) probably was a Barrow's Goldeneye.

Early fall Oct. 29 Denver; late spring June 1 M.H.D.C.

BARROW'S GOLDENEYE   *Bucephala islandica* (Gmelin). [152]

RECOGNITION.—Length 16.5–21 inches. *Adult male*: head glossed with purple; white *crescent* in front of yellow eye instead of rounded spot of white. *Female and young*: not distinguishable in the field from the Common Goldeneye. (Plate 21)

RANGE.—Breeds irregularly from Alaska across Canada to Greenland and Quebec, and from California, Washington, and Oregon to Nevada and northwest Wyoming. Winters along the Pacific coast from southern Alaska to central California, and on the Atlantic coast from the Gulf of St. Lawrence to Massachusetts; irregularly from British Columbia and northern Montana to southern Colorado.

Nebraska: rare visitor; New Mexico: one observed at Bitter Lake Dec. 22, 1956, and one near Clayton Feb. 23, 1957 (Ligon, 1961); Utah: rare migrant and winter visitor, but reported common near Logan during 1955–56 (seventeen on Christmas Count, A.F.N. 11:215); Wyoming: common transient, and breeds along mountain streams.

COLORADO.—A rare straggler in the Upper Sonoran, and formerly nesting into the Canadian Zone. Listed as a resident in Dolores Co. (Morrison, 1888). There are five Carter collected skins in the Museum, a female (no. 940) taken in Middle Park with the first set of eggs on June 17, 1876, and four high-plumaged males from near Breckenridge. Two were shot Mar. 26, and the others Apr. 1 and 2, 1877. Few specimens have been collected since Carter's time. Species formerly nested in Grand, Park, and Summit Counties.

BUFFLEHEAD   *Bucephala albeola* (Linnaeus). [153]

RECOGNITION.—Length 13–15 inches; from a distance appearing as a miniature Goldeneye. *Adult male*: small round-headed duck, mainly dark above and white below with much white in wings; head with large white patch, eye brown. *Adult female*: very small with under parts grayish-white, and white cheek spot and wing patch; downy young Plate 19; adults Plate 21.

RANGE.—Breeds from southern Alaska, British Columbia, Saskatchewan, Manitoba, and Ontario south to California and northern Montana; formerly east to Wisconsin and Iowa. Winters from Alaska to central Mexico and casually in nearly all of the states east of the Rockies, and from New Brunswick south along the Atlantic coast to Florida.

Nebraska: uncommon transient; Kansas: fairly common migrant, and occasional winter resident; New Mexico: widely distributed during migration, and a few in winter; Utah: uncommon migrant and winter resident; Wyoming: common transient, nesting in northwest.

COLORADO.—Regular migrant and winter visitor in the Upper Sonoran and Transition Zones.

Early fall Oct. 3 Barr Lake (no. 19480); late spring May 23 Ft. Collins.

OLDSQUAW   *Clangula hyemalis* (Linnaeus). [154]

RECOGNITION.—Length: male, 20–23 inches; female, 16–18 inches. *Adult male* in winter: crown, neck, and belly white; head patch around eye pale brown, bordered on lower side by patch of dark brown; eye brown to reddish; breast, wings, back, and middle tail feathers blackish-brown; central tail feathers conspicuously long. *Adult female* in winter: head white except for brown crown, ear patch, and throat; upper parts dark brown shading into grayish-brown on breast; neck and under parts white; tail feathers not elongated. (Plate 21)

RANGE.—Breeds in northern Alaska and Canada, Sweden, Norway, Finland, Russia, and Greenland, south through Bering Sea, the Siberian coast, Aleutian Islands, and east across Canada to Labrador. Winters in open water from southern part of its breeding range to Italy, Yugoslavia, the Black Sea, Iran, China, and Japan, and casually through most of the interior of the United States, occasionally to the Gulf coast.

Nebraska: a rare migrant, most numerous in east; Kansas: uncommon transient state-wide; Utah: rare migrant; Wyoming: straggler.

COLORADO.—Uncommon winter visitor on reservoirs of the Upper Sonoran Zone. Recorded in the literature are reports of birds observed or shot in Adams, Arapahoe, Boulder, El Paso, Larimer, Morgan, and Weld Counties, and there are ten specimens in the Museum.

Early fall Oct. 16 Loveland; late spring Mar. 7 Larimer Co.

HARLEQUIN DUCK   *Histrionicus histrionicus* (Linnaeus). [155]

RECOGNITION.—Length 15.5–20 inches. A small duck conspicuously marked with white on head, breast, and back. *Adult male*: head and neck dark bluish, with crown black and a chestnut border at nape; two white patches behind reddish-brown eye and one white patch before; back and under parts mainly grayish-blue with sides bright chestnut; wing with four white patches and dark blue speculum. *Adult female*: plumage mainly dusky brown, with two small white patches before brown eye and one behind the eye; belly mottled with grayish-white; downy young Plate 19; adults Plate 22.

RANGE.—Breeds in Alaska, Siberia, Labrador, and northwestern and western Canada, and south to California. Winters from the Aleutian Islands to central California and from Labrador to Massachusetts and casually on Lake Ontario, Lake Erie, and in the interior, in Idaho, Nebraska, and Missouri with stragglers recorded from Ohio, South Carolina, and Florida.

Nebraska: three records from Omaha area (Sept. 16, 1893 and Sept. 19, 1895); Wyoming: male (no. 258) in this Museum, mounted in the synoptic collection, was collected near Cody June 2, 1912 by R. Richardson, breeds on the mountain streams of the northwest.

COLORADO.—Straggler, rare; Upper Sonoran and Transition Zones. Carter collected a pair May 21, 1876 on Michigan Creek, Jackson Co., and both specimens are in the Museum collection.

* COMMON EIDER   *Somateria mollissima dresseri* Sharpe. [160]

RECOGNITION.—Length 23–26 inches. *Adult male*: head white except crown black; neck, breast, and upper parts white, black below, eye brown. *Adult female*: head, throat, and breast brown, back black; barred brown below. (Plate 22)

RANGE.—Breeds along the coasts of Labrador, eastern Quebec, and Newfoundland, south to Maine. Winters from Newfoundland and the Gulf of St. Lawrence south to New York and casually to North Carolina.

Kansas: one specimen from Douglas Co. Nov. 3, 1891.

COLORADO.—Cooke (1898) reported a bird killed by W. G. Smith at Loveland some time before 1892, on the authority of William Osburn. Bergtold (1932) listed a male eider observed on Marston Res. Feb. 25, 1932, which was in company with several hundred ducks of various species.

WHITE-WINGED SCOTER   *Melanitta deglandi deglandi* (Bonaparte). [165]

RECOGNITION.—Length 19–23 inches. *Adult male*: a large black duck with white patch behind eye and white speculum, eye white to gray. *Adult female*: plumage blackish-brown with white speculum and sometimes with white in front of and behind the brown eye. (Plate 22)

RANGE.—Breeds from the Mackenzie delta and British Columbia across Canada south to North Dakota and Washington. Winters from Aleutian Islands to Baja California, and from the Gulf of St. Lawrence to South Carolina; winters sporadically in British Columbia, on the Great Lakes, the Atlantic coast and recorded from Louisiana and Florida.

Nebraska: uncommon fall transient; Kansas: uncommon fall migrant (nine specimens from Douglas and Leavenworth Counties, 1927–1938); New Mexico: rare migrant, with at least three specimens taken; Utah: rare migrant and winter resident; Wyoming: rare transient.

COLORADO.—Winter visitor. There are many records of scoters shot on reservoirs of eastern counties; five were seen in Mesa Co. in Oct. 1912, and one collected on Grand Lake in the fall of 1937. Numerous observations are listed in *Colorado Bird Notes* from 1955 into 1966. The nine skins in the Museum series were secured in Adams, Boulder, Larimer, Morgan, and Weld Counties.

SURF SCOTER   *Melanitta perspicillata* (Linnaeus). [166]

RECOGNITION.—Length 18–21 inches. *Adult male*: black with white crown and occipital patches; bill varicolored with red, yellow, white, and black; eye white. *Adult female*: plumage generally blackish-brown with under parts lighter; sides of head with grayish-white patches; eye brown. (Plate 22)

RANGE.—Breeds from northwestern Alaska across Canada to Labrador, Hudson and James Bays, British Columbia, and Saskatchewan. Winters on the coast from Alaska to Baja California and from Bay of Fundy to Florida; on the Great Lakes and irregularly in many states in the interior, and rarely south to Louisiana.

Nebraska: straggler; Kansas: rare migrant (eight specimens from Douglas and Sedgwick Counties); New Mexico: one observed near Los Lunas Oct. 31, 1959 (Ligon, 1961, 307). Utah and Wyoming: rare migrant.

COLORADO.—Straggler, rare. Reports include one shot in Denver Oct. 1887, one found dead in North Park Nov. 2, 1951, a female observed Nov. 26–Dec. 4, 1954 in Cherry Creek, Denver, and a male in Denver Dec. 29, 1962. There are nine specimens in the Museum collection from Adams, Larimer, Logan, and Weld Counties.

COMMON SCOTER   *Oidemia nigra americana* Swainson. [163]

RECOGNITION.—Length 17–21 inches. *Adult male*: entirely black without conspicuous markings, except for a large yellow swelling on base of upper bill and silvery flight feathers; eye dark brown. *Adult female*: dark brown and grayish-brown below, with cheek patch whitish. (Plate 22)

RANGE.—Breeds from central Siberia eastward and south along the Bering Sea coast; and from northern Alaska to Hudson Bay and Newfoundland. Winters from Maine to New Jersey, from the Aleutian Islands to California, and casually in interior states south to Louisiana, and rarely in Florida.

Nebraska: straggler in fall and winter; Kansas: rare migrant, one adult male shot by a hunter in Brown Co. in early 1930's, identified by L. B. Carson; Wyoming: rare migrant.

COLORADO.—Straggler, rare. One shot in Adams Co. about Oct. 2, 1909; a female killed in Boulder Co. Oct. 18, 1925; one taken in Weld Co. Oct. 30, 1917, and an immature was found dead Nov. 24, 1960 on Watson Lake, five miles northeast of Fort Collins.

RUDDY DUCK   *Oxyura jamaicensis rubida* (Wilson). [167]

RECOGNITION.—Length 14–16 inches; a small, stout-bodied duck with stiff, pointed tail feathers. *Adult male*: crown and nape black; cheeks and chin white; upper parts and neck bright chestnut; bill bright blue; eye yellowish to red-brown. In fall and winter the plumage is mainly dark brown above, marked with gray. *Adult female*: plain grayish-brown above with crown darker; cheeks whitish, with a dark stripe extending from the bill nearly to the nape; under parts grayish with sides more brownish; downy young Plate 19. Note: caption under adults (Plate 17) should read *adult winter male, adult male and female*.

RANGE.—Breeds from British Columbia across southern Canada and in northern states, Illinois, Ohio, and Pennsylvania, south to Baja California and east to Texas. Winters from Chesapeake Bay to Florida; from southern British Columbia to Costa Rica; and in the southern states.

Nebraska: common transient and breeder in Garden, Morrill, and Cherry Counties; Kansas: common migrant, rare in winter, and breeding reports from Barton, Stafford, and Grant Counties; New Mexico: common migrant, and breeder on high mountain lakes of north; Utah: transient, and common summer resident in north, especially Bear River marshes; Wyoming: common breeder and migrant.

COLORADO.—Fairly common summer resident in the Upper Sonoran and Transition Zones, rare in winter. Breeds regularly throughout eastern counties, in San Luis Valley, in North Park, and Brown's Park.

HOODED MERGANSER   *Lophodytes cucullatus* (Linnaeus). [131]

RECOGNITION.—Small saw-billed duck; length 16–19 inches. *Adult male*: head and neck black, with a white triangular patch extending from behind the yellow eye into the rounded crest; breast and belly white; sides reddish-brown finely barred with black; back black. *Adult female*: grayish-brown above, and brownish below except for white belly; wings and tail dark brown; speculum white, crest small and yellowish-brown; eye yellowish-brown. (Plate 23)

RANGE.—Breeds locally from southeastern Alaska and British Columbia across southern Canada to New Brunswick, south to Oregon, Idaho, Wyoming, Iowa, and Missouri to Louisiana and Florida. Winters from northern states southward into Mexico.

Nebraska: uncommon migrant and winter resident in east, with several early breeding records; Kansas: uncommon transient and winter resident; New Mexico: uncommon winter visitor; Utah: uncommon transient and winter resident; Wyoming: rare migrant, and a breeding record.

COLORADO.—Numerous birds observed on reservoirs and lakes of the Upper Sonoran Zone. The thirteen specimens in the Museum series were from Adams, Boulder, Kiowa, Morgan, Washington, and Weld Counties.

COMMON MERGANSER   *Mergus merganser americanus* Cassin. [129]

RECOGNITION.—Length 21–27 inches, a large, saw-billed duck mainly dark above and white below; crest small. *Adult male*: head dark glossy green; eye dark red; neck and under parts white, tinged with pale buffy; upper back and primaries black; lower back and tail gray; most of wing white with a black bar. *Adult female*: upper neck and crested head cinnamon-brown; chin and throat white; breast and belly whitish or pale buffy; under parts and sides gray; speculum white; downy young Plate 19; adults Plate 23.

RANGE.—The species breeds in northern Europe, Russia, and Siberia; and the American race from Alaska across Canada, south to Maine, South Dakota, northern New Mexico, and central California. Winters from Alaska south over the United States to Florida and northern Mexico.

Nebraska: common migrant and local winter resident; Kansas: common transient and winter resident; New Mexico: frequent winter resident, several recent breeding records; Utah: fairly common transient and possibly breeds; Wyoming: common migrant and resident.

COLORADO.—Common winter and rare summer resident. Breeds along rivers of Archuleta and La Plata Counties and a female and five young in the Museum collection were taken on the Pine River July 3, 1945. Wampole saw a female with three downies in North Park in 1951, and a downy from Lake Granby, Grand Co., in the R.Mt.N.P. collection is dated July 12, 1961. Three females and two half-grown young, observed on the Colorado River near Dotsero, Eagle Co., July 2, 1967 by Harold Holt (pers. comm.).

RED-BREASTED MERGANSER   *Mergus serrator serrator* Linnaeus. [130]

RECOGNITION.—Length 20–25 inches; a saw-billed duck with a double-pointed crest averaging smaller than that of the Common Merganser. *Adult male:* head and crest dark glossy green; eye vivid red; collar white; upper back and primaries black; breast dark brown with black spots; under parts whitish with sides lined with black; wing with considerable white. *Adult female:* head and crest pale brown; eye straw or red; upper parts brownish; wing with black primaries and white speculum; breast and under parts white, with sides gray; females in the field, unaccompanied by males, would be very difficult to separate from *M.m. americanus*. (Plate 23)

RANGE.—The species ranges over much of the Northern Hemisphere, and this race breeds from Alaska and Greenland, Scandinavia, Russia, and Siberia, and across Canada and the northern United States from Maine to British Columbia. Winters in the Old World from Iceland and Scandinavia south along the coast of Europe to Morocco and east to Greece, Egypt, the Caspian Sea, China, and Japan; in the New World from southern Alaska, Canada, and northern states south to Baja California and the Gulf coast.

Nebraska: rare migrant; Kansas: uncommon transient; New Mexico and Utah: uncommon migrant, and winter visitor; Wyoming: uncommon transient.

COLORADO.—An uncommon migrant and winter resident on reservoirs and streams.

Early fall Oct. 24 Denver; late spring June 4 Ft. Morgan.

Order FALCONIFORMES: Vultures, Hawks, Falcons

Family CATHARTIDAE: American Vultures

TURKEY VULTURE   *Cathartes aura meridionalis* Swann. [325a]

RECOGNITION.—Length 26–32 inches; a large black vulture with small head. *Adult:* plumage rusty-black; flight feathers grayish on under surface; naked head dull red; sexes alike. (Listed as *C.a. teter* in caption of Plate 24.)

RANGE.—Species breeds from southern Canada south to the Straits of Magellan and this race from British Columbia, southwestern Canada, Minnesota, Wisconsin, and western states to Texas and the interior of Mexico. Winters from California to Nebraska and southward.

Nebraska: irregular throughout the state, and one breeding record from Nuckolls Co.; Kansas: common transient, and summer resident west to Clark Co.; New Mexico, Utah, and Wyoming: fairly common summer resident.

COLORADO.—Fairly numerous in summer, and uncommon in winter. Several nesting records.

* BLACK VULTURE   *Coragyps atratus* (Bechstein). [326]

RECOGNITION.—Length 23–27 inches; base of head and body black; bill black with yellowish tip; tail short and square; wings shorter than in Turkey Vulture, with conspicuous white patches toward tips. (Plate 24)

RANGE.—Resident from southern Illinois, Indiana, Ohio, and West Virginia south along the Gulf coast states to Argentina and Chile, wandering northward to Quebec and Nova Scotia.

Nebraska: one record; Kansas: former resident of the southeast, recent sight records.

COLORADO.—Two noted in flight near Pueblo by R. P. Fox May 27, 1953 (pers. comm.).

Family ACCIPITRIDAE: Hawks, Kites, Eagles, and Harriers

SWALLOW-TAILED KITE   *Elanoides forficatus forficatus* (Linnaeus). [327]

RECOGNITION.—Length 19–25 inches; a gray-black and white hawklike bird with pointed wings and deeply forked tail. *Adult:* white, with back, wings, upper tail coverts and tail gray-black, glossed with purple. *Young:* more brownish above and with narrow black streaks on some of the white body feathers. (Plate 25)

RANGE.—Breeds locally from South Carolina to Florida, southern Texas, and Louisiana south through Mexico to Guatemala. Formerly bred from Minnesota and Wisconsin down the Mississippi Valley to Alabama. Straggler in interior of United States and Canada.

Nebraska: formerly uncommon summer resident in east, occasionally breeding; Kansas: formerly summer resident in southeast, last specimen being taken in Greenwood Co. May 17, 1914; New Mexico: three records listed by F. M. Bailey, the last about 1907.

COLORADO.—Straggler. Aiken observed one near Leadville, Lake Co., in Aug. 1871, and two specimens were brought to him—one had been shot at Colorado Springs Aug. 8, 1877, and the other at Manitou Park on Trout Creek, Teller Co., presumably during the same month (Sclater, 1912); Aiken in a margin in Sclater corrected the above date of 1871 to 1872. Cooke (1898) reported one killed near Colorado Springs in August 1883; and Harold Webster and Duncan MacDonald (pers. comm.) reported observations of single birds west of Hereford in June 1939 and near Lookout Mountain west of Denver July 2, 1947.

* MISSISSIPPI KITE   *Ictinia misisippiensis* (Wilson). [329]

RECOGNITION.—Length 14–16 inches; a medium-sized gray hawk with long wings. *Adult:* plumage mainly bluish-gray, becoming whitish on head; primaries and square tail almost black, with some of the wing quills edged with chestnut. *Young:* blackish above with markings of gray, brown, and white; head, neck, and under parts light-colored, lined with dark brown; tail black with three gray bands. (Plate 25)

RANGE.—Breeds locally in South Carolina, Kansas, Iowa, Oklahoma, Tennessee, and the Gulf states. Winters from Texas, Florida, and the Gulf coast to Guatemala.

Nebraska: two records from Adams and Douglas Counties; Kansas: common summer resident in south-central, west to Morton Co.; New Mexico: first record for state in 1955 and several since, a summer observation indicating the species probably nests.

COLORADO.—Casual. Breninger saw a specimen in Denver which was said to have been taken near Trinidad (Cooke, 1897), and Aiken observed a bird in Dead Man's Canyon, southwest of Colorado Springs, during the summer of 1873 (Warren and Aiken, 1914).

GOSHAWK   *Accipiter gentilis atricapillus* (Wilson). [334]

RECOGNITION.—Length 20–28 inches. *Adult:* dark slate-blue above with crown black; white line over eye extending around head; under parts gray, finely barred and streaked with black; tail crossed with three or four dark bands. Iris red in the male and yellowish-brown in the female. *Young:* brownish-black above marked with buffy and white; under parts yellowish-white, broadly streaked with dusky; iris yellow. (Plate 26)

RANGE.—Breeds from Alaska across Canada and south into the northern states and to California and Arizona. Winters from Alaska and southern Canada southward to California, Nevada, Minnesota, Michigan, Pennsylvania, Maryland, Arizona, and in Mexico.

Nebraska: uncommon winter visitor; Kansas: rare and irregular in winter; New Mexico: widely distributed in the mountainous forests above 7000 feet with several breeding records; Utah: uncommon resident breeding in mountains and transient in the valleys; Wyoming: rare resident in the mountains.

COLORADO.—Resident, not common, from the Upper Sonoran into the Canadian Zone. Nests regularly in the coniferous forests with center of abundance in the Upper Transition Zone.

SHARP-SHINNED HAWK   *Accipiter striatus velox* (Wilson). [332]

RECOGNITION.—Length 10–14 inches. *Adult:* upper parts dark slate-blue; tail tipped with white and crossed with three or four dark bands, and tip *straight* across in contrast to the *rounded* tail of Cooper's Hawk; under parts whitish, heavily barred with reddish-brown; iris yellow to red depending on age. *Young:* dark brown above marked with rusty and white; under parts whitish streaked with reddish and dusky. (Plate 26)

RANGE.—Breeds from northwestern Alaska throughout much of Canada and the United States to Louisiana, Texas, and Arizona. Winters from southeastern Alaska and British Columbia throughout the United States south to Guatemala.

Nebraska: common migrant, breeding in Sioux Co., and a few wintering; Kansas: uncommon resident, and one nest found in Cloud Co.; New Mexico: common migrant in summer with nesting records from near Santa Fe; Utah: common resident and migrant; Wyoming: uncommon migrant and resident.

COLORADO.—Uncommon resident, fairly numerous migrant in Upper Sonoran and Transition Zones in winter; breeds uncommonly from the Transition into the Canadian Zone in summer.

COOPER'S HAWK   *Accipiter cooperii* (Bonaparte). [333]

RECOGNITION.—Length 14–20 inches. *Adult:* much like the Sharp-shinned, but larger, with crown almost black and upper parts much clearer blue-gray; end of tail *rounded*. *Young:* plumage similar to that of the young Sharp-shinned. (Plate 26)

RANGE.—Breeds from British Columbia east across southern Canada, and south through the United States to northern Mexico. Winters throughout the United States and Mexico to Costa Rica.

41

Nebraska: resident and breeding locally; Kansas: resident, breeding west to Cloud Co.; New Mexico: migrant and nests throughout the state; Utah: summer resident with a few in winter; Wyoming: rare resident and migrant.

COLORADO.—Resident, not common from the Upper Sonoran throughout the Canadian Zone, breeding regularly, usually in the Transition Zone.

RED-TAILED HAWK   *Buteo jamaicensis calurus* Cassin. [337b]

RECOGNITION.—Length 19–25 inches. Adults with varied plumage. *Light phase:* dark brown above, marked with light brown and white; under parts whitish or pale buffy, streaked on sides and belly with rust; tail bright red-brown with a dark band near the tip. *Dark phase:* uniformly dusky-brown except red-brown tail. The intermediate plumage has more reddish-brown on the belly and sides and the back is not so dark. *Young:* dark brown above; whitish under parts marked with blackish; tail gray or brownish with nine or ten dark bands. (Plate 27)

RANGE.—The species breeds from central Alaska across Canada and south to Panama, and this race from central Alaska, Yukon, Mackenzie, Saskatchewan, Ontario, and Quebec, and from Montana and Wyoming south to Baja California. Winters from southern British Columbia to Guatemala and east to Louisiana.

Nebraska: as a species a common resident; Kansas: common transient and summer resident, with the eastern race the breeding form, and probably *B.j. calurus* in west along the river bottoms; New Mexico: widely distributed and nesting in lower parts of state; Utah: common resident from lowlands into high mountains; Wyoming: common migrant, uncommon breeder, and occasionally winters.

COLORADO.—Common migrant and resident from the plains into the Canadian Zone, nesting throughout its range.

Buteo jamaicensis kriderii Hoopes. [337a]

RECOGNITION.—Length 19–22 inches; a Red-tailed Hawk with an albinistic appearance. *Adult:* grayish-brown above, marked with whitish; head sometimes very white; under parts white, lightly streaked with brown; tail pale reddish and usually without a dark tip. *Young:* similar to adult, but tail crossed by nine or ten dark bands. (Plate 27)

RANGE.—Breeds in southern Alberta, Saskatchewan, Manitoba, and Ontario south to Montana, Minnesota, and Nebraska. Winters from South Dakota and Minnesota to Louisiana, Texas, and Mexico.

Nebraska: migrant; Kansas: transient and winter resident; New Mexico: rare; Utah: transient; Wyoming: probably migrant, and breeding uncommonly.

COLORADO.—Migrant, rare in Upper Sonoran Zone. Sclater (1912) lists two immatures killed near Colo. Spgs., one on Sept. 12, 1902, the other at Manitou Park Aug. 29, 1906. There is a light specimen in C.S.U. Museum (no. 408) which may be this form, and there is an immature male (no. 7002) in this Museum, taken by Carter at Breckenridge on Oct. 10, 1891.

HARLAN'S HAWK   *Buteo harlani* (Audubon). [337d]

RECOGNITION.—Length 19–25 inches. *Adult:* plumage variable, but with the tail usually mottled with white, brown, and dusky, and a tendency toward longitudinal streaks. The upper parts vary from a gray to almost black, while the under parts may be very light with dark spotting to almost uniform dusky. *Young:* tail barred as in the young Red-tails with dark brown or black. (Plate 27)

RANGE.—Breeds from the Yukon and Mt. Logan area, Alaska, to British Columbia and Alberta. Winters in the Mississippi Valley to the Gulf states.

Nebraska: rare migrant; Kansas: uncommon transient.

COLORADO.—Straggler, rare in the Upper Sonoran and Transition Zones. There are two specimens in the Museum collection, a male from Arapahoe Co. secured Oct. 16, 1918, and another from Baca Co. July 25, 1921. In addition, there are three dark females with barred tails from Adams, Jackson, and Lincoln Counties. Sight records are not reliable.

RED-SHOULDERED HAWK   *Buteo lineatus lineatus* (Gmelin). [339]

RECOGNITION.—Length 18–22 inches; upper parts dark, edged with rufous and whitish; primaries barred with black and white, and wing coverts conspicuously rufous; tail dark with four or five bands of white. (Plate 28)

RANGE.—Breeds from southeastern Canada to North Carolina, west to Minnesota, Nebraska, and Kansas. Winters casually over much of the eastern United States south to Texas.

Nebraska: uncommon migrant; Kansas: uncommon transient, and breeding records from Leavenworth and Woodson Counties; Utah: one taken at Elgin Sept. 28, 1939.

COLORADO.—A specimen in the Museum of Northern Arizona was taken in El Paso Co. by Breninger. Listed in the literature are reports of individuals observed at Weldona Mar. 18, 1941 and Mar. 29, 1942, one near Johnstown, Weld Co. July 14, 1948, and one seen near Boulder May 22, 1963 and June 23.

BROAD-WINGED HAWK   *Buteo platypterus platypterus* (Vieillot). [343]

RECOGNITION.—Length 13–18 inches; size of Cooper's Hawk, but heavier; broad-winged, with two to four gray bands in tail. *Adult:* dark grayish-brown above; throat, under-tail and under-wing surfaces white; breast and belly barred with reddish-brown; tail banded. *Young:* much like the adult, but more brown; breast and sides streaked with dusky; tail with several dark bands. (Plate 28)

RANGE.—Breeds from Alberta and Saskatchewan east to Quebec and Nova Scotia, south to North Dakota, Oklahoma, Texas, and Gulf coast states; winters from Florida through Mexico to northern South America.

Nebraska: uncommon migrant and occasional breeder; Kansas: fairly common in migration, breeding regularly in east: Wyoming: straggler; New Mexico: rare, a specimen taken forty miles south of Portales by J. S. Ligon Oct. 3, 1945.

COLORADO.—Uncommon spring and fall migrant in the Upper Sonoran Zone east of the foothills.

Early spring Apr. 15 Longmont; summer June 5 Denver; winter Dec. 1 Denver.

SWAINSON'S HAWK   *Buteo swainsoni* Bonaparte. [342]

RECOGNITION.—Length 19–22 inches. *Adult male:* in normal plumage the upper parts are dark grayish-brown, with tail crossed by nine or ten bands; throat white, breast rusty, and belly buffy. *Adult female:* like the male, but breast grayish-brown. There is a dark phase in which the plumage is a nearly uniform blackish, and intermediate stages occur between this dark phase and the light plumage. *Young:* dark brown above, mottled with buff and blackish; head, neck, and under parts buffy, streaked with dusky; tail banded. (Plate 28)

RANGE.—Breeds from Alaska, Mackenzie, Saskatchewan, Manitoba, and Minnesota, interior British Columbia to Great Slave Lake, south in western states to Mexico. Winters casually south from Colorado with majority going through Mexico to southern South America.

Nebraska: common transient, breeding in central and western counties; Kansas: abundant migrant in west, and nesting commonly, less numerous in east; New Mexico: very common summer resident; Utah: common summer resident in valleys; Wyoming: common migrant and breeder.

COLORADO.—Common summer resident, abundant in migration, and rare in winter from Upper Sonoran to the Hudsonian Zone.

ROUGH-LEGGED HAWK   *Buteo lagopus s. johannis* (Gmelin). [347a]

RECOGNITION.—Length 20–24 inches. *Adults in light phase:* head, neck, breast, and back buffy, with head streaked and back mottled with dusky; wings and tail darker except for white base of tail; belly solid blackish; wrist-mark under wing black. *Adults in dark phase:* uniform blackish with base of tail white; forehead sometimes white. (Plate 29)

RANGE.—The species breeds in both the Old and New Worlds, and this race from the Aleutian Islands, northern Alaska, and northern Canada to Labrador and Newfoundland. Winters from southern Canada south to Georgia, Texas, Arizona, and southern California.

Nebraska: uncommon in winter; Kansas: fairly common winter resident; New Mexico: common to uncommon midwinter visitor; Utah: winter resident in valley of central and northern parts; Wyoming: common in winter.

COLORADO.—Winter resident throughout the state in Upper Sonoran and Transition Zones.

Early fall Aug. 25 Sedalia (C.B.N. 11:105; late spring June 4 Adams Co. (H. Holt, pers. comm.).

FERRUGINOUS HAWK   *Buteo regalis* (Gray). [348]

RECOGNITION.—Length 22–25 inches. *Adult in light plumage:* flanks, leg feathers, and upper parts bright rust, with head streaked, back mottled, and leg feathers barred with dusky; primaries and secondaries dark gray with black markings; tail white at base and tip, with middle portion light rusty; throat and breast white with rusty streakings on sides; *dark phase:* uniform dark brown, with base of tail and area at base of primaries white. *Young:* much less rusty, and tail with several dark bands. (Plate 29)

RANGE.—Breeds from eastern Washington, southern Alberta, Saskatchewan, and Manitoba south to eastern Oregon, Nevada, southern Arizona, Oklahoma, and Texas. Winters from Manitoba and California to northern Mexico.

Nebraska: uncommon breeding resident in west, rare in east; Kansas: common migrant in west, rare in east, and nesting records in west; New Mexico: resident, nesting sparingly throughout the state; Utah: rather uncommon resident; Wyoming: uncommon breeder and migrant, and occasionally winters.

COLORADO.—Summer resident and a few in winter in the Upper Sonoran and Transition Zones. Nests regularly in trees or on escarpments.

* HARRIS' HAWK   *Parabuteo unicinctus harrisi* (Audubon). [335]

RECOGNITION.—Length 17.5–26. *Adult:* dark sooty-brown above, *shoulders, under wing coverts, and thighs reddish-brown. Black* tail tipped with *white* and rump white. *Young:* under parts streaked, shoulders reddish, and base of tail white (not illustrated in color).

RANGE.—Resident from southern Texas south through eastern Mexico and Central America to Colombia and western Ecuador.

Kansas: male from Sedgwick Co. Dec. 14, 1918 and female, Douglas Co. Dec. 25, 1918, and nesting in Meade County in 1963; New Mexico: recorded nesting near Carlsbad at about 3000 feet altitude June 2, 1919, and numbers seen along New Mexico-Texas line Jan. 5, 1919, and "great numbers" Jan. 7 twenty miles northwest of Jal (F. M. Bailey, 1928); one Bosque Refuge Feb. 7–14, 1964 (A.F.N. 18: 377); Utah: one observed at Parawan, in the southern part of the state Apr. 11, 1963 (A.F.N. 17: 422).

COLORADO.—Straggler. One observed by Catherine Bonner in Denver January 14, 1963 (C.B.N. 11:14).

GOLDEN EAGLE   *Aquila chrysaetos canadensis* (Linnaeus). [349]

RECOGNITION.—Length 30–42 inches. *Adult:* plumage uniform dark brown with crown and occipital feathers edged with golden-buff; primaries and tail feathers darker, with a whitish area at base of primaries; legs feathered to toes; females larger than males; weight between eight and ten pounds. *Young:* like adult, but base of tail white. (Plate 30)

RANGE.—Species occurs in Northern Hemisphere in Scotland, Norway, Lapland, and Russia, and from Morocco and Tunis across Asia to Japan, and in North America this race breeds locally from northern Alaska across Canada and throughout much of the mountainous terrain of the United States, south to central Mexico; casually in the Canadian provinces east of the Rocky Mountains. Winters south to the Gulf coast.

Nebraska: uncommon migrant and winter resident, occasionally nesting; Kansas: common winter resident in west, rare in east, and record of nesting in Comanche Co. prior to 1891; New Mexico: occurs throughout the state, nesting along precipitous ledges; Utah: uncommon resident, formerly common; Wyoming: common resident except in northwest.

COLORADO.—Resident from the Upper Sonoran to the Arctic-Alpine Zone, nesting in trees or on cliffs. Eagles have gradually diminished in numbers and are sadly in need of better protection.

BALD EAGLE   *Haliaeetus leucocephalus alascanus* Townsend. [352a]

RECOGNITION.—Length 34–44 inches. *Adult:* uniformly dark brown, with head, neck, tail, and tail coverts *white;* tarsi unfeathered. *Young:* generally brownish-black, with whitish mottling on the under parts and white tail base. (Plate 30)

RANGE.—Breeds locally from northwestern Alaska and across Canada to Labrador and Newfoundland, and in the northern tier of states from Oregon to New Jersey. Winters from Alaska to Washington and in southern part of breeding range.

Nebraska: uncommon migrant and winter resident and formerly a common breeder in east; Kansas: uncommon transient and winter resident in east, fairly common in west, and L. B. Carson reports an unsuccessful nesting attempt in 1960–61 at the Kirwin Wildlife Refuge; New Mexico: winter resident, locally fairly numerous, and two nesting records; Utah: winter resident; Wyoming: uncommon in winter and breeds in northwest.

COLORADO.—Winter visitor and rarely a summer resident. There are several reports of nesting but none entirely satisfactory. As with other "birds of prey" this species has decreased in numbers.

MARSH HAWK   *Circus cyaneus hudsonius* (Linnaeus). [331]

RECOGNITION.—Length 17–22 inches; a medium-sized hawk with diagnostic white rump patch. *Adult male:* pale bluish-gray above and on neck; breast and under parts white with faint reddish markings on sides; tail gray with several dusky bands. *Adult female:* generally brown, brighter on shoulders and streaked with reddish; under parts clear cinnamon. (Plate 31)

RANGE.—The species occurs throughout much of the Northern Hemisphere, and this race breeds from northwestern Alaska across Canada and south to Baja California, Arizona, and Texas. Winters from southern British Columbia to New Hampshire, and south throughout the United States, to Cuba and Colombia.

Nebraska and Kansas: common breeding resident, less numerous in winter; New Mexico: the most common hawk in the state in fall and winter, and nests locally; Utah: common resident, abundant locally; Wyoming: common migrant and breeder, and occurs occasionally in winter.

COLORADO.—Common resident in Upper Sonoran. Nests on the plains and wanders in late summer to the tundra and rock slopes above timberline. All species of hawks, falcons, eagles, and owls have decreased, not only in Colorado, but throughout our country.

GOLDEN EAGLE
Nesting escarpment on McArthur's Ranch, Douglas County

Family PANDIONIDAE: Ospreys

OSPREY   *Pandion haliaetus carolinensis* (Gmelin). [364]

RECOGNITION.—Length 21–24 inches. *Adult:* dark brown above and white below; crown white, streaked with black; broad dusky stripe through eye; tail with several dark bars; dark wrist mark; legs and feet bluish. *Young:* like the adult, but mottled with white on the upper parts and showing more buffy below. (Plate 31)

RANGE.—The Osprey has a cosmopolitan distribution. Five subspecies have been described and this race breeds locally from northwestern Alaska, western and southern Canada, along both coasts to Baja California, western Mexico, and the Florida Keys. Winters from the Gulf states through Mexico to the West Indies and Central America.

Nebraska: uncommon migrant, and one breeding record from Carr Co.; Kansas: irregular transient; New Mexico: migrant, occasionally nesting; Utah: transient and irregular summer resident; Wyoming: uncommon migrant, breeding along a few northwestern lakes and streams.

COLORADO.—Uncommon but regular straggler and summer resident in Upper Sonoran and Transition Zones. Recorded by Scott (1879) nesting at Twin Lakes near Granite in Lake Co., nest on the ground in San Luis Valley in 1959 by J. H. Brandt (pers. comm.); and reported nesting on Electra Lake, near Durango for five years 1961 through 1965 (Oppie Reames, pers. comm.).

Family FALCONIDAE: Caracaras and Falcons

CARACARA   *Caracara cheriway audubonii* (Cassin). [362]

RECOGNITION.—Length 20–25 inches. *Adult:* compressed, slightly hooked beak, skin of face orange and nearly bare; horizontal crest, whitish neck collar; body blackish-brown; tail white with narrow bars, broad black terminal band; tarsus long and bare. *Young:* body brown and white cape dingy. (Plate 24)

RANGE.—Florida, southwestern Texas, Arizona, south through Mexico to Panama.

New Mexico: casual straggler recorded nesting in 1953 in center of state.

COLORADO.—One record near Glenwood Springs (Matteson, 1951).

* GYRFALCON   *Falco rusticolus obsoletus* Gmelin. [354b]

RECOGNITION.—Length 21–22 inches. Dark phase: dark slate-gray above with faint buffy to grayish bars; tail barred and mottled with grayish; under parts light, streaked with fuscous. *Immatures:* dark gray-brown above; head and neck streaked; white under parts more heavily streaked. White phase: white head streaked with black; broad bars of "slaty fuscous" on scapulars and wing coverts. Immatures gray-brown above; tail barred, and under parts streaked (not illustrated in color).

RANGE.—An Arctic species which breeds in both the Old and New Worlds and is distributed from northern Alaska east to Greenland and south to Southampton Island, northern Quebec, and Labrador. Winters in the far north, but wanders irregularly south to British Columbia, Montana, Wisconsin, eastward to New York.

Nebraska: one specimen, Johnson Co. in 1885 and one in white phase near Chadron Nov. 27, 1965 (A.F.N. 20:65); Kansas: one specimen, Ashland, Clark Co. Dec. 1, 1880.

COLORADO.—There have been occasional reports of the species from the state, but with little confirming data. One was observed at Palmer Lake in 1956, one at Dan Lake one mile east of Barr Lake in 1958, and a bird in the white phase at Weldona Mar. 9, 1961.

PRAIRIE FALCON   *Falco mexicanus* Schlegel. [355]

RECOGNITION.—Length 18–20 inches; a falcon of medium size, pale brown with pointed wings. *Adult:* pale brown above, mottled with dusky; cheeks buffy-white with a dark brown, faintly streaked with dusky. *Young:* like adult, but more ruddy above and with broader stripes below. The Prairie Falcon is browner than the Peregrine Falcon, and the under parts are lined rather than barred. (Plate 32)

RANGE.—Breeds from British Columbia, Alberta, Saskatchewan, and North Dakota south to Texas and Baja California. Winters from the northern part of its breeding range south into northern half of Mexico.

Nebraska: common migrant, and breeding rarely in Dawes and Sioux Counties; Kansas: rare in summer and more numerous in winter; New Mexico: common breeding bird along suitable cliffs or canyon walls; Utah: fairly common summer resident throughout the state; Wyoming: uncommon resident.

COLORADO.—Resident, common in summer and less so in winter. Nests on escarpments of the plains and seldom in the mountains. Unfortunately many young are taken annually by falconers, and breeding pairs are in need of better protection.

Above: PRAIRIE FALCON FAMILY AT McARTHUR'S RANCH
Below: ALBINISTIC FEMALE NEAR HEREFORD, WELD COUNTY

PEREGRINE FALCON   *Falco peregrinus anatum* Bonaparte. [356a]

RECOGNITION.—Length 15–22 inches; a medium-sized, dark bluish hawk with pointed wings. *Adult:* dark slate-blue above, barred with black on the back; side of head with black moustache; throat, foreneck and breast whitish; under parts buffy to gray, barred with black; tail with several dark bands. *Young:* like the adult, but mottled with rusty above; under parts, except throat, lined with dark brown. Resembles the preceding species in color pattern and actions, but adults of this form have bluish-gray upper parts and barred belly, while the Prairie Falcon is pale brown with lined under parts. (Plate 32)

RANGE.—The species is nearly cosmopolitan, and this race, formerly known as the Duck Hawk, has a wide breeding range from northern Alaska, Canada, and southern Greenland southward through Alaska, British Columbia to Baja California. Recorded breeding locally in Arizona, Texas, Arkansas, Louisiana, Tennessee, Alabama, and Georgia. Winters from British Columbia, Ontario, and New Brunswick southward through Central America and the West Indies to Argentina and Chile.

Nebraska: transient and occasional winter visitor; Kansas: rare migrant and winter visitor; New Mexico: migrant and rare breeder (Lake Buford). Utah: rare summer resident and migrant; Wyoming: rare migrant and winter visitor, and known to have nested.

COLORADO.—Uncommon summer resident; occasional in winter; more often seen in migration. A nest near Pueblo in 1895 (Cooke, 1897); Garden of the Gods near Colorado Springs records (Sclater, 1912); Archuleta Co. in 1943 (B. & N., 1946); near Boulder (French, 1951); six occupied nests in Colorado in 1964 (J. H. Enderson, pers. comm.).

PIGEON HAWK   *Falco columbarius richardsonii* Ridgway. [357b]

RECOGNITION.—Length: 10–13 inches; a small, pale blue or brown, pointed-winged hawk. *Adult male:* pearl-gray above with black streaks; nape brownish, throat white with rest of under parts buffy, streaked with brown; tail with *six narrow light* gray bands. *Adult female and young:* like the male, but upper parts dull dusky-brown. Plate 33 shows *bendirei* left, *richardsonii* middle, and *suckleyi* right.

RANGE.—The species (eleven subspecies) ranges through much of the northern part of the Northern Hemisphere. This western race breeds from Alberta, Saskatchewan, and Manitoba south to Montana and northwestern North Dakota. Winters south into western Texas to northwestern Mexico.

Nebraska: rare migrant; Kansas: fairly common transient in west, *F.c. columbarius* most frequent in east; New Mexico: fairly common in winter; Utah: rare migrant and in winter; Wyoming: uncommon migrant, winter visitor, and occasional breeder. Harold Webster reported to us a nest "east of Laramie in a conifer in June 1961—thirty feet from the ground, nest small, about twelve inches across—and a female noted near Colorado border north of Cowdrey, July 23, 1961."

COLORADO.—Regular migrant and uncommon winter resident on the plains and in the mountains. Twenty-one skins of this race, all from the eastern prairies, are listed in the Museum catalogue, and there are two nesting reports for the species, one in Grand Co. May 26, 1877, and La Plata Co. July 3, 1887.

Early fall Sept. 5 Platteville; late spring May 23 Boulder.

Falco columbarius bendirei Swann. [357c]

RECOGNITION.—Length 10–13 inches. Similar to *F.c. richardsonii,* but darker above and below, with three light gray bands in tail, instead of six. (Plate 33)

RANGE.—Breeds from northwestern Alaska, northern Yukon, Mackenzie, Alberta, and Saskatchewan south through eastern British Columbia, Washington, Oregon, and northern California. Winters south from California, Nevada, and Texas to Baja California and northeastern Mexico. Casual to Louisiana, Florida, and the Bahamas.

Nebraska: rare migrant; Kansas: one specimen from Ellis Co. Oct. 1875; Utah: uncommon transient, and rare summer resident in north; Wyoming: one specimen.

COLORADO.—Migrant and winter resident; not common. Some of the numerous observations listed under *F.c. richardsonii* may well have been birds of this race. There are eight specimens in the Museum.

Early fall Sept. 1 Weld Co.; no definite spring records for race.

Falco columbarius suckleyi Ridgway. [357a]

RECOGNITION.—*Adult male:* blackish-brown above, tail black with *three grayish bars* and white tip; under parts blackish-brown with tawny markings; wing coverts, tertials and tail coverts slaty. *Female and young:* lighter blackish-brown above and heavily marked with dusky below; tail bars indistinct or lacking. (Plate 33)

RANGE.—Breeds in western British Columbia, wintering southward through Washington to southern California.

Utah: rare migrant and winter visitor (also specimen, *F.c. columbarius,* Salt Lake City, Mar. 9, 1937 recorded in Wilson Bull., 75: 451).

COLORADO.—Straggler, one record (Bailey, 1942). A beautiful dark adult female (no. 22391), collected Dec. 14, 1940 by Lloyd Triplet at Weldona, Morgan Co., is the only specimen from the state. It is an interesting record, for the bird was far east of its normal range.

SPARROW HAWK   *Falco sparverius sparverius* Linnaeus. [360]

RECOGNITION.—Length 9–12 inches; a small falcon showing considerable reddish-brown. *Adult male:* crown blue-gray with chestnut patch in center; upper parts and tail reddish-brown, with black bars on back and broad black tip on tail; wings bright gray-blue marked with black; throat and cheeks white, with two vertical black cheek stripes and three black patches across nape; under parts buffy and sides spotted with black: *Adult female:* like the male, but back, wings, and tail brownish, barred with black. *Young:* like adults. (Plate 33)

RANGE.—Breeds from Alaska, northern Mackenzie, Manitoba, Ontario, and Quebec, to Nova Scotia southward to the Gulf states, Baja California, and northern Mexico. Winters from southern British Columbia, and northern states to Massachusetts, south through Mexico to Panama.

Nebraska and Kansas: common migrant, resident and breeder; New Mexico: common resident with preferred nesting areas between 5000 and 7000 feet; Utah: abundant in migration and common resident; Wyoming: abundant migrant, common breeder and occasional visitor in winter.

COLORADO.—Resident, common except in winter, chiefly in the Upper Sonoran but ranging to the Alpine Zone.

Order GALLIFORMES: Gallinaceous Birds
Family TETRAONIDAE: Grouse and Ptarmigan

BLUE GROUSE   *Dendragapus obscurus obscurus* (Say). [297]

RECOGNITION.—Length 16–23 inches; a large, dark grouse. *Adult male:* plumage mainly dark blue-gray, mottled above with brown and gray; white on sides of neck and white edgings on flank feathers; tail black, tipped with a broad slate-gray band; orange comb over eye; flesh-colored neck pouch becomes purple in breeding season; feathered legs grayish-brown. *Adult female:* more brownish than the male and with black and white mottling above. *Young:* like the female, with under parts whitish, marked with black on the chest and sides. (Plate 34)

RANGE.—The species has a wide breeding range in the west from southeastern Alaska, southern Yukon, southwestern Mackenzie and Alberta, on islands off Alaska to Vancouver Island, and south in California mountains. This race is resident in mountainous regions from central Wyoming and western South Dakota, south through Colorado to central Arizona.

New Mexico: resident in north-central and in western part of state above 8000 feet; Utah: uncommon resident in central and eastern mountains (*D.o. oreinus* in west); Wyoming: common in mountains.

COLORADO.—Resident, formerly common in mountains from 7000 to 10,000 feet. Center of abundance during nesting season in the Transition and Hudsonian Zones.

* SPRUCE GROUSE   *Canachites canadensis franklinii* (Douglas). [299]

RECOGNITION.—Length 14–17 inches: *Adult male:* blackish-gray upper parts and brownish wings barred with black; under parts and tail black; sides and flanks brown with white mottling; upper tail coverts tipped with white. *Adult female:* blackish above, mottled with rusty and gray; under parts barred with tawny, black, and white. (Plate 35)

RANGE.—The species occurs from central Alaska, Yukon, Mackenzie, and northern Alberta across Canada to Labrador, and this race is resident from southeastern Alaska, central British Columbia, and western Alberta to Oregon, Idaho, and Montana.

Wyoming: rare in northwestern part of the state.

COLORADO.—One record, a bird said to have been shot at Palmer Lake in Sept. 1896.

* RUFFED GROUSE   *Bonasa umbellus incana* Aldrich and Friedmann. [300g]

RECOGNITION.—Length 15–19 inches; a large gray grouse with black neck ruffs. *Adult male:* upper parts gray, finely mottled with black and buffy; neck ruffs black; under parts buffy or whitish, barred with brown; gray tail, with a broad black subterminal band. *Adult female:* like male, but ruffs smaller. (Plate 35)

RANGE.—The species ranges in forested areas from central Alaska and the Yukon, across Canada to Labrador and Nova Scotia, south to northern Georgia, Arkansas, and Tennessee, and in northern states from California to Virginia. This race is a local resident in Idaho, Wyoming, Utah, Colorado, and North and South Dakota.

Nebraska and Kansas: race *B.u. umbellus* formerly resident; Utah: uncommon resident in central and northern mountains; Wyoming: common in mountain areas except in the Medicine Bow and Snowy Ranges.

COLORADO.—Few occur in Colorado, and so far as we have been able to determine, there are no specimens from the state, but there are satisfactory observations. An old bird with young was observed in Estes Park Aug. 12, 1899 (Cooke, 1900), and there is a report of an adult with chicks in the Uncompahgre National Forest in 1948 (Paul Gilbert, pers. comm.).

Photographs by Patricia Bailey Witherspoon

Above: NEST AND EGGS OF WHITE-TAILED PTARMIGAN (July 8)
Below: FEMALE UPON HER NEST NEAR SUMMIT LAKE (July 8)

WHITE-TAILED PTARMIGAN   *Lagopus leucurus altipetens* Osgood. [304c]

RECOGNITION.—Length 12–13 inches; a medium-sized grouse inhabiting the alpine tundra areas. Completely white in winter except black bill, eyes, and claws. *Adults in summer:* plumage mottled with brown, black, and white, except for the all-white wings, tail, belly, and legs. Male has a small red comb over the eye which is most conspicuous during breeding season. *Young:* tail gray. (Plate 36)

RANGE.—The Rocky Mountains from Montana through Wyoming to northern New Mexico. Utah: Reported from Uinta Mountains, but no specimens collected; Wyoming: uncommon on highest mountains.

COLORADO.—Resident, local in the high alpine areas, dropping to the Hudsonian Zone in winter. Numerous nests have been located on the wind-swept Arctic-Alpine slopes.

GREATER PRAIRIE CHICKEN   *Tympanuchus cupido pinnatus* (Brewster). [305]

RECOGNITION.—Length 17–19 inches; a large grouse with mottled plumage, long, ornamental neck feathers, and tip of black tail feathers rounded. *Adult male:* buffy-brown and white above, barred with black; white below, barred with brown, neck pouch orange-yellow. *Adult female:* like male, but ornamental neck feathers short; rounded tail feathers brown. (Plate 37)

RANGE.—Resident from central Alberta, southern Saskatchewan, Manitoba, Ontario, Wisconsin, and Michigan south to eastern Colorado, Arkansas, Missouri, Illinois, Indiana, and formerly Ohio, Kentucky, and Tennessee to Texas.

Nebraska: common locally in the grasslands north of the Platte River; Kansas: local resident but absent in southwest; Wyoming: rare on eastern border.

COLORADO.—Resident in northeastern Colorado; formerly common locally but now scarce.

LESSER PRAIRIE CHICKEN   *Tympanuchus pallidicinctus* (Ridgway). [307]

RECOGNITION.—Length 16–18 inches; smaller than the Greater Prairie Chicken, plumage similar, but paler and the barring composed of two narrow dark bars enclosing a brown bar. Neck pouch of male reddish instead of orange as in the Greater Prairie Chicken. (Plate 37)

RANGE.—The Great Plains from southeastern Colorado and Kansas, western Oklahoma, to east-central New Mexico and west-central Texas.

Nebraska: formerly resident of grassland areas; Kansas: local resident in southwest counties, set of ten eggs in this Museum (no. 5193) from Angelus, Sheridan Co.; New Mexico: formerly locally numerous over eastern grasslands, now most common in Lea and Roosevelt Counties.

COLORADO.—Resident and formerly common locally in southeastern Baca Co.; first specimens from the state collected in 1914 (Lincoln, 1918).

SHARP-TAILED GROUSE   *Pedioecetes phasianellus jamesi* Lincoln. [308e]

RECOGNITION.—Length 15–19 inches; a brown and buffy-colored grouse with pointed tail. *Adult:* buffy-gray above, barred with black; wings more brown, mottled with black and white; foreneck, breast, and sides heavily mottled with dark V-marks; belly white; comb over eye yellow, and neck pouch purple in the male. Distinctly paler than other races. (Plate 37)

RANGE.—The species is resident from north-central Alaska, Yukon, Mackenzie, Manitoba, Ontario, and Quebec south to Oregon and east to South Dakota, Minnesota, Wisconsin, and Michigan, and this race from north-central Alberta and Saskatchewan to Wyoming, eastern Colorado, Kansas, Nebraska, and New Mexico.

Nebraska: fairly common in sand hills and grasslands of the west; Kansas: formerly resident in the west but now nearly extirpated; New Mexico: uncommon and confined to Johnson Mesa and areas east of Raton; Wyoming: common on native grasslands of northeast.

COLORADO.—Resident, formerly common locally upon the eastern plains, but now rare. Courtship performances are at their height in late April and early May.

Pedioecetes phasianellus columbianus (Ord). [308a]

RECOGNITION.—Smaller and more grayish above than *P.p. jamesi;* darker breast and flanks.

RANGE.—Resident from British Columbia south to northern California, western Montana, eastern Oregon, Nevada, and locally east to Utah, western Colorado, and northern New Mexico.

New Mexico: on mesas at 8000 to 9000 feet in northern part of state; Utah: local in northern original grasslands; Wyoming: uncommon in southern and western counties.

COLORADO.—Resident locally to 9500 feet west of the Continental Divide from Transition into the Canadian Zone.

GREATER PRAIRIE CHICKEN
These grouse assemble on strutting grounds and the males, with tufts erect, perform on their arenas

Photographs by the authors

LESSER PRAIRIE CHICKEN

SAGE GROUSE *Centrocercus urophasianus urophasianus* (Bonaparte). [309]

RECOGNITION.—Length 22–30 inches; a large grouse with black belly. *Adult male:* brownish-gray above, mottled with black; patch of white cottony feathers on side of neck; breast blackish in breeding season and becoming white later; belly black, neck pouch and comb yellow; tail feathers long and spiked. *Adult female:* smaller and lacks the neck plumes, pouch, and comb. (Plate 38)

RANGE.—Resident locally in western Saskatchewan and eastern Alberta to east-central California, northwestern Nebraska, and formerly to the Oklahoma Panhandle.

Nebraska: formerly rare resident in extreme northwestern counties; New Mexico: formerly in sage habitats in northwest, and 310 birds introduced by 1933 and 1936; Utah: fairly numerous in sagebrush habitats throughout the state; Wyoming: locally common to abundant.

COLORADO.—Resident, common locally in sage habitats west of the Continental Divide and North Park; rarely east of the foothills. These large grouse are dependent upon a sage habitat, and are noted for their "arena" courtship performances.

Family PHASIANIDAE: Quail and Pheasants

BOBWHITE *Colinus virginianus taylori* Lincoln. [289d]

RECOGNITION.—Length 9–11 inches; a pale form with grayish-brown upper parts. *Adult male:* crown, hind neck, back, breast, and sides pinkish-brown variously marked with black and white; superciliary line and throat white; wings brown; under parts white, barred with dusky. *Adult female:* like male, but superciliary line and throat buffy instead of white. Less heavily marked with black above and below. (Plate 39)

RANGE.—The species ranges over much of eastern states, and this race is a resident of the Great Plains from South Dakota and eastern Colorado, western Kansas and Nebraska, Arkansas and Oklahoma, to north-central Texas.

Nebraska: common resident except in far west; Kansas: common locally in east, less so in west; New Mexico: locally numerous in plum thickets about Portales and Logan; Utah: introduced unsuccessfully; Wyoming: resident of North Platte and Laramie River valleys near Wheatland.

COLORADO.—Local resident from Yuma Co. south into Baca Co. and west to Jefferson, Boulder, and Larimer Counties, to the edge of the foothills.

SCALED QUAIL *Callipepla squamata pallida* Brewster. [293]

RECOGNITION.—Length 10–12 inches; a pale blue quail with a white-tipped crest. *Adult:* plumage generally pale blue-gray or brownish above; short, erect crown patch tipped with white; under parts whitish, scaled with brown; sides lined with white; lower belly patch buffy or rusty. *Young:* plumage more rufous, with under parts barred with dusky. (Plate 39)

RANGE.—Resident from southern Colorado, northern New Mexico, western Oklahoma, Arizona, and western Texas to northwestern Mexico.

Kansas: locally common breeding in the southwest; New Mexico: widespread resident of arid country below 7000 feet.

COLORADO.—Resident, common locally in southeastern counties from north of the Arkansas River south into Baca Co., west into Las Animas and north into El Paso Counties. Nest with twelve eggs thirty feet from highly traveled Garden of the Gods road north Colo. Spgs. July 15, 1966 (Robert M. Stabler, pers. comm.).

GAMBEL'S QUAIL *Lophortyx gambelii sanus* Mearns. [295a]

RECOGNITION.—Length 10–12 inches; a small quail having chestnut sides streaked with white. *Adult male:* crown uniform brown; forehead and throat black, bordered by white; black head plume decurved; upper parts and foreneck bluish-gray, with hind neck lined; breast buffy; belly black. *Adult female:* similar, but lacks the brown crown and black face and with head plume shorter. (Plate 39)

RANGE.—Resident in western Colorado in the drainages of the Uncompahgre, Gunnison, and upper Colorado Rivers.

Utah: species fairly common resident in the Colorado River drainage.

COLORADO.—Resident, locally common in western Colorado in the Upper Sonoran into the Transition Zone.

CALIFORNIA QUAIL *Lophortyx californicus californicus* (Shaw). [294a]

RECOGNITION.—Length 10–12 inches. Generally similar to Gambel's Quail, but forebreast windsor-blue; belly with scaly pattern; short *head plumes curving forward.* (Plate 40)

RANGE.—Resident from southern Oregon and western Nevada south to Baja California.

Utah: Introduced about 1872, and fairly common resident in northern part of state.

COLORADO.—Introduced into Larimer and Weld Counties.

Photographs by the authors

STRUTTING MALE SAGE GROUSE WITH FEMALES

RING-NECKED PHEASANT   *Phasianus colchicus* Linnaeus. [309.1]

RECOGNITION.—*Male:* Length 22–36 inches; head and neck iridescent green except grayish-brown crown and naked red patch about eye; back mainly chestnut marked with black and white; elongated tail brown, barred with black; breast metallic bronze shading to yellow on the sides and flanks and marked with black. *Female:* Length 20–24 inches; plumage mainly brown, mottled with black above; buff below. (Plate 40)

RANGE.—Native locally in southern Russia, Mongolia, Manchuria, and Japan south to Armenia, Iran, Afghanistan, southern China, and Formosa. Introduced and established widely through much of Europe, and North America from southern Canada and northern states south to Texas, Arizona, and northern Baja California.

Nebraska and Kansas: common resident locally; New Mexico: resident in north, uncommon; Utah: first introduced in 1912 and now a common resident; Wyoming: common in cultivated areas.

COLORADO.—Introduced resident, common locally throughout the state in Upper Sonoran into the Transition Zone.

CHUKAR   *Alectoris graeca* (Meisner). [288.2]

RECOGNITION.—Length 12–14 inches. Crown, back, and breast light vinaceous-drab mixed with brown; sides of face and throat white with sharp black line, sides heavily barred; beak, legs, and eyering red. (Plate 40)

RANGE.—Resident locally in France, Switzerland, Italy, east Turkey, Iraq, and Inner Mongolia. Established in Washington, Idaho, California, Nevada, Wyoming, and Colorado.

New Mexico: several thousand released in southern parts of the state but apparently nowhere fully established; Utah: many importations and well established statewide; Wyoming: locally common in many places.

COLORADO.—Introduced into the western part of the state and some eastern counties.

* RED-LEGGED PARTRIDGE   *Alectoris rufa hispanica* (Seoane).

RECOGNITION.—Like the chukar but darker. Lower throat black and heavily striped. Eyering more conspicuously red than shown in color plate. (Plate 40)

RANGE.—Northern and northwestern Spain and northern Portugal. Introduced in the United States but apparently has not become well-established.

Utah: introduced unsuccessfully.

COLORADO.—Introduced into Larimer Co. March 9, 1955.

* GRAY PARTRIDGE   *Perdix perdix perdix* (Linnaeus). [288.1]

RECOGNITION.—Length 12–14 inches. Crown, neck and breast dark and light gray; face, chin and throat brown with dark superciliary line; flanks barred; back light and dark brown mixed; belly gray with dark patch in center. (Plate 40)

RANGE.—An Old World species introduced widely into Canada and the United States.

Utah: introduced, rare in north; Wyoming: introduced birds common locally.

COLORADO.—Introduced but not established.

Family MELEAGRIDIDAE: Turkeys

WILD TURKEY   *Meleagris gallopavo merriami* Nelson. [310]

RECOGNITION.—Length about 35–50 inches. *Adult male:* head and neck naked; bluish-white on crown, becoming red on wattles and neck, back dark brown with iridescent reflections; upper tail coverts white to buff; breast and under parts metallic bronze, marked on belly with black; pendant tuft of black bristles on breast. *Adult female:* smaller and with less iridescence. (Plate 41)

RANGE.—The species once occurred locally over much of the eastern half of the United States into Mexico, and west to Colorado, New Mexico, and Arizona. *M.g. merriami* is a resident locally in mountain areas of Colorado south to Arizona and southwestern Texas, and has been introduced into other states.

Nebraska: species formerly resident, and re-established in Pine Ridge; Kansas: re-established in Barber, Cowley, and Linn Counties; New Mexico: common locally over much of the conifer-oak forests; Utah and Wyoming: introduced birds common locally.

COLORADO.—Formerly resident in the southeastern counties from the prairies into the foothills north to Larimer Co. and in Black Forest of Elbert and El Paso counties. Now confined for the most part to the southern half of the state in the Transition Zone, except where reintroduced.

Order GRUIFORMES: Cranes, Rails, and Allies
Family GRUIDAE: Cranes

WHOOPING CRANE   *Grus americana* (Linnaeus). [204]

RECOGNITION.—Length 50–56 inches. *Adults:* plumage entirely white except gray nape and black primaries; naked forehead and cheek stripe red. *Young:* head feathered, and plumage mottled with rusty. All cranes are distinguished from herons in flight by outstretched neck. (Plate 42)

RANGE.—Formerly bred from southern Mackenzie to Alberta, Saskatchewan, Manitoba, North Dakota, and Iowa; and also in Louisiana. Now breeds in south-central Mackenzie and migrates south to the Aransas Refuge in Texas.

Nebraska: The majority of this species pass through the central part of the state in migration, resting along the Platte River and near the Harlan County Reservoir; Kansas: the main migration seems to pass regularly through the east-central counties; New Mexico: former rare migrant; Wyoming: rare straggler.

COLORADO.—Casual migrant. There is a specimen in the C.C. Museum taken at Colo. Spgs. about 1880; another is in the C.S.U. Museum with no date; W. G. Smith saw one at Loveland Apr. 8 to 16, 1890; one was seen June 20, 1931 near Ft. Collins; a male specimen in the Museum (no. 18609), probably killed in the 80's has notation by W. C. Ferril, "said to be from Colorado." Observed in eastern Colorado in Oct. 1941 (Auk 59:307), and one at Orchard, Morgan Co., Oct. 18, 1965 (C.B.N. 13:21).

Early spring Apr. 8 Loveland; late fall Oct. 15 Cheyenne Co.

SANDHILL CRANE   *Grus canadensis canadensis* (Linnaeus). [205]

RECOGNITION.—Length 34–38 inches; a long-legged, long-necked bird with a naked red forehead and slate or brownish-gray plumage. *Young:* head feathered, and plumage chocolate-brown with some rusty. The small Sandhill Crane and the larger are indistinguishable in the field. This race has an exposed culmen of 69–110 mm. and weighs eight to ten pounds, and *G.c. tabida* has a culmen of 113–159 mm. and weighs about twelve pounds. (Plate 42)

RANGE.—Breeds from northeastern Siberia, northern and western Alaska to southern Alaska, Mackenzie, and Southampton Island. Winters from California and Texas to northern Baja California and northern Mexico. Migrates through the interior of Canada and the United States. Spring and fall migrant.

Nebraska: a common spring migrant locally in the Platte River valley with a peak of 240,000 recorded; Kansas: common transient in west, rare in east; New Mexico: common migrant and winter resident; Utah and Wyoming: status of this race little known, but probably migrant in spring and fall.

COLORADO.—Regular transient in both the eastern and the western parts of the state.

Early spring Mar. 20 Weld Co.; early fall Sept. 9 Platteville; late fall Nov. 15, 29 Crowley Co., and 3000 to 6000 on Prewitt Res. October into December 1963.

Grus canadensis tabida (Peters). [206]

RECOGNITION.—Length 40–48 inches; similar to *G.c. canadensis,* but larger; weight about twelve lbs; exposed culmen 113–159 mm. (*G.c. canadensis* 69–110 mm.). (Plate 42)

RANGE.—Former territory and numbers of birds much reduced. Breeds in southern Canada, California, Oregon, Nevada, Utah, Idaho, Wyoming, Colorado, and North Dakota to Michigan. Winters from California, Texas, and Louisiana south to Mexico.

Nebraska and Kansas: probably regular transient; New Mexico: spring and fall migrant; Utah: uncommon migrant, former resident; Wyoming: regular breeder in northwest, elsewhere rare.

COLORADO.—Regular migrant, particularly in western counties. Nested formerly in mountain parks of Colorado up to 9500 feet but few breeding pairs remain. Present nesting populations occur in Routt County in the Snake Creek drainage of California and Slater Parks, and along the Floyd, Larson, and Beaver Creeks and Circle Basin of the Hahns Peak area north of Steamboat Springs.

Family RALLIDAE: Rails, Gallinules, and Coots

VIRGINIA RAIL   *Rallus limicola limicola* Vieillot. [212]

RECOGNITION.—Length 8–11 inches; a long-billed, reddish-brown rail. *Adult:* olive-brown above, streaked with black; cheeks gray, chin white, throat and breast reddish-brown; wing patch rufous; flanks black, barred with white. *Young:* wing patch rufous as in adults, but plumage more blackish. (Plate 43)

RANGE.—Breeds from Nova Scotia across southern Canada south to Baja California, and Oklahoma; eastern North Carolina, West Virginia, Missouri, Illinois, and Arizona. Winters from British Columbia, Washington and Oregon south to Baja California and North Carolina, south to Gulf states and southward through Mexico.

Nebraska and Kansas: Uncommon transient and summer resident; New Mexico and Utah: summer resident and occasional in winter; Wyoming: uncommon breeder.

COLORADO.—Resident, common in summer, but rare in winter in marsh areas of the Upper Sonoran Zone.

SORA   *Porzana carolina* (Linnaeus). [214]

RECOGNITION.—Length 8–10 inches; a short-billed rail, with "face" black. *Adult:* plumage olive-brown above, with black and white markings; mid-crown, face and chin black; cheeks and breast gray; sides blackish, barred with white; belly white; under tail coverts buffy. *Young:* like the adult, but breast and cheeks buffy, lacking the black "face." The short, stout bill and absence of reddish color distinguishes this bird from the Virginia Rail. (Plate 43)

RANGE.—Breeds from British Columbia across southern Canada to New Brunswick; south in northern states from West Virginia, Indiana, and Illinois to Arizona and Baja California into South America. Winters occasionally in north, but usually south from California, Arizona, Texas, and Florida to Venezuela and Peru.

Nebraska: common migrant and occasional breeder, especially in east; Kansas: common transient and two breeding records; New Mexico: summer resident around all marshes; Utah: summer resident, and possibly wintering in south; Wyoming: common migrant and breeder.

COLORADO.—Summer resident, common locally. Breeds along marshy areas on the plains and occasionally in the mountains to 10,000 feet. Occurs rarely in winter.

YELLOW RAIL   *Coturnicops noveboracensis noveboracensis* (Gmelin). [215]

RECOGNITION.—Length 6–8 inches; a small yellowish rail with a conspicuous white wing patch; buffy above, marked with black and brown; back barred with fine white lines; wings dusky with white patch; under parts with belly whitish. (Plate 43)

RANGE.—Breeds locally across southern Canada and from Alberta to New Brunswick south to Massachusetts, Connecticut, Ohio, Illinois, North Dakota, Wisconsin, Minnesota, and east-central California. Winters in the Gulf states north to North Carolina and in California.

Nebraska: rare migrant; Kansas: rare with records from eastern part of the state only.

COLORADO.—Straggler. A specimen (no. 957) was taken at Barr in July 1906 by L. J. Hersey (Lincoln, 1914).

* BLACK RAIL   *Laterallus jamaicensis jamaicensis* (Gmelin). [216]

RECOGNITION.—Length 5–6 inches. Blackish, speckled with white above; bill black. (Plate 43)

RANGE.—Breeds from Kansas, Indiana, and Ohio eastward to Massachusetts and south to Florida. Winters along the Gulf coast.

Nebraska: a rare migrant and summer resident; Kansas: rare summer resident with seven specimens from scattered localities, two breeding records from Riley and Finney Counties, and "several nests at our famous Cheyenne Bottoms in central Kansas" in June 1963 (D. P. Parmelee, pers. comm.).

Colorado.—One collected by David Bruce near Denver in the mid-1890's, and one was observed two miles NE of Longmont Oct. 18, 1964.

PURPLE GALLINULE   *Porphyrula martinica* (Linnaeus). [218]

RECOGNITION.—Length 12–14 inches. *Adult:* head (except bluish forehead plate), neck, and under parts deep purple; bill red, tipped with yellowish; back, wings, and tail bluish-green; under tail coverts white and legs yellow. Immatures with upper parts dark, light below, and dark bill. (Plate 44)

RANGE.—Breeds from Tennessee and South Carolina south through the Gulf states, Mexico, and Central America, and south through South America to Argentina and Peru. Winters in the Gulf states and southward. Irregular in summer north to Canada.

Kansas: rare summer resident; New Mexico: one observed near Caprock June 12, 1953, and another at Roswell May 10, 1958 (Ligon, 1961); Utah: a female collected in Salt Lake Co. Nov. 23, 1924.

COLORADO.—Straggler. A male was taken at Florence, Fremont Co., June 17, 1911 (Cooke, 1912).

* COMMON GALLINULE   *Gallinula chloropus cachinnans* Bangs. [219]

RECOGNITION.—Length 12–14 inches. *Adult:* neck and under parts slate-gray; head blackish; frontal plate red; back dusty-brown; flanks streaked with white. *Young:* grayer below, with belly and chin whitish; frontal plate small. (Plate 44)

RANGE.—Breeds locally from central California to northern Baja California, Arizona, and into Mexico and Panama; and in Texas and the Gulf states north to Iowa, Minnesota, southern Ontario, New York, and Vermont. Winters in the southern states southward.

Nebraska: a rare summer resident, breeding locally, especially in southeast counties; Kansas: rare summer resident with breeding records from Coffey and Douglas Counties; New Mexico: first record July 14, 1928 and well established by 1940 in Rio Grande valley, and nest May 15, 1955 near Las Cruces (Ligon, 1961); Utah: nine near St. George Dec. 19, 1963, and Mar. 12, 1964 (A.F.N. 18: 377).

COLORADO.—Straggler. One was seen "in the flesh" at Colo. Spgs. on May 9, 1882 (Allen and Brewster, 1883); one was observed near Golden on Lathrop Lake in 1883 by E. L. Berthoud (Cooke, 1898); and two were noted on Lily Lake, R.Mt.N.P., Aug. 8 and 25, 1939 (Packard, 1945); one Ft. Morgan by D.F.O. June 6, 1965 (D. Thatcher).

AMERICAN COOT   *Fulica americana americana* Gmelin. [221]

RECOGNITION.—Length 13–16 inches; stout-bodied, dark bird with pointed ivory-colored beak. *Adult:* head and neck blackish; rest of body dark slate, with under tail coverts white; bill white, with small reddish spots, frontal plate white blending to brown and red. *Young:* more brownish above and under parts mottled; frontal plate small. While swimming, the coot has a decided forward and backward motion of the head. (Plate 44)

RANGE.—Breeds across the southern half of Canada south through the United States to the Gulf coast, locally, to Baja California; also in southern Mexico, West Indies, and Nicaragua. Winters from southeastern Alaska, southern British Columbia across northern states to the Atlantic coast and south through Mexico to Panama.

Nebraska: common summer resident and uncommon in winter; Kansas: abundant in migration and uncommon summer resident; New Mexico and Utah: summer resident and transient; Wyoming: abundant migrant and breeder.

COLORADO.—Resident; common in summer and uncommon in winter. Breeds mainly on the plains, but occasionally in the mountains to 10,000 feet.

ORDER CHARADRIIFORMES: Shore Birds, Gulls, and Allies
Family CHARADRIIDAE: Plover, Turnstones

SEMIPALMATED PLOVER   *Charadrius semipalmatus* Bonaparte. [274]

RECOGNITION.—Length 6.5–7.5 inches; a small plover, with a single breast band. *Adult:* dark brown above, with neck encircled by a black collar; forehead with two black bars enclosing a white bar; under parts white. *Adult winter:* black replaced by dark gray. *Young:* more buffy above. Dark cheeks and dark brown upper parts separate this bird from the Piping Plover; the small size and single breast band from the Killdeer. (Plate 45)

RANGE.—Breeds from northern Alaska and along the Arctic coast to Labrador and the Gulf of St. Lawrence and west locally across Canada to British Columbia. Winters from central California, Louisiana, and South Carolina to South America.

Nebraska: a regular transient; Kansas: common migrant; New Mexico, Utah, and Wyoming: uncommon migrant.

COLORADO.—Uncommon migrant, spring and fall.

Early spring Apr. 18 Cherry Creek Res. (C.B.N. 12:16); late fall Oct. 8 Longmont; winter: Dec. 7 Denver.

PIPING PLOVER   *Charadrius melodus circumcinctus* (Ridgway). [277a]

RECOGNITION.—Length 6–7.5 inches; a small, short-billed plover, with an incomplete breast band. *Adult:* pale fawn-brown above, with forecrown black; forehead, cheeks, neck, and under parts white; black shoulder mark meeting across the back of the neck in a narrow line. (Plate 45)

RANGE.—Breeds locally from central Alberta, southern Saskatchewan, and Manitoba east to southern Newfoundland, Michigan, Illinois, North and South Dakota, and Nebraska. Winters along the Gulf coast from Texas eastward along the shores of Lakes Michigan and Erie, and the Atlantic coast south to Virginia, and from South Carolina to Florida and the Bahamas to Puerto Rico.

Nebraska: uncommon transient breeding locally in east; Kansas: rare; New Mexico: recorded Aug. 10, 1964 from Lake Avalon (A.F.N. 18:527); Wyoming: casual.

COLORADO.—Irregular summer resident and transient. First state specimen collected at M.H.D.C., Adams Co., May 6, 1939. First mention of the species: one observed near Julesburg "between 4:30 p.m. May 16 and 4:30 p.m. May 17, 1899" (W. L. Dawson, Wilson Bull. 11:49–50). Other records include one Marston Res. May 21, 1955; one Bonny Res. May 23, 1959 and May 13, 1961; two Union Res. near Longmont Aug. 31, 1961 and two May 18, 1963. A nest with three eggs was located at Prewitt Res., Washington Co., June 26, 1949.

Early spring May 6 M.H.D.C.; no fall records.

SNOWY PLOVER *Charadrius alexandrinus nivosus* (Cassin). [278]

RECOGNITION.—Length 6–7.5 inches; average slightly smaller and lighter above than the Piping Plover; neck band reduced to side patch, and legs grayish-black. (Plate 45)

RANGE.—The species occurs from southern England, Sweden, Russia, and Siberia to southern Japan, south to South Africa, Ceylon, and Australia. Thirteen races are recognized and this subspecies breeds locally in Kansas, Oklahoma, and Texas west to Washington and south to Baja California. Winters from Oregon and central California south along the coast into Mexico and from Texas east to Mississippi.

Nebraska: straggler, two specimens taken at Lincoln; Kansas: uncommon summer resident with one old breeding record (1886); New Mexico: summer resident along borders of alkali lakes of the Rio Grande, Estancia, and Pecos valleys; Utah: transient and summer resident in north, especially Bear River Sanctuary; Wyoming: straggler.

COLORADO.—Casual summer resident and transient. Three nesting reports, three eggs (no. 6406) along shores of Nee Grande Res., Kiowa Co., June 5, 1939 and three downy young in another nest Aug. 3; and two downy young banded July 4, 1965 at San Luis Lake by R. A. Ryder (pers. comm.).

KILLDEER *Charadrius vociferus vociferus* Linnaeus. [273]

RECOGNITION.—Length 9.5–11 inches; a rusty-tailed plover, with two breast or neck bands; mainly brown above with rump and tail rusty-brown; tail edged with white and with a dark subterminal band; forehead white bordered above by black; dusky band from bill below eye to nape; under parts white, with two neck bands; conspicuous white wing bar. Iris brown circled with orange eyering. (Plate 46)

RANGE.—Breeds from British Columbia east across southern Canada and south to Florida, central Mexico, and southern Baja California. Winters from southern British Columbia and New York to South America.

Nebraska, Kansas, New Mexico, Utah, and Wyoming: common migrant and summer resident, and a few in winter.

COLORADO.—Very common summer resident throughout the state in the Upper Sonoran and less numerous in the Transition Zone. Recorded regularly on Christmas Count. Nest with three eggs on roof of Denver Museum May 23, 1958.

MOUNTAIN PLOVER *Eupoda montana* (Townsend). [281]

RECOGNITION.—Length 8–9 inches; a plain, light brown plover inhabiting the shortgrass prairie. *Adults:* light brown above, with forecrown black and forehead and superciliary line white; under parts white with breast and sides pale buffy; tail with dark subterminal band. *Young:* black feathers broadly edged with buffy and under parts more tawny. (Plate 50)

RANGE.—Breeds from northern Montana and North and South Dakota south through eastern Wyoming and western Nebraska, and western Oklahoma to northwestern Texas. Winters from northern California, southern Arizona, and Texas to southern Baja California and central Mexico.

Nebraska: possibly formerly rare summer resident; Kansas: summer resident in west; New Mexico: irregular summer resident, breeding on shortgrass uplands; Utah: uncommon transient; Wyoming: summer resident of the basins and Laramie Plains.

COLORADO.—Summer resident on the eastern plains, and occasionally into mountain parks. Formerly numerous, becoming rare over much of breeding territory. Nests on the shortgrass prairie, the center of abundance being in Weld and Larimer Cos. with fewer birds in Adams, Arapahoe, Elbert, Morgan, and Park Cos. Fifty (39 adults & 11 young) observed in Weld Co. by members of D.F.O. June 10, 1967 (Nancy Hurley, pers. comm.).

Early spring Mar. 25 Weld Co. (AMB); late fall Oct. 5 Morgan Co. (no. 23959).

AMERICAN GOLDEN PLOVER *Pluvialis dominica dominica* (Muller). [272]

RECOGNITION.—Length 10–11 inches; a black-bellied plover, spotted above with golden-yellow. *Adult summer:* plumage mainly black, spotted above with golden-yellow; white forehead and superciliary line extending into a patch on side of neck; tail dark brown, barred with gray; axillars gray. *Adult winter:* less golden above, and with under parts mottled. *Young:* like the winter adult, but more golden above and with yellow-tinged breast. (Plate 46)

RANGE.—The western race nests in Siberia east to Alaska from Kotzebue Sound south along the shores of Bering Sea; and this form breeds from Point Barrow east along the Arctic coast to Baffin Island and south to south-central Alaska, Yukon, Mackenzie, Manitoba, and Southampton Island. Winters from Bolivia, Paraguay, and Brazil to Argentina. Fall migration chiefly from Nova Scotia over the Atlantic Ocean to South America. Spring migration through Central America and Mexico and up the Mississippi Valley.

Nebraska: uncommon but regular migrant; Kansas: regular transient in east, especially in spring; New Mexico: irregular transient; Utah: uncommon migrant; Wyoming: rare transient.

COLORADO.—Uncommon spring and fall migrant along lakes and reservoirs of the prairies.

Early spring Mar. 30 Barr Lake; late fall Nov. 5 Longmont.

BLACK-BELLIED PLOVER *Squatarola squatarola* (Linnaeus). [270]

RECOGNITION.—Length 11–13.5 inches; a stout-bodied, black and white plover. *Adult summer:* head, hind neck, and shoulders white, with crown spotted and lined with dusky; rest of upper parts spotted with black and white; dark below except for white lower belly and under tail coverts; rump whitish and tail barred with dusky; under wing surfaces white with axillars *black. Young:* like the winter adult, but with some pale yellow spotting above. In flight, the white under wing surfaces and *black* axillars are diagnostic. (Plate 46)

RANGE.—Breeds on the Arctic tundras of North America, Russia, and Siberia. Winters from the Mediterranean to South Africa, in India and Australia, and from southern British Columbia, California, Louisiana, and North Carolina to central South America. Nonbreeding birds occur in summer in the Old World south to the British Isles; in the New World south to California, Panama, Ecuador, Galapagos Islands, and the coast of the Gulf of Mexico.

Nebraska and Kansas: regular transient in both states; New Mexico: uncommon visitor; Utah and Wyoming: regular transient in eastern counties.

COLORADO.—Regular but uncommon spring and fall migrant upon the prairies.
Early spring Apr. 11 Morgan Co. (no. 20988); winter Dec. 28 Loveland (no. 106).

RUDDY TURNSTONE *Arenaria interpres morinella* (Linnaeus). [283a]

RECOGNITION.—Length 8.5–10 inches; a conspicuously marked russet-red, black, and white shore bird. *Summer adult:* head and hind neck mainly white, with crown streaked; black facial markings extending into the black breast; under parts, rump, and middle of tail white; back and wings mixed variously with rusty and black; upper tail coverts and subterminal band in tail black. (Plate 47)

RANGE.—The species breeds from northern Alaska across Canada, Ellesmere Island, Greenland, Iceland, northern Scandinavia, and south in the New World to Southampton and Bristol Bay, Alaska. Nonbreeding birds occur south to Pacific coasts of South America. Winters from Atlantic coast and the southern states to Brazil and Chile.

Nebraska: rare spring migrant in east; Kansas: rare to regular transient in spring and fall; Utah: rare transient; Wyoming: uncommon migrant; New Mexico: one collected near Carlsbad May 7, 1962 (Auk, 81:227).

COLORADO.—Rare spring and fall migrant.
Early spring April 26 Denver; late fall Barr Lake Sept. 28.

Family SCOLOPACIDAE: Woodcock, Snipe, and Sandpipers

AMERICAN WOODCOCK *Philohela minor* (Gmelin). [228]

RECOGNITION.—Length 10–12 inches; a stout-bodied, long-billed bird, mainly rusty-brown in color. *Adult:* crown, neck, and scapular edges gray; rest of upper parts rusty-brown, barred and mottled with black; uniformly ruddy below, with mid-belly buffy; tail tipped with white; inhabits moist woodlands. The Woodcock resembles the Common Snipe, but is slightly larger. (Plate 48)

RANGE.—Breeds from southeastern Canada east to Nova Scotia and south locally from the Dakotas, Nebraska, and Illinois to Texas and Florida. Winters in the Ohio Valley to Texas and central Florida.

Nebraska: rare migrant, breeding occasionally in Missouri bottomlands; Kansas: uncommon transient in east; New Mexico: one collected in Dona Ana Co. Jan. 25, 1964 (Auk, 82:649); Wyoming: rare straggler.

COLORADO.—A specimen (no. 14760) was taken near Denver Aug. 9, 1885; one was observed near Denver in Oct. 1885; one near Boulder in the fall of 1887; one Denver June 8, 1895; one east of Boulder May 24 & 30, 1905; a female (no. 24766) collected east of Bennett on Kiowa Creek Sept. 16, 1945; three noted at Cherry Creek Res. Apr. 19, 1959; five recorded in Conejos Co. Dec. 3, 1959 and one Nov. 6, 1960; and one reported from Evans Ranch, Clear Creek Co., Apr. 17, 1965.

COMMON SNIPE *Capella gallinago delicata* (Ord). [230]

RECOGNITION.—Length 10–11 inches; a long-billed shorebird inhabiting marshy grasslands. Upper parts dark brown, with head stripes buffy-white and back mottled with black, buffy, and white; neck and breast streaked and mottled with buffy and dusky; under parts white, with broad black bars on sides and flanks; tail rufous with a black subterminal band and white tip. (Plate 48)

RANGE.—The species ranges over much of the Northern Hemisphere of both the New and Old Worlds from the British Isles, Scandinavia, Finland, Russia, Siberia, southern Europe, the Himalayas to the Amur River, and the Kurile Islands. This North American race breeds from northwestern Alaska, northern Yukon, and east across Canada to central Labrador, south through northern states from West Virginia to California and eastern Arizona. Winters from Alaska, western Canada, and the western and southern states to Central and South America.

Nebraska: migrant, and uncommon in winter, with breeding record from Garden Co.; Kansas: common transient and occasional winter visitor; New Mexico: migrant and winter resident; Utah: summer resident, and a few in winter; Wyoming: common resident.

COLORADO.—Summer resident in small numbers from plains to the lower Canadian Zone; numerous in migration, and often many in winter at low elevations. Nests in suitable moist environment throughout the state.

LONG-BILLED CURLEW   *Numenius americanus americanus* Bechstein. [264]

RECOGNITION.—Length 20–26 inches; a large, dark brown wader with a long decurved bill. Plumage pale cinnamon with crown and hind neck streaked, and back and wings barred with dusky; chin white; neck and breast streaked; belly plain fawn-brown; cinnamon axillars, and a uniformly marked crown, instead of a dark crown with light median stripe as in the Whimbrel. (Plate 49)

RANGE.—Breeds from northwestern Nevada and southern Idaho to Iowa and southern Wisconsin, and south to Oklahoma and southern Texas. Winters from central California, Texas, Louisiana, South Carolina, and Florida south on both coasts of Mexico to Guatemala.

Nebraska: common migrant and summer resident in west, rare in east; Kansas: uncommon summer resident, transient in west, and breeding records from Morton and Stanton Cos.; New Mexico: summer resident and transient; Utah: transient and common summer resident in north; Wyoming: uncommon migrant and breeder in south.

COLORADO.—Summer resident and migrant on the eastern plains; few west slope records. Recorded nesting in Middle and South Parks in the 1870's; fresh eggs in Boulder Co. May 4, 1886; newly hatched young near Parker in Douglas Co. June 4, 1931; four eggs in Arapahoe Co. May 30, 1956. Four eggs in the Museum (no. 3699) were taken in Morgan Co. in June 1903, and another set (no. 4505) in Baca Co. May 18, 1921.

Early spring Apr. 10 Larimer Co.; late fall Oct. 24 Kiowa Co. (no. 22179).

WHIMBREL   *Numenius phaeopus hudsonicus* Latham. [265]

RECOGNITION.—Length 16–18 inches. Smaller and browner than the Long-billed Curlew; bill decurved, crown dark with distinctive median crown stripe; upper parts grayish-brown, mottled and barred with dusky; hind neck streaked; under parts whitish, with sides and flanks barred with buffy and dusky, legs blue-gray. (Plate 49)

RANGE.—The species breeds from Iceland, Norway, Finland, Russia, and Siberia, and this race on the coast of Alaska from the mouth of the Yukon northward and locally east along the Arctic coast to northern Mackenzie, northern Manitoba, and along the west side of Hudson Bay to James Bay. Migrates along the Atlantic and Pacific coasts, and regularly in the interior in spring. Winters locally from central California and Baja California to Honduras and northern South America.

Nebraska, Kansas, New Mexico, Utah, and Wyoming: rare transient. Flock of 28 birds noted on a sandbar at Montez Creek, Uintah Co., Utah May 18, 1963, and female collected (Condor, 68:305).

COLORADO.—Spring and fall migrant, rare. One was shot near Pueblo about 1885, one near Fort Lyon in May 1888, and one near Colo. Spgs. Sept. 23, 1900. One seen near Berthoud May 25, 1952; six observed and one collected May 15, 1953 in Weld Co., and five seen May 14, 1954; two recorded at Barr and one M.H.D.C. May 18, 1954; six at Longmont May 14, 1961, seven at Bonny Res. and one at M.H.D.C. May 18; one at Colo. Spgs. Apr. 5, 1964, and one at Cherry Creek Res. May 7; one Bonny Res. May 8, 1965, two May 22, Park Co. (C.B.N. 13:12).

ESKIMO CURLEW   *Numenius borealis* (Forster). [266]

RECOGNITION.—Length 12–14.5 inches. Similar to the Whimbrel, except smaller, legs dusky green, bill shorter; top of head black, streaked with buff along median line. Primaries not barred. (Plate 49)

RANGE.—Nearly extinct. Formerly bred in northern Mackenzie and possibly northern Alaska migrating southward to Argentina and Chile.

Nebraska and Kansas: formerly a common migrant in eastern counties; Montana: rare straggler.

COLORADO.—One record (Jewett, 1942), a female (no. 6903) in his collection deposited in the San Diego Natural History Museum, collected by Dwight D. Stone in Denver Apr. 29, 1882. Actually, there were two birds, the other being a male (no. 6960) in the H. B. Conover collection in the Field Museum of Natural History.

UPLAND PLOVER   *Bartramia longicauda* (Bechstein). [261]

RECOGNITION.—Length 11–13 inches; a brown-colored, long-legged, round-headed, and short-billed "wader." *Adult:* head and neck streaked and rest of upper parts mottled with brown, black, and white; tail brown, barred with black and tipped with white; chin and belly white, with breast and sides buffy, barred with dark brown. *Young:* like adult, but the back feathers are darker and edged with white. (Plate 50)

RANGE.—Breeds locally from Alaska, southwestern Yukon, Mackenzie, Saskatchewan, Manitoba, Ontario, Quebec, Maine, Virginia, Michigan, Illinois, Missouri, and Oklahoma to Washington and Oregon. Winters in southern South America to Argentina and Chile.

Photograph by Patricia Bailey Witherspoon

LONG-BILLED CURLEW
The male occasionally took his turn upon the eggs

Nebraska: an uncommon migrant, breeding locally; Kansas: common transient and summer resident; New Mexico: formerly common in migration, now rare; Utah: rare summer resident; Wyoming: uncommon breeder in eastern half of state.

COLORADO.—Uncommon except on eastern border of state, where it is a fairly numerous summer resident. Breeds regularly in small numbers in the eastern grassland counties; two young east of Platteville July 26, 1965 (C.B.N. 13:17).

Early spring Apr. 14 Weld Co.; late summer Sept. 2 Bent Co.

SPOTTED SANDPIPER   *Actitis macularia* (Linnaeus). [263]

RECOGNITION.—Length 7–8 inches; a small shore bird with a conspicuous white wing bar and a teetering action. *Adult:* upper parts olive-brown, marked with dusky; white superciliary line; under parts white, dotted with *round dark spots;* outer tail feathers white, barred with dusky. *Winter adult:* under parts unspotted. (Plate 48)

RANGE.—Breeds from northwest Alaska, Yukon, Mackenzie, Manitoba, Ontario, Quebec, and Labrador south to southern California, Arizona, central Alabama, and northern South Carolina. Winters from southern British Columbia, Washington, Arizona, and Gulf coast states to northern South America, and occasionally to Argentina.

Nebraska, Kansas, New Mexico, Utah, and Wyoming: a common migrant and summer resident.

COLORADO.—Common summer resident throughout the state from the prairies into the mountains to 10,600 ft. at Echo Lake.

Early spring Apr. 15 Colo. Spgs. (C.B.N. 25, no. 9); late fall Oct. 13 Denver (C.B.N. 11:7).

SOLITARY SANDPIPER   *Tringa solitaria cinnamomea* (Brewster). [256a]

RECOGNITION.—Length 7–9 inches; a small sandpiper finely patterned with black and white, with dark wings, and white tail feathers showing in flight. *Adult:* dark olive-gray above with head and neck streaked; white eyering; throat and belly white; sides and flanks marked with dusky; mainly *white tail, barred* with *black; wings dark,* with axillars and under wing linings heavily barred with black and white. *Young:* like the adults, but under parts more extensively streaked, and back marked with buffy. (Plate 51)

RANGE.—The species breeds locally from central Alaska, northern and central Mackenzie, British Columbia, Yukon, and Manitoba, to central Quebec and Labrador, and this race has a more westerly distribution. Migrates through the western intermountain region east to Montana and Colorado, and winters in Baja California south to Ecuador, Bolivia, and central Argentina.

Nebraska and Kansas: common spring and fall transient; New Mexico and Utah: uncommon in migration; Wyoming: common transient.

COLORADO.—Regular and sometimes a common migrant and nonbreeding summer resident in suitable environment throughout the state in Upper Sonoran and Lower Transition Zones.

Early spring Mar. 29 Denver (C.B.N. 12:16); late summer Oct. 1 Longmont (C.B.N. 12:49).

WILLET   *Catoptrophorus semipalmatus inornatus* (Brewster). [258a]

RECOGNITION.—Length 14–16.5 inches; a large gray and white wader. Head and neck whitish, streaked with dusky; back mottled with gray and black; upper tail coverts and base of tail white; tail barred with dusky and tipped with gray; wings blackish with a *conspicuous wide white band* through secondaries and primaries; belly white, with breast and sides marked with dusky. (Plate 50)

RANGE.—The species breeds locally from southern Canada to the Gulf of Mexico, and this western race from eastern Oregon, Idaho, Alberta, Saskatchewan, Manitoba, south to California, east to Nevada, South Dakota, and formerly in Minnesota and Iowa. Winters on the Gulf coast, and from California south to the Galapagos Islands and southern South America.

Nebraska and Kansas: transient, sometimes locally common; New Mexico: rather common migrant in spring and fall; Utah: common migrant and breeding summer resident; Wyoming: common transient and uncommon breeder.

COLORADO.—Uncommon migrant and summer resident in the Upper Sonoran Zone and rarely at higher elevations. Twenty-five at Antero Res. (about 8900′) May 5, 1956 observed by D. G. Davis (pers. comm.). Breeding records: young at M.H.D.C., Adams Co., June 15, 1931 and Aug. 19, 1936.

Early spring Apr. 11 Boulder Co. (C.B.N. 10:35); late fall Oct. 20 Cherry Creek Res. (C.B.N. 12:49).

GREATER YELLOWLEGS   *Totanus melanoleucus* (Gmelin). [254]

RECOGNITION.—Length 12–15 inches; a large black and white shore bird with *long, yellow legs* and *white* tail coverts. Upper parts mottled, and head and neck streaked with black and white; breast and sides marked with dusky; throat, belly, tail coverts, and base of tail white; tail barred toward tip. (Plate 51)

RANGE.—Breeds in central-southern Alaska, British Columbia, and Alberta east to Quebec, Labrador, and Newfoundland. Nonbreeding birds occur in summer south to South America. Winters from British Columbia, central California, and the southern states to Patagonia.

Nebraska, Kansas, and New Mexico: common migrant; Utah: fairly common transient and occasional in winter in the north; Wyoming: uncommon migrant.

COLORADO.—Migrant and nonnesting summer resident, chiefly in the Upper Sonoran and Lower Transition Zones.

Early spring Mar. 22 Longmont (C.B.N. 11:28); late fall Nov. 18 Ft. Collins (A.F.N. 21:52).

LESSER YELLOWLEGS   *Totanus flavipes* (Gmelin). [255]

RECOGNITION.—Length 10–11 inches; similar to Greater Yellowlegs, but smaller, and bill shorter. (Plate 51)

RANGE.—Breeds from north-central Alaska, northern Yukon, Mackenzie, Manitoba, Ontario, and Quebec, south to east-central British Columbia, Alberta, and Saskatchewan. Winters in Louisiana, Texas, and Florida south to Chile and Argentina. Migrates mainly east of the Rocky Mountains, and more rarely on Atlantic and Pacific coasts.

Nebraska, Kansas, and New Mexico: common migrant; Utah: uncommon transient; Wyoming: common in migration.

COLORADO.—Migrant and nonnesting summer resident throughout the state from the Upper Sonoran Zone into mountain parks and upward to an altitude of 10,000 feet.

Early spring Mar. 29 Cherry Creek Res. (C.B.N. 12:17); late fall Nov. 8 Latham Res.

KNOT   *Calidris canutus rufa* (Wilson). [234]

RECOGNITION.—Length 10–11 inches. Stout-bodied, short-billed, and short-legged shore birds about size of dowitchers; breast red in spring, but white in fall. (Plate 47)

RANGE.—Breeds from Victoria Island and Melville Peninsula south to Southampton Island. Migrates along both coasts and through the interior of the United States. Winters irregularly from Massachusetts to Florida, Texas, Mexico, Central America, and south to Tierra del Fuego.

Nebraska, Kansas, Utah, and Wyoming: rare migrant; New Mexico: one observed near Clayton Aug. 12, 1954, and five (three collected) in Eddy Co. to Sept. 2, 1962 (Auk, 81:227).

COLORADO.—Rare straggler. Observations include: one at Barr Lake Sept. 6, 1941; noted near Berthoud Aug. 9, 10, and 15, 1952; one collected May 18, 1953, Weld Co.; one observed at Bonny Res. May 13, 1961 and one at Longmont May 14; one taken from a group of four on Timnath Res., Larimer Co., Sept. 5, 1962; one recorded at Cherry Creek Res. May 7, 1964 and Sept. 12–13.

PECTORAL SANDPIPER   *Erolia melanotos* (Vieillot). [239]

RECOGNITION.—Length 8–9.5 inches; this sandpiper inhabits wet, grassy marshes. The head, neck, and upper parts are streaked and mottled with buffy-brown and black; the breast-band is buffy; the throat and belly white; rump and upper tail coverts black; under tail coverts white; legs and feet yellowish-green; iris brown. (Plate 52)

RANGE.—Breeds from Arctic Siberia, northern Alaska, and northern Canada to Southampton Island and Hudson Bay. Fall migrant in the Mississippi Valley and on the Atlantic coast, and rarely on the Pacific coast. Winters in South America and casually to Patagonia, New Zealand, and Australia.

Nebraska, Kansas, and New Mexico: common in migration; Utah: transient; Wyoming: common fall migrant.

COLORADO.—Uncommon, but regular migrant and nonnesting summer resident in shortgrass marsh areas on both sides of the Continental Divide, chiefly in the Upper Sonoran Zone.

Early spring Apr. 2 Boulder; late fall Nov. 17 Longmont.

WHITE-RUMPED SANDPIPER   *Erolia fuscicollis* (Vieillot). [240]

RECOGNITION.—Length 7–8 inches; this sandpiper resembles the Pectoral, but is smaller, and distinguished by the *white upper tail coverts*, conspicuous in flight. The feet and legs are greenish-black, the eyering is white, and the iris brown. (Plate 52)

RANGE.—Breeds locally along the Arctic coast from Pt. Barrow to Hudson Bay. Migrates mainly through the Mississippi Valley. Winters in southern South America.

Nebraska and Kansas: common transient; New Mexico: rare migrant; Wyoming: rare migrant.

COLORADO.—Regular spring and summer visitor along the shores of the lakes and reservoirs of the eastern plains.

Early spring May 7 Prowers Co. (no. 2612); late fall Oct. 21 Morrison.

BAIRD'S SANDPIPER   *Erolia bairdii* (Coues). [241]

RECOGNITION.—Length 7–8 inches; a small sandpiper with a streaked buffy breast, and the light brownish back feathers edged with light pale buffy which give a scaly appearance. The sides and under parts white; upper tail coverts dusky-brown; legs and feet blackish; iris brown. (Plate 52)

RANGE.—Breeds along the Arctic coast of northeastern Siberia and from western Alaska to Baffin Island and northwestern Greenland. Winters locally in the Andes of Bolivia to Chile and along the coast of Patagonia. Migrates from the Mississippi River west to the Rocky Mountains, in autumn it is irregular along the Atlantic and Pacific coasts.

Nebraska and Kansas: common in migration; New Mexico and Utah: uncommon transient; Wyoming: common migrant.

COLORADO.—Common migrant and less numerous nonbreeding summer resident on the eastern prairies; rare in winter. Ranges from the plains to 13,000 feet in the mountains.

Early spring Mar. 10 Barr Lake (C.B.N. 10:35); late fall Oct. 28 Platteville; winter Jan. 2 Barr Lake (no. 23966).

LEAST SANDPIPER   *Erolia minutilla* (Vieillot). [242]

RECOGNITION.—Length 5–7 inches; a very small sandpiper with a streaked breast. *Adult:* brownish above, streaked on head and neck, and mottled on back with dusky; breast buffy, lined with dusky; superciliary line, chin, and belly white; rump and upper tail coverts black. *Winter adult and young:* more grayish above, with breast streaks indistinct. As the name indicates, this is the smallest of our sandpipers. The short, thin bill and the greenish or yellow legs distinguish it from the larger Western Sandpiper, which has darker greenish legs. The Semipalmated Sandpiper has a short but heavier bill and legs similar to the Western. (Plate 53)

RANGE.—Breeds locally from northwestern Alaska and northern Alaska, northern Mackenzie southeastward to Hudson Bay, Quebec, and Labrador, and Alaska Peninsula, Yakutat Bay, and northeastern Manitoba. Winters from Oregon, Washington, and Nevada, and in the southern states to Central America and Patagonia.

Nebraska, Kansas, New Mexico, Utah, and Wyoming: common migrant.

COLORADO.—Common transient and less numerous nonnesting summer resident on the plains to 8000 ft. in the foothills. Recorded from both sides of the Continental Divide.

Early spring Apr. 16 Marston Res.; late fall Nov. 30 Cherry Creek Res. (C.B.N. 11:53).

DUNLIN   *Erolia alpina pacifica* (Coues). [243a]

RECOGNITION.—Length 7–8 inches. *Adult:* head (except crown), neck, and breast white, streaked with dusky; crown, back and upper tail coverts *rusty* and somewhat streaked; wings grayish-brown; *belly black. Winter adult:* gray above and faintly streaked; breast light gray and obscurely streaked; under parts, upper tail coverts, and sides of rump white. This sandpiper is distinguished by the slightly decurved bill, somewhat longer than the head. (Plate 52)

RANGE.—The species breeds in the northern part of both the New and Old Worlds and winters from the British Isles, the Mediterranean and Red Seas, northern Africa, India, and Formosa. The North American race breeds from Cape Prince of Wales and Arctic Alaska across northern Canada and from the mouth of the Yukon to Hudson Bay. Winters on the Pacific coast from southern British Columbia to southern Baja California, and on the Atlantic coast from New Jersey to Florida and Texas.

Nebraska, Kansas, New Mexico, Utah, and Wyoming: uncommon to rare migrant.

COLORADO.—Rare migrant on the eastern prairies. Three specimens are in the Museum collection: a male (no. 17172) from M.H.D.C. May 2, 1937, a female (no. 26132) secured by R. Ryder in Saguache Co. May 5, 1950, and one in winter dress (no. 33715) collected by A. Collister five miles east of Longmont Dec. 30, 1958. Two noted in Larimer Co. Apr. 18, 1965, and one M.H.D.C. May 6 (C.B.N. 13:12).

LONG-BILLED DOWITCHER   *Limnodromus scolopaceus* (Say). [232]

RECOGNITION.—Length 11–12 inches; a long-billed shore bird with rusty under parts in spring plumage. *Adult:* dark brown above, mottled and streaked with reddish-brown and dusky; lower back, rump, and tail white, with tail barred; whitish line over eye; under parts tawny, heavily spotted on breast and barred on sides. *Winter adult:* gray throughout except white eye line, white rump and belly. Differs from the Short-billed Dowitcher in having longer beak—females average 72.6 mm. and males 62.2 as against an average of 61.6 mm. for females and 56.9 for male Short-billed Dowitchers. Further distinguished by having the breast and belly more or less uniform salmon with many feathers tipped with white and ventral spotting confined to throat region and sides of the breast; sides and breast barred heavily. The next form has scanty spotting not confined to the throat and general color below has yellowish tinge. See Pitelka (1950) for comparisons too varied to describe here. (Plate 54)

RANGE.—Breeds in northeastern Siberia along the coast of Alaska from the Yukon north to Pt. Barrow, and east across Canada to Hudson Bay. Migrates chiefly through the western half of the continent and winters in southern states and Mexico to Panama and Ecuador.

Nebraska, Kansas, New Mexico, Utah, and Wyoming: fairly common transient.

COLORADO.—Migrant in spring and fall, not common in summer. All records are from the eastern prairies but the species probably occurs in western counties.

Early spring Mar. 27 Berthoud; late fall Nov. 21 Denver; winter one M.H.D.C. Jan. 28, 1967 (T. Marsh, pers. comm.).

SHORT-BILLED DOWITCHER   *Limnodromus griseus hendersoni* Rowan. [231a]

RECOGNITION.—Similar to *L. scolopaceus*, but yellowish-salmon color below, neck and sides less heavily dotted, the dark marks scattered over under parts; wing slightly longer, and bill, according to Rowan, averages shorter as follows:

L. scolopaceus female 68–78 mm. (72.6); male 58–66 mm. (62.2)
L.g. hendersoni female 57–66 mm. (61.6); male 53–61 mm. (56.9)

RANGE.—Breeding from Mackenzie, British Columbia, and northern Alberta east to Manitoba. Winters along the Gulf coast.

Nebraska, Kansas, New Mexico, and Utah: probably rare migrant, or at least its status little known.

COLORADO.—Rare transient. There are two specimens in the Museum collection, an immature female (no. 987) from Barr Lake, Aug. 14, 1909, and an adult female (no. 17645) taken at Barr Lake July 16, 1938.

STILT SANDPIPER   *Micropalama himantopus* (Bonaparte). [233]

RECOGNITION.—Length 7–9 inches; a medium-sized, long-legged sandpiper, with spring adults having barred under parts; head streaked with gray and dusky, a rufous patch below the eye; upper parts mottled with black and brown; upper tail coverts white, barred with gray and black. *Winter adult:* mainly gray above, marked with white; superciliary line, tail coverts, and under parts white. *Young:* breast and sides washed with buffy. (Plate 51)

RANGE.—Breeds from northeastern Alaska, northern Mackenzie, Manitoba, northern Ontario, and probably southern Canada to Hudson Bay. Migrates in spring through Central America, Mexico, and the western Mississippi Valley; in fall through the lower Great Lakes region and the Atlantic coast states. Winters in South America to Argentina.

Nebraska and Kansas: common migrant locally; New Mexico: uncommon, sixteen observed Lake McMillan and two collected May 17, 1963 (A.F.N. 17:424); Utah and Wyoming: uncommon transient.

COLORADO.—Fairly common spring and fall migrant along the ponds and reservoirs of eastern counties. There are a few early-day reports from Grand and Park Counties.

Early spring Apr. 20 Berthoud; late fall Oct. 12 Barr Lake (C.B.N. 11:53); winter Dec. 13 Barr Lake (no. 977).

SEMIPALMATED SANDPIPER   *Ereunetes pusillus* (Linnaeus). [246]

RECOGNITION.—Length 6–7 inches. *Adult:* pale brown above, closely resembling the Least Sandpiper, but generally grayer, the bill slightly longer and heavier, and the legs are black instead of olive-green. *Winter adult:* dull gray above, faintly streaked with dusky; white below, with breast gray. *Young:* like winter adult, but back feathers edged with white. (Plate 53)

RANGE.—Breeds from the Arctic coast of Alaska, northern Yukon, Mackenzie, Baffin Island, Labrador, Manitoba, and Hudson Bay. Migrates through the interior of the United States and Canada. Winters from South Carolina and the Gulf states through eastern Mexico and South America to Chile and Paraguay.

Nebraska and Kansas: common migrant; New Mexico: one record near Socorro Sept. 10, 1926; Utah: transient; Wyoming: rare visitor.

COLORADO.—Common migrant in spring and fall with a few nonbreeding birds present during the summer months along the ponds and reservoirs of eastern counties and in Middle and South Parks.

Early spring Apr. 15 Longmont; late fall Oct. 21 Morrison.

WESTERN SANDPIPER   *Ereunetes mauri* Cabanis. [247]

RECOGNITION.—Length 6–7 inches; a small, rusty-backed sandpiper. *Adult:* nape and back chestnut-red, streaked and mottled with black; *neck streaked* and *breast spotted* with dusky; belly white; wings mainly gray, with primaries black. Bill longer than that of the Semipalmated and Least Sandpipers. *Winter adult:* brownish-gray above, streaked with black, and feather edgings white; white below with breast streaked. (Plate 53)

RANGE.—Breeds on the coasts of northern and western Alaska from Nunivak Island and Seward Peninsula to Point Barrow and Camden Bay. Winters from the coasts of California and North Carolina south to both coasts of Mexico, Central America, and northern South America. Migrates chiefly along the Pacific coast, and uncommonly in the interior from southern Ontario and North Dakota southward, and regularly in fall along the south Atlantic coast.

Nebraska and Kansas: numerous in the west, uncommon migrant in east; New Mexico, Utah, and Wyoming: common transient.

COLORADO.—Regular migrant and nonbreeding summer resident along the shores of lakes and reservoirs from the Upper Sonoran Zone into the Transition. Less common west of the Continental Divide than in eastern counties.

Early spring Mar. 23 Denver; late fall Oct. 17 Longmont.

BUFF-BREASTED SANDPIPER　*Tryngites subruficollis* (Vieillot). [262]

RECOGNITION.—Length 7–9 inches; a small sandpiper with clear buffy under parts. *Adult:* above grayish-brown, marked with buffy; crown and hind neck streaked; cheeks and under parts clear buffy; underwing surfaces gray and somewhat mottled. *Young:* like adults but with white-edged back feathers. (Plate 50)

RANGE.—Breeds along the Arctic coast from northern Alaska to northern Mackenzie and Bathurst Island south to King William Island. Winters in South America south to Argentina. Migrates in spring through the western interior of the United States and Canada, and in fall east to Hudson Bay and south from North Dakota and Missouri to Louisiana and eastern Mexico; a few from Ontario, Ohio, and New England states south to Florida.

Nebraska and Kansas: rare in spring and uncommon but regular in fall in eastern counties; New Mexico: one observed near Clayton May 19, 1957 (Ligon, 1961); Wyoming: rare, six Casper Sept. 2, 1962 (A.F.N. 17:54).

COLORADO.—Straggler. L. J. Hersey (1911) collected two females at Barr Lake Aug. 25 and Sept. 4, 1910, out of flocks of three and five respectively, and these specimens (nos. 465–6) are in the Museum collection. Two were seen, one on each side of Cherry Creek Res. on Sept. 8 and 9, 1962, by Mildred and Charles Snyder, and Harold Holt (pers. comm.)

MARBLED GODWIT　*Limosa fedoa* (Linnaeus). [249]

RECOGNITION.—Length 16–20 inches; a large brown wader with a long, slightly upturned bill. *Adult:* plumage mainly light brown, mottled above with black; under side of wing *rich brown;* breast, sides, and flanks finely barred with dark brown or blackish; superciliary line and throat white. *Young:* more buffy, with under parts plain. (Plate 54)

RANGE.—Breeds from central Alberta, southern Saskatchewan, and Manitoba to Montana, South Dakota, and Minnesota. Winters from central California, Nevada, and the southern states south on the coast of Mexico, Guatemala, and British Honduras, and rarely to Ecuador, Peru, and Chile. Migrates in spring through the western interior and California, and returns in fall over the same route, with a few along the east coast and south via islands of Caribbean.

Nebraska: uncommon, but occasionally locally numerous in migration; Kansas: common transient east-central counties; New Mexico: uncommon in migration; Utah: uncommon transient; Wyoming: common migrant.

COLORADO.—Regular spring and fall migrant in the Upper Sonoran and Transition Zones.

Early spring Apr. 11 M.H.D.C.; late fall Nov. 25 Barr Lake (no. 104).

HUDSONIAN GODWIT　*Limosa haemastica* (Linnaeus). [251]

RECOGNITION.—Looks like an extra large, very dark dowitcher. Length 14–17 inches; long, slightly upcurved bill; back blackish, with conspicuous *white band* on upper tail coverts; under parts dark cinnamon with tips of feathers finely barred with black. *Female:* lighter below; immatures and fall plumage gray above and whitish below. (Plate 54)

RANGE.—Breeds locally from the mouth of the Mackenzie River to northeastern Manitoba. Winters in southern South America to Tierra del Fuego and the Falkland Islands. Casual at Point Barrow, Bermuda, and New Zealand. Recorded from Grant Co., Washington, Sept. 12, 1959 (Murrelet, 41:16).

Nebraska: uncommon migrant in eastern counties; Kansas: common transient in east-central counties; New Mexico: two records, one collected near Estancia May 22, 1951 and one observed at Buttes Lake Refuge May 18, 1958 (Ligon, 1961).

COLORADO.—Straggler. One observed on a pond west of Jackson Res., Morgan Co. May 22, 1955; and a male (no. 28293) collected at M.H.D.C. May 26, 1956.

SANDERLING　*Crocethia alba* (Pallas). [248]

RECOGNITION.—Length 7–8.5 inches; a small gray or brown sandpiper with a conspicuous long *white wing band* showing in flight. *Summer adult:* head, neck, and back tawny, streaked on neck and mottled on back with black; wings gray with a white wing band; breast, belly, and outer tail feathers white. *Winter adult:* forehead and under parts clear white; gray above, with hind neck streaked and back mottled with black. *Young:* breast washed with buffy. May be recognized in flight in any plumage by the *white band* extending the length of the wing. (Plate 47)

RANGE.—Breeds in Siberia, Spitsbergen, Iceland, Greenland, and the Arctic islands north of Canada to Hudson Bay. Winters in the southern states to South America.

Nebraska: rare migrant; Kansas: common transient; New Mexico and Utah: uncommon transient; Wyoming: common in migration.

COLORADO.—Regular, but uncommon spring and fall migrant along the shores of eastern lakes and reservoirs.

Early spring Apr. 15 Denver; late fall Nov. 5 Longmont.

Family RECURVIROSTRIDAE: Avocets and Stilts

AMERICAN AVOCET   *Recurvirostra americana* Gmelin. [225]

RECOGNITION.—Length 15–18.5 inches; a large, long-legged, long-billed wader. *Adults:* head, neck, and breast fawn-brown; back, tail, and under parts white; wings black with conspicuous white bar; bill black and curved upward; legs and feet bluish. *Winter adult* and *immature:* clear white below; fawn-brown absent on neck and replaced above by gray. (Plate 55)

RANGE.—Breeds locally from southern Saskatchewan, Manitoba, and Alberta to eastern Washington and California, east from Nevada to North Dakota, and south to Oklahoma and Texas; formerly in southern Mackenzie, Minnesota, Wisconsin, Iowa, and New Jersey. Winters from central California and southern Texas to Baja California and Guatemala.

Nebraska: migrant and commonly breeding in the Sandhill Lakes area; Kansas: regular migrant and summer resident in west and central counties; New Mexico and Utah: common migrant and summer resident; Wyoming: common migrant and breeder, locally abundant.

COLORADO.—Summer resident breeding throughout the state adjacent to ponds and reservoirs of the Upper Sonoran into the Transition Zone.

Early spring Mar. 15 M.H.D.C.; late fall M.H.D.C. Nov. 30 (no. 12609).

BLACK-NECKED STILT   *Himantopus mexicanus* (Muller). [226]

RECOGNITION.—Length 13–16 inches; a long-legged, black and white wader. *Adult male:* dark above, glossed with greenish and purple; forehead, rump, tail coverts, and under parts white; bill black, legs and feet pinkish-red; iris red. *Adult female:* like male, but more brownish on back and without glossy reflections. (Plate 55)

RANGE.—Breeds from Oregon and southern Saskatchewan south locally to the Gulf coast, and through the West Indies to South America.

Nebraska and Kansas: rare migrant; New Mexico: migrant and summer resident in south; Utah: migrant and summer resident in north; Wyoming: rare migrant and breeder.

COLORADO.—Rare summer visitor in eastern and western counties. One Boulder Apr. 29, 1965 (C.B.N. 13:12); one with 25 Willets west side of Antero Res. (about 8900′) May 5, 1956 (D. G. Davis, pers. comm.). Recorded breeding northwest of Ft. Garland June 21, 1873 by Henshaw (1875).

Early spring Apr. 14 Berthoud; late fall Sept. 12 Latham Res.

Family PHALAROPODIDAE: Phalaropes

RED PHALAROPE   *Phalaropus fulicarius* (Linnaeus). [222]

RECOGNITION.—Length 7–9 inches. *Summer male:* mottled with black and brown above; side of head whitish; entirely dark reddish-brown below; wing bluish-gray with a white band; female more colorful than male, with forehead, crown, and hind neck black. *Winter adult:* head and under parts white, with a dark area at nape and around eye; rest of upper parts bluish-gray. (Plate 56)

RANGE.—Circumpolar in distribution, breeding in North America from the Yukon delta northward along the Alaskan coast and east to Baffin Island, Ellesmere Island, northern Quebec, Labrador, and northern Mackenzie. Winters off the coasts of South America, Arabia, West Africa, and New Zealand. Migrates along the coasts of the United States, but well offshore.

Nebraska: one specimen from Cherry Co.; Kansas: a specimen from Douglas Co. Nov. 5, 1905, and one from Franklin Co. Oct. 25, 1926, several records Barton and Shawnee Counties, 1959 and 1963; New Mexico: first specimen from the state collected in Lea Co. Oct. 4, 1962 (Condor, 66: 518); Utah: casual, with two record specimens; Wyoming: straggler.

COLORADO.—Rare straggler. A female (no. 5152) was collected at Loveland July 25, 1895 by E. A. Preble (Cooke, 1909); another female was seen in Kiowa Co. June 27, 1938 (B. & N., 1938); and an adult at Federal Center Lake, West Denver, May 28, 1959 by Dennis Carter (C.B.N. 7:9).

WILSON'S PHALAROPE   *Steganopus tricolor* Vieillot. [224]

RECOGNITION.—Length 8–10 inches; gray and white wader, the female chestnut on neck, shoulders, and wings. *Summer male:* gray above, with upper tail coverts white; foreneck buffy; breast light gray shading into white belly. *Summer female:* more colorful than male, with wide black stripe behind eye extending into side of neck and becoming *chestnut* on *lower neck* and *back;* wide chestnut band on wings. *Winter adult:* face and under parts white, with gray breast; pale bluish-gray above, except white tail coverts. *Young:* dusky above, streaked with brown; white below, with breast buffy. (Plate 56)

RANGE.—Breeds locally from British Columbia, Alberta, Manitoba, Minnesota, Wisconsin, Michigan, and Ontario, south to Indiana and west to Oregon and California. Winters in southern South America.

Nebraska: abundant summer resident; Kansas: summer resident, breeding in Barton Co.; New Mexico: common transient; Utah and Wyoming: common breeding summer resident.

COLORADO.—Common breeding birds locally in short growth along prairie marshes, and in mountain parks on both sides of the Continental Divide.

Early spring Apr. 9 Longmont (C.B.N. 11:30); late fall Nov. 12 Jackson Res. (no. 19498).

NORTHERN PHALAROPE   *Lobipes lobatus* (Linnaeus). [223]

RECOGNITION.—Length 6.5–8 inches; small gray and white wader with a chestnut neck patch. *Summer male:* dark gray above, with a light line over eye and buffy markings on the wings; breast, sides, and flanks gray; throat, belly, and wing bar white; side of neck chestnut. *Summer female:* more colorful than male, darker above, and with chestnut and buffy patches richer and more pronounced. *Winter adult:* face, eyeline and under parts white; mainly gray above with crown and cheek patch darker. *Young:* back, wings, and breast extensively marked with buffy; the *white wing stripe* distinguishes it from the Wilson's Phalarope. (Plate 56)

RANGE.—Breeds in northern areas of the New and Old Worlds, in North America from Pribilof Islands and from the Aleutians north across Arctic Alaska and Canada south to northern Quebec and Labrador. Migrates along both coasts as well as in the interior. Winters off the coasts of South America, Arabia, India, Japan, and China south to New Zealand.

Nebraska, Kansas (regular transient in Barton Co.), and New Mexico: uncommon to rare migrant; Utah and Wyoming: common transient.

COLORADO.—Regular migrant throughout the state, the center of abundance being along the ponds and reservoirs of the Upper Sonoran Zone, but ranging in the mountains to above 9500 feet.

Early spring Mar. 18 Barr Lake (no. 958); late fall Oct. 23 El Paso Co.

Family STERCORARIIDAE: Jaegers and Skuas

POMARINE JAEGER   *Stercorarius pomarinus* (Temminck). [36]

RECOGNITION.—Length 21–24 inches; sexes alike; adult Pomarine and Parasitic Jaegers have light and dark color phases and are distinguished from gulls by their falconlike flight; Pomarine Jaegers are larger than the next two; they are about the size of Ring-billed Gulls, and the central tail feathers of adults are broad and twisted; immatures dusky above, dorsal feathers edged with brown; dusky brown below; under tail coverts light brown, conspicuously barred with black; legs light blue, feet dusky. (Plate 57)

RANGE.—Breeds north of the Arctic Circle from northern Alaska and Canada, and islands northward, to Arctic areas of the Old World. Migrates along both coasts, and casually in the interior of the United States.

Nebraska: casual straggler; Kansas: one specimen from Douglas Co. Oct. 10, 1898.

COLORADO.—Several observations, and one record specimen collected at Cherry Creek Res. Sept. 30, 1963. Included in the sight records are one at Marston Res. Sept. 24 and 30, 1955, and one in the same area Sept. 23, 1956, Oct. 12, and Nov. 11. Three observed Cherry Creek Res. Sept. 15 to Sept. 30, 1963; a crippled immature (no. 33798) was collected Sept. 30, and one was seen Oct. 18. One reported near Grand Junction Oct. 15, 1965 (A.F.N. 20:77).

* PARASITIC JAEGER   *Stercorarius parasiticus* (Linnaeus). [37]

RECOGNITION.—Length *adult:* 18–21 inches, *immature:* 15 inches. *Light adult:* dark slate above, darker on crown, wings, and tail; side of neck or entire neck washed with yellow, foreneck and shoulders grayish, throat and under parts white; under surface of primaries and secondaries white at base; two central tail feathers elongated and pointed. *Dark adult:* blackish-slate, with crown, wings, and tail darker. *Young:* dark with head and neck streaked and under parts barred with rusty. (Plate 57)

RANGE.—Breeds in Arctic areas of both the New and Old Worlds. In North America, in southwestern Alaska to Hudson Bay and Labrador. Winters offshore from California and Florida to South America, and from Europe to southern Africa, Australia, and New Zealand.

Nebraska: one specimen collected at Lincoln in 1898; Kansas: one collected at Cheyenne Bottoms Oct. 16, 1965 (D. H. Parmelee, pers. comm.); Utah: casual straggler, one record specimen; Wyoming: one Casper Sept. 2, 1962 (A.F.N. 17:54).

COLORADO.—Rare transient. A specimen taken in Boulder Co. prior to 1874 was in Mrs. Maxwell's collection; an immature male was shot at Sloan Lake, Denver, during the fall of 1889; Lowe collected one near Pueblo in the fall of 1894; an adult was seen at Marston Res. Oct. 25, 1953; one July 1, 1955 near Longmont, an adult in light phase Sept. 25 at Marston Res., and another light adult was chasing Ring-billed Gulls at Cherry Creek Res. Aug. 24, 1964.

LONG-TAILED JAEGER *Stercorarius longicaudus* Vieillot. [38]

RECOGNITION.—*Length adult:* 20–23 inches, *immature:* 13 inches; differs from adults of the preceding by having longer central tail feathers. Adults have a light phase only, but immatures have both light and dark phases. (Plate 57)

RANGE.—Breeds in Arctic Europe and Asia, and in North America from western and interior Alaska, northern Yukon to Ellesmere Island, south to Southampton Island and northern Quebec. Winters offshore in the Atlantic and in the Pacific off the South American coasts to 50° S.

Nebraska: one specimen from Lincoln in 1952; Kansas: one specimen from Barton Co. June 22, 1935; New Mexico: one listed from Bosque Refuge Sept. 24, 1957 (Ligon, 1961); Utah: A. F. Fisher observed one in Bear River Marshes Oct. 26, 1926 (Auk, 54: 389).

COLORADO.—One specimen (no. 20153) was collected at Windsor Res., Weld Co., Oct. 18, 1902, and one was photographed near Rocky Ford, Otero Co., May 29, 1963.

Family LARIDAE: Gulls and Terns

GLAUCOUS GULL   *Larus hyperboreus barrovianus* Ridgway. [42.1]

RECOGNITION.—Length 26–32 inches; a large white gull with a gray mantle and *light* to *white* primaries. *Summer adult:* plumage mainly white, with mantle pearl-gray; primaries and secondaries white, bill yellow with red spot on lower mandible; legs and feet red. *Winter adult:* like the summer adult, but with grayish streaks on head and neck. *Young:* plumage brownish. (Plate 59)

RANGE.—The species breeds in high latitudes of both the New and Old Worlds, and this race occurs in the nesting season from northern Mackenzie to Herschel Island and Point Barrow south along the Alaskan coast to the Pribilofs. Winters from the Aleutian Islands to California and the Great Lakes. Casual in the interior of the continent.

Nebraska: one specimen and several sight records from the eastern part of the state; Kansas: well authenticated sight record from Shawnee Co. Jan. 27, 1951, and several days later; Utah: one specimen from Utah Lake Mar. 3, 1934, one collected Bear River Refuge Mar. 16, 1955 (Condor, 58:340), and one observed near Salt Lake City Apr. 7, 1963 (A.F.N. 17:422); Wyoming: straggler.

COLORADO.—Rare winter resident. Two specimens collected at Barr: a female (no. 18799) was taken Mar. 28, 1938, a male (no. 18800) Apr. 1, and another noted on later date (B. & N., 1939). In addition, Dr. John Chapin saw one over a little lake southeast of Morrison on December 26, 1954 (C.B.N. 2, no. 5, 2); Mrs. Marjorie Lett observed a pure white bird several times near Platteville in February and March 1, 1958 (6:33); and Allegra Collister and Edith Myers identified one at Longmont Feb. 9, 1962, and another in different plumage Feb. 17 (A.F.N. 16: 345).

ICELAND GULL   *Larus glaucoides kumlieni* Brewster. [45]

RECOGNITION.—Length 23–24 inches. Paler than the Herring Gull, and has gray wing tips instead of black. (Plate 58)

RANGE.—Breeds in southern Baffin Island and extreme northwestern Ungava. Winters from southern Labrador to New Jersey and casually inland along the Great Lakes.

Nebraska: one from Salina Co. Jan. 15, 1907.

COLORADO.—Rare winter visitor. An immature male (no. 18886) was collected by AMB at Barr Lake April 20, 1938 for the only record from the state.

* WESTERN GULL   *Larus occidentalis* Audubon. [49]

RECOGNITION.—Length 24–26 inches. White except dark, slaty back; primaries black tipped with white; eyelid vermilion; bill chrome-yellow with vermilion spot toward tip; feet and legs flesh-colored. (Plate 58)

RANGE.—The members of this species breed on the coast and islands from Washington and California south to Baja California. Three races are recognized.

COLORADO.—Two reports, a bird shot at Loveland Sept. 30, 1889 (Cooke, 1897), and several noted near Granby, Grand Co., in the summer of 1965 by Allegra Collister (pers. comm.).

HERRING GULL   *Larus argentatus smithsonianus* Coues. [51a]

RECOGNITION.—Length 22–26 inches; a large white gull with pearl-gray mantle and black primaries. *Summer adult:* white, with mantle pearl-gray, and primaries black, tipped with white; bill yellow with *red spot* on lower mandible; legs and feet pinkish. *Winter adult:* head and neck washed with grayish-brown. *Young:* upper parts dark grayish, mottled with brown and streaked with white on head and neck; primaries and tail dark; bill black. (Plate 59)

RANGE.—Breeds from southern and south-central Alaska, southern Yukon, northern Mackenzie to southern Baffin Island and to Labrador, Ontario, and Quebec, northern British Columbia, North Dakota, Wisconsin, Michigan, and New York. Winters from southern Alaska southward over much of the United States.

Nebraska and Kansas: rather uncommon but regular transient in the east and rare elsewhere; New Mexico: rare winter visitor; Utah: casual transient in winter; Wyoming: rare migrant.

COLORADO.—Migrant and winter resident occasionally numerous.

Late spring May 17 Longmont; early fall Sept. 19 Denver (C.B.N. 12:50).

Larus argentatus thayeri Brooks. [51b]

RECOGNITION.—Length 22–24 inches; a small race of the Herring Gull, the primaries being *gray* instead of *black;* wing tips darker than *L.g. kumlieni,* and, like *L.a. smithsonianus,* have white spots on primaries.

RANGE.—Breeds in Arctic America from Banks and Ellesmere Islands to Mackenzie and Melville Peninsula and islands in Frozen Strait. Migrates offshore along the Alaskan coast and winters from British Columbia to southern California, and occurs casually to Quebec, Ohio, and New Jersey.

COLORADO.—Rare migrant and winter resident. An immature (no. 880) in the Museum collection was taken in Weld Co., Nov. 3, 1912; two others were collected by AMB in 1938—a male (no. 13798) March 27, and a first-year immature (no. 18886), one of two flying together on Apr. 20. Probably will be considered a species in next A.O.U. Check-list.

CALIFORNIA GULL   *Larus californicus* Lawrence. [53]

RECOGNITION.—Length 20–24 inches; a white gull with a dark mantle and black primaries. *Adult:* plumage mainly white with mantle dark gray and primaries black, *tipped with white;* bill yellow with a red and *black* spot on lower mandible, iris yellow with eyelids red; *legs* and *feet greenish-yellow. Young:* plumage mottled and streaked with dusky, gray, and whitish; primaries and tail dusky; bill dark, tipped with black. The greenish legs and the red spot with a black center on the lower mandible distinguish this bird from the Herring and Ring-billed Gulls, but field identification is difficult. (Plate 59)

RANGE.—Breeds on inland lakes from Great Slave Lake, Canada, North Dakota, Great Salt Lake, and Mono Lake, California. Winters from southern British Columbia to Baja California and Texas.

Kansas: straggler, one specimen from Reno Co. Oct. 20, 1880; Utah: common summer resident in north, breeding on numerous islands; Wyoming: common migrant and breeder.

COLORADO.—Summer resident, casual in winter. A rare species prior to 1950, and fairly common since. Noted breeding in a pelican colony on a small island in Riverside Res., Weld Co. by D. G. Davis Apr. 28, 1963; and forty-six young banded in 1966 (A. Collister, pers. comm.).

Early spring Mar. 11 Boulder; late fall Nov. 14 Longmont (C.B.N. 6:14); winter Dec. 26 Longmont.

RING-BILLED GULL   *Larus delawarensis* Ord. [54]

RECOGNITION.—Length 18–20 inches; a medium-sized gull with pearl-gray mantle and black primaries. *Adult:* white with mantle pearl-gray; primaries black, tipped with white; bill yellow, with black ring near tip; *legs* and *feet yellow. Young:* head and neck streaked with dusky and white; upper parts mottled with dusky and gray; tail gray with black subterminal band and white tip. (Plate 59)

RANGE.—Breeds from Oregon, Washington, and northern California east locally through Ontario, Quebec, and Labrador, south to Utah, South Dakota, Wisconsin, Michigan, and New York. Winters from British Columbia throughout much of the United States to the Gulf coast and south into Mexico.

Nebraska, Kansas, New Mexico, and Utah: common migrant and regular winter visitor; Wyoming: migrant and occasional summer resident.

COLORADO.—Migrant and nonbreeding resident; ranging from the plains into the Canadian Zone.

* LAUGHING GULL   *Larus atricilla* Linnaeus [58]

RECOGNITION.—Length 15–17 inches. *Adult:* dark head and mantle; primaries black, tipped with white; feet dark. Larger than Franklin's Gull and has a *dark mantle* and *white border* at the tips of the secondaries. *Young:* plumage brownish-gray with throat and belly buffy; back feathers edged with buffy; tail gray, with black subterminal band and white tip. (Plate 60)

RANGE.—Breeds from Nova Scotia, Maine, and Massachusetts to Florida, islands of the Caribbean, and islands and shores of the Gulf of Mexico to Texas, southeastern California, and the east coast of Mexico to Venezuela. Winters from South Carolina and along the Gulf coast south to South America.

Nebraska: straggler; Kansas: one specimen from Marion Co. May 15, 1933, and sight records from Barton and Shawnee Counties; New Mexico: one taken at Wingate examined by Coues in June 1864 (F. M. Bailey, 1928).

COLORADO.—Rare straggler. One collected at Ft. Lyon prior to 1880; one shot at Sloan Lake, Denver, in December 1889; and one in adult plumage observed at Cherry Creek Res. Aug. 7 and 27, 1964.

FRANKLIN'S GULL   *Larus pipixcan* Wagler [59]

RECOGNITION.—Length 13–16 inches; a white gull with a dark head and dark slate mantle. *Summer adult:* head blackish-slate with incomplete white eyering; mantle dark slate; first primary edged with black, first four black on ends tipped with white, secondaries edged with white border; bill and feet dark red. *Winter adult:* head white, with nape streaked and patches on ear coverts dark. *Young:* upper parts brownish with lighter feather edgings; forehead and under parts white; tail gray, with black *subterminal band,* which is broader than in Laughing Gull. (Plate 60)

RANGE.—Breeds locally from southeastern Alberta, Saskatchewan, Manitoba, Montana, North and South Dakota, southern Minnesota, and Iowa. Winters from the Gulf coast of Louisiana and Texas to South America.

Nebraska, Kansas, and New Mexico: common transient; Utah: summer resident, breeding in Bear River.

COLORADO.—Migrant in spring and fall and exceedingly abundant late summer resident on the eastern plains. Two noted at Ft. Collins Mar. 28, 1965 (C.B.N. 13:12).

Early spring Mar. 28 Ft. Collins (above); late fall Nov. 22 Longmont.

BONAPARTE'S GULL   *Larus philadelphia* (Ord). [60]

RECOGNITION.—Length 12–14 inches; a small, white gull with gray mantle and dark head. *Summer adult:* head blackish-slate, with incomplete white eyering; mantle pearl-gray with distinctive *outer primaries white* with outer edges and tip black; rest of plumage white; bill dark; feet orange-red. *Winter adult:* head white, with nape grayish and ear coverts dusky; feet flesh color. *Young:* plumage mainly white, with crown, back, and ear coverts dusky; tail with black subterminal band and white tip. (Plate 60)

RANGE.—Breeds in the interior from northwestern Alaska to central British Columbia, eastward to Mackenzie, Alberta, Saskatchewan, and Manitoba. Winters from southeastern Alaska to Baja California and from Massachusetts to Florida and Yucatan.

Nebraska, Kansas, New Mexico, Utah, and Wyoming: uncommon transient.

COLORADO.—Regular spring and fall migrant in small numbers from the plains into the Transition Zone.

Early spring Apr. 8 Loveland; early fall Sept. 4 Latham Res.; late fall Nov. 24 Ft. Collins.

IVORY GULL   *Pagophila eburnea* (Phipps). [39]

RECOGNITION.—Length 16–19 inches. Plumage pure white; legs black. *Young:* white with gray face, and upper parts spotted with dusky; tail with narrow dark subterminal band. (Plate 58)

RANGE.—Breeds locally on islands in high Arctic latitudes from Prince Patrick Island, Baffin Island, northern Greenland, Spitsbergen, Franz Josef Land, Novaya Zemlya, and North Land. Winters over open leads of the Arctic Ocean and Bering Sea, and wanders casually south to New York, Wisconsin, and New Jersey. Straggler to British Columbia, Manitoba, Ontario, Wisconsin, northern France, and Switzerland.

COLORADO.—Straggler; one record, a male (no. 11700) found dead near Strasburg, Adams Co., Jan. 2, 1926 (Bailey, 1926).

BLACK-LEGGED KITTIWAKE   *Rissa tridactyla tridactyla* (Linnaeus). [40]

RECOGNITION.—Length 16–18 inches; a medium-sized white gull with pale gray mantle and black primaries; nape and hind neck washed with gray; primaries gray, the longest tipped with black; bill greenish-yellow; legs black. *Young:* mainly gray above, with dusky ear patch, hind-neck collar, and wing patch; white below; tail white, broadly tipped with black. (Plate 58)

RANGE.—Breeds on Arctic islands of the Old and New Worlds south to the British Isles, Channel Islands, Brittany, Helgoland, and Norway, and from northeastern Canada to the Gulf of St. Lawrence. Winters along the coast and at sea from the Gulf of St. Lawrence to New Jersey and ranges casually in the interior; and in the Eastern Hemisphere south through the Mediterranean and off the west coast of Africa.

Nebraska: one record; Kansas: an immature observed by L. B. Carson and O. S. Pettingill, Jr. in Shawnee Co., Oct. 20, 1951; Wyoming: reported from Douglas in A.O.U. Check-list.

COLORADO.—Straggler. There was a specimen in Mrs. Maxwell's collection supposed to have been killed in Boulder Co. in Dec. prior to 1874 (Sclater, 1912); a Denver taxidermist claimed to have received one or two of this species to mount during his Denver residence (Felger, 1909); an immature male (no. 12262) was collected by Robert L. Landberg at Eastlake, western Adams Co., Nov. 13, 1932.

SABINE'S GULL   *Xema sabini sabini* (Sabine). [62]

RECOGNITION.—Length 13–14 inches; a small white gull with a dark head and gray mantle, differing from Bonaparte's by having a *white triangular* patch in secondaries and black *outer primaries; tail forked.* *Winter adult:* head is white except for the dusky ear coverts and nape. *Young:* brownish-gray above, with gray feather edgings. (Plate 60)

RANGE.—Breeds from Wales, Alaska, along the entire Arctic coast to Southampton Island, and from Spitsbergen and the New Siberian Islands south to the Taimyr Peninsula and the Lena Delta. Migrates along the Pacific coast from Alaska and California to Peru, and from Iceland south along the coasts of Europe. Numerous records through the interior of the United States.

Nebraska, Kansas, New Mexico, Utah, and Wyoming: rare transient.

COLORADO.—Uncommon spring and fall migrant from the eastern plains and rarely to the Alpine Zone. One near Longmont Dec. 11 to Dec. 28, 1965 (A.F.N. 20:437).

FORSTER'S TERN *Sterna forsteri* Nuttall. [69]

RECOGNITION.—Length 14–16 inches. *Summer adult:* White below and pale gray above, with crown and nape black; bill orange with tip blackish and feet orange-red. *Winter adult:* crown white and nape gray; dusky stripe over eye and ear coverts. *Young:* like the winter adult, but upper parts tinged with brown. This tern has a gray tail with *outer web* of outer tail feathers *lighter* than inner, while the Common Tern has a white tail and outer web of the outside feathers *darker* than the inner. (Plate 61)

RANGE.—Breeds from southern Alberta, Saskatchewan, and Manitoba south through eastern Washington to central California, east locally to the northern Mississippi Valley, in eastern Maryland and Virginia, and from Texas and Louisiana into eastern Mexico.

Nebraska: common migrant, breeding locally; Kansas: locally common transient, nesting Barton Co. in 1962; New Mexico: uncommon migrant; Utah: fairly common summer resident locally in north; Wyoming: common in migration and local breeder.

COLORADO.—Summer resident on both sides of the Continental Divide, nesting in small colonies in marsh growth.

Early spring Mar. 17 El Paso Co. (Sam Gadd); late fall Oct. 19 Cherry Creek Res.

COMMON TERN *Sterna hirundo hirundo* Linnaeus. [70]

RECOGNITION.—Length 14–16 inches. Generally similar to *S. forsteri*, but with *outer web* of outside tail feather *darker* than inside web. Bill red *at base* instead of orange as in *S. forsteri*. (Plate 61)

RANGE.—Breeds from central Mackenzie and Saskatchewan east to Labrador and south into northeastern United States to North Carolina, Pennsylvania, Ohio, Indiana, to North and South Dakota; also on the coast of Texas, Alabama, and the Florida Keys; Europe, western Asia, and Siberia south to the Azores, the Mediterranean, Black, and Caspian seas, east through Syria, Iraq, northern Iran, and Turkestan. Winters in Florida, western Mexico, and both coasts of South America to the Straits of Magellan; in Eastern Hemisphere from the west coast of Africa and western India south to Cape of Good Hope and the Arabian Sea.

Nebraska, Kansas, New Mexico, Utah, and Wyoming: rare transient.

COLORADO.—Uncommon spring and fall migrant. Eight specimens have been collected in eastern counties. One noted in Lathrop St. Park, Huerfano Co., June 10, 1967 (Hugh Kingery, pers. comm.).

* ARCTIC TERN *Sterna paradisaea* Pontoppidan. [71]

RECOGNITION.—Length 14–17 inches. Much like the Common Tern; bill and legs red; under parts much grayer. The darker *gray breast* and *red bill* distinguish this from Forster's and Common Terns. (Plate 61)

RANGE.—Breeds in Arctic America and northern Canada, British Columbia, southeastern Alaska, Mackenzie, and Alberta to Labrador, to Maine and Massachusetts; also Arctic Asia and Europe. Migrates offshore and winters in the subantarctic and antarctic waters of the Atlantic, Pacific, and Indian Oceans.

COLORADO.—Rare visitor. This species has been recorded in Colorado twice; a specimen taken on Marston Res. near Denver in 1887 was mounted in the Todenworth Taxidermy Shop, and identified by Robert Ridgway (H. G. Smith, 1896); the other was an adult male shot at Loveland July 9, 1889 (Cooke, 1897). Unfortunately, there is no record of the disposition of the specimens.

LEAST TERN *Sterna albifrons athalassos* Burleigh and Lowery. [74b]

RECOGNITION.—Length 9–10 inches. *Summer adult:* pearl-gray above with crown and nape black; forehead and under parts white; outer primaries dusky; *bill* yellow, tipped with black; legs yellow. *Winter adult:* crown grayish. *Young:* nape dusky and upper parts pale gray marked with dusky. (Plate 61)

RANGE.—Breeds as a species from central California south through Baja California to Peru, along inland river systems of Nebraska, Iowa, Missouri, Tennessee, and Kentucky; along the Atlantic coast from Massachusetts to Florida, eastern Mexico, islands of the Caribbean to Brazil, locally through Europe and the Mediterranean area east to Japan, south to Australia and west Africa. This race occurs in interior states from Kansas, Nebraska, Iowa, and Ohio southward to Texas and Louisiana.

Nebraska: uncommon migrant, breeding on larger river bars; Kansas: uncommon resident, with five nests in Hamilton Co., and others in Rooks and Barton Cos.; New Mexico: uncommon, one breeding record from Bitter Lake Refuge June 28, 1951; Wyoming: uncommon straggler.

COLORADO.—Rare summer visitor. One observed at M.H.D.C. June 9, 1907; one found dead (U.C. no. 3351) in Boulder May 26, 1935; seven noted at Jackson Res. Aug. 10, 1940 and three collected (nos. 21696, 7, 8); three over Bluff Lake near Denver Sept. 30, 1955; one at Bonny Res. May 20, 1961; and one Elbert Co. May 22, 1965 (C. & M. Snyder, C.B.N. 13:29).

BLACK TERN *Chlidonias niger surinamensis* (Gmelin). [77]

RECOGNITION.—Length 9–10 inches. *Summer adult:* head, neck, under parts, and primaries black; mantle dark gray. *Winter adult:* bluish-gray above, head and under parts white; eye patch and ear coverts dusky. *Young:* like the winter adult, but nape dusky and scapulars edged with brown. (Plate 61)

RANGE.—The species breeds over much of the northern part of the Old World, and this race from British Columbia south to California and east across southern Canada, locally to Ontario and New Brunswick, and in northern United States to Maine, Vermont, and New York. Winters south to northern South America.

Nebraska: migrant and abundant breeder in Sandhill Lakes region; Kansas: recorded nesting in Barton Co.; New Mexico: common migrant; Utah: uncommon migrant, breeding in small numbers in the north; Wyoming: common migrant and breeding locally.

COLORADO.—Summer resident, ranging from the plains into the Transition Zone. Although a common bird over eastern marsh areas, only a few nesting occurrences are listed in the literature.

Early spring Apr. 25 Longmont; late summer Oct. 2 Cherry Creek Res. (H. Holt, pers. comm.).

Family ALCIDAE: Auks, Murres, and Puffins

ANCIENT MURRELET *Synthliboramphus antiquum* (Gmelin). [21]

RECOGNITION.—Length 9–11 inches. *Summer:* small, short-billed water bird with black head, black throat, and white stripe above and behind eye; white on side of neck and under parts; back slate-colored and sides black. *Winter:* lacks black throat. (Plate 57)

RANGE.—Breeds on islands of the north Asiatic coast, the Kuriles, Korea, and along the Aleutians locally to southeastern Alaska and British Columbia. Straggler in Oregon, Nevada, Idaho, Ohio, Minnesota, Wisconsin, southern Ontario, southern Quebec, and Illinois (Auk, 81: 443).

Nebraska: one record from the Missouri River in Burt Co.; Utah: one at Logan, a female found dead Nov. 24, 1962 (Condor, 68:510).

COLORADO.—Straggler. One (C.U. no. 6282) found dead Nov 28, 1957 on highway just south of Lafayette, Boulder Co., and a second specimen (no. 33827), a bird in winter plumage, was collected by Allegra Collister Oct. 14, 1965 on Union Res., Weld Co., three miles east of Longmont.

Order COLUMBIFORMES: Sand-grouse, Pigeons, and Doves

Family COLUMBIDAE: Pigeons and Doves

BAND-TAILED PIGEON *Columba fasciata fasciata* Say. [312]

RECOGNITION.—Length 15–16 inches; a large, stout-bodied pigeon with head and under parts purplish-brown; hind neck iridescent green bordered above with white; grayish-brown above; wings slate-blue with primaries dusky; tail tipped with a broad, pale gray band. *Young:* lacks the white and green on the neck; breast washed with brown. (Plate 62)

RANGE.—The species breeds from southwestern British Columbia, Washington, Oregon, and California to Texas and the southwestern states, to Mexico and Guatemala. This race from Utah and Colorado south to Guatemala. Winters from New Mexico and Arizona into Mexico and Central America.

Kansas: One observed in Clark Co. July 19, 1963 (Hibbard, 1964); New Mexico: breeding to 10,000 feet, uncommon in winter; Utah: resident in south and casual elsewhere.

COLORADO.—Common locally in the lower mountains of the state in summer; rare in winter. Nests in Transition Zone, usually in lodgepole or ponderosa pines.

ROCK DOVE   *Columba livia* Gmelin. [313.1]

RECOGNITION.—Length 13 inches. Upper parts pale slate, with head, neck, breast, and tail darker, and rump white. Tail with broad, blackish terminal band. Some individuals with much white, others almost entirely white (not illustrated).

RANGE.—Resident from British Isles, Norway, Russia south to Egypt, east to Burma; introduced into North America.

Nebraska, Kansas, New Mexico, Utah, and Wyoming: introduced common resident.

COLORADO.—Occurs wild in cities and in suitable rocky habitat, in or along the edge of the plains, occasionally in steep, rocky canyons in low mountains. Breeds commonly in suitable natural openings in cliffs such as Denver's Red Rocks Park, Garden of the Gods, in barns, and under bridges throughout the state.

WHITE-WINGED DOVE   *Zenaida asiatica mearnsi* (Ridgway). [319a]

RECOGNITION.—Length 11–12.5 inches; a slim-bodied, broad-tailed, brown dove, with a conspicuous white wing patch and black primaries; rump and tail bluish-gray; narrow dusky band and white tip on tail. *Young:* Upper feathers with light edgings and a tawny wash on breast. (Plate 63)

RANGE.—Breeds from southern Nevada, southern Arizona, southeastern California, Baja California, and south into Mexico. Uncommon in winter north of Mexico.

New Mexico: summer resident, most numerous in south; Utah: casual, possibly breeding in extreme southwest; Wyoming: straggler with a record from Casper.

COLORADO.—Casual visitor. One or two were shot from a small flock near timberline at 11,500 feet on Cub Creek in July 1869 by E. L. Berthoud (Coues, 1877); another was said to have been taken in Wet Mt. Valley in Sept. 1899 by A. D. Baker (Cooke, 1900); a male (no. 9910) was collected in Prowers Co. Nov. 23, 1921, and State Game Warden Scott saw one on Barela Mesa near Trinidad in Aug. 1945, according to Johnson Neff, an authority on the species. One was observed on a fence and in flight at Sunbeam, Moffat Co. July 3, 1967 by H. Holt (pers. comm.).

MOURNING DOVE   *Zenaidura macroura marginella* (Woodhouse). [316a]

RECOGNITION.—Length 11–13 inches; a slim-bodied dove; long, tapering pointed tail, with white tips on shorter feathers; upper parts mainly brown, with a few black spots on back and wings; crown olive or blue-gray, under parts light brown, sides of neck iridescent. *Young:* generally grayish-brown, and some feathers edged with white. (Plate 63)

RANGE.—Breeds from southeastern Alaska, British Columbia east to Manitoba, Minnesota, and south to Arkansas, Texas, and Baja California, and through Mexico. Winters over much of breeding range to Panama and northern South America.

Nebraska, Kansas, New Mexico, Utah, and Wyoming: common in summer and less so in winter.

COLORADO.—Resident; abundant in summer and casual in winter. A very common nesting bird throughout the state from the plains into the Transition Zone.

* GROUND DOVE   *Columbigallina passerina pallescens* (Baird). [320a]

RECOGNITION.—Length 6.25–7.25 inches; smallest of our doves, usually seen on ground, and when in flight showing rufous through the wings. (Plate 63)

RANGE.—The species breeds in southern states from South Carolina and Florida westward to California and southward.

Kansas: one observed in Pottawatomi Co. Nov. 11, 1954, a specimen from Anderson Co. Nov. 28, 1958, and male collected near Toronto Nov. 20, 1963, and a Nov. specimen from Wabaunsee Co. (D. Parmelee, pers. comm.); New Mexico: uncommon in southern part.

COLORADO.—One sight record by F. M. Brown at Fountain Valley School, El Paso Co., Apr. 25, 1937 (pers. comm.).

* INCA DOVE   *Scardafella inca* (Lesson). [321]

RECOGNITION.—Length 7–8 inches. Small pale dove with outer tail feathers showing white and wings rufous when bird is in flight.

RANGE.—Breeds in southern New Mexico, Arizona, and Texas, south over the Mexican lowlands to Costa Rica and Nicaragua, wintering within the nesting range.

Kansas: recorded daily at Halstead, Harvey County between Nov. 10, 1951 and Jan. 21, 1952, and one seen at Topeka, Shawnee Co., the latter part of June 1952, and a specimen in Kansas State University collected in Meade Co. Mar. 26, 1957; New Mexico: recorded breeding; Utah: one collected in Washington Co. July 9, 1963 (Condor, 68:396).

COLORADO.—One report, a bird observed near Bonny Res., Yuma Co., May 13, 1961 by Ray E. Olson (pers. comm.).

Order PSITTACIFORMES: Parrots and Parakeets
Family PSITTACIDAE: Parrots and Macaws

* CAROLINA PARAKEET   *Conuropsis carolinensis ludoviciana* (Gmelin). [382a]

RECOGNITION.—Length 13 inches. Bright green parakeets with yellow heads and pointed tails (not illustrated).

RANGE.—Now extinct. The species formerly occurred from New York south to Florida, Alabama, and Georgia, and this race from Mississippi, Louisiana, and Texas, up the Mississippi Valley to Iowa, Illinois, Indiana, Ohio, North Dakota, Wisconsin, Nebraska, Kansas, and Colorado.

Nebraska and Kansas: formerly common.

COLORADO.—A former straggler to the foothills. Recorded by Berthoud (1887) who stated:

In 1855–56 the Carolina Parrot, (Psittacus Carolinensis) was a bird by no means uncommon near Ft. Leavenworth, Kansas, and all along the Kansas River as far as where now stands Fort Ellsworth. As late as 1865 I saw a flock on the Smoky Hill three miles above Ft. Ellsworth. In 1860–61 it was seen by me in Jefferson County (Colorado), repeatedly, in small flocks along Vasquez Fork of Platte River, on Bear Creek, St. Vrain, etc. In 1863–64 it was not uncommon on the Arkansas and the Huerfano. A few years later it seems to have disappeared, and we did not see one until 1877, when two or three were noticed near Longmont in a wheat field.

Order CUCULIFORMES: Cuckoos and Plantain-eaters
Family CUCULIDAE: Cuckoos and Roadrunners

YELLOW-BILLED CUCKOO   *Coccyzus americanus americanus* (Linnaeus). [387]

RECOGNITION.—Length 11–13 inches; a long-tailed, slender bird with a rather stout bill. *Adult:* olive-brown above and white below; inner webs of primaries rufous; outer tail feathers broadly tipped with white spots; lower mandible yellow. *Young:* tail paler and white markings smaller. (Plate 64)

RANGE.—The species breeds throughout much of North America and this race from Quebec, Ontario, and North Dakota to eastern Colorado, Louisiana, and the Florida Keys into the West Indies. Winters in South America to Ecuador and Argentina.

Nebraska and Kansas: common summer resident; New Mexico and Utah: the race *occidentalis* listed as uncommon.

COLORADO.—Uncommon summer resident, arriving in early May, and the majority departing during the first weeks of September. Occurs throughout the state, the majority of records being from the Upper Sonoran Zone into the Lower Transition Zone.

Early spring May 8 Platteville; late fall Nov. 18 Lyons (A.F.N. 21:53).

BLACK-BILLED CUCKOO   *Coccyzus erythropthalmus* (Wilson). [388]

RECOGNITION.—Length 11–13 inches; similar to preceding species, but has a black bill and lacks rufous wing linings; tail feathers narrowly edged with white instead of broadly spotted. *Young:* dull brown above with wings rusty. (Plate 64)

RANGE.—Breeds from south-central Canada east to Quebec and Nova Scotia and south to Kansas, Wyoming, Arkansas, South Carolina, and Georgia. Winters in northwestern South America.

Nebraska and Kansas: uncommon migrant and summer resident; Utah: straggler, one record; Wyoming: common summer resident.

COLORADO.—Uncommon summer resident in eastern Colorado in the Upper Sonoran and Transition Zones. A nest found in Denver July 23, 1951, and one on farm of Mr. and Mrs. Sullivan on Valmont Road, NE of Boulder June 26, 1966 with one egg and one newly hatched young. Photographs secured by Robert Wright.

Early spring May 18 Franktown (C.B.N. 11:30); late fall Oct. 19 Longmont.

ROADRUNNER   *Geococcyx californianus* (Lesson). [385]

RECOGNITION.—Length 19–25 inches; a large ground bird with a long tail and a stout bill. Upper parts streaked with black, brown, white, and glossy green; crest brownish-black, under parts brownish, streaked with dark brown on neck and breast; naked skin about eye pale blue, bordered posteriorly by orange-red. (Plate 64)

RANGE.—Resident locally in California, Nevada, Utah, Colorado, Kansas, Oklahoma, Arkansas, Louisiana, and Texas south into Mexico.

Kansas: resident, uncommon locally in south; New Mexico and Utah: fairly common in southern parts.

COLORADO.—Resident in small numbers in southern Colorado and a casual straggler northward; recorded nesting in El Paso, Las Animas, Baca, and Bent Counties.

Order STRIGIFORMES: Owls

Family TYTONIDAE: Barn Owls

BARN OWL   *Tyto alba pratincola* (Bonaparte). [365]

RECOGNITION.—Length 15–20 inches; a pale-colored, long-legged owl without ear tufts; iris dark brown; yellowish-brown above, mottled with gray and spotted with black and white; facial disc pale buffy, narrowly bordered with dusky; under parts pale yellowish-buff, spotted with black. (Plate 66).

RANGE.—As a species, *Tyto alba* is nearly cosmopolitan in distribution, being found on the larger land masses of the world, ranging from the British Isles, Baltic area and southern Russia, south through Africa; from Palestine, Iraq, and Burma south to Australia. The race *pratincola* breeds from southern British Columbia, North Dakota east to southern Ontario, Quebec, and Massachusetts south to the Gulf states, and through Mexico and Baja California to Guatemala.

Nebraska: uncommon resident throughout the state; Kansas: common resident in northwest and probably in southwest; New Mexico, Utah, and Wyoming: uncommon resident.

COLORADO.—Summer resident occasionally wintering on the plains, not common; few records from the western slope. Nests in crannies in cliffs, and in buildings.

Family STRIGIDAE: Typical Owls

SCREECH OWL   *Otus asio maxwelliae* (Ridgway). [373e]

RECOGNITION.—Length 8–10 inches; a small, light gray owl with ear tufts. *Adult:* brownish-gray above, streaked and mottled with black; pale gray below, streaked with black; scapulars edged with white. *Young:* plumage grayish, banded with dusky. Field identification of races of this species would be unsatisfactory. (Plate 65)

RANGE.—The species is resident from southeastern Alaska across southern Canada south into Mexico; this race occurs on the plains and adjacent foothills from central and eastern Montana south to east-central Colorado.

Nebraska, Kansas, and New Mexico: species resident with several races represented; Utah: races *O.a. inyoensis* northwest and *cineraceus* in south; Wyoming: species rare in eastern half of state.

COLORADO.—Uncommon resident in northeastern Colorado. This light race, with type locality Boulder Co., was named for Mrs. M. A. Maxwell, pioneer collector of Colorado birds. One banded by Berene Sullivan at Boulder in 1960 retrapped in 1966 (pers. comm.).

Otus asio aikeni (Brewster). [373g]

RECOGNITION.—Length 8–9 inches; similar to *O.a. maxwelliae,* but slightly smaller and much darker; gray with dark fine markings above and below.

RANGE.—From the plains of central Colorado and western Kansas south through eastern New Mexico and southeastern Colorado, with the southern limit of the race unknown.

COLORADO.—Uncommon resident of the plains and foothills of southern and east-central Colorado south of Denver. The type of this race, a female, was secured by C. E. Aiken in El Paso Co. May 29, 1872.

Otus asio naevius (Gmelin). [373m]

RECOGNITION.—Similar to *O.a. maxwelliae,* but darker and slightly smaller, and has both a gray and red phase. Lighter than *O.a. aikeni,* but indistinguishable in the field except when in red plumage.

RANGE.—Breeds locally in northern states from Nebraska, Kansas, and Missouri, eastward to southern Quebec and Maine.

COLORADO.—Status in the state unknown but likely to occur along the eastern border. One specimen in the red phase (no. 26008) was collected in Colorado Springs Jan. 9, 1904 by C. E. Aiken.

FLAMMULATED OWL   *Otus flammeolus flammeolus* (Kaup). [374]

RECOGNITION.—Length 6–7 inches; a very small, gray owl having short *ear tufts* and *dark eyes. Red phase* not known from Colorado. (Plate 65)

RANGE.—Southern British Columbia to California, Idaho, Texas, Mexico, and Guatemala.

New Mexico: uncommon; Utah: several records.

COLORADO.—Uncommon from the foothills into the mountains. Nests from the Transition into the Canadian Zone. Adult caught in mist net and banded by Berene Sullivan (pers. comm.) May 11, 1967 at 8323 Valmont Dr., Boulder Co. at elevation of 5400′. The same bird, another adult, and 2 young observed in nearby willows June 8.

GREAT HORNED OWL   *Bubo virginianus occidentalis* Stone. [375j]

RECOGNITION.—Length 19–25 inches; a large, grayish-brown owl with long ear tufts. Upper parts mottled with grayish and brown with light tawny background; throat patch white; eyes yellow, facial disc brown, bordered with dusky; under parts tawny-white, barred and marked with brown; primaries and tail banded. (Plate 66)

RANGE.—Breeds locally from central Alberta, Saskatchewan, and Manitoba and from Oregon, California, Nevada, Idaho and Minnesota to Kansas.

Nebraska, Kansas, New Mexico, Utah (in the north), and Wyoming: common resident locally.

COLORADO.—Fairly common resident on the plains, and less so in the mountains to about 10,000 ft.; possibly intergrading with *B.v. pallescens* in the southern part of the state.

Bubo virginianus lagophonus (Oberholser). [375i]

RECOGNITION—Length 19–23 inches. Plumage similar to *B.v. occidentalis,* but decidedly darker.

RANGE.—Breeds in southeastern and interior Alaska to eastern Washington, northeastern Oregon, Idaho, and Montana.

Nebraska: casual winter migrant; Utah: casual, several records (*B.v. pallescens* resident south, *B.v. pacificus* casual); Wyoming: probably a winter straggler.

COLORADO.—Uncommon fall and winter visitor, ranging west into the foothills and mountain parks. There are ten specimens in the Museum collection.

Bubo virginianus virginianus (Gmelin). [375]

RECOGNITION.—Length 19–23 inches. Plumage similar to that of *B.v. occidentalis,* but browner with less tawny background.

RANGE.—Southeastern Canada to the Gulf coast and eastern Texas.

Nebraska and Kansas: several races recorded from each state, with this subspecies nesting in eastern counties.

COLORADO.—Straggler. There are five specimens in the Museum as follows: a female (no. 4256) from Golden Oct. 2, 1909; three (nos. 1167-1184-9754) from Wray were taken Aug. 23–24, 1911 and Nov. 2, 1923; and an adult male from Littleton collected by R. W. Hendee on Nov. 14, 1924.

Bubo virginianus wapacuthu (Gmelin). [375b]

RECOGNITION.—Length 19–23 inches. Similar to *B.v. occidentalis,* but plumage much whiter.

RANGE.—Breeds from tree limit in Mackenzie Valley to Hudson Bay, and in northeastern British Columbia south to central Alberta, Saskatchewan, Manitoba, and Ontario. Winters to Idaho, Wisconsin and casually to New York and Massachusetts.

COLORADO.—Numerous early records, listed as *B.v. arcticus* or *B.v. subarcticus,* which are no longer considered as valid subspecies, probably were of this race. There is a beautiful light-colored male (no. 33777) in the Denver Museum collected near Haxton, Phillips Co., Nov. 22, 1959, and another (no. 35810) from Baca Co. Feb. 8, 1967.

SNOWY OWL   *Nyctea scandiaca* (Linnaeus). [376]

RECOGNITION.—Length 21–27 inches; a large white owl without ear tufts; iris yellow; plumage white, more or less barred with grayish-brown. (Plate 66)

RANGE.—Breeds on the tundras of Norway, Sweden, Russia, Siberia, northern Alaska, Canada, Greenland, south in the Western Hemisphere to the Yukon delta, northern Manitoba, Quebec, and Labrador. Winters to southern Canada and irregularly in the United States, and as a straggler to Texas and Louisiana.

Nebraska and Kansas: rare and irregular; Utah: one record from near Provo, Dec. 1908; Wyoming: irregular winter straggler.

COLORADO.—Irregular winter visitor from the plains into the foothills.

PYGMY OWL   *Glaucidium gnoma californicum* Sclater. [379a]

RECOGNITION.—Length 6.5–7.5 inches; a very small owl with yellow eyes and *lacking ear tufts. Adult:* dark grayish-brown above, spotted with white on crown and wings; black patch on each side of back of head; white below streaked with dark brown; tail with several narrow light bars. *Young:* like adult, but crown clear gray. (Plate 65)

RANGE.—British Columbia, western Alberta, Washington, and mountains of California; mountainous portions of Montana and Idaho to New Mexico and Arizona.

New Mexico and Utah: uncommon resident from the Transition Zone into higher mountains; Wyoming: recorded in northwest mountains.

COLORADO.—Uncommon resident in the mountains throughout the state.

BURROWING OWL   *Speotyto cunicularia hypugaea* (Bonaparte). [378]

RECOGNITION.—Length 9-11 inches; a pale brown and white prairie owl, usually seen on the ground far from trees. (Plate 66)

RANGE.—The species occurs on the plains and in unforested areas from British Columbia south through Baja California and Central America to Tierra del Fuego. This race ranges from British Columbia, Saskatchewan, and Manitoba south through Washington, Oregon, and California and offshore islands to Baja California, and from Minnesota and Iowa south to Oklahoma, Texas, and Louisiana. There is a local race in Florida. Winters over much of the southern portions of the breeding range.

Nebraska, Kansas, New Mexico, Utah, and Wyoming: formerly common but numbers gradually decreasing, due, to a great extent, to the disappearance of prairie dog villages.

COLORADO.—Summer resident, formerly very common locally on the prairies of eastern and western Colorado, especially in association with prairie dog "towns." There are several winter records including one within the city limits of Aurora from Dec. 19, 1965 through Mar. 25, 1966 (Chas. and Mildred Snyder, pers. comm.).

BARRED OWL   *Strix varia varia* Barton. [368]

RECOGNITION.—Length 19–24 inches; a large, dark brown owl *without ear tufts;* mottled and barred with buffy and white and long dark streaks on belly; primaries and tail banded with brown and white; facial disc grayish and *eyes brown;* under parts buffy, broadly streaked with brown. (Plate 67)

RANGE.—As a species, breeds from British Columbia across southern Canada to Nova Scotia, and from central Montana and eastern Wyoming to Texas, Louisiana, Florida, and the mountains of Mexico and Central America.

Nebraska: rare in west, uncommon in east; Kansas: common locally in east; Wyoming: straggler in east.

COLORADO.—Rare straggler. An adult and two eggs were taken near Holyoke, Phillips Co., in Mar. 1897 by B. G. Voight (Aiken, 1900), and the eggs (no. 6668) are in this Museum. Two were seen at Bonny Res. May 21, 1960 (C.B.N. 8:49), and one on Spring Count May 16, 1964 (12:8). One at Bonny May 13, 1967 (Hugh Kingery, pers. comm.).

SPOTTED OWL   *Strix occidentalis lucida* (Nelson). [369b]

RECOGNITION.—Length 16–18 inches; a large, dark brown owl without ear tufts, much like the Barred Owl. Dark brown above, spotted with white on head, back, and wings; primaries and tail barred with brown and white; facial disc grayish-brown and eyes brown; throat white; under parts barred with brown and white, while the Barred Owl has lengthwise streaks of brown. (Plate 67)

RANGE.—Resident locally from British Columbia southward into Mexico and eastward to Colorado and western Texas.

New Mexico: Uncommon resident; Utah: one record from San Juan Co. Aug. 13, 1936.

COLORADO.—Rare straggler. There are four state specimens including one (C.C. no. 6074) June 1873, and a male (C.C. no. 5765) May 24, 1919, both from El Paso Co.; a male in the C.S.C. collection at Greeley from Pitkin Co., Nov. 1903; and (no. 34437) in this Museum, the first Denver record, Dec. 31, 1958. About eight observations from eastern foothills are listed in the literature.

LONG-EARED OWL   *Asio otus wilsonianus* (Lesson). [366]

RECOGNITION.—Length 13–16 inches. Eyes yellow; tawny facial disc and prominent ear tufts; brownish-black above, mottled with grayish; barred tail and wings and under parts light with dark shafts and barring. Males much lighter under parts then females. The western race differs from the eastern in being paler. (Plate 67)

RANGE.—The species breeds across southern Canada from Manitoba east to Nova Scotia and south to Virginia, Arkansas, and Oklahoma; winters south to Mexico. This race occupies the eastern part of the range from southern Manitoba to Nova Scotia and south to Oklahoma and Arkansas. Winters from eastern Canada and the Great Plains to Texas and Louisiana.

Nebraska, Kansas, and New Mexico: uncommon in summer, and winter resident; Utah and Wyoming: common resident in lower valleys (probably western race *A.o tuftsi*).

COLORADO.—Common resident on eastern plains, and less so in foothills, breeding throughout the state.

LONG-EARED OWL

Photograph by Patricia Bailey Witherspoon

SHORT-EARED OWL   *Asio flammeus flammeus* (Pontoppidan). [367]

RECOGNITION.—Length 14–17 inches; a medium-sized, pale brown owl with *short ear tufts*. *Adult:* buffy-brown above, lined on head and neck with dusky, back mottled, and wings and tail barred with dusky; facial disc bordered with white; eyes yellow; under parts buffy-white. *Young:* dark brown above with pale brown feather edgings; under parts dull buffy. (Plate 67)

RANGE.—The species breeds in the northern portions of the Old World, and this race from northern Alaska and Canada to California, Nevada, Missouri, and Illinois to New York and New Jersey. Winters from northern states to Louisiana, Cuba, and Guatemala, and in the Old World south through breeding range to Africa, India, and China.

Nebraska and Kansas: uncommon resident but more numerous in winter; New Mexico: winter resident; Utah and Wyoming: rather uncommon summer resident.

COLORADO.—Uncommon resident, occasionally numerous locally in winter. Young collected in Arapahoe Co. in 1919 and 1943; two nests near Monte Vista in June 1950, and Monte Vista Wildlife Refuge in 1954; and young in Adams Co. July 12, 1962.

BOREAL OWL   *Aegolius funereus richardsoni* (Bonaparte). [371]

RECOGNITION.—Length 9–12 inches; a medium-sized, sepia-brown owl *without ear tufts*. *Adult:* profusely spotted with white on the crown; wings with large white spots and scapulars tipped with white; throat white; eyes lemon-yellow; under parts gray, broadly streaked with dark rusty. *Young:* dull brown above, with dark facial disc and sharply contrasting superciliary line; plain brown below. (Plate 65)

RANGE.—The species breeds in the northern parts of the Old World and this race from northern Alaska and northwestern Canada to British Columbia, and eastward across Canada to Nova Scotia. Winters south to southern Canada and casually to northern states.

Nebraska: two records from Lincoln Dec. 10, 1892 and Oct. 19, 1907.

COLORADO.—There are two specimens in this Museum, a male (no. 6338) collected at Crested Butte, Gunnison Co., Oct. 14, 1896, and a male (no. 11894) from Fraser, Grand Co., on Nov. 11, 1929. A mounted bird in the C.S.U. Museum at Greeley, a female, was secured in Pitkin Co. in Nov. 1903; and a juvenal was collected one mile SW of Deadman Lookout, Larimer Co., August 14, 1963, at an elevation of 10,700 feet.

SAW-WHET OWL   *Aegolius acadicus acadicus* (Gmelin). [372]

RECOGNITION.—Length 7–8.5 inches; smaller and more rusty than the Boreal Owl. *Adult:* bright chocolate-brown above, with crown and neck finely lined with white; eyes yellow; back and wings spotted with white; under parts whitish, streaked with reddish. *Young:* dark gray-brown, with face darker and belly buffy. (Plate 65)

RANGE.—Breeds from southern Alaska and across southern Canada to Quebec and Nova Scotia, and south to Maryland, Ohio, Missouri, Oklahoma, California, and the mountains of Mexico.

Nebraska: uncommon winter visitor; Kansas: rare, and one breeding record from Wyandotte Co. in 1951; New Mexico, Utah, and Wyoming: uncommon resident in mountains.

COLORADO.—Resident, not common. Ranges on wooded slopes of the Upper Sonoran into the Transition Zone. Ten records of nesting in eastern foothills from Pueblo County to Estes Park.

Order CAPRIMULGIFORMES: Goatsuckers and Allies

Family CAPRIMULGIDAE: Whip-poor-wills, Poor-wills, and Nighthawks

WHIP-POOR-WILL   *Caprimulgus vociferus vociferus* Wilson. [417]

RECOGNITION.—Length 9–10 inches; like a nighthawk in appearance, but ground-inhabiting in shady woods. *Adult:* Plumage generally mottled with gray, black, and brown; throat black bordered below by white; primaries brown, barred with black; three outer tail feathers mainly white, the white much more extensive in the male. Whip-poor-wills and Poor-wills differ from nighthawks in having rounded tails, while the latter have notched tails and conspicuous wing bars. (Plate 68)

RANGE.—Breeds from Saskatchewan, Manitoba, and Ontario to Nova Scotia, and southeast of the Great Plains from South Dakota to Oklahoma, Texas, Louisiana, Georgia, North Carolina, and Virginia. Winters in southern part of breeding range through eastern Mexico and Central America.

Nebraska and Kansas: locally common in eastern counties; New Mexico: four specimens (Wilson Bull., 68:213); Utah: one at Pine Lake near Bryce Canyon Natl. Park July 6 and 9, 1965 (A.F.N. 20:77).

COLORADO.—Straggler. There are only three records from the state, a female (no. 6399) which was found dead near Ft. Collins Sept. 14, 1903; one observed at Bonny Res. May 23, 1959 (C.B.N. 7:3), and one May 13, 1967 (Hugh Kingery, pers. comm.).

POOR-WILL   *Phalaenoptilus nuttallii nuttallii* (Audubon). [418]

RECOGNITION.—Length 7–8.5 inches. Differs from the nighthawk in having a rounded tail and lack of white in the wings. *Adult:* Plumage soft grayish-brown, heavily marked with black; cheeks and chin black; throat white, bordered below by black; under parts barred, with under tail coverts buffy or rusty; outer tail feathers tipped with white, but more extensive in the males. *Young:* pale gray above, washed with rusty; throat buffy. (Plate 68)

RANGE.—Breeds from British Columbia, Alberta, Montana, and east to South Dakota, south to eastern California, central Texas, Arizona, and northern Mexico. Winters from southeastern California and southern Texas to central Mexico.

Nebraska and Kansas: common summer resident in ponderosa pine country of the west; New Mexico: breeds from the southern part of the state northward, ranging to 9000 feet; Utah: fairly common in summer in lower valleys and foothills; Wyoming: common breeder on dry slopes of pine and juniper.

COLORADO.—Common but inconspicuous summer resident, nesting locally, with center of abundance in the Transition Zone among scrub oaks.

Early spring Apr. 23 Platteville (C.B.N. 8:37); late fall Oct. 29 Golden (C.B.N. 11:7).

COMMON NIGHTHAWK   *Chordeiles minor minor* (Forster). [420]

RECOGNITION.—Length 8.5–10 inches; slender, long-winged, erratically flying birds, with conspicuous white wing patches across primaries. *Adult male:* white throat and blackish chest patch, barred with black and white; tail with white band across tip except central pair of feathers. *Adult female:* similar, except throat patch tawny and no white tail band. Races not identifiable in field. (Plate 68)

RANGE.—Breeds from southeastern Alaska to Vancouver Island, across southern Canada and northern states from Washington eastward to Minnesota, Indiana to Virginia, North Carolina, Georgia, and Oklahoma. Winters southward in Mexico, West Indies, and Central America to South America.

Nebraska and Kansas: nesting in east; Utah: transient.

COLORADO.—Probably regular migrant in eastern and southern counties; six specimens.

Chordeiles minor hesperis Grinnell. [420d]

RECOGNITION.—Similar to *C. m. minor* but less blackish; white and buff mottling, above finer and more abundant; less blackish below and bars narrower and lighter. Female more buffy.

RANGE.—Breeds from British Columbia, Alberta through northern Washington, Montana, Nevada, and Utah to extreme northern Colorado and western Wyoming.

Utah and Wyoming: summer resident.

COLORADO.—Breeds in North Park and other areas of extreme northern part, west of the Front Range, and a more or less common migrant throughout the state. Garfield, Rio Blanco, and Moffat Counties (Felger, 1910).

Chordeiles minor sennetti Coues. [420c]

RECOGNITION.—Palest of races, differing from *C.m. hesperis* in lighter ground color; finer mottlings, grayer under parts, and narrow and lighter ventral bars; female more brownish and lighter than male.

RANGE.—Breeds from eastern Montana, southern Saskatchewan, and Manitoba to North Dakota, Minnesota, and Iowa. Winters in South America.

Nebraska and Kansas: migrant throughout the state; Wyoming: breeding in southeast.

COLORADO.—Summer resident in northeastern corner, and migrant through eastern counties.

Chordeiles minor howelli Oberholser. [420e]

RECOGNITION.—Length 9.2–9.5 inches; "a variable race more or less intermediate between *henryi* and *sennetti*." Ground color and dorsal mottlings buffier than *sennetti*; ground color browner and dorsal mottling more abundant and finer, under parts lighter, and wing patch larger than *henryi*.

RANGE.—Breeds from northern Texas, western Oklahoma and Kansas into eastern Colorado, and in less typical form in central Colorado, northeast Utah, and Wyoming. Intergrades with other races.

Nebraska and Kansas: summer resident in west; New Mexico: summer resident in northeast; Utah: transient and breeding in northeast; Wyoming: breeds in north-central part.

COLORADO.—Summer resident throughout the state with numerous nesting records from both sides of the Continental Divide.

Early spring Apr. 30 Jackson Res.; late fall Nov. 5 Boulder.

Chordeiles minor henryi Cassin. [420a]

RECOGNITION.—Slightly smaller and differing from *C.m. hesperis* in browner and rufescent ground color with less black; coarser dorsal mottlings, tawny instead of white or buff; white on wing usually smaller than in other races.

RANGE.—Breeds from northern Mexico north through western Texas, Arizona, New Mexico, southwestern Colorado, and Utah.

New Mexico: occurs throughout the state, the type of the race was taken at Fort Webster; Utah: summer resident in the southeast.

COLORADO.—Breeds in southwestern counties. There are ten specimens in the Museum collection from Archuleta, La Plata, and Mesa Counties.

LESSER NIGHTHAWK   *Chordeiles acutipennis texensis* Lawrence. [421]

RECOGNITION.—Length 8.2–9.3 inches. Smaller than races of *C. minor;* color pattern much like that of the other nighthawks, but paler brown; *wing band nearer tip* of primaries. (Plate 68)

RANGE.—Breeds from north-central California, southern Nevada, and southern Utah to central Texas, south-central Mexico, Arizona, and Baja California. Winters from central Mexico to Panama.

New Mexico: summer resident in southern part of the state, nesting locally; Utah: summer resident in southwestern Washington Co.

COLORADO.—Rare migrant. Aiken collected an adult female (no. 26006) at Hoehne, near Trinidad, Las Animas Co., June 11, 1908, and an immature (no. 26007) at Colo. Spgs. Aug. 25, 1922.

Order APODIFORMES: Swifts and Hummingbirds
Family APODIDAE: Swifts

BLACK SWIFT   *Cypseloides niger borealis* (Kennerly). [422]

RECOGNITION.—7–7.5 inches; a dark, swallow-like bird with long pointed wings. *Adult male:* blackish, with forehead and crown grayish-white; lores velvety; tail forked. *Adult female:* belly feathers and under tail coverts edged with white, except in worn plumage. *Immature:* feathers lightly tipped with white. (Plate 69)

RANGE.—Breeds from southeastern Alaska to California, eastward to southern and central Colorado, and to southern Mexico.

New Mexico: rare migrant and nesting species; Utah: five nesting sites and specimens (U. of Utah) Aug. 2, 1960 (Wilson Bull., 75:453); Montana: five nests in Mission Valley of Mission Range; Wyoming: nesting in Tetons.

COLORADO.—Summer resident locally in southern and central Colorado to R. Mt. Nat. Park (three or more Loch Vale Lake July 1, 1967, W. K. Reeser, pers. comm.). Nest sites usually in pockets of steep cliffs near waterfalls at elevations of over 9000 feet. Data covering numerous areas in *Birds of Colorado* (1965).

Early spring May 16 (11 birds) Niagara Gulch near Silverton (John A. Murphy, notes); late summer Sept. 12 when 9 young were banded between Sept. 4 and 9, 1963, and fledgling noted in nest Sept. 24, 1967 in Cataract Gulch, South Mineral Creek.

CHIMNEY SWIFT   *Chaetura pelagica* (Linnaeus). [423]

RECOGNITION.—Length 5–5.5 inches. *Adult:* dark sooty gray, spiny-tailed swift with throat and foreneck whitish; lores black. *Young:* like adult, but with rump and upper tail coverts lighter. (Plate 69)

RANGE.—Breeds from southeastern Saskatchewan across Canada to Nova Scotia, south to southeastern Texas and the Gulf coast to Florida. Winters in the Upper Amazon drainage.

Nebraska: abundant in east with western limit in Scottsbluff region; Kansas: common transient and summer resident in east; New Mexico: two specimens taken at Riconada May 1, 1904 and May 22, 1921 in Luna Co. (F. M. Bailey); Utah: casual, one record specimen; Wyoming: uncommon in eastern half of state, two Cheyenne June 17, 1962 (C.B.N. 10:40).

COLORADO.—Uncommon summer resident. Numerous records from eastern counties with 5 definite breeding reports from Boulder in 1956 and 1957. Three observed Glenwood Springs May 28, 1964 (O. A. Knorr, pers. comm.); three at Longmont May 5, 1965 (C.B.N. 13:14) and 12 Denver Sept. 8, 1965 (13:20).

Nesting along Cataract Creek, San Juan Co. Colorado

→

BLACK SWIFT
Photographs by John A. and Jack A. Murphy

WHITE-THROATED SWIFT   *Aeronautes saxatalis sclateri* Rogers. [425a]

RECOGNITION.—Length 6–7 inches. *Adult:* black-brown with throat, breast, mid-belly, sides of rump, and basal wing edgings white. *Young:* similar but with less contrast. (Plate 69)

RANGE.—The species breeds from British Columbia and southern Alberta south in the mountains to Guatemala and to El Salvador. This race ranges from Montana and South Dakota to Nebraska and Colorado. Winters in Mexico.

Nebraska: common summer resident and breeder in Scottsbluff and Pine Ridge areas; New Mexico and Utah: common summer residents locally (*A.s. saxatalis*); Wyoming: local common breeder.

COLORADO.—Common summer resident, locally, nesting on escarpments throughout the state.

Early spring Mar. 19 Garden of the Gods, El Paso Co. (Sam Gadd, pers. comm.); late fall Red Rocks Oct. 13 (C.B.N. 11:50).

FAMILY TROCHILIDAE: HUMMINGBIRDS

BLACK-CHINNED HUMMINGBIRD   *Archilochus alexandri* (Bourcier and Mulsant). [429]

RECOGNITION.—Length 3.40–3.75 inches. *Male:* gorget black with metallic purple border below, white collar; metallic green above, sides and flanks gray-green, outer tail feathers dark purple. *Female:* metallic green above, whitish below, throat dusky, tail green with lateral white tips. *Young:* similar to adult female, with under parts washed with buff, male usually with traces of a gorget. (Plate 70)

RANGE.—Breeds from British Columbia, Montana, Idaho, south to Arizona, southwestern Texas, and northern Mexico. Winters from southeastern California into Mexico.

New Mexico and Utah: summer resident in lower valleys, and occasionally in foothills.

COLORADO.—Summer resident in southwest, with stragglers to the northward and east. A few nesting records from La Plata, Montezuma, Montrose, and Gunnison Counties.

Early spring Apr. 21 Hotchkiss, Delta Co.; late fall Sept. 22 Hotchkiss.

BROAD-TAILED HUMMINGBIRD   *Selasphorus platycercus platycercus* (Swainson). [432]

RECOGNITION.—Length 4–4.5 inches. *Male:* iridescent magenta gorget, back and sides metallic green, dull white below, outer tail feathers dusky, edged with brown. *Female:* throat speckled, metallic green above, sides pale cinnamon, under parts dull white, outer tail feathers brown at bases with white tips. *Young:* generally similar to adult female. The rapidly moving wings, due, possibly to the sharp-pointed, notched outer primaries, make a loud "trilling" sound, unique with the species. (Plate 70)

RANGE.—Breeds from east-central California and northern Nevada to Colorado, south to Texas and northern Mexico. Winters in Mexico.

Nebraska: uncommon migrant; New Mexico, Utah, and Wyoming: common migrant and summer resident.

COLORADO.—A common summer resident from the plains adjacent to the foothills well into the Transition Zone, especially in a ponderosa pine habitat.

Early spring Apr. 27 Denver; late fall Oct. 24 Boulder.

RUFOUS HUMMINGBIRD   *Selasphorus rufus* (Gmelin). [433]

RECOGNITION.—Length 3.2–3.6 inches; smaller than Broad-tailed. *Male:* gorget metallic reddish-copper, crown iridescent green; nape, back, sides, and tail *bright rufous*, wings and edge of tail black. *Female:* iridescent green above, dull white below, sides rufous; throat with a few iridescent feathers; tail feathers brown at base, outer edges tipped with white. *Young:* like the adult female; male with tail and upper coverts more rufous, female with dorsal feathers slightly tipped with buff. (Plate 70)

RANGE.—Breeds from coastal Alaska and southern Yukon to east-central British Columbia, southern Alberta, Washington, Oregon, California, and Montana. Migrates through Wyoming, Colorado, and Texas. Winters in Mexico.

Nebraska: rare migrant, two sight records; New Mexico and Utah: common late summer migrant (July and August); Wyoming: common migrant in late summer in west.

COLORADO.—Common migrant in late July and August in mountains and southern valleys.

Early spring May 16 Black Forest; early summer July 11 Daniels Park; late fall Sept. 28 Denver.

CALLIOPE HUMMINGBIRD   *Stellula calliope* (Gould). [436]

RECOGNITION.—Length 3–3.5 inches. *Adult male:* iridescent green above, but wings and tail dusky, gorget purplish with feathers white basally, forming iridescent rays against white; breast and belly dull white; sides gray-green. *Adult female:* green above, with bases of all but two middle tail feathers brown, and three outer feathers tipped with white; throat spotted whitish; under parts whitish-cinnamon. (Plate 70)

RANGE.—Breeds in mountains from northern British Columbia, southwestern Alberta, and Montana to Baja California and New Mexico. Winters in Mexico.

Nebraska: female found dead near North Platte Apr. 8, 1962 reported by Gail Shickley (pers. comm.); Kansas: rare transient in the west (one record Morton Co.); New Mexico and Utah: common summer resident and migrant in mountains; Wyoming: breeds in northwest and Big Horn Mts.

COLORADO.—Uncommon summer resident in foothills and mountains, and occasionally in the Upper Sonoran Zone. One banded eight miles west of Longmont in Sept. 1966 (A. Collister).

RIVOLI'S HUMMINGBIRD   *Eugenes fulgens aureoviridis* van Rossem. [426]

RECOGNITION.—Length 4.5–5 inches. *Male:* Gorget bright *green;* metallic purple crown; plumage olive-black, darker at nape and belly; under tail coverts barred with white. *Female:* olive-green above; white under parts with spots on throat; gray-green sides; white line behind eye; outer tail feathers tipped with white. (Plate 70)

RANGE.—Breeds from mountains of southwestern New Mexico and southern Arizona south to Guatemala and Nicaragua. Winters from central Mexico south.

New Mexico: recorded from the southwestern corner (Ligon, 1961).

COLORADO.—Uncommon summer visitor in mountains, with a first record from Jackson Co. in 1942; subsequently at least ten appearances in eight different years. A female (no. 33825) and two eggs (no. 6669) collected by Dexter Landau in Boulder Co. July 22, 1965 (see p. 846 *Birds of Colorado*). Additional observations not recorded by Bailey and Niedrach (1965) include one observed at Cedaredge, Delta Co., July 27, 1965 (C.B.N. 13:18), and a female photographed June 10, 1967 by Harold Holt along Soda Creek, 4 mi. SE of Idaho Spgs. which had been a regular visitor at the Shaller home feeder for the two previous years, in 1966 being accompanied by two young (H. Holt, pers. comm.).

Order CORACIIFORMES: Kingfishers and Allies

Family ALCEDINIDAE: Kingfishers

BELTED KINGFISHER   *Megaceryle alcyon alcyon* (Linnaeus). [390]

RECOGNITION.—Length 11–14 inches; a stocky, gray-blue bird with crested head. *Male:* head, upper parts, breast band, and sides slate-blue; wide collar and under parts white; small white spot before the eye; wings and tail spotted with white. *Female:* sides and flanks cinnamon, forming a band across the lower breast and belly. (Plate 71)

RANGE.—Breeds in the Yukon and British Columbia, and east of the Rocky Mountains in Saskatchewan, Manitoba, and Ontario to Labrador, south to Texas and the Gulf coast. Winters from much of summer range, south to Central America and the islands of the Caribbean.

Nebraska and Kansas: common summer resident, uncommon in winter; New Mexico: widespread in migration, uncommon in summer, with no definite breeding records; Utah: race *caurina* fairly common; Wyoming: uncommon resident.

COLORADO.—Fairly common in summer and winter along the watercourses of the state.

Order PICIFORMES: Woodpeckers and Allies

Family Picidae: Woodpeckers

YELLOW-SHAFTED FLICKER   *Colaptes auratus luteus* Bangs. [412a]

RECOGNITION.—Length: 12–14 inches. *Male:* crown and hind-neck gray, with red crescent on nape; face, cheeks, and foreneck pinkish-brown, with *malar patch black;* back and wings dull brown, barred with black; tail black, with under surface yellow; underwing surfaces yellow; breast crescent black; under parts buffy, spotted with black. *Female:* similar, but lacks the black malar patch. (Plate 71)

RANGE.—Species breeds from the northern limit of trees in central Alaska to southern Labrador and southeast of the Rockies to Texas, the Gulf coast, and Cuba. This race nests from eastern Montana, North Dakota, and southern Canada southeast of the Rocky Mountains to Missouri, Kentucky, Virginia, Tennessee, North Carolina and northern Texas.

Nebraska and Kansas: common summer resident, less numerous in winter, with hybridism between this species and *C. cafer* in the west; New Mexico: rare (three recorded by Ligon, 1961); Utah: several intermediates and one showing "no indication of hybridism" (Condor, 56: 362); Wyoming: uncommon resident of central and northeast counties.

COLORADO.—Uncommon resident east of the Continental Divide. There are six specimens in the Museum collection from Baca, Denver, Park, Prowers, and Yuma Counties. Hybridizes commonly with *C. c. collaris*.

RED-SHAFTED FLICKER   *Colaptes cafer collaris* Vigors. [413]

RECOGNITION.—Length 12–14 inches. *Male:* generally similar to male Yellow-shafted Flicker, except *malar patch red instead of black,* no red crescent on nape, and undersurface of wings and tail red. *Female:* like male, but with malar patch light brown. (Plate 71)

RANGE.—The species breeds locally from southeastern Alaska, British Columbia, Alberta, and southwestern Saskatchewan, southward along the western part of the Great Plains to Baja California. This race nests from southern British Columbia south to Washington, Oregon, and California to Baja California, and east to the Great Plains, western Texas, and northern Mexico. Winters throughout range.

Nebraska and Kansas: common resident in west, intergrading with Yellow-shafted; New Mexico, Utah, Wyoming: common resident.

COLORADO.—Common breeding resident from plains into the mountains, with center of abundance in the Upper Sonoran and Transition Zones.

* PILEATED WOODPECKER   *Dryocopus pileatus picinus* (Bangs). [405c]

RECOGNITION.—Length 16–19 inches; large, black woodpecker with red crest, and male with bright red malar stripe, wing-patch and underwing coverts white. Female differs in having front of head and malar stripe blackish instead of red. (Plate 73)

RANGE.—The species occurs locally in forested regions from southern Mackenzie, Manitoba, and Ontario to Nova Scotia, and south to central California, central Texas, and the Gulf coast. The race *D.p. picinus* ranges from British Columbia to the Rocky Mountains, south through western states to northern Arizona.

Nebraska: formerly uncommon resident; Kansas: formerly common, with several recent observations, with a definite nesting report from Linn Co.; New Mexico: one specimen labeled from the Rio Grande within the state "more than half a century ago" (F. Bailey, 1928); and one reported from Bosque Refuge Apr. 30, 1954 (Ligon, 1961); Utah: a specimen now in the American Museum of Natural History was collected at Bluff on the San Juan River May 21, 1892.

COLORADO.—Sight records from near the Kansas border, from Gunnison Co. Aug. 15, 1959 (A. S. Hyde, pers. comm.), and from Pitkin Co. in the Snowmass Lake area in the summer of 1958 and 1960.

RED-BELLIED WOODPECKER   *Centurus carolinus zebra* (Boddaert). [409a]

RECOGNITION.—Length 9–10 inches. *Male:* crown to nape *bright red;* wings, back, rump, and tail barred with black and white; cheeks and under parts fawn-gray with *mid-belly reddish. Female:* like male, but with gray forecrown. *Young:* red restricted, belly buff. (Plate 72)

RANGE.—The species is resident over much of the eastern half of the United States, and this race from southeastern Minnesota, southwestern Ontario east to New York, and south through the Mississippi Valley to Mississippi, Louisiana, and central Texas.

Nebraska and Kansas: common resident east and expanding to western counties.

COLORADO.—Resident locally upon the plains and the eastern foothills, rare west of the Continental Divide.

RED-HEADED WOODPECKER   *Melanerpes erythrocephalus caurinus* Brodkorb. [406a]

RECOGNITION.—Length 8.5–10 inches. *Adult:* head and neck bright red; wing patch, rump, and under parts white; back, wings, and tail deep blue-black. *Young:* head and neck gray-brown; breast gray streaked with black; upper parts barred with brown. (Plate 72)

RANGE.—As a species, breeds from southern Saskatchewan, Manitoba, and western Ontario, Quebec, New Hampshire, and New York to Florida, the Gulf coast, and Texas. This race ranges south through central Montana, Wyoming, and eastern Colorado.

Nebraska and Kansas: common migrant and resident; New Mexico: recorded as most numerous in Pecos and Rio Grande Valleys; Utah: casual, with several records; Wyoming: common in eastern half of state.

COLORADO.—Uncommon summer and winter resident along the watercourses of eastern counties.

LEWIS' WOODPECKER   *Asyndesmus lewis* (Gray). [408]

RECOGNITION.—Length 10–11.5 inches. *Adult:* glossy green-black above; face dull red; neck collar gray; breast and under parts rose-red; crow-like flight. *Young:* similar, but lacking red face and gray collar; under parts grayish. (Plate 73)

RANGE.—Breeds from southern British Columbia and Alberta, South Dakota and Montana, south to California and central Arizona. Winters casually in breeding range south to Baja California and northern Sonora.

Nebraska: rare in summer and occurs occasionally in winter; Kansas: several specimens and observations in western counties; New Mexico: common breeding bird and migrant; Utah: common summer resident in north and transient throughout the state; Wyoming: common migrant, breeder in mountains.

COLORADO.—Rather uncommon breeding resident of the Upper Sonoran Zone into the Transition throughout the state.

YELLOW-BELLIED SAPSUCKER   *Sphyrapicus varius nuchalis* Baird. [402a]

RECOGNITION.—Length 8–9 inches. *Male:* crown, feathers of nape below black occiput line, and throat red; upper parts black faintly marked with white; primaries and tail spotted with white; wing patch and rump white; black bib; belly yellow; sides gray marked with black. *Female:* like male, but chin, and sometimes upper throat white; immature male with white throat marked with red. *Young:* dark crown, throat gray-brown; black bib lacking. (Plate 72)

RANGE.—The species breeds from southern Canada over much of the United States, and this western race from central British Columbia, southern Alberta to northeastern California, east to Colorado and south to Arizona and western Texas. Winters to Baja California and central Mexico.

Nebraska: rare summer resident, and occasionally present in winter; Kansas: three specimens of this race from western Wallace and Morton Counties; New Mexico: fairly numerous summer resident in Transition Zone, and migrant at lower elevations in fall; Utah: common summer resident in north, and regular transient; Wyoming: common migrant, and breeder in the mountains.

COLORADO.—Migrant on plains and common summer resident in mountains, and a few regularly in winter.

Sphyrapicus varius varius (Linnaeus). [402]

RECOGNITION.—Length 8–8.5 inches. *Male:* similar to *S.v. nuchalis*, but back with more white and nape line white or brown instead of red. *Female:* like male but has white throat. (Plate 72)

RANGE.—Breeds across southern Canada from Cape Breton Island to northeastern British Columbia, and from New York, northern Indiana, and Illinois casually to eastern Nebraska, south to Missouri and North Carolina. Winters from Wisconsin and Connecticut south to Gulf of Mexico.

Nebraska: uncommon in east and very rare straggler in west; Kansas: uncommon transient in east.

COLORADO.—Casual on the plains to the foothills; possibly resident.

WILLIAMSON'S SAPSUCKER   *Sphyrapicus thyroideus nataliae* (Malherbe). [404a]

RECOGNITION.—Length 9–9.5 inches. *Male:* black above, with rump and wing patch white; white line over eye meeting at nape and white stripe below eye; chin red; breast black; yellow belly. *Female:* head brown; upper parts barred with black and white, except white rump; breast black, belly yellow; sides and flanks barred with black. (Plate 72)

RANGE.—A western species, this race occupying the eastern part of the range from southeastern British Columbia and mountains of Idaho to Utah, New Mexico, and central Arizona. Intergrades with *S.t. thyroideus* where races meet. Winters from southern New Mexico and western Texas into Mexico and Baja California.

Nebraska: observations in Adams Co. Mar. 24, 1939, Douglas Co. Feb. 18, 1945, and North Platte in 1962; Kansas: adult male noted Apr. 4, 1935 in Cloud Co.; New Mexico: common breeding bird of high mountains; Utah: fairly common summer resident in mountains; Wyoming: uncommon in the high forests.

COLORADO.—Common summer resident in the ponderosa pine forests, rare on plains.

Early spring Feb. 26 Fort Morgan; late summer Sept. 24 Park Co.

HAIRY WOODPECKER   *Dendrocopos villosus monticola* (Anthony). [393e]

RECOGNITION.—Length 8.5–10.5 inches. *Male:* blue-black above, with red nape; under parts, two head stripes, broad stripe down back white; *wing coverts not dotted with white,* and outer tail feathers white. *Female:* red nape lacking. *Young:* like adult female; occasionally male with red streaks in crown. The eastern Hairy and eastern subspecies of Downy Woodpeckers have the wings conspicuously spotted with white, while in the Rocky Mountain forms of Hairy and Downy Woodpeckers, the wing coverts are unspotted. (Plate 74)

RANGE.—The species occurs throughout much of North America from central Alaska across central Canada south to western Panama. This race is resident in the Rocky Mountains from central British Columbia to eastern Washington, Alberta, Montana, Nevada, Idaho, and western South Dakota, south to northern New Mexico.

Nebraska: occurs uncommonly in western part of the state; New Mexico: breeds rather commonly in northern mountains; Utah: common resident in central and northern mountains (*D.v. leucothorectis* in south); Wyoming: common resident.

COLORADO.—Resident, breeding in mountains throughout the state and wintering at lower elevations.

Dendrocopos villosus villosus (Linnaeus). [393]

RECOGNITION.—Length 8.5–10 inches. Similar to the mountain race *D.v. monticola,* but *wing coverts spotted with white.* (Plate 74)

RANGE.—Breeds from central North Dakota, Minnesota, and across southeastern Canada to Nova Scotia and northeastern United States, Missouri, northern Tennessee, western Carolinas, and Virginia. Winters irregularly southward from breeding range to northern Alabama.

Nebraska and Kansas: fairly common resident.

COLORADO.—Resident in eastern Colorado; not common.

Dendrocopos villosus septentrionalis (Nuttall). [393a]

RECOGNITION.—Similar to *D. v. villosus,* but averages slightly larger.

RANGE.—Breeding from the Canadian Zone of Alaska and Canada south to British Columbia, Montana, and North Dakota. South in winter casually to Colorado and Nebraska.

COLORADO.—Rare winter resident on the eastern plains. Five specimens collected in Adams, Baca, and Morgan Counties.

DOWNY WOODPECKER   *Dendrocopos pubescens leucurus* (Hartlaub). [394b]

RECOGNITION.—Length 6–8 inches. Members of this species appear as miniature Hairy Woodpeckers. This race has greater wing coverts *black* with few or no white spots. (Plate 74)

RANGE.—Breeds in Kenai Peninsula and southern Alaska to British Columbia, east of the Cascades to northeastern California, western Nebraska, and northern New Mexico.

Nebraska: racial distribution little known, this form ranging to western counties, according to A.O.U. Checklist; New Mexico: uncommon resident in summer between 6000 and 8000 ft., and lower in winter; Utah and Wyoming: common resident in mountains and wintering at lower elevations.

COLORADO.—Fairly common summer resident in mountains. Majority winter in the Upper Sonoran Zone.

Dendrocopos pubescens medianus (Swainson). [394c]

RECOGNITION.—Length 6–7 inches. Similar to *D.p. leucurus,* but much smaller; under parts smoky-white and white outer tail feathers spotted with black, *wing coverts with conspicuous white spots.* Colorado birds tend to be whiter on under parts than eastern birds. (Plate 74)

RANGE.—Breeds from southern Alberta, Manitoba, Ontario, and Quebec south to Kansas, Missouri, Tennessee, Kentucky, Virginia, and western North Carolina.

Nebraska: common summer resident; Kansas: *D.p. pubescens* in southeast, *D.p. medianus* in rest of state.

COLORADO.—Uncommon resident in eastern Colorado.

Dendrocopos pubescens nelsoni (Oberholser). [394d]

RECOGNITION.—Length 7–7.5 inches. Resembles *D.p. medianus,* but slightly larger, with under parts whiter and less barring in outer tail feathers.

RANGE.—Breeds from north-central Alaska and southwestern Mackenzie to northern British Columbia and central Alberta. Southward in winter irregularly to eastern Colorado, Minnesota, Michigan, and New England.

COLORADO.—Winter visitor in eastern Colorado.

Early fall Sept. 9 Jackson Res. (no. 22272); late spring Apr. 21 Denver (AMB).

LADDER-BACKED WOODPECKER   *Dendrocopos scalaris symplectus* (Oberholser). [396]

RECOGNITION.—Length 7–8 inches. *Male:* crown red, anteriorly marked with black streaks and white spots; upper parts black, barred with white except black central tail feathers; white stripe extending from eye onto neck, another from bill to cheek; under parts dusky, spotted with black on both sides. *Female:* black crown. *Young:* similar to adult female, male with some red in crown. (Plate 74)

RANGE.—The species is an uncommon resident in the desert areas from southeastern Colorado, Nevada, and western Oklahoma south through western Texas, and into northern Mexico and Baja California. This race occupies the eastern part of the range.

Kansas: common resident in southwest but no nests recorded; New Mexico: race *cactophilus* listed as common below 6300 ft. in central counties in south, northward casually to Taos; Utah: race *cactophilus* in southwest.

COLORADO.—An uncommon resident in southeastern part of state.

NORTHERN THREE-TOED WOODPECKER   *Picoides tridactylus dorsalis* Baird. [401b]

RECOGNITION.—Length 8.5–9.5 inches. *Male:* black above with broad white stripe down back; crown *yellow;* malar and postocular stripes, primary spots, outer tail feathers, and under parts white; *sides and flanks barred with black. Female:* crown black, under parts more dusky. *Young:* like adult female, but male with yellow streaks in crown. (Plate 73)

RANGE.—Resident in boreal forests of the Rocky Mountains from Montana and Nevada to central Arizona.

Nebraska: straggler, one specimen Scotts Bluff Co. June 15, 1916; New Mexico: uncommon resident in higher mountains south to the Mogollon Range; Utah: uncommon resident in high mountains; Wyoming: resident in high forests.

COLORADO.—An uncommon resident in the coniferous forests above 8000 feet. Male observed at 10,000 ft. east of Nokhu Crags, Jackson Co., June 30, 1967 (Mrs. Terry Cole, pers. comm.). Nesting cavity 5 ft. from ground in lodgepole pine at Echo Lake (10,500 ft.) and adults & young photographed July 14, 1952 (AMB & RJN, 1965).

Order PASSERIFORMES: Perching Birds
Family TYRANNIDAE: Tyrant Flycatchers

EASTERN KINGBIRD   *Tyrannus tyrannus* (Linnaeus). [444]

RECOGNITION.—Length 8.5–9 inches. Upper parts blackish; under parts and conspicuous tip of tail white; concealed orange-red streak on crown. (Plate 77)

RANGE.—Breeds from Nova Scotia across Canada to British Columbia, and south to eastern Washington, Oregon, California, Nevada, Idaho, the Gulf coast, and southern Florida. Winters in South America from Peru to Bolivia.

Nebraska and Kansas: common transient and summer resident; New Mexico and Utah: uncommon summer resident; Wyoming: migrant and summer resident.

COLORADO.—Common in summer throughout the state in Upper Sonoran Zone and less numerous in foothills.

Early spring Apr. 24 Longmont (7:9); late summer Sept. 19 Weldona (8:9); late fall Oct. 12 El Paso Co. (Sam Gadd).

WESTERN KINGBIRD   *Tyrannus verticalis* Say. [447]

RECOGNITION.—Length 8–9.5 inches; upper parts pearl-gray, throat white, breast pale gray, and abdomen sulphur-yellow; wings brownish; tail blackish with *white edges;* concealed orange-red crown patch. (Plate 77)

RANGE.—Breeds from British Columbia, southern Alberta, Saskatchewan, and Manitoba south to Michigan, Wisconsin, Minnesota, Texas, northern Baja California, Sonora, and Chihuahua. Winters chiefly from western Mexico to Nicaragua but casually from South Carolina to Florida.

Nebraska and Kansas: common transient and summer resident in west, less common in east; New Mexico and Utah: abundant summer resident; Wyoming: common migrant and breeder.

COLORADO.—Common summer resident throughout the state in the Upper Sonoran Zone.

Early spring Apr. 6 Denver (C.B.N. 3:59); late summer Sept. 28 eastern plains (6:1).

CASSIN'S KINGBIRD   *Tyrannus vociferans vociferans* Swainson. [448]

RECOGNITION.—Length 8.5–9 inches. Similar to the Western Kingbird, but upper parts darker, more olive-gray; tail tipped with whitish, but lacks white edges of outer tail feathers. (Plate 77)

RANGE.—Breeds from southeastern Montana, Wyoming, east to Kansas, south to western Texas and northern Arizona, and from central California south into Mexico. Winters from central California south into Baja California, and Mexico to Guatemala.

Nebraska and Kansas: transient and uncommon summer resident in west; New Mexico: migrant and summer resident to 8000 feet; Utah: summer resident in south; Wyoming: rare in southeastern counties.

COLORADO.—Uncommon summer resident; more numerous in southern half of the state.

Early spring Apr. 17 Golden; late summer Sept. 23 Weldona.

SCISSOR-TAILED FLYCATCHER   *Muscivora forficata* (Gmelin). [443]

RECOGNITION.—Length 10.5–14.5 inches; size of Eastern Kingbird, but with an extremely long tail. Ashy-gray above, whitish below, sides, under wings and lower tail coverts pink. Sexes much alike, but female less colorful and tail shorter. (Plate 76)

RANGE.—Breeds from southeastern Colorado, eastern New Mexico, Nebraska, southeastern Kansas, western Oklahoma, Arkansas, western Louisiana, and Texas. Winters from southern Mexico to Panama.

Nebraska: rare summer resident in south with breeding records from Adams, Gage, Lancaster, and Logan Counties; Kansas: common in summer in southern and central parts, breeding west to Morton Co., and range extended northward in recent years; New Mexico: confined to eastern and southeastern counties; Utah: one sight record (Behle); Wyoming: one three miles north Cheyenne June 30, 1959 (C.B.N. 8:11).

COLORADO.—Casual straggler on eastern plains north to Longmont and Fort Collins. Recorded nesting in Baca Co. June 1, 1923 by RJN and nest observed near Campo June 23, 1962 by Charles and Mildred Snyder.

Early spring Bonny Res. Apr. 24; late fall Nov. 9 Longmont.

GREAT CRESTED FLYCATCHER   *Myiarchus crinitus boreus* Bangs. [452a]

RECOGNITION.—Length 8–9 inches. Upper parts, grayish olive-brown, with reddish-brown tail and primaries, and two yellowish wing bars; under parts, from grayish-white at throat and breast to sulphur-yellow abdomen. Head more conspicuously crested than those of others of family; darker, and tail more rufous than Western Kingbird. (Plate 75)

RANGE.—Breeds from southeastern Saskatchewan, Manitoba, and Ontario south to Georgia, Louisiana, and Texas; ranges west to the Great Plains. Winters in Mexico, and south to South America.

Nebraska: a common resident and breeder in east, rare in west; Kansas: common transient and summer resident; New Mexico: uncommon; Wyoming: straggler.

COLORADO.—Straggler. Occurs regularly in vicinity of Bonny Res., Yuma Co. A specimen was taken in Weld Co. Aug. 17, 1911, one at Bonny Res. May 24, 1959, and one observed in Jeff. Co. May 14, 1966 (D.F.O., 1:no. 9).

Early spring Apr. 30 Baca Co.; late summer Sept. 12 banded at Sedalia by Chas. and Mildred Snyder (C.B.N. 12:51).

ASH-THROATED FLYCATCHER   *Myiarchus cinerascens cinerascens* (Lawrence). [454]

RECOGNITION.—Length, 7.5–8.5 inches. Resembles Great Crested Flycatcher, but is smaller, with throat whiter and yellow abdomen paler; wing bars white. (Plate 75)

RANGE.—Breeds from southwestern Oregon, eastern Washington, and southwestern Wyoming to Texas, and winters from southeastern California and central Arizona south to southern Mexico and Central America.

Kansas: a few records from Morton Co.; New Mexico: common breeding bird except in extreme east; Utah: common, widely distributed summer resident, especially in the south; Wyoming: casual in southern part.

COLORADO.—Rather common summer resident in pinyon-juniper country throughout the state.

OLIVACEOUS FLYCATCHER   *Myiarchus tuberculifer olivascens* Ridgway. [455a]

RECOGNITION.—Length 6.5–7 inches; small olive-colored flycatcher, tail rufous, pale yellow below, with throat gray. (Plate 75)

RANGE.—Breeds in southwestern New Mexico, southeastern Arizona, casually in Brewster Co., Texas, south into Mexico.

New Mexico: few records only.

COLORADO.—Rare straggler. One was taken at Fort Lyon, Bent Co., May 11, 1883 (Thorne, 1889).

92

EASTERN PHOEBE *Sayornis phoebe* (Latham). [456]

RECOGNITION.—Length 6.5–7 inches; upper parts brownish-gray, darkest on head. Under parts grayish-white, with yellow wash on abdomen. Lack of conspicuous wing bars and its *tail wagging* habit help to distinguish it from other flycatchers. (Plate 75)

RANGE.—Breeds from northeastern British Columbia, Alberta, Manitoba, Ontariö, Quebec, and New Brunswick south to western Oklahoma, Texas, Alabama, and South Carolina. Winters from Virginia and the Gulf coast and casually northward, south into Mexico.

Nebraska and Kansas: common summer resident in east and less so in west; New Mexico: casual summer resident; Utah: one Zion Canyon Oct. 21, 1963 (A.F.N. 18:60) and two collected in Washington Co. Mar. 27 and Dec. 17, 1965 (Condor, 68:519); Wyoming: straggler.

COLORADO.—Rare summer resident on eastern prairies west to the foothills (Pueblo, Morrison, Golden, Boulder, Longmont, and Fort Collins).

Early spring Mar. 11 Golden; late fall Oct. 1 Bonny Res.

SAY'S PHOEBE *Sayornis saya saya* (Bonaparte). [457]

RECOGNITION.—Length 7.5–8 inches. Upper parts dark gray, with blackish tail; breast grayish and *abdomen orange-brown*. Has the Phoebe tail-wagging habit, and a plaintive "pee-ur" voice, slurring downward, generally having no resemblance to the notes of the Eastern Phoebe. (Plate 75)

RANGE.—Breeds from northeastern British Columbia eastward in Mackenzie, Alberta, Saskatchewan, and Manitoba, south over the central plains from North Dakota to Texas, and from southern California into Mexico. Winters north to California and southeastern New Mexico into Mexico.

Nebraska: common migrant and summer resident in western third of state; Kansas: common transient and summer resident in west; New Mexico and Utah: common summer resident; Wyoming: common breeder away from forests.

COLORADO.—Common migrant, a summer resident in the Upper Sonoran and Transition Zones; occasional in winter. Nests in and on buildings, under bridges, or on ledges. One Weldona Mar. 31, 1965; pair Apr. 1 started repairing old nest on house, and had young May 31 (Howard Rollin, C.B.N. 13:24).

TRAILL'S FLYCATCHER *Empidonax traillii* (Audubon). [466]

RECOGNITION.—Length 5.5–6.5 inches. The small flycatchers of the genus *Empidonax* are so similar in size, coloring, and habits that it is generally impossible to identify them with certainty in the field, except by their notes, seldom heard during migration, and by their breeding habits. All are olive-gray or green, with more or less brownish cast above, and grayish-white below with a whitish eyering and two light wing bars; sexes colored much alike. This species has end of tail rounded, while others of the genus are notched (emarginate). Light lower mandible of *traillii* differs from other species except *E. wrightii*. (Plate 78)

RANGE.—Central Alaska and western Canada east to Newfoundland, south to Virginia, Missouri, and California; winters from southern Mexico to Argentina.

Nebraska: common, but status of races not well known; Kansas: transient, breeding in Doniphan and Wyandotte Cos. in 1963, *E.T. brewsteri* in west and *E. t. traillii* in east; New Mexico: few, probably *E.t. brewsteri;* Utah: fairly common summer resident and transient (races *E.t. extimus, adastus,* and *traillii*); Wyoming: species common breeder of mountain willows and alders.

COLORADO.—The 1957 A.O.U. Check-list recognizes two races only, but several others have been reported by Phillips (1948) and Aldrich (1951). *E. t. traillii* (= *E. t. campestris?*) is a common migrant upon the plains and there are ten specimens in the Museum collection; *E. t. brewsteri* (= *E. t. adastus?*) ranges throughout the state in migration, and nests in the mountains (fifteen specimens in the Museum collection); and *E. t. extimus* (five specimens) migrates over the eastern prairies and in western counties. Data for all the above are given by B. & N., 1965.

Early spring May 2 Longmont; late fall Sept. 19 Pagosa Springs.

LEAST FLYCATCHER *Empidonax minimus* (Baird and Baird). [467]

RECOGNITION.—Length 5–5.5 inches. Similar to preceding species, but smaller, grayer above, whiter below and both mandibles dark; throat less white than *E. traillii:* wing bars whiter. (Plate 78)

RANGE.—Breeds from southwestern Yukon, central Mackenzie, and northeastern Alberta east across Canada, south to British Columbia, Montana, Wyoming, and South Dakota, east to central New Jersey, West Virginia, and Tennessee. Winters through Mexico to Panama.

Nebraska: common transient and rare breeder, Kansas: common migrant; Wyoming: common migrant and breeder in eastern half of state.

COLORADO.—Regular migrant over the eastern plains.

Early spring May 3 Denver; late summer Sept. 23 Kiowa Co.

HAMMOND'S FLYCATCHER　*Empidonax hammondii* (Xantus). [468]

RECOGNITION.—Size 5.5–5.75 inches. This species and the next seldom can be distinguished from each other in the field, but both are less brownish than Traill's, less grayish than the Least and Gray, and less yellowish below than the Western. Hammond's has a dark breast band and an indistinct whitish web on tail, it is somewhat more olive above and yellowish below, and has a shorter beak than the Dusky. (Plate 78)

RANGE.—Breeds from central Alaska, Yukon, British Columbia, and western Alberta south through Montana, Yellowstone Park, northeastern Nevada, central Utah, south-central California, and northern New Mexico. Winters from southern Arizona into Mexico to Nicaragua.

Nebraska: one record Dawes Co.; New Mexico: resident in north; uncommon migrant; Utah: uncommon summer resident; Wyoming: uncommon breeder in mountains over 8000 feet.

COLORADO.—Migrant in the Upper Sonoran Zone and breeding bird of the Transition into the Canadian Zone.

Early spring Apr. 4 west Denver (H. Holt, pers. comm.); late summer Sept. 20 Longmont (banded by A. Collister).

DUSKY FLYCATCHER　*Empidonax oberholseri* Phillips. [469]

RECOGNITION.—Length 5.5–6 inches. Similar to *hammondii*, except the latter has the back and tail a uniform olive-brownish while some specimens of *oberholseri* show the brown tail differing from the back, and the throat of this species averages whiter. The *outer web* of the outer tail feather is whiter than the inner, and there is a distinct white eyering in some individuals. (Plate 78)

RANGE.—Breeds from southern Yukon, British Columbia, Alberta, and Saskatchewan south to southern California, southern Nevada and to central Arizona. Winters from Arizona into Mexico.

Kansas: rare transient, three specimens Morton Co. in 1952; New Mexico and Utah: summer resident in mountains, often associated with aspens; Wyoming: common breeder in western half.

COLORADO.—Migrant at low elevations and breeding in mountain thickets of Transition and Canadian Zones.

GRAY FLYCATCHER　*Empidonax wrightii* Baird. [469.1]

RECOGNITION.—Length 5.25–5.75 inches. Coloration similar to the Dusky Flycatcher, but more gray above, breast slightly lighter and lower mandible light; the pinyon-juniper habitat of this species during the breeding season is distinctive. (Plate 78)

RANGE.—Breeds from Oregon, southern Idaho, southwestern Wyoming, and western Colorado south to central-eastern California, Nevada, Arizona, and central New Mexico. Winters in southern California and Arizona and south into Mexico.

New Mexico and Utah: Local summer resident in pinyon-juniper associations; Wyoming: one recorded from Cody (A.O.U. Check-list), and breeding in the southwest (Ned K. Johnson, pers. comm.).

COLORADO.—Summer resident, common locally in the western part of the state in pinyon-junipers.

WESTERN FLYCATCHER　*Empidonax difficilis hellmayri* Brodkorb. [464b]

RECOGNITION.—Length 5.5–6 inches. Similar to the other species of *Empidonax* but generally more yellowish below, and the only member of the genus with the throat yellowish instead of white. (Plate 78)

RANGE.—The species breeds from southeastern Alaska, British Columbia, Idaho, western Montana, Nevada, and South Dakota south to southwestern California, the mountains of western Texas, Arizona, and Baja California. This race occupies the eastern part of the range from Montana and South Dakota south into Mexico.

Kansas: rare, two specimens from Morton Co.; New Mexico: summer resident in the mountains; Utah: uncommon summer resident; Wyoming: common breeder in eastern half of state.

COLORADO.—Fairly common summer resident from the Transition into Canadian Zone.

Early spring Apr. 7 Boulder (no. 27539); late summer Sept. 9 Denver (8:55).

EASTERN WOOD PEWEE　*Contopus virens* (Linnaeus). [461]

RECOGNITION.—Length 6–6.75 inches. Dark olive-gray above, with two whitish wing bars, no eyering, under parts light olive-gray, with distinctive lighter line down center of breast and lighter abdomen. Slightly larger than the species of *Empidonax*, and wings proportionately longer. Distinguished from next species by yellowish lower mandible and by its notes. Lacks tail-wagging habit of the phoebes.

RANGE.—Breeds from southern Manitoba east to Nova Scotia and south through eastern North and South Dakota, south to the Gulf coast and Florida. Winters in Central America to Ecuador and Peru.

Nebraska: a common summer resident in the eastern counties; Kansas: a common transient and summer resident in the east, rare in west.

COLORADO.—Casual in eastern Colorado.

WESTERN WOOD PEWEE   *Contopus sordidulus veliei* Coues. [462]

RECOGNITION.—Length 6–6.5 inches. Closely resembles the Eastern Wood Pewee, but grayer, less olive above and darker below, with both mandibles blackish. (Plate 78)

RANGE.—Breeds in western North America from eastern Alaska and southwestern Canada east to North Dakota, and south to central Texas and Baja California. Winters from Panama into northern South America.

Nebraska: a common migrant and breeder in the Panhandle region; Kansas: a common transient and probably a summer resident in west, but no breeding records; New Mexico: common summer resident, nesting in the mountains; Utah: common widely distributed summer resident; Wyoming: abundant nesting species in mountains.

COLORADO.—Common summer resident from plains into the mountains to 10,000 feet.

Early spring Apr. 11 Larimer Co. (A.F.N. 18:465); late fall Morrison Oct. 21 (C.B.N. 8:8).

OLIVE-SIDED FLYCATCHER   *Nuttallornis borealis* (Swainson). [459]

RECOGNITION.—Length 7–8 inches. A large-headed flycatcher, dark olive grayish-brown above and dark olive-gray below; bill large, throat light, *chest patches dark* with whitish line through middle of abdomen. No wing bars. Conspicuous patches of yellowish-white, *down feathers* on flanks, sometimes concealed when the bird is perched, are good field marks. Has a distinctive, loud, three-note phrase, "hip'-three cheers," also a sharp call note, "pip, pip, pip." (Plate 78)

RANGE.—Breeds from northern and western Yukon across Canada to Newfoundland, and in northern states from Nevada to New York, south to Arizona and Baja California. Winters in South America.

Nebraska: rare migrant; Kansas: uncommon transient; New Mexico and Utah: fairly common summer resident in high mountains; Wyoming: uncommon in forests.

COLORADO.—Migrant on the plains, fairly common in summer in the Canadian Zone, and frequent in the Transition Zone throughout the state.

Early spring May 7 Denver; late summer Sept. 20 Golden.

VERMILION FLYCATCHER   *Pyrocephalus rubinus flammeus* van Rossem. [471a]

RECOGNITION.—Length 5.5–6.5 inches. *Male:* with blackish upper parts, and top of head and under parts bright scarlet. Female brown above, white below streaked with brown, the abdomen washed with yellowish or salmon-pink. (Plate 78)

RANGE.—Breeds from southeastern California, southern parts of Nevada, Utah, Arizona, New Mexico, and western Texas south into Mexico. Occasionally wanders northward in early fall.

Nebraska: two records from Omaha and North Platte; New Mexico and Utah: uncommon summer resident in south, and occurs occasionally in winter.

COLORADO.—Straggler with reports from Adams, El Paso, Gunnison, and Rio Grande Counties, including Christmas Count in the Denver area in 1957. Male recorded at Bowles Lake, Denver, Oct. 16, 1965, Dec. 1 and Dec. 8 (Chas. and Mildred Snyder, pers. comm.).

Family ALAUDIDAE: Larks

HORNED LARK   *Eremophila alpestris leucolaema* Coues. [474c]

RECOGNITION.—Length 6.5–8 inches; a pinkish-brown, ground-loving bird, with short, black, horn-like head feathers; mainly brown above, with crown, wing shoulder, and upper tail coverts pinkish-brown; horn tufts, crown crescent, lores, cheek stripe, and breast patch black; forehead and eyeline yellow; throat pale yellow, and belly white, with sides and flanks pinkish-brown; tail black, outer feathers edged with white. Walks, not hops, on the ground. (Plate 79)

RANGE.—The Horned Lark occurs throughout most of the Northern Hemisphere on all continents. This race breeds from Alberta, Saskatchewan, and Montana south to Idaho, Utah, and Wyoming to northwestern Texas; it withdraws in winter from the most northern areas and the high mountains.

Nebraska and Kansas: very common migrant and resident as a species (five races recorded from both states); New Mexico: common in winter and nests on plains; Utah: winter resident, nesting in the northeast (five other races recorded); Wyoming: numerous in summer, many in winter, and several races are migrants.

COLORADO.—An abundant resident throughout the lower areas of the state, nesting commonly upon the prairies, and in fewer numbers on the grasslands of mountain parks and alpine slopes.

Family HIRUNDINIDAE: Swallows

VIOLET-GREEN SWALLOW   *Tachycineta thalassina lepida* Mearns. [615]

RECOGNITION.—Length 5–5.5 inches; upper parts dark metallic-green and violet, with a conspicuous white mark on the side of the rump; under parts white. (Plate 79)

RANGE.—Breeds from Alaska, Yukon, British Columbia, Montana, and South Dakota to Arizona, and into Mexico. Winters from southern California and Mexico to Central America.

Nebraska: summer resident in Pine Ridge region, Wildcat Hills, and Scottsbluff area; Kansas: five noted Shawnee Co. Apr. 14, 1947 by L. B. Carson; New Mexico and Utah: common summer resident; Wyoming: common migrant and breeder.

COLORADO.—Common spring and fall migrant at low elevations, and nesting from the foothills into the mountains to near timberline.

Early spring Apr. 1 Jefferson Co.; late fall Oct. 9 Longmont.

TREE SWALLOW   *Iridoprocne bicolor* (Vieillot). [614]

RECOGNITION.—Length 5–6 inches; upper parts dark iridescent greenish-blue; under parts pure white. The lack of *white side patches* distinguishes it from the Violet-green Swallow. (Plate 79)

RANGE.—Breeds throughout North America from the northern half of the United States north to the limit of tree growth. Nests casually south to Arkansas, Louisiana, and Mississippi. Winters from southern states to Central America.

Nebraska: rare breeder in Missouri River valley, common migrant in east; Kansas: migrant in east, summer resident in northeast; New Mexico: migrant; Utah: transient and summer resident; Wyoming: common migrant and uncommon breeder.

COLORADO.—Migrates in spring over the plains and nests from the lower edge of the foothills to near timberline.

Early spring Apr. 4 Denver (H. Holt, pers. comm.); late fall Oct. 9 Longmont.

BANK SWALLOW   *Riparia riparia riparia* (Linnaeus). [616]

RECOGNITION.—Length 4.75–5.25 inches; upper parts plain brown; under parts white, with a conspicuous brown band between throat and breast. (Plate 80)

RANGE.—The species is wide-ranging in the Northern Hemisphere from northern Alaska, Canada, the British Isles, northern Scandinavia, northern Russia and Siberia to northwestern Africa, Abyssinia, Iraq, Iran, India, and Japan. In North America it breeds throughout much of the United States except in extreme southeast, north to tree line. Winters in the New World in South America.

Nebraska and Kansas: common summer resident and migrant in east; New Mexico and Utah: summer resident locally and transient; Wyoming: migrant and common colonial breeder.

COLORADO.—Occurs locally throughout the state from the Upper Sonoran into the Transition Zone.

Early spring Apr. 7 Longmont; late summer Oct. 9 Platteville (C.B.N. 5:9).

ROUGH-WINGED SWALLOW   *Stelgidopteryx ruficollis serripennis* (Audubon). [617]

RECOGNITION.—Length 5–5.5 inches; plain brown above; throat and breast brownish, belly white, lacking the white throat and contrasting band of the Bank Swallow. Has a rasping squeak, repeated frequently in flight, which is easily distinguished from notes of other swallows. Outer web of outer primaries *roughened*. (Plate 80)

RANGE.—Breeds from British Columbia across southern Canada south to Florida, and in southern Arizona and California. Winters from Louisiana into Central America to Panama.

Nebraska and Kansas: common migrant and summer resident; New Mexico: migrant, breeding locally; Utah: fairly common summer resident and transient; Wyoming: common migrant and breeder.

COLORADO.—Summer resident locally throughout the state in the Upper Sonoran into the Transition Zone, nesting in holes along banks, or in crannies of buildings.

Early spring Apr. 1 Arapahoe Co. (C.B.N. 10:37); late fall Oct. 20 Weldona (C.B.N. 6:4).

BARN SWALLOW   *Hirundo rustica erythrogaster* Boddaert. [613]

RECOGNITION.—Length 6–7.5 inches; above glossy purplish-blue; below rich chestnut at throat to salmon at abdomen. Distinguished from the other swallows by its deeply forked tail and long outer tail feathers. (Plate 80)

RANGE.—Breeds from northwestern Alaska, Yukon, western Mackenzie, Saskatchewan, and Manitoba to Newfoundland, south to Baja California, North Carolina, Mississippi, Louisiana, and into Mexico. Winters from Panama to Chile.

Nebraska: common migrant and breeder; Kansas: summer resident and common migrant; New Mexico: migrant and widely distributed breeder from plains into the mountains; Utah: common migrant and summer resident in valleys; Wyoming: uncommon migrant and breeder.

COLORADO.—Common summer resident from the plains into the mountains to about 10,000 feet.

Early spring Apr. 2 Denver (H. Holt, pers. comm.); late fall Oct. 20 Ft. Collins.

CLIFF SWALLOW   *Petrochelidon pyrrhonota pyrrhonota* (Vieillot). [612]

RECOGNITION.—Length 5–6 inches. Above dark blue; below, reddish-brown at throat to whitish near tail. *Whitish forehead, buffy rump,* and *square tail* distinguish it from other swallows. (Plate 80)

RANGE.—Breeds in southwestern British Columbia across southern Canada to Nova Scotia, south except extreme southeastern states, to northern Alabama, eastern Arizona, and California. Winters in South America.

Nebraska and Kansas: common migrant and breeding locally; New Mexico and Utah: common summer resident locally; Wyoming: abundant summer resident and migrant.

COLORADO.—Common summer resident locally from the plains to 9000 feet in mountain parks. The mud nests are placed along cliffs, arroyos, under bridges and eaves of buildings.

Early spring Apr. 1 Jeff. Co. (C.B.N. 10:37); late fall Oct. 10 Weldona.

PURPLE MARTIN   *Progne subis subis* (Linnaeus). [611]

RECOGNITION.—Length 7–8.5 inches. *Male:* purplish black, with the wings and tail somewhat brownish. *Female:* part of head, wings, and tail dark brown, under parts and forehead gray to whitish. Tail deeply notched. (Plate 79)

RANGE.—Breeds west of the Cascade Range and Sierra Nevada from British Columbia, western Washington, Oregon, and Nevada through California to Mexico; east of the Rockies (absent from much of the Great Basin) from British Columbia across southern Canada to Quebec, and from Minnesota, Wisconsin, and Michigan south to the Gulf coast, Texas, and Arizona; migrates through Mexico to Central and South America.

Nebraska and Kansas: locally common migrant and breeder in east, uncommon in west; New Mexico: migrant and fairly common breeder in Transition Zone to 9000 ft.; Utah: uncommon summer resident in northern mountains (Condor, 60: 406), fifteen at Heber July 10, 1963 (A.F.N. 17:474); Wyoming: formerly reported from east.

COLORADO.—Uncommon summer resident. Recorded breeding in Las Animas and La Plata Counties. Majority of the observations were made in western counties; female noted near Ft. Collins Sept. 1, 1965 (C.B.N. 13:23).

Family CORVIDAE: Jays, Magpies, and Crows

GRAY JAY   *Perisoreus canadensis capitalis* Ridgway. [484a]

RECOGNITION.—Length 10.5–13 inches; a large gray jay with uncrested head. Head and neck white, with dusky occipital patch; back dull gray; wings and tail dark gray, with wing edgings and tip of tail white; belly and sides dark gray. *Young:* plumage brownish-gray, with feathers of under parts tipped with whitish. (Plate 81)

RANGE.—The species occurs from the edge of the northern forests of Alaska and Canada south into northern states, and is resident of the southern Rocky Mountain region from eastern Idaho, southern Montana, western and southern Wyoming south through eastern Utah, mountains of Colorado, and Arizona. Winters at lower elevations in breeding range.

Nebraska: uncommon winter visitor in northwest and along Niobrara River; New Mexico: resident in mountains of the north; Utah: fairly common resident in central and northern mountains; Wyoming: common resident in mountains.

COLORADO.—Common bird of the coniferous forests, nesting from 8500 feet to timberline.

97

BLUE JAY   *Cyanocitta cristata cyanotephra* Sutton. [477c]

RECOGNITION.—Length 11–12 inches; a pale blue jay with a prominent crest. *Adult:* head and neck dark grayish-lavender; wings and tail blue, barred with black and marked with large white feather edges on wings and tip of tail; narrow black line encircling crown and extending across cheeks to breast; throat, cheeks, and under parts pale gray. *Young:* duller than the adult. (Plate 81)

RANGE.—The species breeds from central Alberta across southern Canada to Newfoundland, south through the Dakotas and eastern Wyoming to Texas, the Gulf coast, and southern Florida. This race is resident, so far as is known, from the northwestern corner of the Panhandle of Texas, northern Oklahoma, Kansas, Nebraska, and Colorado to the foothills of the Rockies.

Nebraska: *C.c. bromia* in northeast, and *C.c. cyanotephra* elsewhere; Kansas: *C.c. bromia* a common resident locally in east; New Mexico: uncommon straggler; Wyoming: common in the northeast and lower Platte Valley, elsewhere rare; Utah: one Cedar City Oct. 29, 1966 (A.F.N. 21:63).

COLORADO.—Formerly uncommon but many recent reports, and the species is fairly common resident east of the Front Range.

STELLER'S JAY   *Cyanocitta stelleri macrolopha* Baird. [478b]

RECOGNITION.—Length 12–13.5 inches; a dark blue jay with black head crested. Crest, head, and neck almost black; back and scapulars dusky-gray; forehead streaked with white and small white line over eye; wings and tail deep blue, barred with black; under parts and rump clear dark blue. The crested head distinguishes the species from Scrub and Pinyon Jays, and its dark plumage from the Blue Jay. (Plate 81)

RANGE.—The species has a western range from southeastern Alaska east to South Dakota and south to Texas and California, and south through Mexico to southern Nicaragua. This race is resident in the eastern portion of the range from southern Nevada, Arizona, and into Mexico.

Nebraska: a rare winter visitor in the west; Kansas: sight records from the southwest; New Mexico and Utah: common resident; Wyoming: common resident in mountains.

COLORADO.—Common bird of the foothills into the mountains.

SCRUB JAY   *Aphelocoma coerulescens woodhouseii* (Baird). [480]

RECOGNITION.—Length 11–13 inches; a blue and gray jay with uncrested head. *Adult:* blue above, with back and scapulars dusky-gray; narrow white streak over eye; cheek and ear patches black; throat and breast streaked with white and bluish; under parts gray. *Young:* gray above, with wings and tail blue; brownish-gray below, with breast darker. (Plate 81)

RANGE.—As a species, southwestern Washington, Oregon, southern Idaho, and Wyoming south to Texas, and Arizona through Mexico, including Baja California. *A.c. woodhouseii* is resident from Wyoming, Utah, and Colorado south to northern Chihuahua.

Kansas: an uncommon winter resident locally; New Mexico: permanent resident; Utah: resident in east; Wyoming: rare in southern part of state.

COLORADO.—Common resident in scrub oak, sage, serviceberry or pinyon in the west and southern half of the state.

BLACK-BILLED MAGPIE   *Pica pica hudsonia* (Sabine). [475]

RECOGNITION.—Length 17–21 inches, *Adult:* plumage black, glossed with green, blue, purple, and bronze; belly, sides, scapulars, and bar in primaries white. *Young:* plumage duller, but wings and tail metallic; scapulars washed with rusty. (Plate 83)

RANGE.—As a species, the magpie is a well-known bird of the Northern Hemisphere in Europe, Asia, and North America. This race is resident from Alaska, the middle Yukon, and southwestern Canada to the eastern slope of the Sierra Nevada, western North Dakota, south to western Oklahoma, casual east of normal range to New York and Florida.

Nebraska and Kansas: common resident in west, and uncommon through eastern counties in winter; New Mexico: common to 10,500 feet in summer in north, straggling to southern part in winter; Utah: permanent resident; Wyoming: abundant resident.

COLORADO.—Common species of the Upper Sonoran Zone into the Transition, occasionally ranging to timberline.

COMMON RAVEN   *Corvus corax sinuatus* Wagler. [486]

RECOGNITION.—Length 21–26 inches. *Adult:* plumage black, somewhat glossed with blue, green, and purplish. *Young:* plumage lusterless and belly brownish. (Plate 82)

RANGE.—The species ranges through much of northern Europe, Asia, and North America. This race is resident from the mountains of south-central British Columbia, Oregon, Montana, and North Dakota south through western Oklahoma, Arizona, Texas, California, and Mexico (except Baja California) to Nicaragua.

Nebraska: no record since 1900; Kansas: formerly on high plains, no recent records; New Mexico: rather uncommon resident of mountains and lower canyons and mesas; Utah: fairly common in desert regions, especially in west and southeast; Wyoming: common resident northwest mountains, uncommon elsewhere.

COLORADO.—A fairly common bird of the mountains and western areas of the state.

WHITE-NECKED RAVEN   *Corvus cryptoleucus* Couch. [487]

RECOGNITION.—Length 19–21 inches. Like the Common Raven, but smaller, and larger than the Common Crow. The white bases of the neck feathers are concealed and are not good field marks. Bent (1948) states they may be distinguished from crows by the raven's "less open-throated and distinctly lower-pitched and gutteral voice." (Plate 82)

RANGE.—Resident on the dry plains area of southeastern Colorado, ranging southward through New Mexico and southern Arizona into Mexico.

Nebraska: an uncommon resident in Adams and Kearney Counties; Kansas: common summer resident in west, rare in winter; New Mexico: common in summer and breeding on the arid unforested eastern and southeastern part of the state; Wyoming: uncommon migrant, breeds locally, and occasionally winters.

COLORADO.—Formerly abundant on the eastern plains along the foothills but now absent from much of the former range.

COMMON CROW   *Corvus brachyrhynchos brachyrhynchos* Brehm. [488]

RECOGNITION.—Length 17–20 inches; *Adult:* plumage black, glossed with blue, green, and purple. *Young:* plumage browner. (Plate 82)

RANGE.—The species occurs from British Columbia across southern Canada to Quebec and Newfoundland, south to southern Florida, along the Gulf of Mexico to Texas, and to Arizona and Baja California. This race has a wide breeding range from the east coast of North America to Alberta, Montana, Wyoming, and Arizona, southward to the Gulf of Mexico.

Nebraska and Kansas: occurs commonly in both states in eastern counties, and less so in west; New Mexico: breeds in north and east, and winters in numbers south to Las Cruces; Utah: uncommon resident in valleys and common locally in winter; Wyoming: uncommon migrant, breeding locally and occasionally wintering.

COLORADO.—Common resident in the northeastern prairie counties, and casually throughout the rest of the state.

PINYON JAY   *Gymnorhinus cyanocephalus* Wied. [492]

RECOGNITION.—Length 10–11.5 inches; uniformly blue with uncrested head. *Adult male:* plumage grayish-blue, brightest on head, and with gray streaked throat. *Adult female:* plumage grayer. *Young:* like female, with only wings and tail blue. (Plate 83)

RANGE.—Resident from central Oregon, Montana, and western South Dakota south through eastern California to Baja California, Nevada, western Texas, and western Oklahoma. Wanders throughout the Great Basin to southwestern Saskatchewan.

Nebraska: fairly common breeder in the Panhandle, occasionally wintering in Lincoln and Logan Counties; irregular visitor, more frequent in the west; New Mexico: breeding in pinyon from 5500 to 7400 feet, and wandering widely in nonnesting season; Utah: fairly common resident of the pinyon-juniper belt; Wyoming: locally common in pinyon-juniper associations; Kansas: irregular winter visitor.

COLORADO.—Common breeding bird of pinyon-juniper areas, occasionally wandering in flocks at other seasons.

CLARK'S NUTCRACKER   *Nucifraga columbiana* (Wilson). [491]

RECOGNITION.—Length 12–13 inches; plumage gray, except black wings and middle tail feathers; face, tips of secondaries, and outer tail feathers white. *Young:* plumage duller, with wing coverts tipped with brownish and breast speckled with white. (Plate 83)

RANGE.—Resident from central British Columbia and southwestern Alberta south through central Montana, Nevada, Washington, and eastern California to Baja California, and south in the Rocky Mountains to eastern Arizona.

Nebraska: occasional records throughout the state; Kansas: irregular winter visitor; New Mexico: resident in mountains from 8,000 feet to timberline; Utah: fairly common summer resident in mountains; Wyoming: resident in mountains.

COLORADO.—Common resident of the coniferous forests to timberline.

Family PARIDAE: Chickadees, Titmice, and Bushtits

BLACK-CAPPED CHICKADEE   *Parus atricapillus septentrionalis* Harris. [735a]

RECOGNITION.—Length 4.75–5.5 inches. Upper parts grayish, under parts whitish, with throat and top of head black, and sides washed with buff. (Plate 84)

RANGE.—The species ranges from Central Alaska across Canada south to Virginia and North Carolina to eastern Tennessee. This race is resident from southern Yukon, British Columbia, Alberta, Mackenzie, Saskatchewan, Manitoba, and Montana to North Dakota, wandering in winter to Oklahoma and northern Texas.

Nebraska: *P.a. atricapillus* common resident; Kansas: *P. a. atricapillus* in east and *septentrionalis* in west; New Mexico: fairly common summer resident in northern mountains, but only one nest recorded; Utah: species permanent resident, with race *garrinus* in east and *nevadensis* in west; Wyoming: common in mountainous areas, and at lower elevations in winter.

COLORADO.—Resident, nesting from the plains and foothills to 9000 feet, and wintering mostly below 8000 feet in the eastern two-thirds of the state, being replaced by *P.a. garrinus* or intermediates in western counties.

Parus atricapillus garrinus Behle. [735h]

RECOGNITION.—Differs from the preceding form by having a browner back without the gray tone.

RANGE.—Breeds in eastern Idaho, southwestern and south-central Montana, central and western Wyoming, central and western Colorado, northern New Mexico, and eastern Utah.

COLORADO.—Occurs in the west-central and southwestern part of the state.

MOUNTAIN CHICKADEE   *Parus gambeli gambeli* Ridgway. [738]

RECOGNITION.—Length 5–5.5 inches. Similar to Black-capped Chickadee, but with a *white line over the eye;* under parts usually grayer. (Plate 84)

RANGE.—Resident in the Rocky Mountains from Montana and Wyoming south to southeastern Texas and eastern Arizona.

New Mexico: common summer resident in mountains; Utah: species resident in mountains; Wyoming: common in mountains in summer, and lower elevations in winter.

COLORADO.—Common resident in the coniferous forests from foothills to timberline; many occur on the plains and in low valleys in winter.

PLAIN TITMOUSE   *Parus inornatus ridgwayi* Richmond. [733a]

RECOGNITION.—Length 5–5.5 inches. Plain, unmarked gray, with a conspicuous crest. (Plate 84)

RANGE.—The species inhabits the lower mountains of western United States, south to Baja California, usually being confined to the pinyon-juniper forest or, in far west, to oaks. The easternmost race *P.i. ridgwayi* is resident locally from northeastern Nevada and southeastern Idaho to southeastern California, and from Wyoming to western Oklahoma, western Texas, and northeastern Arizona.

New Mexico: common resident of wooded foothills between 4000 and 7000 feet; Utah: permanent resident of the pinyon-juniper belt; Wyoming: uncommon, in the lower Green River valley only.

COLORADO.—Common in the pinyon-juniper country of the southern and western parts of the state.

COMMON BUSHTIT   *Psaltriparus minimus plumbeus* (Baird). [744]

RECOGNITION.—Length 4–4.5 inches. A small, uncrested, plain bird with a long tail; brownish-gray above and lighter below. (Plate 84)

RANGE.—Species resident from southern British Columbia east to Colorado and south to Texas, Sonora, and through Baja California. The race *plumbeus* from Oregon south through eastern California, east to Colorado, western Oklahoma, and Texas.

New Mexico and Utah: fairly common resident, chiefly in the pinyon-juniper association; Wyoming: straggler.

COLORADO.—Fairly common resident in the dry chaparral and pinyon-juniper areas of southern and western counties, ranging northward in winter along the east slope of the foothills.

Family SITTIDAE: Nuthatches

WHITE-BREASTED NUTHATCH   *Sitta carolinensis nelsoni* Mearns. [727c]

RECOGNITION.—Length 5–6 inches. Top of head and neck black in male, grayish-black in female; rest of upper parts grayish-blue; under parts white, with rusty flanks and abdomen. Nuthatches often work with heads downward. (Plate 85)

RANGE.—The species occurs from British Columbia across southern Canada to New Brunswick and south, except over the treeless Great Plains, to Baja California and Mexico. The race *S.c. nelsoni* is a resident of the Rocky Mountain region from Montana and South Dakota south to western Texas and Arizona.

Nebraska: resident in the Pine Ridge region; Kansas: three races recorded with *nelsoni* listed from Morton Co.; New Mexico: summer resident between 7000 and 8000 feet, ranging lower in winter; Utah and Wyoming: fairly common resident in mountains.

COLORADO.—Resident, nesting on the plains and commonly from the foothills to 9500 feet, and less frequently at higher altitudes.

RED-BREASTED NUTHATCH   *Sitta canadensis* Linnaeus. [728]

RECOGNITION.—Length 4–4.5 inches. Smaller than White-breasted Nuthatch. Has a conspicuous black line through the eye, with white line above it, and under parts chestnut, except throat white. (Plate 85)

RANGE.—Breeding chiefly in the Canadian Zone of Canada, southern Alaska, and the northern states, and in western mountains to California and Arizona, and through the Appalachians to eastern Tennessee; winters throughout much of its lower breeding range to Arizona and the Gulf coast.

Nebraska: common winter visitor in east, less so in west; Kansas: uncommon migrant and winter visitor; New Mexico: uncommon in fall and winter; Utah: fairly common resident in mountains; Wyoming: common resident of mountains, often ranging to lower elevations.

COLORADO.—Occurs on the plains in winter and breeds in Transition Zone, ranging upward to timberline in summer.

PYGMY NUTHATCH   *Sitta pygmaea melanotis* van Rossem. [730b]

RECOGNITION.—Length 4–4.5 inches. Upper parts blue-gray, top of head brownish and nape white; dull white below. The unusually short tail aids in identification, especially when the bird is in flight. Has a constant chattering of high-pitched notes, "tee-dee, tee-dee," quite unlike those of the other nuthatches. (Plate 85)

RANGE.—Resident of the Transition Zone of western United States from southern British Columbia east to South Dakota and south to Texas, Arizona, and into the highlands of Mexico.

Nebraska: resident in the Pine Ridge region; Kansas: specimen Sedgwick Co. Dec. 30, 1961, and observed in Wichita winter of 1961–62 (L. B. Carson); New Mexico and Utah: common breeding bird and winter resident; Wyoming: uncommon resident of southern mountains, more widely distributed in mountains in winter.

COLORADO.—Common in the ponderosa pine forests of the Transition Zone throughout the state.

Family CERTHIIDAE: Creepers

BROWN CREEPER   *Certhia familiaris montana* Ridgway. [726b]

RECOGNITION.—Length 5–5.5 inches. Plain brownish above and white below, with a slender, down-curved bill and long, stiff tail feathers. (Plate 85)

RANGE.—The species is circumpolar in distribution; in North America occurs in the coniferous forests throughout Canada and the northern states, and south in the western mountains into New Mexico. The race *C.f. montana* breeds from southern Alaska, central British Columbia, Oregon, and Washington east to central Saskatchewan and southward to western Texas and Arizona, and individuals winter at lower elevations, or south of their nesting range.

Nebraska: *C.f. americana* common winter visitor in the east, and *C.f. montana* rare in Pine Ridge region; Kansas: *C.f. americana* fairly common transient and winter visitor; New Mexico and Utah: fairly common resident; Wyoming: uncommon resident, common migrant and winter visitor.

COLORADO.—Resident, breeding from 7000 feet to timberline, and wintering from 9000 feet to the plains.

Family CINCLIDAE: Dippers

DIPPER   *Cinclus mexicanus unicolor* Bonaparte. [701]

RECOGNITION.—Length 7–8 inches. Chunky, short-tailed, plain slate-colored, and lighter below; usually found near water. (Plate 86)

RANGE.—The species is resident from the Aleutian Islands, north-central Alaska, central Yukon, Alberta, Montana, and South Dakota south to southern California, Arizona, and through the highlands of Mexico to Panama.

Nebraska: specimen collected in Chase Co. June 2, 1903, and sight record in Sioux Co.; New Mexico: common along many of northern streams; Utah: common resident along mountain streams throughout the state; Wyoming: common breeder, occasionally wintering at lower elevations.

COLORADO.—Occurs from the foothills to timberline along streams in summer, and ranges in winter along open water at lower elevations.

Early nesting: May 6, 1967 fully-fledged young out of nest under bridge near Morrison at approx. 6000 ft. elevation (Harold Holt, pers. comm.).

Family TROGLODYTIDAE: Wrens

HOUSE WREN   *Troglodytes aedon parkmanii* Audubon. [721a]

RECOGNITION.—Length 4.5–5 inches. *Adults:* gray-brown above, with fine black barring on back, wings, and tail; under parts washed with gray-brown, lighter on throat; superciliary line lacking; faint barring on flanks. *Young:* similar to adults, but breast feathers edged with brown. (Plate 86)

RANGE.—The species occurs across southern Canada south throughout much of the central states into Mexico. This race breeds from eastern British Columbia, Alberta, southern Saskatchewan, Manitoba, and central Ontario south to Arizona and Baja California. Winters from extreme southern United States to southern Mexico.

Nebraska and Kansas: common migrant and summer resident in east, less so in west; New Mexico: common summer resident, breeding between 7000 and 8500 feet; Utah: fairly common summer resident in the mountains, wintering in southern valleys; Wyoming: common breeder and migrant.

COLORADO.—Common summer resident, breeding from the plains into the mountains to 10,000 feet; occasionally winters.

Troglodytes aedon baldwini Oberholser. [721b]

RECOGNITION.—*Adult:* Similar to the western race, but much browner above.

RANGE.—Breeds from Michigan, southern Ontario, and southwestern Quebec south to South Carolina, Kentucky, Tennessee, and Georgia. Winters south of breeding range to Texas and the Gulf coast.

COLORADO.—Recorded breeding in Morgan Co. July 19, 1947.

WINTER WREN   *Troglodytes troglodytes pacificus* Baird. [722a]

RECOGNITION.—Length 4–4.5 inches. Upper parts dark brown, with wings and tail finely barred with blackish, and a buffy line over the eye. Under parts brownish, the flanks heavily barred with black and white. Tail very short, square, and held erect. Bobs continually. (Plate 86)

RANGE.—The species ranges through regions of Europe, Asia, and North America. This western race breeds in southeastern Alaska and the Yukon, British Columbia south along the Pacific Coast to central California and casually to western Montana. Winters from breeding range south to southern California, Nevada, and rarely to Arizona.

Nebraska and Kansas: *hiemalis* listed as uncommon migrant and winter resident; New Mexico, Utah, and Wyoming: *pacificus* considered the wintering race.

COLORADO.—Uncommon winter resident.

Late spring May 21 M.H.D.C.; early fall Sept. 23 Julesburg.

BEWICK'S WREN   *Thryomanes bewickii eremophilus* Oberholser. [719b]

RECOGNITION.—Length 5–5.5 inches. Upper parts deep cinnamon-brown, tail and wings finely barred with blackish; under parts grayish-white, with brownish flanks. Tail rounded, with outer feathers white-tipped; conspicuous white line over eye. (Plate 86)

RANGE.—This wren, as a species, is resident from British Columbia, Washington, eastern California, Nevada, Utah, and Wyoming east to Ontario, Pennsylvania, and Virginia, south to Gulf states and into Mexico. In winter wanders to deserts of the Southwest and southward.

Nebraska: this subspecies rare summer resident in western third of the state, *T.b. bewickii* uncommon in southeast; Kansas: species common in south, but status of races poorly known; New Mexico: resident from 4000 to 7000 feet in oak, pinyon, and juniper; Utah: common in south, rare in north; Wyoming: uncommon breeder of lower Green River valley only.

COLORADO.—Birds of this race are fairly numerous in the pinyon-juniper country of the southern and western parts of the state.

CAROLINA WREN   *Thryothorus ludovicianus ludovicianus* (Latham). [718]

RECOGNITION.—Length 5.5–6 inches. Upper parts reddish-brown, wings and tail finely barred with blackish, and a white line over the eye; under parts buffy, and throat white. (Plate 86)

RANGE.—Resident locally from eastern Nebraska, Minnesota, Wisconsin, Michigan, and southern Ontario east to Massachusetts, and south to the Gulf coast and Texas.

Nebraska: uncommon summer resident in southeast, recorded west to North Platte and north to Stapleton; Kansas: common resident in south, fewer in north and west; New Mexico: rare visitor, with five records, principally Pecos and Rio Grande Valleys.

COLORADO.—Rare visitor. The ten records include observations from Ft. Morgan, Colo. Springs, Palmer Lake (El Paso Co.), Platteville, Weldona, and a specimen (C.U. no. 6203) collected in Boulder Nov. 18, 1956; one observed at Lakewood several times in summer of 1964 and June 6–7, 1965 (C.B.N. 13:18); one at Bonny Res. Apr. 30, 1966 (A.F.N. 20:524); one banded at Lyons by Allegra Collister July 14, 1966 (pers. comm.); and one for 3 weeks in Wheat Ridge from Mar. 17, 1966 (Mrs. R. M. Wilson, pers. comm.).

LONG-BILLED MARSH WREN   *Telmatodytes palustris plesius* (Oberholser). [725c]

RECOGNITION.—Length 4.5–5.5 inches. Upper parts brown, the top of the head very dark, and the middle of the back streaked with white and blackish-brown; under parts white, with buffy sides; a white line over the eye. (Plate 87)

RANGE.—The species ranges across southern Canada from British Columbia to Quebec and throughout much of the United States except the southern Great Plains. Winters mostly in southern part of breeding range and south to Central Mexico, a few wintering almost throughout the summer range. This race occurs from British Columbia east to Wyoming and Nebraska, and south to central-eastern California and southwestern Texas.

Nebraska: migrant, and common breeder in Sandhill Lakes region; Kansas: *T.p. dissaeptus* uncommon transient and breeder; New Mexico: migrant, and nests locally along lakes near Grants; Utah: common resident in marshes; Wyoming: common summer resident with few in winter.

COLORADO.—Winter resident in Upper Sonoran marshes throughout the state, and breeds in San Luis Valley.

SHORT-BILLED MARSH WREN   *Cistothorus platensis stellaris* (Naumann). [724]

RECOGNITION.—Length 4–4.5 inches. Upper parts brown, streaked with black and white; under parts buffy, darker on sides. Streaked crown and lack of light line over the eye distinguish it from the Long-billed Marsh Wren. (Plate 87)

RANGE.—The species breeds locally from Saskatchewan eastward across much of Canada to New Brunswick, and southward in northern states through South Dakota to Virginia, west to Arkansas, and south through central Mexico, Central America, and South America to Tierra del Fuego and the Falkland Islands. The North American race winters to the Gulf coast and southern Florida.

Nebraska: uncommon migrant and rare breeder in eastern counties; Kansas: uncommon migrant in east, with one breeding record from Douglas Co. Aug. 30, 1950; Wyoming: straggler.

COLORADO.—Alamosa Co. (Cary, 1909, 184). One observed along Bonny Reservoir May 19, 1957 (C.B.N. 4:73), and a pair along Latham Reservoir Aug. 9, 1957 (5:9). Reported nesting in Monte Vista Wildlife Refuge in July 1965 by H. W. Goard (pers. comm.), and observed at Bonny Res. Mar. 30, 1966 (A.F.N. 20:524).

CANYON WREN   *Salpinctes mexicanus conspersus* Ridgway. [717a]

RECOGNITION.—Length 5–5.5 inches. Upper parts brown, the head grayer than the back, and the tail bright reddish-brown with blackish bars; throat conspicuously white, and under parts dark chestnut. (Plate 87)

RANGE.—Resident in the lower mountains and hills from British Columbia, California, Washington, and Oregon east to South Dakota, and south to Oklahoma and Texas, into Mexico and Baja California.

New Mexico and Utah: fairly common resident locally; Wyoming: uncommon summer resident.

COLORADO.—A fairly numerous resident of the dry canyons and escarpments of the southern two-thirds of the state at elevations below 8000 feet.

ROCK WREN   *Salpinctes obsoletus obsoletus* (Say). [715]

RECOGNITION.—Length 5–6 inches. Upper parts grayish-brown, finely spotted with black and white, the rounded tail browner, barred with black and tipped with white or pale buff; under parts dull white, the flanks buffy, and the breast finely streaked. (Plate 87)

RANGE.—A western species with six recognized races, three of which are island forms. This subspecies breeds locally from British Columbia, Alberta, Saskatchewan, and North Dakota, and southeast of the coast ranges from Washington to Baja California; winters in parts of northern breeding ranges.

Nebraska and Kansas: a common migrant, resident in the western counties and rare in east; New Mexico and Utah: common summer resident, wintering in smaller numbers; Wyoming: almost an abundant summer resident.

COLORADO.—Common migrant in April on the plains and in low valleys, breeding to 12,000 feet.

Early spring Mar. 3 Denver; late fall Nov. 13 Denver; numerous winter references.

Family MIMIDAE: Mockingbirds and Thrashers

MOCKINGBIRD   *Mimus polyglottos leucopterus* (Vigors). [703a]

RECOGNITION.—Length 9.5–11 inches. A slender bird with a long tail; gray above, lighter below, with conspicuous white wing patches and outer tail feathers. (Plate 88)

RANGE.—The species is resident throughout much of the United States into Mexico, except in the mountains, and most common in the southern half of its range. The race *M.p. leucopterus* occurs locally from California and Oregon south to Baja California and east to central Texas and South Dakota. Winters generally throughout the breeding range.

Nebraska: both races occur uncommonly, *M.p. leucopterus* in the Panhandle and in Lincoln and Logan Counties, and *polyglottos* in the east; Kansas: both races resident, with *M.p. leucopterus* in west (majority of specimens intermediate); New Mexico and Utah: statewide resident; Wyoming: uncommon summer resident in the south, and occasionally winters.

COLORADO.—Uncommon summer resident in southern half of the state on both sides of the Continental Divide. Occurs occasionally in winter.

CATBIRD   *Dumetella carolinensis* (Linnaeus). [704]

RECOGNITION.—Length 8–9 inches. Dark gray, with top of head blackish and under tail coverts chestnut. (Plate 88)

RANGE.—Breeds from southern British Columbia across southern Canada to Nova Scotia, and from eastern Washington and Oregon to Utah and Colorado, south to Arizona and east to Florida, and in Bermuda. Winters occasionally in much of breeding range, but usually from southern states through eastern Mexico to Panama.

Nebraska: common migrant and summer resident, except uncommon in the Panhandle region; Kansas: common migrant and summer resident; New Mexico: uncommon summer resident; Utah: fairly common in the north, uncommon elsewhere; Wyoming: common summer resident.

COLORADO.—Common migrant in mid-May, and summer resident on the eastern plains and in foothills; less numerous in the west.

Early spring Apr. 19 Boulder (C.B.N. 3:64); late fall Nov. 13 Boulder Co. (no. 28049).

BROWN THRASHER   *Toxostoma rufum longicauda* (Baird). [705a]

RECOGNITION.—Length 10–11.5 inches. Upper parts bright rufous-red, under parts streaked with brown; iris yellow, tail long, and bill curved. (Plate 89)

RANGE.—The species breeds across southern Canada from southeastern Alberta to southwestern Quebec and south through New England states and Montana to Texas and the Gulf coast. This race occupies the western part of the range. Winters from eastern Oklahoma to Louisiana, and casually in breeding range.

Nebraska and Kansas: common migrant, and summer resident in west (both races occur); New Mexico: rather uncommon in migration; Utah: casual (four specimen records); Wyoming: common summer resident and migrant, rarely wintering.

COLORADO.—A fairly common summer and occasional winter resident in the eastern part of the state. Recorded from Gunnison Co. Oct. 12, 1952.

LONG-BILLED THRASHER   *Toxostoma longirostre sennetti* (Ridgway). [706]

RECOGNITION.—Length 10.5–12 inches. Upper parts dark brown; under parts white, streaked with black. Tail long, and bill somewhat curved. The darker color and longer bill distinguish it from the Brown Thrasher. (Plate 89)

RANGE.—Resident from southern Texas south into northeastern Mexico.

COLORADO.—Female (no. 2359) collected by L. J. Hersey at Barr, Adams Co., in May 1906 (Lincoln, 1919). One observed in Red Rocks Park west of Denver by D. M. Thatcher on Aug. 21, 1949 (pers. comm.).

BENDIRE'S THRASHER   *Toxostoma bendirei* (Coues). [708]

RECOGNITION.—Length 9–10.5 inches. Pale gray-brown above, and under parts paler, tinged with rust on flanks; breast faintly spotted, wing bars indistinct; iris yellow. *Young:* similar to adults, but under parts streaked. (Plate 89)

RANGE.—Breeds from southeastern California, Nevada, and Arizona south to Sinaloa. Winters from southern Arizona into Mexico.

New Mexico: fairly common in southwest in thorn and cactus environment; Utah: probably occurs regularly in San Juan area, reported Apr. 20 to May 15, 1966 (A.F.N. 20:536).

COLORADO.—Female (no. 6729) collected in El Paso Co. on May 8, 1882.

CURVE-BILLED THRASHER   *Toxostoma curvirostre celsum* Moore. [707]

RECOGNITION.—Length 9.5–11 inches. Above *brownish-gray,* tail darker, with outer feathers *tipped with white;* two narrow white wing bars; bill curved, throat white, and breast and sides spotted with dark gray; iris reddish. (Plate 89)

RANGE.—Semidesert region of southern New Mexico, western Oklahoma, western Texas, and southeastern Arizona, southward into Mexico.

Nebraska: several observed and one collected near North Platte in spring of 1936 (*T.c. palmeri*); New Mexico: resident in northeastern and southern dry valleys.

COLORADO.—One record, an adult male taken Mar. 25, 1951 two miles southwest of Granada, Prowers Co., the specimen being in the collection of Western State College at Gunnison; and an observation at Barr Lake May 15, 1967, reported by Lois Webster (pers. comm.).

SAGE THRASHER   *Oreoscoptes montanus* (Townsend). [702]

RECOGNITION.—Length 8–9 inches. Gray-brown above, with wings and tail darker, two wing bars and outer tail feathers tipped with white; under parts white to buff, streaked on breast and sides with brown; iris yellow. *Young:* browner above, more streaking below. (Plate 89)

RANGE.—Breeds from southern British Columbia and central Idaho east to Wyoming, south through eastern Washington and Oregon to central-southern California, western Oklahoma, and northern Texas. Winters from southern California and central Texas into Mexico and casually northward to Nevada and Colorado.

Nebraska: rare resident in Sioux Co., and casual migrant; Kansas: uncommon transient in west (two specimens, Finney Co., 1954, nesting in Morton Co. in 1963); New Mexico: fairly common summer resident in sage habitat; Utah and Wyoming: common summer resident in sage areas.

COLORADO.—Common spring and fall migrant on both sides of the Continental Divide, but more abundant in western counties, breeding commonly in sage habitats. Occurs occasionally in winter—Dec. 31 Durango and Feb. 10 Cherry Creek Res. (C.B.N. 9:9, 26).

Family TURDIDAE: Thrushes, Bluebirds, and Solitaires

ROBIN   *Turdus migratorius propinquus* Ridgway. [761a]

RECOGNITION.—Length 9.5–11 inches. *Male:* head, wings, and tail gray-black, with back olive-gray; under parts bright cinnamon except black and white streakings on throat; little, if any, white on end of tail. *Female:* head grayer and under parts duller. *Young:* spotted below, streaked above. (Plate 90)

RANGE.—The species breeds throughout much of North America from the limit of trees to Mexico and Guatemala, and this western race from southeastern British Columbia, Alberta, Saskatchewan, Montana, and South Dakota south to southern California and northern Mexico. Winters from the southern half of breeding range to Baja California, Sonora, and Durango.

Nebraska: as a species, common in summer and locally common in winter, with both this race and *T.m. migratorius* represented; Kansas: three subspecies recorded, this form more common in west, especially in migration, and irregular in winter; New Mexico: breeding in mountains above 6500 feet, and occurring throughout the state in migration; Utah: abundant summer resident from valleys into the mountains, small numbers in lowlands in winter; Wyoming: common summer resident, with few in winter.

COLORADO.—Common in summer from plains into the mountains; few in winter, these probably being migrants from the north. Center of abundance throughout the state in the Upper Sonoran Zone but recorded breeding to timberline.

Turdus migratorius migratorius Linnaeus. [761]

RECOGNITION.—Length 9.5–11 inches. Similar to the western Robin but with considerable white on tips of tail.

RANGE.—Breeds from northwestern Alaska, northern Yukon, Mackenzie, Manitoba, Quebec, and Nova Scotia south to British Columbia, Alberta, Saskatchewan, and North Dakota, south to Oklahoma, and east locally throughout the Appalachians to northwestern Virginia. Winters from South Dakota, Iowa and Missouri to Tennessee, and from eastern Massachusetts south to Florida, the Gulf coast, and Mexico.

Nebraska: common summer resident, probably most numerous in east and local in winter; Kansas: common transient and summer resident, and local winter resident; Wyoming: straggler only.

COLORADO.—Uncommon. Occasionally occurs in eastern Colorado.

* VARIED THRUSH   *Ixoreus naevius meruloides* (Swainson). [763a]

RECOGNITION.—Length 9–10 inches. *Male:* dark slate-blue above; eyeline, wing bars, and under parts orange-rust; white spots on lateral tips of tail. *Female:* duller, with breast band obscure. (Plate 90)

RANGE.—Breeds from northern Alaska, Yukon, and Mackenzie south to the Alaskan Peninsula, British Columbia, southwestern Alberta, Washington, and Oregon, and east to northern Idaho and Montana. Winters from British Columbia and Idaho south to Baja California. Casual birds have been recorded east to New York, and AMB (1948) recorded a specimen (no. 22977) from Point Barrow, Alaska.

Nebraska: straggler, several in Lincoln Co. in Dec. 1935 and one collected; Kansas: one specimen taken Finney Co. Oct. 17, 1891; New Mexico: one observed by George Willett on the Rio Grande Bird Reserve Dec. 1, 1916 (Bailey, F. M., 1928); Utah: three sight records; Wyoming: straggler.

COLORADO.—Uncommon winter visitor. Observed near Boulder Dec. 5, 1909; one near Ft. Collins Apr. 11, 1951; one at Fort Morgan between Jan. 15 and Mar. 6, 1957; one at Wheat Ridge Feb. 26 and Mar. 5, 1961; one Boulder Co. May 5, two Golden May 13, and one banded by Allegra Collister in Boulder in Dec. 1961; one in Denver Jan. 1 to Apr. 4, 1962; and one Loveland 1966 Christmas Count (C.F.O., no. 1).

WOOD THRUSH   *Hylocichla mustelina* (Gmelin). [755]

RECOGNITION.—Length 7.5–8.5 inches. *Adult:* rich brown above, particularly on the head; white below, with breast and sides marked with large dark spots; white eyering. *Young:* crown and breast more buffy; wing coverts tipped with rusty. (Plate 90)

RANGE.—Breeds from southern South Dakota, Michigan, southern Ontario, Quebec, and Maine to southern Oklahoma, eastern Texas, Louisiana, Mississippi, and northern Florida. Winters from southern Texas and Florida into Mexico and Panama.

Nebraska and Kansas: common migrant and summer resident in east; Wyoming: straggler, one Casper week of May 29, 1958 (A.F.N. 12:373); Utah: female taken in Salt Lake City Oct. 14, 1963 (Condor, 68:396).

COLORADO.—Casual migrant in eastern counties. One banded in Boulder Oct. 14, 1966 by Berene Sullivan (pers. comm.).

Early spring May 2 Loveland; late fall Nov. 11 Denver.

HERMIT THRUSH   *Hylocichla guttata auduboni* (Baird). [759a]

RECOGNITION.—Length 7–8 inches. Olive-brown above with a diagnostic dark reddish tail which separates this species and its various races from other thrushes. *Young:* breast and sides buffy, spotted with brown; lower belly white. (Plate 91)

RANGE.—The species breeds from central Alaska and southern Yukon across Canada to Newfoundland, south to southern California and New Mexico, and this race from the Transition and Canadian Zones of British Columbia to Montana, south through Idaho and Nevada to Arizona and western Texas. Winters from Mexico south to Guatemala.

Nebraska: occasional in extreme west; Kansas: species uncommon transient, this race probably in west; New Mexico: fairly common breeder in coniferous forests; Utah: common in mountains in summer; Wyoming: migrant and common breeder in mountains.

COLORADO.—Summer resident in the coniferous forests. Breeds commonly in the Transition and Canadian Zones.

Early spring Apr. 12 Golden; late fall Oct. 27 (No. 20541) Morgan Co.; winter Dec. 17 Boulder (C.B.N. 4:42).

Hylocichla guttata oromela Oberholser. [759+]

RECOGNITION.—Length 6–7 inches. Gray above, smaller than *H.g. auduboni,* but cannot be distinguished in the field from other small races.

RANGE.—Breeds from central-northern California, north through central and western Oregon, and central and western Washington, to central British Columbia. Winters south to Baja California and central Texas. Probably a regular migrant east of the Rockies, and of casual occurrence in New Mexico.

Status in neighboring states not determined. Four races listed from New Mexico by F. M. Bailey (1928), and three from Utah by W. H. Behle.

COLORADO.—Probably a regular spring and fall migrant over the eastern prairies.

Hylocichla guttata guttata (Pallas). [759]

RECOGNITION.—Length 6–7 inches. Back dark grayish-brown, slightly smaller than *H.g. auduboni.* May be identified only by comparison of specimens.

RANGE.—Breeds from Nushagak and the Alaskan Peninsula and Kodiak Island east through Cross Sound to southeastern Yukon and south-central British Columbia. Migrates southward in fall through California, Nevada, Colorado, and Texas into northern Mexico. Status of the various small races in states bordering Colorado undetermined.

COLORADO.—Regular migrant in small numbers, probably on both eastern and western slopes.

Early spring Apr. 18 Denver; late fall Oct. 13 Weld Co.

Hylocichla guttata euboria Oberholser. [759+]

RECOGNITION.—Length 6–7 inches. Similar to *H.g. guttata,* "but larger excepting its relatively smaller bill." Not included in the 1957 A.O.U. Check-list.

RANGE.—Breeds from north to southern Yukon, south to central British Columbia. Winters from northern Oklahoma, south-central Texas, and central-western Nuevo Leon.

COLORADO.—Five specimens have been identified as belonging to this race.

Early spring Apr. 22 Adams Co. (no. 10974); late fall Oct. 5 Denver (no. 13549).

Hylocichla guttata crymophila Burleigh and Peters. [759g]

RECOGNITION.—Length 7 inches. Generally similar to *H.g. auduboni,* but slightly smaller and darker. Not possible to distinguish between races in the field.

RANGE.—Breeds throughout Newfoundland. Winter range not known, but recorded in migration in Virginia and Georgia.

COLORADO.—One specimen (no. 19869) found dead in west Denver Feb. 8, 1939.

SWAINSON'S THRUSH *Hylocichla ustulata almae* Oberholser. [758b]

RECOGNITION.—Length 6.5–7.5 inches. Uniformly olive-gray or olive above with conspicuous buffy eyering; sides of head buffy; chest buff with dark streaks, sides olive-brown and belly white. *Young:* breast spotted with dark. (Plate 91)

RANGE.—As a species, breeds from central Alaska across northern Yukon to Quebec, Labrador, and Newfoundland, south to California, and east to Virginia. This race nests from British Columbia, Yukon, western Mackenzie, and west-central Alberta, south through the mountains to Colorado and northwestern Utah. Probably migrates in spring and fall along the Mississippi Valley to the Gulf coast states.

Nebraska and Kansas: species common in migration and status of races uncertain. New Mexico: uncommon summer resident, with one nesting record on the Brazos River July 15, 1951 by Ligon (1961); Utah: uncommon in summer in willows of mountain parks; Wyoming: common migrant and breeder in mountains.

COLORADO.—Common migrant; breeding in mountains.

Early spring Apr. 29 Longmont; late fall Oct. 25 Barr Lake; winter Feb. 18, 1965 (C.B.N. 13:9).

Hylocichla ustulata swainsoni (Tschudi). [758a]

RECOGNITION.—"Resembles *H.u. almae* Oberholser in nuptial plumage except that the upper parts are decidedly more reddish, less grayish olive; sides of head and breast are more buffy and spotting of breast paler. In autumn plumage it is separable by the deep reddish olive of its upper parts, distinctly different from the grayish to brownish olive of *almae* at the same season of the year" (Bond, 1963).

RANGE.—Breeds from eastern Alberta eastward to Newfoundland, and south in the mountains to West Virginia.

Data are lacking for races occurring in states bordering Colorado.

COLORADO.—Probably a regular spring and fall migrant in eastern Colorado.

Early spring May 12 Baca Co. (3772); no fall record.

Hylocichla ustulata ustulata (Nuttall). [758]

RECOGNITION.—Length 6.5–7.5 inches. In breeding season brownish-umber above, buff eyering and cheeks faintly rusty; buffy below, spotted from throat to lower breast with brown; sides gray-brown and lower belly white. Lacks the olive of *swainsoni* and the grayish- to olive-brown upper parts of *almae*.

RANGE.—Breeds from Juneau, Alaska south to northwestern Oregon. Winters mainly to western mainland of Mexico.

New Mexico: one record, May 3, 1892 (F. M. Bailey, 1928, 569).

COLORADO.—There is but one specimen of this far western bird from the state, a female (no. 14631) found dead in City Park, Denver, on Sept. 22, 1934 by H. H. Nininger.

* GRAY-CHEEKED THRUSH   *Hylocichla minima minima* (Lafresnaye). [757]

RECOGNITION.—Length 7–8 inches. Swainson's Thrush is olive-gray above with buffy cheeks and eyering, while this species has gray cheeks and no apparent eyering. (Plate 91)

RANGE.—Breeds locally in northeastern Siberia and to the limit of trees across North America, south to British Columbia, Mackenzie, Saskatchewan, and eastern Quebec. Winters in northern South America.

Nebraska: a common migrant throughout the state; Kansas: fairly common transient in the east: Wyoming: migrant and recorded from Laramie, Cheyenne, and Torrington.

COLORADO.—One observed at Boulder May 20, 1957 (C.B.N. 5:10); one near Golden Apr. 9, 1962 (H. Holt, pers. comm.); one near Lamar May 7, 1963 (C. Snyder, pers. comm.); one at Boulder May 20, 1963 and one near Golden May 24 (11:29); one Golden Apr. 13 & May 31, 1964 (12:17); one Bear Creek, Jeff. Co., May 8, 1965 (13:13); one Denver May 14, 1966 (D.F.O. I, #9); and two Spring Count at Glen Eyrie, Colo. Sprgs. May 14, 1967 (Paul Nesbit party).

VEERY   *Hylocichla fuscescens salicicola* Ridgway. [756a]

RECOGNITION.—Length 6.5–7.5 inches. Uniform brown above; breast buffy, indistinctly spotted with light brown on upper portion; sides washed with gray and belly white. (Plate 91)

RANGE.—Breeds from southern British Columbia, central Alberta, southern Saskatchewan, Manitoba, Ontario, and Quebec south locally across northern states from Oregon to Michigan, and in northeastern Arizona. Winters in northern South America.

Nebraska: uncommon migrant, *H.f. fuscescens* in the east and *H.f. salicicola* more numerous in west; Kansas: migrant, rare in east, fairly common in west; New Mexico: apparently two sight records only; Utah: uncommon summer resident in the north; Wyoming: uncommon migrant in eastern half, breeding in northeast.

COLORADO.—Common in migration; uncommon summer resident.

Early spring May 7 Golden; late fall Oct. 26 Denver.

Hylocichla fuscescens subpallida Burleigh and Duvall. [756c]

RECOGNITION.—"Differs from all other races of *Hylocichla fuscescens* in having upper parts duller, with a gray wash entirely lacking in any other race of Veery examined; crown darker than in *salicicola* . . . buff of throat averaging paler, and less heavily marked with dusky" (Burleigh and Duvall, 1959).

RANGE.—Breeds in northern Washington, east of the Cascades, northern and central Idaho, and western Montana west of Continental Divide.

COLORADO.—Probably a casual migrant through the state. Only one specimen recorded, a female collected in Rio Blanco County September 20, 1948.

EASTERN BLUEBIRD   *Sialia sialis sialis* (Linnaeus). [766]

RECOGNITION.—Length 6.5–7.5 inches. *Male:* bright blue above, under parts cinnamon, and lower belly white. *Female:* gray-blue above, with wings, rump, and tail brighter; under parts duller. *Young:* dark gray above, whiter below; breast and side feathers edged with gray. (Plate 92)

RANGE.—Breeds from southern Saskatchewan, Manitoba, Ontario, southern Quebec, and Nova Scotia south locally to southeastern Texas, Louisiana, and Florida. Winters occasionally from northern states south to the Gulf coast.

Nebraska: common migrant and summer resident, with a few wintering; Kansas: common transient and breeder; New Mexico: straggler, five, two collected at Carlsbad Cavern Dec. 19, 1962 (A.F.N. 17:260); Wyoming: rare migrant and summer resident in eastern third of state.

COLORADO.—Fairly common summer resident along watercourses of eastern prairies; uncommon near foothills.

Early spring Mar. 19 Denver (AMB); late fall Nov. 29 Denver (A.F.N. 17:46).

WESTERN BLUEBIRD   *Sialia mexicana bairdi* Ridgway. [767a]

RECOGNITION.—Length 6.5–7 inches. *Male:* head, throat, and upper parts blue, except rufous back and scapulars; breast and sides rufous; mid-belly gray-blue fading to white below. In winter the blue is obscured by brown feather edgings. *Female:* blue subdued to gray-brown except on wings, rump, and tail; under parts duller. *Young:* plumage gray, flecked with white; blue tint on wings and tail. (Plate 92)

RANGE.—The species breeds from British Columbia and Montana, southern Nevada, Utah, and Colorado south to Mexico. *S.m. bairdi* ranges from Utah, Colorado, New Mexico, and west-central Texas to Durango and Zacatecas, Mexico. Winters from southern Utah and southern Colorado to Sonora and Zacatecas, Mexico.

Nebraska: occasional migrant in west; Kansas: no specimen but possible winter straggler; New Mexico: summer resident throughout the forested areas and common in winter; Utah: common summer resident; Wyoming: rare migrant and summer resident in southwest.

COLORADO.—Fairly common summer resident in Transition Zone throughout the state. Occurs occasionally in winter.

MOUNTAIN BLUEBIRD   *Sialia currucoides* (Bechstein). [768]

RECOGNITION.—Length 6.5–7.5 inches. *Male:* bright cerulean-blue, paler below, with belly white. *Female:* upper parts gray-brown, with primaries, rump, and tail pale blue; under parts washed with gray, with belly dull white. *Young:* plumage gray flecked with white; wings and tail pale blue. (Plate 92)

RANGE.—Breeds from central Alaska, southern Yukon, southern Mackenzie, Saskatchewan, and Manitoba south along the eastern slope of coast ranges and Rocky Mountains to southern California and Nevada to Arizona. Winters from British Columbia, California, and Montana south into Mexico.

Nebraska: common summer resident in western third of state, and in winter where food is available; Kansas: common winter resident in west and irregular in east; New Mexico: common in mountains, and at lower elevations in winter; Utah: common summer resident in valleys, uncommon in high mountains, and a few winter; Wyoming: common migrant and breeder, and wintering except in severe weather.

COLORADO.—Common summer resident, occasionally numerous in winter.

* WHEATEAR   *Oenanthe oenanthe oenanthe* (Linnaeus). [765]

RECOGNITION.—Length 5.5–6 inches. *Male:* ashy gray above; black on wings and end of tail; basal two-thirds of tail white (except middle feathers); forehead, superciliary stripe, and upper tail coverts white. *Female:* duller, with black replaced by dusky. (Plate 91)

RANGE.—Breeds in northern Alaska, northern Canada, British Isles, Sweden, Finland, Russia, and Siberia, south to France, and from Italy to Turkestan.

COLORADO.—Minot (1880) writes "one specimen at Boulder," taken May 14, 1880.

TOWNSEND'S SOLITAIRE   *Myadestes townsendi townsendi* (Audubon). [754]

RECOGNITION.—Length 8–9.5 inches. Gray-brown with wings and tail darker; white eyering; two buff wing patches; lateral edges of tail white. *Young:* similar to adults, but spotted above and below with white. (Plate 92)

RANGE.—Breeds from east-central Alaska, southern Yukon, Mackenzie, mountains of Alberta, Montana, Nevada, and California, south through the Rockies to Arizona. Winters from British Columbia, Montana, and lower part of breeding range to Baja California.

Nebraska: an irregular migrant, locally common in winter where food is available, and uncommon summer resident in Pine Ridge region; Kansas: winter resident in small numbers; New Mexico: fairly common nesting bird in the mountains, especially in the Sangre de Cristo Range, wintering at lower elevations; Utah: common summer resident in mountains, wintering occasionally in the valleys; Wyoming: common resident in the mountains and foothills.

COLORADO:—Common summer resident in Transition to Hudsonian Zone; occasional in winter at lower elevations and far out on the plains.

Family SYLVIIDAE: Old World Warblers, Gnatcatchers, and Kinglets

BLUE-GRAY GNATCATCHER   *Polioptila caerulea amoenissima* Grinnell. [751b]

RECOGNITION.—Length 4–5 inches. *Male:* blue-gray above, with black U-shaped forehead mark; wings darker with pale edgings; tail black with outer tail feathers white; under parts white to gray. *Female:* plumage duller and black forehead mark lacking. *Young:* like the female but browner above. (Plate 93)

RANGE.—Breeds from northern California and central Nevada east to Colorado below 7000 feet, and south into Mexico. Winters from southern California, Nevada, and Arizona southward into Mexico.

Nebraska: uncommon migrant, but a fairly common breeder along streams of eastern counties; Kansas: common transient and summer resident in east; New Mexico: common summer resident of the brushy canyons of the central and southwest counties between 5000 and 6500 feet; Utah: common summer resident of the pinyons and junipers; Wyoming: rare summer resident in southern half.

COLORADO.—Fairly common summer resident in southern and western counties.

Early spring Apr. 16 R.Mt.N.P. (A.F.N. 20:536); late fall Nov. 14 Denver.

GOLDEN-CROWNED KINGLET   *Regulus satrapa amoenus* van Rossem. [748c]

RECOGNITION.—Length 3.5–4 inches. *Male:* olive-green above with wings and tail dusky; crown patch orange-red bordered successively by yellow, black, and white lines; two pale yellow wing bars; under parts yellow-white. *Female:* like the male but mid-crown yellow. *Young:* plumage browner; head grayer with crown colors lacking. (Plate 93)

RANGE.—The species breeds from the Kenai Peninsula, southeastern Alaska, British Columbia, and across southern Canada to Newfoundland, south to southern California, western North Carolina, and Guatemala. This western race occurs from the Kenai and adjacent islands, the interior of British Columbia, southern California, and in the Rocky Mountain region of Nevada, Utah, and Colorado. Winters over much of the breeding range.

Nebraska and Kansas: *R.s. satrapa* common migrant, and uncommon winter resident; New Mexico: *R.s. apache* breeding uncommonly in northern mountains, and winter resident to southward; Utah: fairly common summer resident in coniferous forests.

COLORADO.—Uncommon summer resident in mountains, nesting above 8000 feet. A few in winter upon the plains.

RUBY-CROWNED KINGLET   *Regulus calendula cineraceus* Grinnell. [749c]

RECOGNITION.—Length 3.4–5 inches. *Male:* olive-gray above with crown patch red, rump olive-green, and wings and tail dusky; two wing bars; eyering white, and underparts gray to yellow-white. *Female:* red crown patch lacking. (Plate 93)

RANGE.—The species breeds from northwestern Alaska, Mackenzie, Manitoba, and Ontario to Nova Scotia, and south to New Mexico, Arizona, and central Mexico. This western race breeds from the mountains of British Columbia, Montana, California, and Colorado south into Arizona. Winters from breeding areas south into Mexico.

Nebraska and Kansas: *R.c. calendula* uncommon migrant in east, and rare winter resident; New Mexico: nests from 8000 feet to timberline in the Sangre de Cristo Range, and common winter resident; Utah: common summer resident, wintering in the lowlands; Wyoming: common migrant, and summer resident in mountains.

COLORADO.—Fairly common in migration, in summer, and a few winter.

Family MOTACILLIDAE: Wagtails and Pipits

WATER PIPIT   *Anthus spinoletta alticola* Todd. [697b]

RECOGNITION.—Length 6–7 inches. Olive-brown above, faintly streaked; superciliary line and two wing bars buff; outer tail feathers white; under parts uniform rich buff with few or no streaks on breast in contrast to the dark breasts of the *rubescens*. In winter, browner above and more heavily streaked below. *Young:* similar to adults with heavy streaks on back as well as on breast. (Plate 93)

RANGE.—The species is irregularly distributed on tundras and mountains of Scandinavia, Europe, Asia, northwestern Africa, Alaska, and Canada. This race breeds on the mountaintops from Utah, Colorado, and New Mexico to Arizona. Winter range unknown, but probably south into Mexico and Central America.

Nebraska and Kansas: *A.s. rubescens* regular migrant; New Mexico: widely distributed in spring and fall and occasional in winter, and breeding above timberline in northern mountains; Utah: summer resident in the Uinta Mountains and transient elsewhere; Wyoming: common in summer above timberline, common migrant.

COLORADO.—Common in migration, summer resident of Alpine Zone, and a few on plains in winter. Sub-species *A. s. rubescens* probably migrates through eastern counties.

* SPRAGUE'S PIPIT   *Anthus spragueii* (Audubon). [700]

RECOGNITION.—Length 6.7–7 inches. Similar to Water Pipit, but back conspicuously streaked with black and buff and legs pale or flesh-colored as contrasted with darker legs of the Water Pipit. (Plate 93)

RANGE.—Breeds from northern Alberta, central Saskatchewan, and central Manitoba south to Montana, North Dakota, and northwestern Minnesota. Winters from southern Arizona, Texas, Louisiana, and Mississippi into northern Mexico.

Nebraska: migrant throughout the state, possibly more common in west; Kansas: regular transient with specimens from Trego, Cloud, Greenwood, Woodson, and Anderson Counties; New Mexico: one (two collected in Nov.) at Jal Dec. 20, 1962 (A.F.N.: 17:261); Wyoming: straggler at Laramie, and several observations August 1949 in western Sheridan and eastern Big Horn counties (Mengel, 1952).

COLORADO.—Apparently an uncommon straggler with several sight records by experienced observers. One observed along Tower Rd. north of Aurora Aug. 5, 6, & 13, 1956 by Lois Webster (pers. comm.); two 15 mi. east of Denver Apr. 13, 1966 (W. Reeser, pers. comm.); and four in Weld Co. June 10, 1967, two northeast of Briggsdale and two north of New Raymer (Ruth Dement & Nancy Hurley, pers. comm.).

Family BOMBYCILLIDAE: Waxwings

BOHEMIAN WAXWING   *Bombycilla garrulus pallidiceps* Reichenow. [618]

RECOGNITION.—Length 7.5–8.5 inches. *Adult:* plumage immaculate soft fawn above and below, with wings and tail darker; head crested with forehead and cheeks chestnut; chin, lores, and eyeline black; two *white wing bars,* secondaries often tipped with red, waxlike appendages; portions of primary tips *yellow* to *white;* tip of tail yellow; *under tail coverts chestnut. Young:* duller, with under parts whiter and streaked with brown. (Plate 94)

RANGE.—Species occurs throughout much of the Northern Hemisphere of both the Old and New Worlds. This race breeds in the coniferous forests of west and central Alaska, the Yukon, Mackenzie, and northern Manitoba south to Washington, Idaho, and Montana. Winters from southeastern Alaska and British Columbia east to Nova Scotia, and south to Pennsylvania and California.

Nebraska and Kansas: irregular winter visitor; New Mexico: rare straggler; Utah: occasionally fairly common in north, rare in south; Wyoming: common in winter.

COLORADO.—Irregular winter visitors, sometimes very numerous.

Early fall Nov. 6 Red Rocks (3:18); late spring May 24 Wray (no. 801).

Photograph by Alfred M. Bailey

JOAN WITHERSPOON FEEDS BOHEMIAN WAXWINGS (April 19, 1964)

CEDAR WAXWING   *Bombycilla cedrorum* Vieillot. [619]

RECOGNITION.—Length 6.5–7.5 inches. *Adult:* similar to the Bohemian Waxwing, but smaller, and white and yellow of the wings lacking, flanks and lower belly pale yellow, and under tail coverts *white. Young:* light below with brown streaks. (Plate 94)

RANGE.—Breeds from southeastern Alaska, British Columbia, and Alberta across Canada to Newfoundland, south to North Carolina, Georgia, Alabama, and northwestern California. Winters irregularly throughout most of the United States to Panama.

Nebraska: common migrant and occasional breeder; Kansas: common transient, breeding records from Wyandotte and Shawnee Counties; New Mexico: uncommon; Utah: uncommon summer resident, few in winter; Wyoming: common summer resident, rare in winter.

COLORADO.—Uncommon and irregular resident from the plains into the mountains.

Family PTILOGONATIDAE: Silky Flycatchers

The several species of the Silky Flycatcher family range from southwestern United States through the mountains of Mexico south to Panama. They are sleek, crested birds which feed on berries and insects.

PHAINOPEPLA   *Phainopepla nitens lepida* Van Tyne. [620]

RECOGNITION.—Length 7–7.5 inches. *Male:* glossy black *slender* bird with conspicuous head crest, red eyes, and *white wing patches* on primaries. *Female:* brownish-gray with lighter under parts; white on wings less than in male.

RANGE.—Breeds in California north to San Francisco, southern Nevada, southern Utah, southwestern New Mexico, and western Texas south through Sonora and Baja California.

COLORADO.—One record from near Platteville, Weld Co., August 29–30, 1965. An immature male was observed by Mrs. John Lett on the Lett farm one mile west of Platteville on the above dates. Regional naturalists studied the bird and photographs were secured to verify this first record of the species in Colorado (see page 847 *BIRDS OF COLORADO*).

Family LANIIDAE: Shrikes

NORTHERN SHRIKE   *Lanius excubitor invictus* Grinnell. [621a]

RECOGNITION.—Length 9–10.5 inches. *Adult:* gray above with forehead, superciliary line, scapular edges, and upper tail coverts white; eye stripe, wings, and tail black; one white wing bar; outer tail feathers edged and tipped with white; under parts white with faint barring on breast and sides. *Young:* browner above with black portions gray-brown. (Plate 94)

RANGE.—The species ranges widely in the Northern Hemisphere; in the Old World from Scandinavia and northern Russia south to Africa, Arabia, India, northern China, and Japan, and in the New World from northwestern Alaska, central Yukon, northern Mackenzie, and Manitoba south to British Columbia and northeastern Alberta. Winters irregularly south to California, Arizona, and Texas.

Nebraska and Kansas: uncommon winter visitor in west (*L.e. borealis* in east). New Mexico: uncommon migrant in north; Utah: uncommon in winter; Wyoming: common winter visitor.

COLORADO.—Fairly common winter resident throughout the lower elevations.

Late spring June 1 Weldona; early fall Sept. 24 Allenspark (C.B.N. 12:4).

LOGGERHEAD SHRIKE   *Lanius ludovicianus excubitorides* Swainson. [622a]

RECOGNITION.—Length 8.5–10 inches. Generally similar to the Northern Shrike, but smaller and under parts immaculate or with very faint barring; black eye lines meet over the base of bill. *Young:* duller, black portions tinged with brown. (Plate 94)

RANGE.—The species breeds from British Columbia across southern Canada to Quebec, south through much of the United States into Mexico and Baja California. This race ranges from central Alberta and Saskatchewan south through the Great Plains, and along the eastern slope of the Rocky Mountains to southern Texas. Winters from northern Texas and Louisiana into Mexico.

Nebraska and Kansas: common summer resident in west, *L.l. migrans* in east, with intermediates where ranges meet; New Mexico: breeds commonly in lower parts of the state, intergrading with *L.l. sonoriensis* in southeast; Utah: species summer resident throughout the state, and *L.l. gambeli* winter visitor; Wyoming: common summer resident.

COLORADO.—Common on the plains and low valleys throughout the state, occasionally ranging into the mountains to 9000 feet in summer. There are several winter reports.

Family STURNIDAE: Starlings

STARLING   *Sturnus vulgaris vulgaris* Linnaeus. [493]

RECOGNITION.—Length 7.5–8.5 inches. *Summer adult:* face and cheeks iridescent green; crown, nape, and neck glossy-purple; remaining plumage glossy-green, spotted with buff on back; bill yellow. *Winter adult:* similar, but spotted with white below; bill black. *Young:* similar to winter adult, but duller with less spotting on under parts. (Plate 95)

RANGE.—Breeds from Iceland, the British Isles, Norway, Finland, and Russia, south to France, Italy, and Rumania. Winters from breeding range to northern Africa, Palestine, and Asia Minor. Introduced in New York in 1890, and now ranges throughout southern Canada and most of the United States from Alaska to the Gulf of Mexico.

Nebraska: common resident, first recorded in 1932; Kansas: common, first observed in 1929; New Mexico: abundant, first noted November 1935, and nesting after 1954; Utah: common resident, first February 26, 1939 (Condor, 41:170); Wyoming: very common resident.

COLORADO.—Common throughout much of the state. First flocks reported in Logan Co. (Denver Post, Feb. 16, 1937); first specimen Dec. 7, 1938 at Barr, Adams Co. (Rockwell, 1939); northeastern Colorado (Imler, 1939); in El Paso Co. (Gadd, 1941).

Family VIREONIDAE: Vireos

BELL'S VIREO   *Vireo bellii bellii* Audubon. [633]

RECOGNITION.—Length 4.5–5 inches. Olive-gray above with white eyering, lores indistinct; wings and tail darker, with two white wing bars; under parts washed with yellow, the throat whiter. (Plate 95)

RANGE.—The species breeds locally in its proper habitat from California and southern Nevada east to Wisconsin and Illinois, south to Texas and Louisiana into Mexico and Central America. The local race occurs from eastern Colorado, South Dakota, Minnesota, Wisconsin and from Illinois south to Louisiana, Texas, and Tamaulipas. Winters from Mexico to Nicaragua.

Nebraska: common summer resident in east, occasional in the west; Kansas: common in summer throughout the state; New Mexico: very rare, the race *V.b. arizonae* found in southwest corner only; Utah: rare, two specimens race *V.b. arizonae;* Wyoming: straggler (Lake Como).

COLORADO.—Fairly common summer resident along the eastern border of the state, wandering casually westward to the foothills.

Early spring May 7 Golden; late summer Sept. 7 Sedalia.

GRAY VIREO   *Vireo vicinior* Coues. [634]

RECOGNITION.—Length 5–5.75 inches. Gray above and white below; white eyering and lores inconspicuous; one faint wing bar, sometimes absent. *Young:* browner above with distinct buff wing bar. (Plate 96)

RANGE.—Breeds from south-central California and southern Nevada south to Oklahoma, Texas, and Arizona into Mexico.

New Mexico: summer resident locally, nesting to six feet from the ground in small trees or thorny bushes; Utah: fairly common in summer in southwest, ranging into pinyon-juniper belt.

COLORADO.—Casual in pinyon-juniper associations of the state with records on the western slope from Mesa Verde to the Colorado National Monument.

* YELLOW-THROATED VIREO   *Vireo flavifrons* Vieillot. [628]

RECOGNITION.—Length 5.5–6 inches. Adults bright green above, gray rump, two distinct wing bars; outer web of tail feathers white. Throat and breast bright yellow. (Plate 96)

RANGE.—Breeds from southern Manitoba, northern Minnesota, Wisconsin, and southern Canada to Maine, south to Florida and central Texas. Winters to northern South America.

Nebraska: uncommon migrant and locally uncommon summer resident in eastern half of state; Kansas: uncommon transient and summer resident throughout the state, with nesting records from Woodson, Shawnee, and Douglas Counties.

COLORADO.—Uncommon straggler with observations at Bonny Res., Denver, Boulder, Golden, and Barr Lake.

WARBLING VIREO

Photograph by Alfred M. Bailey

PATRICIA BAILEY WITHERSPOON INTERVIEWS A SOLITARY VIREO

SOLITARY VIREO   *Vireo solitarius plumbeus* Coues. [629b]

RECOGNITION.—Length 5–6 inches. Steel-gray above; eyerings, lores, and two wing bars white, wings and tail dark but edged with white; throat and under parts white with sides olive-gray. *Young:* browner above, with sides and flanks white. (Plate 96)

RANGE.—The species breeds from British Columbia across southern Canada to Nova Scotia, south to Baja California and into Central America. This subspecies nests from eastern Nevada, southern Montana, and southwestern South Dakota south to southwestern Texas and Arizona into Mexico. Winters from the southern part of breeding range into Mexico.

Nebraska and Kansas: uncommon transient, and possible summer resident in west, *V.s. solitarius* in the east; New Mexico: a fairly common breeding bird of the juniper-clad hills into the Transition Zone to over 8000 feet in the west; Utah: uncommon summer resident in Transition Zone; Wyoming: common summer resident in the northeast.

COLORADO.—Common in the east and less so on the western slope in migration, breeding in scrub oak and ponderosa pine habitat.

Early spring Apr. 19 Kiowa (C.B.N. 12:17); late fall Oct. 29 Colorado Springs.

Vireo solitarius cassinii Xantus. [629a]

RECOGNITION.—Length 5–6 inches. Similar to *V.s. plumbeus*, but back olive-green, with wings and tail edged with olive-yellow; more yellow on sides and flanks. *Young:* dull brown above, dull white with yellow wash below.

115

RANGE.—Breeds from southern British Columbia south through Washington, western Montana, Idaho and foothills of California. Winters from Arizona into Mexico.

Kansas: transient in west; New Mexico: spring and fall migrant and breeds in west; Utah: uncommon transient.

COLORADO.—An uncommon migrant through the state.

RED-EYED VIREO   *Vireo olivaceus* (Linnaeus). [624]

RECOGNITION.—Length 5.5–6.5 inches. Olive-green above with *gray crown* bordered with black, eyes red, white superciliary line with dark edgings; no wing bars; throat, breast, and belly white. *Young:* upper parts and sides browner. (Plate 96)

RANGE.—Breeds locally from British Columbia across southern Canada to Nova Scotia and south to northern Oregon, Idaho, and Montana to Texas, and east to Florida. Migrates across the Gulf of Mexico to northwestern South America.

Nebraska and Kansas: a common migrant and summer resident; Utah: uncommon transient; Wyoming: uncommon migrant and summer resident.

COLORADO.—Fairly common summer resident from the plains into the Lower Transition Zone, usually nesting from a few to eight feet from the ground in shrubs or trees.

Early spring May 8 Red Rocks (Denver); late summer Oct. 10, one banded at Sedalia by C. and M. Snyder.

* PHILADELPHIA VIREO   *Vireo philadelphicus* (Cassin). [626]

RECOGNITION.—Length 4.5–5.25 inches. Light olive-green above, white line over eye, and a dark line through the eye; no white on wings; under parts yellowish-buff. (Plate 96)

RANGE.—Breeds from British Columbia and Alberta across Canada to Newfoundland, south to Maine, New Hampshire, Michigan, and North Dakota; winters in Central America.

NEBRASKA: uncommon migrant in east; Kansas: probably regular transient west to Harvey Co.; Montana: recorded from Johnson Lake (A.O.U. Check-list).

COLORADO.—One noted May 19, 1956 at Bonny Reservoir, Yuma Co., by a skilled observer, Dr. John Chapin (C.B.N. 4:5); a bird banded near Sedalia Sept. 8, 1963, and one observed at Barr Lake Oct. 12 (A.F.N. 18:51); one Bonny Res. May 9, 1964 observed by A. Collister, Nancy Hurley, and Lois Webster (pers. comm.); one banded near Sedalia Sept. 5, 1965 (C. and M. Snyder, pers. comm.); one observed near Golden Aug. 23, 1965 and one in Deer Creek Canyon Sept. 29 (C.B.N. 13:22).

WARBLING VIREO   *Vireo gilvus swainsonii* Baird. [627a]

RECOGNITION.—Length 4.5–5.5 inches. Olive-gray above, inconspicuous superciliary line; no wing bars, and white under parts with yellow tinge on sides. *Young:* browner above, sometimes with indistinct buff wing bar. (Plate 95)

RANGE.—The species breeds from northern British Columbia across Canada to Nova Scotia and south to Texas, Louisiana, and Alabama into Mexico. This subspecies has a westerly range from British Columbia, southern Mackenzie, Alberta, and southwestern South Dakota south to southern California, southeastern Arizona, and western Texas. Winters from Mexico into Central America.

Nebraska: common migrant in the west, *V.g. gilvus* in east; Kansas: no record of this subspecies, race *V.g. gilvus* in the east; New Mexico: fairly common summer resident in the mountains; Utah: this race listed by Twomey (1942) from eastern part of state, while *V.g. leucopolius* occurs elsewhere; Wyoming: abundant migrant and summer resident.

COLORADO.—Common on the plains in migration, and breeding in the Transition Zone. Aspens are favorite nesting trees.

Early spring May 8 Archuleta Co. (no. 14723); late fall Oct. 11, 1965 Sedalia (C.B.N. 13:20).

Vireo gilvus gilvus (Vieillot). [627]

RECOGNITION.—Length 5–5.75 inches. Indistinguishable in the field from the western race *V.g. swainsonii*, though slightly larger, and lighter above.

RANGE.—Breeds from southwestern Alberta across southern Canada to New Brunswick, and south from southeastern Montana and South Dakota to Texas, Louisiana, Alabama, and North Carolina. Winters from southern Mexico to South America. Migrates through the Mississippi Valley.

Nebraska and Kansas: common transient, and summer resident in east.

COLORADO.—Probably occurs regularly in eastern counties. There are eight specimens in the Museum collection, including one (no. 13893) from Jefferson Co.

Family PARULIDAE: Wood Warblers

BLACK-AND-WHITE WARBLER   *Mniotilta varia* (Linnaeus). [636]

RECOGNITION.—Length 4.75–5.5 inches. *Adult male:* streaked with black and white; two wing bars, mid-belly, and two spots near under-tip of tail white. *Young male:* markings duller; throat unstreaked white. *Female:* like young male but back duller and under parts gray-white. (Plate 97)

RANGE.—Breeds from British Columbia and Alberta, east across Canada to Newfoundland, and south from Montana and South Dakota to Georgia, Mississippi, Alabama, Louisiana, and Texas. Winters casually from Florida, Texas, and California to Venezuela.

Nebraska: common migrant throughout the state and a local summer resident in the east; Kansas: common transient and reported nesting in Douglas and Leavenworth Counties; Utah: straggler, one record specimen; Wyoming: uncommon migrant.

COLORADO.—Spring and fall migrants through eastern counties, occasionally occurring in winter.

Early spring Apr. 1 Barr Lake (D.F.O. no. 8); summer June 19, 1967 male near Squaw Pass, Clear Creek Co. at 9000 ft. (H. Holt); late fall Nov. 20 Jefferson Co.; winter Dec. 20 Fort Collins.

PROTHONOTARY WARBLER   *Protonotaria citrea* (Boddaert). [637]

RECOGNITION.—Length 5.25–5.75 inches. *Male:* head and under parts bright orange-yellow; hind neck and back olive-yellow; wings, rump, and tail gray; under tail coverts and patches near under-tip of tail white. *Female:* head darker and under parts paler than in male. (Plate 97)

RANGE.—Breeds from central Minnesota, Wisconsin, Michigan, southern Ontario to New York, south to Florida, through Oklahoma and eastern Texas. Winters in Central America and northern South America.

Nebraska: uncommon migrant and rare breeder; Kansas: locally common transient and summer resident; New Mexico: one recorded at Anthony May 6, 1953, and at Bosque Refuge Sept. 9 (Ligon, 1961).

COLORADO.—Straggler in eastern Colorado. Observed in Boulder, El Paso, Logan, and Pueblo Counties; a male (no. 33793) collected in Arapahoe Co. Aug. 25, 1962; one banded near Longmont July 8, 1965 by Allegra Collister; and one noted at Platteville Apr. 30, 1967 (D.F.O., 2: no. 8).

SWAINSON'S WARBLER   *Limnothlypis swainsonii* (Audubon). [638]

RECOGNITION.—Length 5–5.5 inches. *Adult:* olive-brown above, with crown rich brown; line over eye yellow-white; throat and under tail coverts white; breast gray-white; belly yellow-white; flanks and sides olive. (Plate 97)

RANGE.—Breeds locally from northeastern Oklahoma to southern Illinois, east to southern Virginia, Maryland, northern Florida, Mississippi, Alabama, and Louisiana. Winters in Cuba, Jamaica, southern Yucatan, and in British Honduras.

Nebraska: straggler, one specimen from Buffalo Co. Apr. 9, 1905; Kansas: rare, one specimen collected by Ben King and Elizabeth Cole in Johnson Co., 1957 (L. B. Carson), and a second in the southeast in 1965 (D. F. Parmelee, pers. comm.).

COLORADO.—Rare straggler in eastern Colorado. A female (no. 2806) was collected near Holly, Prowers Co., May 12, 1913, and individuals were observed near Golden Sept. 21, 1963, and on Aug. 22, 1964.

WORM-EATING WARBLER   *Helmitheros vermivorus* (Gmelin). [639]

RECOGNITION.—Length 5–6 inches. Adult olive-green above, top of head buffy with blackish stripes on sides; buffy-whitish below. (Plate 98)

RANGE.—Breeds from northeastern Kansas, Iowa, and Illinois east to Massachusetts, south to Georgia and Louisiana. Winters from Florida, Veracruz, and the Bahamas south to Panama. Casual north to Wisconsin, Ontario, Vermont, and Bermuda.

Nebraska: casual summer visitor in southwest to Webster Co., one collected at Scottsbluff; Kansas: rare transient with specimens from Doniphan, Douglas, and Woodson Counties, with a breeding record from Leavenworth Co. on June 7, 1919; New Mexico: one reported from Las Cruces Sept. 14, 1956 (Ligon, 1961); Wyoming: one at Casper May 11–18, 1962 (A.F.N. 16:436).

COLORADO.—Rare straggler. Reported from Ft. Collins May 16, 1959 (C.B.N. 7:10); Durango Oct. 22, 1960 (8:60); one at Golden April 30, 1961 (9:33); one Dinosaur Nat. Monument May 1, 1963 (A.F.N. 17:422); two Golden May 7 and one Gregory Canyon, Boulder, May 9 (11:29); one Morrison Apr. 26, 1964 (12:17); a male in Elbert Co. Apr. 22, 1965 reported by Charles and Mildred Snyder (pers. comm.); one banded at Golden by Geo. Shier (first fall record) Nov. 18, 1965 (C.B.N. 13:24); and one observed at Waterton, Jeff. Co., May 29–30, 1967 (Hugh Kingery, pers. comm.).

* GOLDEN-WINGED WARBLER   *Vermivora chrysoptera* (Linnaeus). [642]

RECOGNITION.—Length 4.5–5 inches. *Male:* crown and *wing patches bright yellow;* throat and cheek band *black;* gray above and white below, sides grayish; inner webs of outer tail feathers white. *Female:* like the male but throat gray. *Young:* olive-gray above; sides of head olive, streaked with yellowish; two narrow yellow-white wing bars. (Plate 98)

RANGE.—Breeds from southeastern Manitoba, central Minnesota, Wisconsin, southeastern Ontario, and Massachusetts to New Jersey, and south from eastern Iowa, Illinois, Indiana, Pennsylvania, and Maryland to Georgia. Casual north to Manitoba, Maine, New Hampshire, and Vermont. Winters in Central America and Venezuela.

Nebraska: rare migrant; Kansas: rare transient in east, one specimen from Douglas Co. May 2, 1921, and one in 1957.

COLORADO.—Rare straggler in eastern Colorado. Sight records from Yuma (1906), Bonny Res. (1961), and Golden, Barr Lake, and Evergreen (1964); and male Red Rocks Park, Denver May 13–15, 1967 (H. Holt and D. Thatcher).

TENNESSEE WARBLER   *Vermivora peregrina* (Wilson). [647]

RECOGNITION.—Length 4.5–5 inches. *Male:* olive-green above, with crown and hind neck dark gray; gray eye line and superciliary line white; under parts clear white. *Female:* like the male but crown greenish, and white areas yellowish. *Young:* olive-green above and olive-yellow below except belly and under tail coverts white. (Plate 98)

RANGE.—Breeds from the southern Yukon, central Mackenzie and British Columbia locally across Canada to Nova Scotia, and south in Wisconsin, Michigan, New York, and New England states. Winters from Mexico south to Colombia and Venezuela.

Nebraska and Kansas: common in migration in eastern counties; Wyoming: uncommon in eastern half.

COLORADO.—Regular spring and near fall migrant on eastern prairies, and rare west of the Continental Divide. One taken near Gunnison on May 9, 1951, and one seen in same location May 22, 1953 and Sept. 25, 1955 (A. S. Hyde, pers. comm.).

Early spring May 2 Weld Co. (C.S.U. no. 5941); late fall Oct. 7 Golden.

ORANGE-CROWNED WARBLER   *Vermivora celata orestera* Oberholser. [646c]

RECOGNITION.—Length 4.5–5 inches. *Male:* dull olive-green above, dingy yellow below; crown dull orange; eyering and superciliary stripe whitish. *Female:* like the male, but crown patch restricted or lacking. (Plate 98)

RANGE.—The species breeds from central Alaska and Mackenzie across Canada to Quebec, and this race occurs in the Rocky Mountains and the mountains of the Great Basin from the Yukon, Alberta, Saskatchewan, and eastern California to Utah and Arizona; winters from southern part of its range into Mexico.

Kansas: common, *V.c. celata* in east and this race in west; New Mexico: rather widely distributed during migration, and breeding uncommonly in northern mountains; Utah and Wyoming: common migrant, and uncommon breeder in the mountains.

COLORADO.—The Rocky Mountain race is fairly common in migration throughout the state and probably breeds in the mountains.

Early spring Apr. 19 Ft. Morgan; late fall Nov. 10 Ft. Collins; winter Dec. 29 Durango and Feb. 1 Denver.

Vermivora celata celata (Say). [646]

RECOGNITION.—Similar to *V.c. orestera* but less yellowish above and below.

RANGE.—Breeds from central Alaska, Yukon, and northwestern Mackenzie south to northern Manitoba, Saskatchewan, Ontario, and Quebec. Winters in the south Atlantic and Gulf states; also from southern California into Mexico.

Nebraska and Kansas: a common migrant throughout both states.

COLORADO.—Spring and fall migrant over the eastern prairies.

NASHVILLE WARBLER   *Vermivora ruficapilla ridgwayi* van Rossem. [645a]

RECOGNITION.—Length 4.5–5 inches. *Male:* head gray with chestnut crown; eyering white; olive-green above, with rump brighter; yellow below. *Female:* like the male, but duller; crown patch restricted or lacking. *Young:* brown-gray above; rump olive; dull yellow below except buffy belly. (Plate 99)

RANGE.—The species breeds from southern British Columbia across Canada to Nova Scotia, and this western race from British Columbia and northwestern Montana to southern Idaho, Oregon, and northern California. Winters from Mexico into Central America.

Nebraska and Kansas: *V.r. ruficapilla* common migrant; New Mexico: one reported from Anthony Sept. 9, 1948 and one Sept. 3, 1953, and one from Roswell in Feb. 1956 (Ligon, 1961); Utah: this race uncommon transient and summer resident; Wyoming: rare migrant.

COLORADO.—Regular but uncommon transient throughout the state from Upper Sonoran into the Transition Zone. One on Spring Count May 22, 1965 Prewitt Res. (C.B.N. 13:31).

Early spring Apr. 24 Denver; late fall Nov. 21 Denver.

VIRGINIA'S WARBLER   *Vermivora virginiae* (Baird). [644]

RECOGNITION.—Length 4.5–5 inches. *Male:* gray above, with crown chestnut; eyering white; rump yellow-green; dull white below with breast spot and under tail coverts yellow. *Female:* like the male but duller; back browner, and crown patch restricted. *Young:* plumage gray, lighter below; rump and under tail coverts yellow; two faint wing bars. (Plate 99)

RANGE.—Breeds in the Transition Zone from southeastern California, southeastern Idaho, and Nevada to Colorado and southeastern Arizona. Winters south into Mexico.

Kansas: casual migrant in Morton County, with two record specimens in 1950; New Mexico: summer resident in northern mountains between 7000 and 8000 feet; Utah: common summer resident from the oak belt into mountain aspen groves; Wyoming: one at Rawlins May 12, 1962 and one at Cheyenne May 28 (A.F.N. 16:435).

COLORADO.—Common summer resident in the foothills throughout the state, the nests being on the ground and well hidden by vegetation. Thirty-seven noted at Waterton Apr. 30, 1967 (Hugh Kingery, pers. comm.).

Early spring Apr. 29 Cherry Creek Res.; late fall Oct. 20, 1960 Longmont.

LUCY'S WARBLER   *Vermivora luciae* (Cooper). [643]

RECOGNITION.—Length 4–4.5 inches. *Summer male:* gray above, with crown and upper tail coverts chestnut; eyering and lores white; white below with breast buffy. *Autumn male:* browner above. *Female:* like the male, but chestnut paler. *Young:* gray above and white below; upper tail coverts buffy. (Plate 99)

RANGE.—Breeds from southern Nevada, Utah, and southwestern Colorado south into Arizona, Mexico, and Baja California. Winters in Mexico.

New Mexico: summer resident of the Lower Sonoran Zone in the southwest; Utah: common in cottonwoods of southern counties.

COLORADO.—Rare summer resident in the southwestern part of the state, the nests being in natural cavities or old woodpecker holes.

PARULA WARBLER   *Parula americana* (Linnaeus). [648]

RECOGNITION.—Length 4–4.5 inches. *Male:* blue-gray above with dorsal saddle olive-green; two wing bars and tail spots white; yellow below except white lower belly, dark breast band, and sides tinged with rust. *Female:* like the male but duller. *Young:* gray above with dorsal saddle olive; yellow below fading to white on belly; two wing bars. (Plate 99)

RANGE.—Breeds from southeastern Manitoba and central Ontario to New Brunswick and Nova Scotia, south to Florida, the Gulf coast, and Texas. Winters in the Bahamas and the West Indies, and southern Mexico to Nicaragua.

Nebraska: rare migrant and local summer resident in east; Kansas: transient and nesting records in eastern counties; New Mexico: three observations, and first known specimen, a male, collected in Lea Co. Apr. 11, 1963 (Auk, 82:649); Wyoming: rare migrant on eastern edge of state.

COLORADO.—Regular but uncommon spring migrant in eastern counties, and an adult male was collected in Gunnison Co. on May 24, 1952. Noted at Barr Lake, Red Rocks, and Waterton Apr. 16, 23, 30, 1967 (Hugh Kingery, pers. comm.).

Early spring Apr. 3 Cherry Creek Res.; late fall Oct. 24 Golden.

YELLOW WARBLER   *Dendroica petechia aestiva* (Gmelin). [652]

RECOGNITION.—Length 4.5–5.25 inches. *Male:* yellow-olive above, bright yellow below; breast and sides streaked with rufous; wings dusky with yellow edgings on primaries. *Female:* duller and streakings often lacking. *Young:* olive-gray above, yellow-white below. (Plate 100)

RANGE.—The species breeds from north-central Alaska, Yukon, and Mackenzie south into Mexico, and this race from southeastern Alberta, southern Saskatchewan, southwestern Manitoba, and southern Ontario to the Atlantic coast, south to southern Montana, Oklahoma, Arkansas, and Georgia. Winters through Central America to northern Brazil.

Nebraska and Kansas: as a species, a common migrant and summer resident (three races recorded from both states); New Mexico: common species, three races reported, with *D.p. morcomi* breeding in the north, and *D.p.*

119

sonorana in the far south; Utah: *D.p. aestiva* an infrequent transient, *D.p. morcomi* a common summer resident; Wyoming: as a species a common breeder.

COLORADO.—Summer resident, the most common nesting warbler in the state. Recorded as a breeding bird from practically every county.

Early spring Apr. 30 Denver; late fall Oct. 7 Morgan Co.

MAGNOLIA WARBLER   *Dendroica magnolia* (Wilson). [657]

RECOGNITION.—Length 4.5–5 inches. *Male:* crown, hind neck, and wings gray; lores, cheeks, back, and tail black; two wing bars and basal portion of all but middle tail feathers white; rump and under parts yellow, with breast and sides streaked with black; under tail coverts white. *Female:* like the male but more olive above and less black. *Young:* breast streakings gray or absent. (Plate 100)

RANGE.—Breeds from Mackenzie and east-central British Columbia across southern Canada, and in northern states south to Virginia and west to Pennsylvania, Ohio, Wisconsin, and Minnesota. Winters from the Gulf coast and islands of the Caribbean into Central America. Migrates west to base of Rocky Mountains.

Nebraska and Kansas: uncommon migrant; Utah: two Salt Lake City Oct. 14, 1962 (A.F.N. 17:54); Wyoming: rare migrant in east, twelve noted near Cheyenne Oct. 9, 1955 (C.B.N. 3:36).

COLORADO.—Uncommon migrant in the eastern part of the state.

Early spring Apr. 25 Ft. Collins; late fall Nov. 13 Denver; winter Dec. 3 Littleton.

CAPE MAY WARBLER   *Dendroica tigrina* (Gmelin). [650]

RECOGNITION.—Length 5–5.5 inches. *Male:* olive-green above streaked with black, rump yellow to greenish-yellow, yellow patch on sides of neck and ear coverts rufous, wing coverts with white patch, under parts yellow streaked with black; tail coverts and lower belly whitish. *Female:* grayish-olive above; no chestnut cheeks. (Plate 101)

RANGE.—Breeds from northeastern British Columbia across much of southern Canada to Nova Scotia south to Maine, Vermont, New York, northern North Dakota, Wisconsin, and Michigan. Migrates through the Mississippi Valley and eastward, and winters on the islands of the Caribbean and in Central America.

Nebraska: straggler, two records in Hall and Douglas Counties; Kansas: rare straggler, one specimen from Douglas Co. Dec. 6, 1954; Arizona and California: straggler (A.O.U. Check-list).

COLORADO.—Two sight records, a male at Boulder May 20, 1953 and another at Kittredge, Jefferson Co. May 10, 1964, photographed by Harold Holt.

BLACK-THROATED BLUE WARBLER *Dendroica caerulescens caerulescens* (Gmelin). [654]

RECOGNITION.—Length 5–5.5 inches. *Male:* dark blue above with white wing patch; cheeks, foreneck, and sides black; under parts and two spots on tail white; *Female:* olive above, with wing patch indistinct yellow; dull white superciliary line; under parts white to pale yellow; tail spots often lacking. *Young:* generally similar to adult female. (Plate 101)

RANGE.—Breeds from Ontario and southern Quebec to Nova Scotia and south to New Jersey, and west in northern states to Wisconsin. Winters from Key West, Bahamas, and Greater Antilles to Colombia.

Nebraska: a rare migrant as far west as Keith Co.; Kansas: rare transient with more records from west than east; New Mexico: straggler, recorded most frequently in Las Cruces area; Wyoming: straggler.

COLORADO.—A casual but often observed visitor in the eastern part of the state, ranging occasionally to the foothills. One banded eight miles west of Longmont in Oct. 1966 (Allegra Collister, pers. comm.).

Early spring May 9 Holly; late fall Boulder Nov. 27.

MYRTLE WARBLER   *Dendroica coronata coronata* (Linnaeus). [655]

RECOGNITION.—Length 5–6 inches. *Summer male:* blue-gray above, with black dorsal streaks; cheeks black; crown, *rump,* and sides yellow; breast heavily streaked with black; *throat* and belly *white;* two wing bars and tail spots white. *Autumn male:* like the female but darker. *Female:* similar to summer male, but paler; brown-gray above. (Plate 100)

RANGE.—The race *D.c. hooveri* breeds in northern Alaska, the Yukon, northwestern and central Mackenzie, southeastern Alaska, and British Columbia, and *D.c. coronata* from north-central Alberta across southern Canada to Labrador, and south into northern states west to Wisconsin, Minnesota, and Massachusetts. Species winters from southern part of the breeding range to Panama, and on the Pacific coast from Oregon to Baja California.

Nebraska and Kansas: common transient and occasional winter visitor; New Mexico: winter resident; Utah: rare straggler; Wyoming: common migrant in eastern two-thirds of the state.

COLORADO.—Common transient and occasional winter visitor throughout the state.

AUDUBON'S WARBLER   *Dendroica auduboni memorabilis* Oberholser. [656a]

RECOGNITION.—Length 5–6 inches. Similar to Myrtle Warbler, but *throat yellow* instead of white. *Young:* similar to the adult female, but often paler. (Plate 100)

RANGE.—Breeds from southeastern British Columbia, southwestern Saskatchewan, and Alberta, southeast of the Cascade Mountains and the Sierra Nevada to central eastern California, southern Nevada, and Wyoming south to Arizona and western Texas, and through Mexico to Guatemala.

Nebraska: common migrant and a breeding record from Sioux Co.; Kansas: common transient in west, with numerous hybrids; New Mexico: abundant summer resident in northern mountains, with a few in winter; Utah: a common summer resident in mountains; Wyoming: common migrant and breeder in the mountains.

COLORADO.—Common migrant and occasional winter resident, breeding in mountains above 8000 feet.

BLACK-THROATED GRAY WARBLER   *Dendroica nigrescens* (Townsend). [665]

RECOGNITION.—Length 4.5–5 inches. *Male:* head and throat black; superciliary and cheek lines white, lores yellow; upper parts gray streaked with black on back; two white wing bars; white below, sides streaked with black, tail patches white, in autumn upper parts tinged with brown. *Female:* like the male but crown grayer, and throat white. *Young male:* like the autumn male, but browner above; throat feathers edged with white. (Plate 101)

RANGE.—Breeds from southern British Columbia, central Oregon, northern Utah, and southwestern Wyoming. Winters from southern California into Baja California, and Mexico to Central America.

Kansas: common transient in extreme west, with five records from Morton Co.; New Mexico: widely distributed but most numerous in mountains in south; Utah: common summer resident in pinyon-juniper forest; Wyoming: uncommon in summer in south.

COLORADO.—Fairly common warbler of the pinyon-juniper habitats of the south and southwest. Ranges casually northward to Boulder, east of foothills; noted Red Rocks May 2, 1965, Jeff. Co. May 12, and one Boulder May 22 (C.B.N. 13:3); observed nesting in Huerfano Co. May 30, 1949 and feeding young at Mesa Verde July 4, 1965 (H. Holt, pers. comm.).

Early spring Apr. 15 Red Rocks Park (H. Holt, pers. comm.); late summer Sept. 7 Sand Dunes.

TOWNSEND'S WARBLER   *Dendroica townsendi* (Townsend). [668]

RECOGNITION.—Length 4.5–5 inches. *Summer male:* olive-green above, marked with black; crown, lores, cheeks, throat, and tail black; lores and cheeks almost circled with yellow; breast yellow, belly white, and sides lined with black; two wing bars and tail patches white. *Autumn male:* black areas obscured; throat often yellow, breast and sides flecked with black. *Female:* like the autumn male, with crown and cheek patch browner. (Plate 101)

RANGE.—Breeds from southern Alaska and the Yukon south along the coast and islands to Washington, Oregon, Idaho, and western Montana. Winters from central California to Nicaragua.

Nebraska: straggler, one specimen Dawes Co. Sept. 19, 1911; Kansas: transient in west, five records (female collected from Morton Co. May 3, 1950); New Mexico: common spring and fall migrant; Utah and Wyoming: uncommon transient.

COLORADO.—Regular spring and fall migrant from the plains into the mountains.

Early spring Apr. 28 Berthoud (C.B.N. 2: no. 9, 6); late fall Oct. 29 Golden.

BLACK-THROATED GREEN WARBLER   *Dendroica virens virens* (Gmelin). [667]

RECOGNITION.—Length 4.5–5 inches. *Male:* olive-green above; olive cheek patch almost encircled with yellow; wings, tail, throat, and breast black; belly yellow-white with black-streaked sides; two wing bars and tail patches flecked with black. *Female:* similar to male with less black on chin and throat. (Plate 101)

RANGE.—Breeds from central Alberta, north-central Saskatchewan, northern Manitoba, and central Ontario to Newfoundland, south to New Jersey and Pennsylvania, west to Minnesota, and south to mountains of Georgia and Alabama. Winters from Texas and Florida south to Mexico and Panama.

Nebraska: uncommon migrant in east; Kansas: uncommon transient, rare in west; New Mexico: reported from Anthony Nov. 1, 1954, Roswell in Feb. 1956, and Bernardo in Oct. 1958 (Ligon, 1961).

COLORADO.—Rare straggler. Specimens have been collected at Barr Lake, Limon, Littleton, and Sedalia, and there are several sight records in eastern counties west to the foothills and R.Mt.N.P.

Early spring Boulder May 4 (C.B.N. 11:29); late fall Nov. 4 (no. 34521) Littleton.

CERULEAN WARBLER   *Dendroica cerulea* (Wilson). [658]

RECOGNITION.—Length 4.5–5 inches. *Male:* pale blue above, with wings and tail darker; under parts white, with dark neck band; two wing bars and tail patches white. *Female:* white line over eye, greenish above, whitish below, wing bars white. (Plate 102)

RANGE.—Breeds locally from southern Ontario, New York, New Jersey, Pennsylvania and southeastern Minnesota south through eastern Oklahoma to Texas, and from North Carolina and Virginia to central Alabama. Winters in South America to Ecuador.

Nebraska: uncommon migrant and summer resident with breeding records; Kansas: uncommon transient and possible summer resident in east.

COLORADO.—Rare migrant. One was seen at Denver on May 17, 1873 (Henshaw, 1875); female taken at Parker in Douglas Co. on Sept. 20, 1936 (Bailey and Niedrach, 1937); and one Denver May 13, 1959 (C.B.N. 7:11).

* BLACKBURNIAN WARBLER   *Dendroica fusca* (Müller). [662]

RECOGNITION.—Length 5–5.5 inches. *Male:* head, tail, and wings black, head stripe, neck patch and under parts orange; outer tail feathers white; wing patch white; sides streaked. *Female:* duller, and wings with two bars. (Plate 102)

RANGE.—Breeds from central Saskatchewan and Manitoba eastward to central Quebec and New Brunswick, and in northern states from Minnesota east to New England states, in the Alleghenies, and from Ohio, Pennsylvania, and New York to Tennessee and Georgia. Winters from Guatemala south through Central America to Peru. Straggler in western Montana.

Nebraska: uncommon migrant in east; Kansas: uncommon in east, rare in west; New Mexico: recorded at Fort Bayard in Sept. 1886 (Ligon, 1961).

COLORADO.—There are twelve or more May observations from eastern counties west to the foothills at Golden, Boulder, Longmont, and Platteville.

Early spring Apr. 30 Platteville (D.F.O., 2: no. 8, 1967); late fall Oct. 1 Ft. Collins (A.F.N. 21:54).

YELLOW-THROATED WARBLER   *Dendroica dominica albilora* Ridgway. [663a]

RECOGNITION.—Length 5–5.5 inches. Back gray; throat yellow; white eye line *without yellow;* white below; wings with two white bars, and sides of head black. (Plate 102)

RANGE.—Breeds from South Carolina, Alabama, Georgia, Mississippi, and Louisiana northward through the eastern part of the Mississippi Valley to Michigan and Wisconsin.

Nebraska: a rare summer resident in the southeast (two races listed); Kansas: a few sight records of species from east, and may breed.

COLORADO.—Straggler. A male (no. 28290) was found dead at Loveland in June or July 1956, one was seen in Chaffee Co. June 2, 1957, and another at Golden May 6–9, 1961.

GRACE'S WARBLER   *Dendroica graciae graciae* Baird. [664]

RECOGNITION.—Length 4.5–5 inches. *Male:* slate-gray above, crown and back streaked with black; lores, throat, and breast yellow; belly white, sides lined with black, two wing bars and tail patches white. In autumn buffier below with a tinge of brown above. *Female:* paler. (Plate 102)

RANGE.—Breeds in the mountains of southern Colorado and Utah south through western Mexico and Central America to Nicaragua. Winter range uncertain but probably northern Mexico to Veracruz.

New Mexico: common and widely distributed summer resident over forested mountains between 7000 and 8000 feet; Utah: uncommon in summer in southern mountains.

COLORADO.—Uncommon summer resident in the southwestern part of the state; straggler elsewhere. Recorded from NE Colorado and Colo. Spgs. May 18, 1957; R.Mt.N.P. Sept. 14, 1958; Colo. Spgs. May 23, 1959; Colo. Spgs. May 16, 1964 and May 16, 1965; one at Denver Nov. 2, 1965 (A.F.N. 20:66); and one in Englewood May 11, 1967 (Roberta C. Ausfahl).

CHESTNUT-SIDED WARBLER   *Dendroica pensylvanica* (Linnaeus). [659]

RECOGNITION.—Length 4.5–5.25 inches. *Male:* crown yellow; back streaked with black over yellow-green; sides of head black and white; wing bars yellowish; sides chestnut; under parts white; white patches in tail. *Female:* similar but paler. (Plate 102)

RANGE.—Breeds from central Saskatchewan across Canada to Nova Scotia, from North Dakota, Minnesota, and Michigan to New York and the New England states, and south locally in the Alleghenies to Tennessee, South Carolina, and Georgia. Winters from Guatemala to Panama and northern South America.

Nebraska: uncommon migrant, and a breeding record from vicinity of Omaha; Kansas: fairly common in east, less so in west; Wyoming: migrant, fairly common west, uncommon in east.

COLORADO.—Uncommon spring migrant in eastern counties, with less than twenty observations recorded in the literature. One at Barr Lake and one near Golden on Spring Count May 22, 1965 (C.B.N. 13:31).

Early spring Apr. 29 Boulder; summer June 1 Longmont and Aug. 25 Weld Co.; late summer Sept. 27, 1966, an immature banded by A. Collister near Longmont (pers. comm.).

* BAY-BREASTED WARBLER   *Dendroica castanea* (Wilson). [660]

RECOGNITION.—Length 5–6 inches. *Male:* olive-gray above, streaked with black; wings and tail brown-black; crown, throat, and sides chestnut; forehead, lores, and cheeks black; buff neck patch; belly buff-white, two wing bars and tail patches white. *Female:* olive-green above, faintly streaked with black; crown and sides tinged with chestnut; no black on head. (Plate 103)

RANGE.—Breeds from central Alberta, Saskatchewan, Manitoba, and northern Ontario to Newfoundland, and from Minnesota and Wisconsin to Maine, New Hampshire, Vermont, and New York. Winters in Panama, Colombia, and Venezuela.

Nebraska: uncommon migrant in east; Kansas: uncommon transient throughout the state; Wyoming: reported several times including one at Cheyenne May 17, 1963 (A.F.N. 17:422); Oregon: first state specimen collected along Upper Klamath Lake July 6, 1963 (A.F.N. 17:474).

COLORADO.—Uncommon spring and fall straggler in the Upper Sonoran and Transition Zones with observations reported from Ft. Morgan, Crook, Bonny Res., Denver, Jefferson Co., Boulder and R.Mt.N.P. Two on Spring Count May 22, 1965 at Boulder (C.B.N. 13:31).

Early spring May 11 Bonny Res.; late fall Oct. 11 Golden (Geo. Shier).

BLACKPOLL WARBLER   *Dendroica striata* (Forster). [661]

RECOGNITION.—Length 5–5.5 inches. *Male:* gray above, heavily marked with black on back, neck, and sides; white cheek patches, white below; *crown solid black,* two wing bars and tail patches white. *Female:* olive-gray above and yellow-white below; back and sides streaked with black; wing bars yellow-white. *Autumn adult and young:* like the female, but yellow-green above; under parts unstreaked. (Plate 103)

RANGE.—Breeds from treeline in northwestern Alaska south to British Columbia and the Yukon, and east across Canada to Labrador and Newfoundland, south in New England states to New York. Winters in Colombia, Ecuador, Peru, and Chile.

Nebraska: common migrant in east; Kansas: common in east in migration, rare in west; New Mexico: reported from Clayton Oct. 3, 1954, Roswell in May 1954 (Ligon, 1961) and Ft. Webster (A.O.U. Check-list).

COLORADO.—Regular but uncommon spring migrant east of the Continental Divide. Twenty-five observed at Bonny Res. May 21, 1967 (Hugh Kingery, pers. comm.).

Early spring Apr. 29 Longmont; late spring May 27 Kit Carson.

PINE WARBLER   *Dendroica pinus pinus* (Wilson). [671]

RECOGNITION.—Length 5–5.75 inches. *Male:* a larger warbler, olive-green above, yellowish below; two conspicuous white wing bars, and inner tips of outer tail feathers white. *Female:* olive-green to brownish above, whitish below with breast yellowish.

RANGE.—Breeds locally in coniferous forests from southern Manitoba east to Quebec, south to northern Gulf coast states, and west to southeastern Texas. Winters in southern part of breeding range.

Nebraska: straggler (Dakota and Lancaster Counties); Kansas: observations reported from Topeka, Cloud Co., Johnson Co., Wyandotte Co., and a specimen collected in Wyandotte Co. Oct. 29, 1964 (Condor 67:444).

COLORADO.—Straggler. One specimen in C. U. Museum collected at Boulder Dec. 11, 1964; a female on Lookout Mtn. Sept. 5, 1965 (C.B.N. 13:8) and one banded at Golden Oct. 7 (A.F.N. 20:66); one banded at Boulder Dec. 6, 1966 (Oakleigh Thorne II, pers. comm.).

PALM WARBLER   *Dendroica palmarum palmarum* (Gmelin). [672]

RECOGNITION.—Length 4.5–5.5 inches. *Adult:* olive-brown above, with deep red-brown crown; back faintly streaked; superciliary line, throat, breast, and rump yellow; breast and sides streaked; two faint wing bars; tail patches white. *Young:* similar to autumn adult, but no wing bars; superciliary line and throat white; under parts yellow-buff. (Plate 103)

RANGE.—Breeds from northeastern British Columbia, northern Alberta, southern Mackenzie, northern Saskatchewan, Manitoba, and across Canada to Nova Scotia, south to Minnesota and Michigan. Winters from North Carolina, Tennessee, Louisiana, and Mississippi south to the Yucatan Peninsula, Honduras, the Greater Antilles, Bermuda, Bahamas, and the Virgin Islands. Casual in migration west to Montana.

Nebraska: uncommon migrant in eastern part of state; Kansas: uncommon transient in east; New Mexico: reported from the White Sands in 1935, and the Bosque Refuge Aug. 31, 1953 (Ligon, 1961); Wyoming: straggler.

COLORADO.—Uncommon visitor with at least twelve records east of the Continental Divide. A female (no. 25375) was collected in Lincoln Co. May 13, 1947, a male (no. 34444) near Estes Park Sept. 16, 1963, and an adult was banded 8 mi. w. of Longmont Oct. 2, 1965 (A. Collister, pers. comm.), and one noted in same area Oct. 12 (C.B.N. 13:24).

Early spring May 12 Denver; fall Nov. 11 Georgetown; winter Dec. 17 Boulder.

OVENBIRD   *Seiurus aurocapillus cinereus* Miller. [674b]

RECOGNITION.—Length 5.5–6 inches. *Adult:* dark gray olive-green above with orange crown patch; crown and occiput narrowly edged with black; white below, streaked on breast and sides with dark gray-brown. *Young:* back less olive and narrowly streaked; buffy below, streaked with dusky on sides. (Plate 103)

RANGE.—The species breeds across north central Canada south locally to northern Gulf states, and the race from southern Alberta, southeastern Montana, and western South Dakota south to eastern Colorado and central Nebraska. Migrates south into Mexico and Central America.

Nebraska: migrant, and summer resident locally across the state; Kansas: common transient and local summer resident with a nesting reported from Leavenworth County; New Mexico: reported from Roswell Aug. 31, 1956 and Sept. 9 (Ligon, 1961); Utah: one sight record; Wyoming: uncommon migrant, common breeder in northwest.

COLORADO.—Rather common along the foothills in scrub oak-ponderosa pine associations. Niedrach found a nest on the ground in Douglas Co. in June 1939, and Knorr one in El Paso Co. June 1, 1948.

Early spring May 6 Denver; late fall Oct. 14 Boulder.

NORTHERN WATERTHRUSH   *Seiurus noveboracensis notabilis* Ridgway. [675a]

RECOGNITION.—Length 5.5–6 inches. *Adult:* sooty-brown above; superciliary line dull white; under parts buffy; streaked on throat, breast, and sides with dark gray-brown; buffy tinge on belly. *Young:* less streaked below and somewhat spotted above. (Plate 103)

RANGE.—Breeds from north-central Alaska, northern Yukon, Mackenzie, northern British Columbia, northern Saskatchewan, Manitoba, Ontario, and north central Quebec to Newfoundland south to Montana, North Dakota, Minnesota, Wisconsin, Michigan, Ohio, Pennsylvania, and Massachusetts. Winters from Baja California south through Central America to northern South America.

Nebraska and Kansas: fairly common migrant through both states; New Mexico: regular spring and fall migrant; Utah and Wyoming: uncommon transient.

COLORADO.—Regular migrant in eastern counties and probably in the west.

Early spring Apr. 15 Platteville; summer Aug. 13 Boulder and Aug. 17 western slope; late fall Oct. 28 El Paso Co.

CONNECTICUT WARBLER   *Oporornis agilis* (Wilson). [678]

RECOGNITION.—Length 5.5–6 inches. *Male:* dark olive-green above; head, neck, and upper breast gray; *eye-ring white;* belly yellow with olive-green sides. *Female:* crown olive with throat and breast brownish. *Young:* like the female, but crown more brownish; breast olive. (Plate 104)

RANGE.—Breeds locally from eastern British Columbia, Alberta, Manitoba, central Ontario, and northwestern Quebec to northern Minnesota, Wisconsin, and Michigan. Winters in Colombia, Venezuela, and northern Brazil.

Nebraska: uncommon in eastern third of state (specimen from Cherry Co., May 27, 1933); Kansas: rare straggler, one specimen Topeka 1955; Utah: one specimen.

COLORADO.—Rare straggler. A male (no. 26000) was collected near Limon by C. E. Aiken on May 24, 1899; a female noted May 28, 1952 at the mouth of Big Thompson Canyon was reported by Jay Arnold, and a male was "carefully observed" at Bonny Reservoir May 21, 1960 by Thompson Marsh and John Chapin.

Early spring May 21 Bonny Res.; no fall records.

MOURNING WARBLER   *Oporornis philadelphia* (Wilson). [679]

RECOGNITION.—Length 5–5.75 inches. Similar to Connecticut and MacGillivray's Warblers but rarely with white on eyering. Male has black on breast.

RANGE.—Breeds from central Alberta eastward to Newfoundland south in northern states from northeast North Dakota east to southern Maine and higher Appalachians to northwestern Virginia.

Nebraska: uncommon migrant in eastern counties, probably breeding in southeast; Kansas: a common transient in east and casually west to Sedgwick and Cloud Counties.

COLORADO.—Ranges irregularly into eastern Colorado. There have been several reports including observations at Golden Sept. 14, 1961 (C.B.N. 11:46), one at Bonny Res. May 18, 1963 (11:29) and one May 16, 1964 (12:10). The Mourning and MacGillivray's Warblers probably are conspecific. The two are so similar field determinations are unsatisfactory, but fortunately there are two specimens, one adult male (no. 34522) collected by Dr. John Chapin at Bonny Res. May 22, 1960 (C.B.N. 8:34), and an immature male (no. 34586) secured by Chas. and Mildred Snyder at Sedalia, Douglas Co. Oct. 18, 1964. The latter was sent to the U.S. National Museum, and the identification was confirmed by Dr. Richard C. Banks.

Early spring May 16 Bonny Res.; fall Oct. 18 Sedalia.

MacGILLIVRAY'S WARBLER   *Oporornis tolmiei monticola* Phillips. [680a]

RECOGNITION.—Length 5–5.5 inches. *Male:* gray head similar to that of the Connecticut Warbler, but lores and breast with black feathering; *eyering incomplete. Female:* head less gray, fading to gray-white on throat. *Young:* crown olive and throat yellowish. (Plate 104)

RANGE.—The species breeds from southern Alaska and the Yukon, British Columbia, Alberta, and Saskatchewan south to Arizona, and this race from southeastern Oregon, southern Idaho, southern Wyoming, and Nevada to Arizona. Winters in Mexico south to Guatemala.

Nebraska: species rare migrant; Kansas: common transient in extreme west; New Mexico: migrant, and rather uncommon widely dispersed summer resident; Utah: common in summer throughout the state in chaparral areas of mountains; Wyoming: common migrant and breeder in wet mountain bogs.

COLORADO.—Common migrant in the Upper Sonoran Zone and nesting summer resident in moist areas of the Transition Zone.

Early spring Apr. 24 Golden; late fall Oct. 8 Denver.

YELLOWTHROAT   *Geothlypis trichas occidentalis* Brewster. [681a]

RECOGNITION.—Length 4.5–5.5 inches. *Male:* olive-green above, with black mask covering forehead and cheeks; mask trimmed with white above and throat yellow. *Female:* lacks the black mask and white trim. (Plate 104)

RANGE.—The species breeds from southern Alaska, southern Yukon and northern Alberta across Canada to Newfoundland and south to the Gulf coast, Mexico, and Baja California. Twelve races have been recognized and this form breeds in the Great Basin region from eastern Oregon, Nevada, Idaho, and Wyoming to central-eastern California, northeastern Arizona, and northwestern Texas. Winters from southern part of breeding range to Guatemala.

Nebraska: species common, with race *occidentalis* breeding in west; Kansas: common transient with *occidentalis* in west and *G.t. brachidactylus* in east; Utah: fairly common summer resident except in southwest, where *G.t. scirpicola* occurs; Wyoming: common migrant and marsh breeder, with *campicola* nesting in Uinta Co. It seems quite likely *campicola* occurs regularly as a spring and fall migrant in Colorado and the above states.

COLORADO.—Common nesting summer resident, chiefly in marshy areas of the Upper Sonoran Zone. Thirty-six noted at Bonny Res. May 21, 1967 (Hugh Kingery, pers. comm.).

Early spring Apr. 18 M.H.D.C.; late fall Oct. 4 Denver.

Geothlypis trichas campicola Behle and Aldrich. [681k]

RECOGNITION.—Grayer than *occidentalis;* "less yellow olive-green upper parts; yellow of under parts less extensive; belly and flanks grayer, averaging more whitish, less buffy."

RANGE.—Breeds east of the Cascade Mountains in northern Oregon, Washington and British Columbia, thence locally through northern Idaho, Alberta, Saskatchewan, Montana, Wyoming, and North Dakota. In migration occurs through Colorado to Mexico.

Nebraska, Kansas, and New Mexico: may occur in migration; Utah: transient; Wyoming: breeding along Muddy Creek in Uinta Co. (A.O.U. Check-list).

COLORADO.—Probably migrates regularly throughout the state. There are specimens in the Museum collection from Montezuma, Morgan, Weld, and Yuma Counties. This western breeding form intergrades with *occidentalis* along the Colorado-Wyoming line.

YELLOW-BREASTED CHAT   *Icteria virens auricollis* (Deppe). [683a]

RECOGNITION.—Length 6.5–7.5 inches. *Adult:* olive-gray above; superciliary and eyering white; lores black, throat and breast orange-yellow; belly white. *Young:* olive above with lores gray; throat and belly white, breast and sides gray. (Plate 104)

RANGE.—The species breeds from British Columbia across Canada to Ontario, and in northern states from North Dakota east locally to Vermont, New Hampshire, and New York. This western race breeds from southern British Columbia to California, northern Idaho, Montana, southern Alberta, Saskatchewan, and North Dakota south through Washington, Oregon and through the western Great Plains into Mexico.

Nebraska and Kansas: fairly common migrant and summer resident in west, probably intergrading with *virens;* New Mexico: widely distributed in summer and local breeder; Utah: common in summer along streams and river valleys; Wyoming: common migrant and summer resident.

COLORADO.—Fairly common migrant throughout the state, nesting in low growth in the Upper Sonoran Zone upward into the Transition Zone to the altitude of about 7000 ft. Thirty-five noted (6 localities) on Spring Count May 22, 1965 (C.B.N. 13:31); four noted along the Dolores River, Mesa Co., May 28, 1967 (Hugh Kingery, pers. comm.).

Early spring May 6 Adams Co.; late fall Oct. 3 Longmont.

Icteria virens virens (Linnaeus). [683]

RECOGNITION.—Length 6.5–7.5 inches. Similar to *auricollis*, but wings and tail shorter, superciliary line less extensive, and back more olive.

RANGE.—Breeds from northeastern South Dakota, southern Minnesota, Wisconsin, Michigan, southern Ontario, Vermont, New Hampshire, and New York south to Florida, the Gulf coast, and eastern Texas. Winters in Mexico and Central America.

Nebraska and Kansas: transient and summer resident in east, intergrading with *I.v. auricollis.*

COLORADO.—Straggler in eastern and southern counties. A specimen (no. 2306) was taken by L. J. Hersey at Wray, May 21, 1911; a female (no. 3340) was secured by H. H. Sheldon along the Animas River in southwestern Colorado June 18, 1913; F. C. Lincoln (1919) obtained a male (no. 2908) at Holly May 24, 1913; and a male (no. 4711) was collected by J. D. Figgins near Wray June 20, 1915.

HOODED WARBLER   *Wilsonia citrina* (Boddaert). [684]

RECOGNITION.—Length 5–5.75 inches. *Male:* dark olive above, with crown, neck, and throat black; forehead, cheeks, and belly yellow; webs of outer tail feathers white. *Female:* like the male, but black absent or if present restricted to nape and breast. *Young:* olive-green above and yellow below. (Plate 105)

RANGE.—Breeds from central Iowa, Illinois, southern Michigan, southern Ontario, northwestern Ontario, Pennsylvania, southern Connecticut, Rhode Island, and New York, south to Florida, the Gulf coast, and southeastern Texas. Winters from Mexico and Central America to Panama.

Nebraska: a very rare migrant and breeder in southeast (eight records), one observed in Dawes Co.; Kansas: formerly numerous in east but now rare, four males collected in Leavenworth and Shawnee Counties; New Mexico: reported from Roswell April 6 and 11, 1953 (Ligon, 1961); Wyoming: straggler.

COLORADO.—Casual migrant. One noted at Boulder May 8–9, 1927; a female (no. 26599) collected at Barr Lake May 3, 1952; one observed at Golden May 16–18, 1961; a male at Ft. Collins May 4, 1963; a male near Golden in mid-April 1964; a male recorded in Denver Apr. 23, 1964; and a male at Barr Lake May 8, 1965 (C.B.N. 13:16). A pair was seen in Bear Creek Canyon, near Colorado Springs May 12, 1966; the male flew into a window, and Dr. Robert Stabler forwarded the bird to this Museum (no. 33848). This is the second specimen from the state and the first report from El Paso Co. A male was banded by Allegra Collister at Lyons July 14, 1966 (pers. comm.), and caught in the net at the same time was a Carolina Wren.

WILSON'S WARBLER   *Wilsonia pusilla pileolata* (Pallas). [685a]

RECOGNITION.—Length 4.5–5 inches. *Male:* bright olive-green above; crown spot glossy black; forehead orange yellow; under parts yellow. *Female:* paler than male; crown patch restricted or wanting. *Young:* olive-brown above; belly white; two white wing bars. (Plate 105)

RANGE.—The species breeds across northern Alaska and Canada to Nova Scotia and New England, and this race from northern Alaska, Yukon, and northwestern Mackenzie south through British Columbia, eastern Oregon, and eastern California, east to central Nevada, Montana, and Wyoming south to New Mexico. Winters from Texas into Mexico.

Nebraska and Kansas: migrant in west (*W.p. pusilla* in east); New Mexico: breeds in northern mountains, and is regular in migration at lower elevations; Utah: fairly common transient, and probably breeds in higher mountains; Wyoming: common migrant, and a breeder in mountains.

COLORADO.—Common spring and fall migrant in the Upper Sonoran Zone, and summer resident, nesting on the ground in moist places of the Upper Canadian into the Alpine Zone.

Early spring Apr. 15 Fort Morgan; late fall Nov. 6 Arapahoe Co.

CANADA WARBLER   *Wilsonia canadensis* (Linnaeus). [686]

RECOGNITION.—Length 5–5.75 inches. *Male:* gray above, marked on crown with black; lores, eyering, and under parts bright yellow except for black breast stripes. *Female and young:* like the male, but black on crown and breast restricted or lacking. (Plate 105)

RANGE.—Breeds from north-central Alberta east to southern Quebec, New Brunswick, and across northern states south through the Appalachian Mountains to eastern Tennessee, and North Carolina to northern Georgia. Winters in northern South America to Ecuador and Peru.

Nebraska: casual migrant in eastern third of state; Kansas: uncommon transient west to Sedgwick and Cloud Counties.

COLORADO.—Straggler. An adult male (C.C. No. 4131) was collected near Limon, Lincoln Co., May 23, 1899, a female (C.U. No. 2778) near Parker Sept. 9, 1913, and a male in high plumage along Clear Creek near Denver May 26, 1917; one was observed in Boulder Co. June 13, 1960 at 8600 ft.; one north of Golden "at close range" Sept. 23, 1963; and one June 18, 1967 at Briggsdale, Weld Co. (Hugh Kingery, pers. comm.).

AMERICAN REDSTART   *Setophaga ruticilla tricolora* (Müller). [687a]

RECOGNITION.—Length 5–5.5 inches. *Male:* glossy black above; belly white; sides, broad wing bar, and patches at base of outer tail feathers salmon-red. *Female:* olive-gray to olive-brown above; crown and cheeks gray; under parts gray-white; color patches yellow. *Young:* like the female, but male with some black breast feathering, and tinge of red in color patches. (Plate 105)

RANGE.—This northern and western race breeds from southeastern Alaska and British Columbia across central southern Canada to Newfoundland south to Washington, Oregon, Idaho, Montana, and Utah. Winters from Mexico and Baja California south to Ecuador and Brazil. The subspecies *S.r. ruticilla* breeds from North Dakota, Minnesota, Michigan, southern Ontario, and New York south to Georgia, Oklahoma, Texas, Louisiana, and Alabama.

Nebraska and Kansas: *S.r. ruticilla* breeding and *S.r. tricolora* a migrant through both states; New Mexico: uncommon as a species, with numerous birds reported from near Carlsbad Caverns; Utah: uncommon summer resident; Wyoming: uncommon migrant in eastern counties, breeding locally.

COLORADO.—Fairly common migrant and rare summer resident east of the Continental Divide.

NESTING.—Found breeding by Trippe near Idaho Springs (Coues, 1874); breeding at Longmont (Bergtold, 1925), and near Loveland in 1930, 31, and 32 (Bergtold, 1935); nested at Boulder in 1927 (Alexander, 1937); nest at Boulder June 5, 1943, and a female on nest near Lyons June 16, 1965 (A. Collister, pers. comm.). Sixteen noted (9 localities) on Spring Count May 22, 1965 (C.B.N. 13:31).

Early spring Apr. 30 El Paso Co.; late fall Nov. 14 Denver.

* PAINTED REDSTART   *Setophaga picta picta* Swainson. [688]

RECOGNITION.—Length 5–5.5 inches. A black warbler, except for red breast, *white wing patch* and white outer tail feathers. (Plate 97)

RANGE.—Breeds from north-central Arizona, southwestern New Mexico, Chisos Mts. in Texas south into Mexico. New Mexico: fairly common in the mountains of the southwest; Utah: one sight record from Zion National Park.

COLORADO.—Straggler. Sight records from El Paso Co. near Fountain Valley School Oct. 25, 1958 and Nov. 8 (F. M. Brown, pers. comm.); and one observed by Geo. Shier at Golden May 16, 1965 (C.B.N. 13:16).

Several other species of warblers have been reported which we mention here, subject to future verification. The Blue-winged Warbler (*Vermivora pinus*) was recorded from north of Golden May 23, 1961 (C.B.N. 11:45) and Lois Webster (pers. comm.) observed one at M.H.D.C. Sept. 18, 1965; Lawrence's Warbler, a supposed hybrid between the Golden and Blue-winged Warblers, north of Golden May 14, 1963 (11:45); a female Hermit Warbler (*Dendroica occidentalis*) from the same area May 12, 1963 (12:46); and several Kentucky Warblers (*Oporornis formosus*) from near Boulder in May and June 1963, and one near Golden May 13, 1964 (12:18).

Family PLOCEIDAE: Weaver Finches

HOUSE SPARROW   *Passer domesticus domesticus* (Linnaeus). [688.2]

RECOGNITION.—Length 6–6.5 inches. *Male:* dark beak, black throat, and chestnut nape. *Female:* brownish above and grayish below, and without black throat. *Young:* similar to female (not illustrated in color).

RANGE.—Resident throughout Europe, Russia, and Siberia. Introduced and widespread in North America, Hawaii, South America, eastern South Africa, New Zealand, and Australia.

Nebraska, Kansas, New Mexico, Utah, and Wyoming: introduced common resident.

COLORADO.—Common throughout the state in settled communities, nesting in mountain towns to 10,000 feet or more. First observed in state at Pueblo Feb. 20, 1895.

Family ICTERIDAE: Meadowlarks, Blackbirds, and Orioles

BOBOLINK   *Dolichonyx oryzivorus* (Linnaeus). [494]

RECOGNITION.—Length 6.5–7.5 inches. *Male:* mainly black; hind neck and dorsal streakings cream-yellow; broad wing bar, rump, and upper tail coverts gray-white. *Female:* yellow-brown above; throat white; under parts creamy yellow with sides sparsely streaked. *Fall adults and young:* like summer female, but streaking darker. (Plate 106)

RANGE.—Breeds from British Columbia across southern Canada to Nova Scotia and south to northeastern California and Arizona, east to northern Nevada, Indiana, Ohio, Pennsylvania, and West Virginia to Maryland and New Jersey. Winters in South America to northern Argentina.

Nebraska: fairly common migrant, breeding throughout the state in small numbers; Kansas: uncommon transient, two pairs noted feeding fledglings in Cloud County in 1940, and nesting in Stafford Co. June 18, 1956; New Mexico: rare visitor, one likely breeding occurrence July 15, 1951; Utah: uncommon summer resident locally; Wyoming: uncommon migrant, but breeder in suitable habitat.

COLORADO.—Irregular summer resident which has been recorded from widespread areas of the state.

Early spring May 4 Limon; late summer Sept. 9 Barr.

NESTING.—Two young collected near Meeker Aug. 17, 1909, first evidence of breeding in the state (Felger, 1910); nest with four young in a meadow two miles southeast of Boulder found by RJN June 19, 1929 (N. & R., 1939); three pairs west of Gunnison and nest and eggs July 1, 1952 (Hyde, 1953).

WESTERN MEADOWLARK　　*Sturnella neglecta neglecta* Audubon. [501.1]

RECOGNITION.—Length 8–10 inches. *Male:* gray-brown above, streaked and barred with dusky; three buff crown stripes; lores, throat, and belly yellow; yellow of throat extending upward to grayish ear-coverts; black breast; crescent and outer tail feathers white. *Female:* paler with breast crescent smaller. *Young:* plumage duller and breast spotted. (Plate 106)

RANGE.—Breeds from southern British Columbia, southern Manitoba, and western Ontario south locally into Wisconsin, Michigan, and Minnesota, south to Baja California, Texas, and Louisiana into Mexico.

Nebraska: a common breeder throughout the state; Kansas: a common transient and resident in the west, nesting east to Flint Hills; New Mexico: resident throughout the state; Utah: common summer resident in the valleys, in winter a few in the north and common in the south; Wyoming: abundant summer resident, with a few in winter.

COLORADO.—Common summer resident throughout the state into the foothills and mountain parks to 8000 or more feet. A few occur regularly in winter at low elevations.

* EASTERN MEADOWLARK　　*Sturnella magna magna* (Linnaeus). [501]

RECOGNITION.—Similar to Western Meadowlark, but darker above and less yellow of throat and none on cheeks.

RANGE.—Breeds in the eastern half of the continent from southwestern South Dakota, Iowa, Minnesota, Ontario, Quebec, and New Brunswick south to North Carolina and through Illinois, Indiana, and Missouri south to northern Texas. Winters through much of the breeding range.

Nebraska: a common breeder throughout the state but less numerous in west; Kansas: common transient and resident in east, nesting locally to Jewell and Barber Counties.

COLORADO.—Probably casual breeding bird of eastern counties. Numerous questionable reports based upon songs.

YELLOW-HEADED BLACKBIRD　　*Xanthocephalus xanthocephalus* (Bonaparte). [497]

RECOGNITION.—Length 9.5–11 inches. *Male:* black, with head, neck, and breast yellow-orange; wing patch white. *Female:* plumage dusky-brown; superciliary line, throat, and upper breast white to pale yellow; lower breast streaked with white; no wing patch. *Young:* plumage dusky; head and breast brown; belly and wing bars whitish. (Plate 106)

RANGE.—Breeds from southern British Columbia, Alberta, Saskatchewan, and Manitoba and from Oregon, Minnesota, Wisconsin, Illinois, and Ohio south to Baja California, Oklahoma, Arkansas, and Arizona. Winters from southwestern states into Mexico.

Nebraska: common migrant and breeder in the Panhandle Region and locally elsewhere; Kansas: transient in west, local summer resident, and uncommon in east; New Mexico: locally common breeder in northern marshes, and a few winter in the south. Utah: common summer resident of the north; Wyoming: common migrant and colonial breeder.

COLORADO.—Common locally in suitable marsh habitat throughout Colorado from the plains into the mountains to above 8000 feet. Occurs occasionally in winter.

RED-WINGED BLACKBIRD　　*Agelaius phoeniceus fortis* Ridgway. [498d]

RECOGNITION.—Length 8–9.5 inches. *Summer male:* black, except the red shoulder edged with buffy. *Winter male:* scapulars edged with rusty. *Summer female:* dark brown above, streaked with buffy and dusky; whitish below, streaked with dark brown; throat white or pinkish. *Winter female:* paler above and under parts more buffy. *Immature male:* like the male, but feathers edged with rusty; epaulettes orange-red marked with black. (Plate 106)

RANGE.—The species breeds across Canada to Nova Scotia south throughout the United States into Central America and some of the islands of the Caribbean. Fourteen subspecies are included in the Check-list and this form breeds east of the Rockies in western Montana, Idaho, and Nevada south to eastern Arizona and northern Texas. Winters mainly in the southern part of the breeding range.

Nebraska: *A.p. fortis* in the west, an abundant breeder as a species, with three races recorded; Kansas: the common race is *A.p. phoeniceus*, with *A.p. fortis* occurring in migration and possibly nesting in west, with two.other races as transients; New Mexico: common nesting species; Utah: *A.p. fortis* common summer resident in central and central-eastern areas; Wyoming: common as a species.

COLORADO.—Common through the state, resident in suitable habitat.

Agelaius phoeniceus arctolegus Oberholser. [498i]

RECOGNITION.—Length 9–10 inches. Similar to *fortis*, but slightly larger; female darker, and streaks more blackish and extensive below; male with wing and tail averaging shorter, bill larger, and buff of wing coverts paler; not distinguishable in the field.

RANGE.—Breeds from British Columbia, Alberta, southeastern Yukon, central Mackenzie, and northeastern Ontario south to Montana, South Dakota, and Iowa. Winters from breeding range to Illinois, Alabama, and Texas.

Nebraska: resident locally (North Platte); Kansas: occurs in migration.

COLORADO.—Winter visitor in northeastern Colorado. A specimen from Semper, Jefferson Co., taken Dec. 29, 1892 (Niedrach and Rockwell, 1939). A female (no. 10237) from Barr Feb. 24, 1924, and another (no. 15646) collected in the same area Feb. 13, 1937 were identified as this subspecies by Dr. H. C. Oberholser.

Agelaius phoeniceus nevadensis Grinnell. [498j]

RECOGNITION.—Length 8–9 inches. Similar to *fortis*, but smaller, with little rusty above in winter.

RANGE.—Breeds from southeastern British Columbia south through Washington, northern Idaho, eastern Oregon, northern and eastern California, and southern Nevada. Winters from its breeding range to western and southern California and southern Arizona to Mexico.

COLORADO.—Straggler. A female (no. 18468) collected by R. L. Landberg at East Lake, Adams Co., Dec. 19, 1937, was identified by Dr. Oberholser as being this form.

ORCHARD ORIOLE   Icterus spurius (Linnaeus). [506]

RECOGNITION.—Length 6–7 inches. *Summer male:* black, except chestnut-red breast, belly, lower back, and wing shoulders. *Winter male:* black obscured with gray feather edgings. *Female:* olive-yellow above; pale yellow below, two whitish wing bars. *Second year male:* like female, but lores and foreneck black. *Young:* similar to female. (Plate 107)

RANGE.—Breeds from south Ontario, southern Manitoba, southern Michigan, north Pennsylvania, New York, and central Massachusetts south through southern North Dakota to the Gulf coast and into Mexico. Winters from southern Mexico to Colombia and Venezuela.

Nebraska: a common migrant and summer resident in the eastern two-thirds of the state, rare summer resident in west; Kansas: common transient and summer resident; New Mexico: occurs regularly in southeastern corner, uncommon and irregular elsewhere; Wyoming: rare summer resident in the northeast.

COLORADO.—Fairly numerous in the eastern part of the state with two records from western counties. Reported nesting southeast of Wray June 5–15, 1906 and three pairs were seen feeding young at Bonny Res. July 14, 1962.

Early spring May 11 Delta Co.; no fall records, probably due to lack of observers.

* HOODED ORIOLE   Icterus cucullatus nelsoni Ridgway. [505a]

RECOGNITION.—Length 7–8 inches. A large oriole, somewhat similar to Bullock's, but male with an *orange crown*. Female with belly yellowish instead of whitish as in the Bullock's Oriole. (not illustrated)

RANGE.—The species occurs throughout much of the southwest from central California, southern Nevada, central and southern New Mexico, and western and southern Texas into Mexico. The race *nelsoni* breeds from southeastern California into Baja California and from New Mexico to central-southeastern Arizona to southern Sonora.

Kansas: one interesting record from near Garden City in Finney Co. about August 5, 1939; New Mexico: ranges in the southwest, north to the Gila River and east to Las Cruces; Utah: reported from the extreme southwest, three specimens recorded (Wilson Bull. 75: 455).

COLORADO.—Observations for two consecutive years from Hotchkiss, Delta County (A.F.N. 15:429).

* SCOTT'S ORIOLE   Icterus parisorum Bonaparte. [504]

RECOGNITION.—Length 7–8 inches. *Male:* black with belly a bright lemon-yellow; white and yellow on wings and tail; upper tail coverts and rump tinged with olive. *Female:* greenish-yellow below, olive-green above, rump yellowish. (not illustrated)

RANGE.—Breeds from southern Nevada, southwestern Utah, New Mexico, Arizona, and western Texas south into Mexico. Nesting records from near Stillwater, Nevada, and Powder Springs, Utah (A.O.U. Check-list).

New Mexico: common locally in southern counties; Utah: rare summer resident, more common in extreme southwest.

COLORADO.—An adult was noted by Mr. and Mrs. Harold R. Holt in Black Canyon National Monument on June 1, 1960 (C.B.N. 8:39), and the bird, or another, had been seen in the same location several times during the previous week by C. Harold Baer (8:49).

BALTIMORE ORIOLE   *Icterus galbula* (Linnaeus). [507]

RECOGNITION.—Length 7–8 inches. *Summer male:* plumage black, except breast, belly, wing shoulders, rump, upper tail coverts, and portions of outer tail feathers are orange; one white wing bar. *Winter male:* scapulars edged with orange; rump and upper tail coverts orange. *Female and young:* dark yellow-brown above, mixed with dusky; rump yellow; under parts dull orange-yellow; two white wing bars. (Plate 107)

RANGE.—Breeds from central Alberta locally across Canada to Nova Scotia and east of the Rocky Mountains south to Oklahoma, Texas, and the Gulf states. Winters from southern Mexico through Central America to South America.

Nebraska: a common migrant and summer resident; Kansas: common transient and summer resident; Wyoming: casual in eastern part of the state.

COLORADO.—A fairly common bird along the eastern border of the state where it hybridizes with Bullock's Oriole.

Early spring May 10 Ft. Collins; no fall records, probably due to lack of observers.

BULLOCK'S ORIOLE   *Icterus bullockii bullockii* (Swainson). [508]

RECOGNITION.—Length 7–8 inches. *Male:* plumage black, except orange-yellow forehead, superciliary line, cheeks, breast, rump, and parts of outer tail feathers; large white wing patch. *Female:* olive-gray above, with crown and occiput brown; cheeks, foreneck, and breast pale yellow, with throat often black; belly gray-white; one white wing bar; tail and upper tail coverts yellowish. *Second-year male:* like female, but lores and throat black; *Young:* like female, but lacking black throat and yellow coloring. (Plate 107)

RANGE.—Breeds from southern British Columbia, Alberta, Saskatchewan, Montana, and North Dakota south to central California in the west, and Oklahoma and southern Texas in the east. Winters from Louisiana, Texas, and California into Mexico.

Nebraska and Kansas: a common migrant and summer resident in the west, intergrading with the Baltimore Oriole; New Mexico: common widespread summer resident over the state up to 7000 feet. Utah: common summer resident in the valleys; Wyoming: common migrant and summer resident.

COLORADO.—Common summer resident from the plains into the foothills, and numerous locally in wooded valleys in western counties.

Early spring Mar. 15 Denver; late fall Nov. 15 Longmont.

RUSTY BLACKBIRD   *Euphagus carolinus carolinus* (Müller). [509]

RECOGNITION.—Length 8.5–9.5 inches. *Male:* glossy black with greenish on head and body; eyes straw yellow. *Winter male:* feathers edged with rusty above and brown below. *Female:* slaty plumage; eye yellow. *Winter female:* brown-gray feather edgings as in male. Young mostly pale rusty. (Plate 108)

RANGE.—Breeds from northern Alaska, northern Yukon, northwestern and central Mackenzie, and British Columbia locally across Canada to Newfoundland, Maine, Vermont, New Hampshire, and New York. Winters from southern Canada and northern states to the Gulf coast.

Nebraska: a common migrant in eastern two-thirds of the state, and rare winter resident; Kansas: common transient and winter resident; New Mexico: occurs rarely in eastern part; New Mexico: recorded from Roswell Nov. 10, 1956 (Ligon, 1961); Utah: casual, one specimen, a male Nov. 24, 1952, Tooele Co. (Condor, 56:363); Wyoming: rare migrant.

COLORADO.—An irregular winter visitor with comparatively few records from the state.

Late spring May 19 Longmont; summer Aug. 29 R.Mt.N.P.; early fall Sept. 28 Weldona.

BREWER'S BLACKBIRD   *Euphagus cyanocephalus* (Wagler). [510]

RECOGNITION.—Length 8.5–10 inches. *Male:* black to blue-green; glossed on head and neck with purple; eyes pale yellow. *Female:* black-brown above; head, neck, and under parts brown-gray; head, wings, and belly faintly glossed; eyes brown. *Young:* like the female, but without gloss. (Plate 108)

RANGE.—Breeds from central British Columbia, central Alberta, Saskatchewan, and central Manitoba to Baja California, east to Michigan and south to Arizona and Texas. Winters from southern British Columbia and Alberta south into Mexico.

Nebraska: a common migrant, and a summer resident in the western half; Kansas: transient and local winter resident, common in the west; New Mexico: widely scattered in north in summer between 6500 and 7500 feet, and common winter resident; Utah: common resident in valleys; Wyoming: common migrant, summer resident, and occasionally in winter.

COLORADO.—Common summer resident from the plains into the mountains, rarely to 10,000 feet; a few occur in winter. Several pairs may nest in close proximity on the ground, in low shrubs, or in trees.

COMMON GRACKLE   *Quiscalus quiscula versicolor* Vieillot. [511b]

RECOGNITION.—Length 11–13.5 inches. *Male:* black, glossed on head and neck with purple or green; body with iridescent bronze; eyes pale yellow; tail wedge-shaped. *Female:* plumage duller than male. *Young:* resembling fall adults or plain dusky-brown. (Plate 108)

RANGE.—Breeds from northeastern British Columbia, southern Mackenzie, Saskatchewan, Ontario, and Quebec to Newfoundland, south to New York, Pennsylvania, Massachusetts, Virginia, Kentucky, and Tennessee; in the west, mostly east of the Rockies to Texas. Winters mainly from Ohio Valley to south Texas, and casually over much of the breeding area.

Nebraska: common migrant and summer resident, occasionally in winter; Kansas: common transient, summer resident, and local winter visitor; New Mexico: not common, recorded nesting in 1951 in NE corner by Ligon (twelve pairs near N. M. and Okla. line); Utah: straggler, one specimen; Wyoming: common migrant, and summer resident in eastern two-thirds of the state.

COLORADO.—Summer resident, and occurs occasionally in winter; common locally upon the eastern plains to the base of the foothills.

BROWN-HEADED COWBIRD   *Molothrus ater artemisiae* Grinnell. [495b]

RECOGNITION.—Length 6–8 inches. *Male:* iridescent black, purple, and green, head and neck dark brown. *Female:* dark brown-gray, lighter below. *Young:* dull gray to brown above; buff-white feather edgings; streaked below with buff-white. (Plate 108)

RANGE.—The species breeds from central and northeastern British Columbia across Canada to Nova Scotia, south into Mexico and Baja California, and this race from British Columbia east in southern Canada to western Ontario, south through Central Washington to eastern California, Nevada, Utah, western Nebraska, Kansas, and western Minnesota to Iowa, south to western New Mexico.

Nebraska and Kansas: both *M.a. ater* and *M.a. artemisiae* recorded; New Mexico: *ater* listed by F. M. Bailey in the east, *artemisiae* in west (Check-list); Utah and Wyoming: *artemisiae* breeding form.

COLORADO.—Common in summer throughout the state at lower elevations, ranging into the Transition Zone. Early spring Mar. 27 Weldona; winter Dec. 28 Arapahoe Co. (RJN), and a male banded Feb. 20 Weld Co.

Family THRAUPIDAE: Tanagers

WESTERN TANAGER   *Piranga ludoviciana* (Wilson). [607]

RECOGNITION.—Length 6–7.5 inches. *Summer male:* head and throat orange-red to crimson; under parts, rump, and upper tail coverts yellow; back, wings, and tail black, one yellow and one white wing bar. *Female:* olive-green above, rump more yellow; wings and tail gray-brown, dull yellow below with olive sides; two white wing bars. *Young:* like female, with under parts streaked, wing bars yellowish. (Plate 109)

RANGE.—Breeds from southern Alaska, northern British Columbia, Mackenzie, Alberta, and Saskatchewan south to Baja California, and from South Dakota to Texas and Arizona. Winters from Baja California and southern Tamaulipas south on the Pacific side of the Continental Divide through Guatemala to Costa Rica.

Nebraska: common migrant in the Panhandle Region, breeding on Pine Ridge; Kansas: fairly common migrant, and perhaps summer resident in the west; New Mexico: widely distributed in summer in the mountains from 7500 to 10,000 feet; Utah: common transient in lowlands, and summer resident in mountains; Wyoming: common migrant, and breeder in conifers.

COLORADO.—Common in migration at low elevations, nesting from the pinyon-juniper areas into the ponderosa pines to 9000 feet.

Early spring May 4 Denver (C.B.N. 12:18); late fall Nov. 27 Boulder; winter Jan. 18 Boulder.

NESTING.—A common breeding form from the pinyon-juniper and scrub oak associations into the ponderosa pines.

SCARLET TANAGER　*Piranga olivacea* (Gmelin). [608]

RECOGNITION.—Length 6.5–7.5 inches. *Summer male:* scarlet, with wings and tail black. *Winter male:* like female, but wings and tail black. *Female:* yellowish-olive above; pale yellow below, wings lighter than in Western and *no* wing bars. *Young:* like female, male with wing coverts dark. (Plate 109)

RANGE.—Breeds from central Nebraska, eastern North Dakota, southeastern Manitoba, western Ontario, southern Quebec, New Brunswick, and Maine south to Oklahoma, Arkansas, Tennessee, Alabama, and South Carolina. Winters from Colombia to Bolivia and Peru.

Nebraska: summer resident and migrant in Missouri River valley, and uncommon elsewhere; Kansas: fairly common transient in east, and uncommon summer resident in northeast; Wyoming: rare visitor.

COLORADO.—Uncommon straggler. At least five specimens have been collected, one from Garfield Co. in the western part of the state, and there have been approximately twenty recorded observations from eastern counties, including a male in R.Mt.N.P. July 1, 1963, and a male by Gilbert J. Mueller near his country home two miles east of Larkspur June 12, 1966 (pers. comm.).

* HEPATIC TANAGER　*Piranga flava dextra* Bangs. [609a]

RECOGNITION.—Length 7–7.80 inches. *Adult male:* upper parts dull red, crown bright red; scarlet below with brownish flanks; *ear coverts grayish-brown. Female:* olive-green above, olive-yellow below. Both sexes differ from *P. rubra* by having a "dull grayish and red back, and grayish-brown ear-coverts, and female of this species has a darkish bill." (Plate 109)

RANGE.—Transition Zone of northwestern Arizona, north-central New Mexico, and western Texas southward through the highlands of Mexico.

COLORADO.—Straggler; one report, a male observed at Boulder May 15, 1956.

SUMMER TANAGER　*Piranga rubra rubra* (Linnaeus). [610]

RECOGNITION.—Length 6.5–7.75 inches. *Male:* rose-red above and bright red below; wings brown-red and bill yellow. *Female:* yellow-olive above and dull orange-yellow below and bill yellowish. *Young:* like female, male with crown, tail, and primary edges tinged with orange. (Plate 109)

RANGE.—Breeds from Oklahoma, Nebraska, Wisconsin, Iowa, Illinois, Ohio, Maryland, New Jersey, and Delaware to Florida and southern Texas. Winters from central Mexico through Central America to northern South America.

Nebraska: uncommon migrant, and summer resident in the southeast; Kansas: common transient and summer resident, but distribution poorly known; New Mexico: ranges north to Albuquerque in the Rio Grande Valley and to Santa Rosa in Pecos Valley; Utah: several observations and female collected in Washington Co. July 24, 1964 (Condor, 68:210); Wyoming: one Cheyenne May 14, 1966 for the first state report (A.F.N. 20:537).

COLORADO.—Uncommon straggler. Four specimens have been collected, and there are about ten observations listed from Colorado Springs, Golden, Boulder, and Longmont, and the latest at 6900 feet at Kittredge, Jeff. Co., May 15, 1967 (H. Holt).

Early spring Apr. 29 Colo. Spgs.; late fall Oct. 19 Colo. Spgs. (no. 33697).

Family FRINGILLIDAE: Grosbeaks, Finches, Sparrows, and Buntings

CARDINAL　*Richmondena cardinalis cardinalis* (Linnaeus). [593]

RECOGNITION.—Length 7.5–9 inches. *Male:* head crested, plumage bright red except black face and chin; back duller red. *Female:* olive-gray, wings, tail, and tip of crest dull red; face gray, brown-gray below, with breast tinged with red. *Young:* similar to female. (Plate 110)

RANGE.—The species ranges from South Dakota, Ontario, Maine, and New York south to Florida and the Gulf coast and from California into Baja California and Mexico. This eastern race is resident and breeding from western New York, Ontario, and lower Hudson Valley west to Minnesota and south to the northern part of the Gulf states. Winters within breeding range.

Nebraska and Kansas: common in the east, rare in west; New Mexico: race *R.c. superba* uncommon; Wyoming: one at Cheyenne May 19, 1962 (A.F.N. 16:436).

COLORADO.—A rare resident in eastern part of state and on the prairies adjacent to the foothills. First recorded, a male (no. 2581), taken near Denver by A. W. Anthony Dec. 5, 1883, and the second one observed at Pueblo Nov. 28, 1895. Since then more than thirty have been observed in eastern counties, and one near Grand Junction May 27–28, 1962. Recorded nesting near Littleton in 1924 and 1926.

ROSE-BREASTED GROSBEAK   *Pheucticus ludovicianus* (Linnaeus). [595]

RECOGNITION.—Length 6.5–7 inches. *Summer male:* plumage black, except white belly, rump, upper tail coverts, wing bars, and patch in primaries; axillars rose, triangular rose-red markings on breast. *Winter male:* wings and tail dusky, axillars pink. *Female:* brown above, streaked with black, axillars yellow; whitish below, streaked on sides; breast tinged with pink. *Young: male:* like adult but wing and some tail feathers brown as in female. (Plate 110)

RANGE.—Breeds from northwestern British Columbia, Alberta, Saskatchewan, and Manitoba east to Quebec and Nova Scotia, south to North Dakota, South Dakota, Missouri, and Tennessee, and from Illinois across northern states to New Jersey, and south to Virginia, North Carolina, Kentucky, and mountains of Georgia. Casual in migration to Arizona and California, and winters from southern Louisiana through Mexico to northern South America.

Nebraska and Kansas: common transient and locally common resident in east; New Mexico: a full-plumaged male observed southeast of Silver City May 20, 1923 (F. M. Bailey, 1928), one at Albuquerque May 5, 1963, and a male collected May 20 at Sitting Bull Falls (A.F.N. 17:424); Utah: a specimen secured in Archer National Monument on May 26, 1965, and another in Juab Co. June 2, 1965. Sight records include one from Kane Co., one from Juab Co. June 4, 1965, and one from Zion Nat'l Park (Condor, 68:396); Wyoming: uncommon in eastern part of state.

COLORADO.—Irregular summer visitor. Four specimens have been collected (Longmont, Daniels Park, W. Denver, Colorado Springs). About forty have been recorded from eastern counties; a male was observed in Jackson Co., June 4, 1946, and another at Gunnison May 26, 1964. Breeds casually (pair Longmont 1889, Loveland 1925; and male feeding two large young, 155 Marion, Denver, July 12, 1966, Elizabeth Flick, pers. comm.). Four banded Sept. 1 to Oct. 26, 1966 and one noted at Longmont Nov. 6 (A.F.N. 21:54); one at Kittredge (6900 ft.) May 16, 1967 (H. Holt); and one at Eldora (8650 ft.) May 30–June 1, 1967 (Gail Shickley).

BLACK-HEADED GROSBEAK *Pheucticus melanocephalus melanocephalus* (Swainson). [596a]

RECOGNITION.—Length 6.5–7.5 inches. *Male:* black above, except cinnamon neck and rump; wing bars, wing and tail patches white; breast, sides, and flanks cinnamon; belly yellow; *Female:* dark brown above, streaked with dusky; wing bars, superciliary, and line below ear white; under parts tawny; sides and flanks streaked; mid-belly yellow-white. *Young:* similar to female. (Plate 110)

RANGE.—Breeds from southeastern British Columbia, Montana, Saskatchewan, Alberta, and North Dakota south to eastern California, Arizona, and western Texas into Mexico.

Nebraska and Kansas: common transient and summer resident in the west; New Mexico and Utah: common breeding summer resident; Wyoming: common migrant and summer resident.

COLORADO.—Common summer resident on the prairies and in low valleys throughout the state, ranging in the foothills to 8000 feet.

Early spring Apr. 26 Loveland; late fall Oct. 10 Sedalia.

BLUE GROSBEAK   *Guiraca caerulea interfusa* Dwight and Griscom. [597a]

RECOGNITION.—Length 6–7.5 inches. *Male:* plumage purple-blue; lores and back streaked with black; wings and tail blue-black; two brown wing bars. *Female:* head and under parts tawny-brown; back olive-brown; wings and tail dusky; flanks faintly streaked; two buff wing bars. *Young:* similar to female. (Plate 110)

RANGE.—The species ranges locally over many of the eastern states and Kansas, South Dakota, Nebraska, Oklahoma, and Texas to Durango, Mexico, and northeastern Baja California. Winters from Sonora south along the Pacific coast of Mexico and Central America to Costa Rica.

Nebraska and Kansas: transient and summer resident, breeding locally; New Mexico: common in the Gila, Rio Grande, and Pecos Valleys; Utah: summer resident in southwest; Wyoming: rare summer visitor.

COLORADO.—Uncommon summer resident, locally, along weed-grown ditches and bushy banks of streams throughout the state in the Upper Sonoran Zone.

Early spring May 14 Cherry Creek Res. (C.B.N. 12:20); late summer Sept. 18 Sedalia.

INDIGO BUNTING   *Passerina cyanea* (Linnaeus). [598]

RECOGNITION.—Length 5–5.75 inches. *Male:* indigo blue, blue in crown and throat; lores black; wings and tail dusky tinged with blue. *Female:* brown above, lighter below with faint streakings on breast. *Young:* like female, but browner. (Plate 111)

RANGE.—Breeds from southwestern South Dakota, Minnesota, southern Manitoba, Ontario, and Quebec to southern New Brunswick, south to Oklahoma, Texas, Georgia, and Florida, and in California (Condor, 60:408). Winters in Cuba and Central America.

Nebraska: uncommon local summer resident; Kansas: common transient and local summer resident west to Finney County; New Mexico: recorded from Anthony May 10, 1953, Silver City May 18, 1955, Carlsbad May 23, 1957, Los Alamos May 18, 1958 (Ligon, 1961), Carlsbad May 9, 1963, and Cedar Crest May 24–27 (A.F.N. 17:425); Utah: casual in southwest, with one specimen record; Wyoming: straggler.

COLORADO.—Numerous records from the eastern plains to the foothills. The first Colorado specimen, a male (no. 25980), was taken by Aiken in El Paso Co. May 8, 1872, and the first nest was found in a tangle of ragweed, thistle, and poison ivy just east of Morrison Aug. 8, 1953. The species hybridizes with the Lazuli Bunting.

LAZULI BUNTING   *Passerina amoena* (Say). [599]

RECOGNITION.—Length 5–5.5 inches. *Male:* head and upper parts cerulean blue, back darker; breast and sides cinnamon, belly white; two white wing bars. *Female:* olive-brown above, rump, tail, and wings tinged with pale blue; under parts buff, chin and belly lighter; two white wing bars. *Young:* gray-brown above; buff below, with breast slightly streaked. (Plate 111)

RANGE.—Breeds from southern British Columbia, southern Saskatchewan, and Montana south to southeastern California, Arizona, and Baja California. Winters from Arizona south into Mexico.

Nebraska and Kansas: common migrant, and summer resident in west; New Mexico: widely distributed summer resident below 7800 feet; Utah and Wyoming: common migrant and summer resident.

COLORADO.—Fairly common on the plains into the foothills to 6500 feet throughout the state and rarely to 9500 feet.

Early spring Apr. 25 Jefferson Co.; late fall Oct. 3 Longmont.

PAINTED BUNTING   *Passerina ciris pallidior* Mearns. [601a]

RECOGNITION.—Length 5–5.5 inches. *Male:* head and neck rich blue, back and scapulars rich green; under parts and rump vermilion red, tail dusky reddish. *Female:* plain green above, and brownish below. Immature male similar to female, but some have a patchy coloring of adult male. (Plate 111)

RANGE.—The eastern race breeds from southern Missouri, Tennessee, and southeastern Texas east to the Gulf coast and southeastern North Carolina; this western subspecies from eastern Kansas, southeastern New Mexico, and Oklahoma on south through western Texas into Mexico. Winters from Mexico to western Panama. Casual in southeastern Arizona.

Nebraska: one collected at Kearney in 1961; Kansas: fairly common summer resident in the east, with several nesting records in Douglas, Shawnee, and Montgomery Cos.; New Mexico: fairly common in southern part of the state; Oregon: a male in high plumage banded at Malheur Wildlife Refuge June 2, 1963 by William A. Bechtel (Western Bird Bander, 38:42).

COLORADO.—Straggler. An immature male was collected in Mesa Verde National Park August 29, 1935 and a male observed in June 1958 near Westcliffe, Custer Co.; AMB banded (no. 66-82019) an adult male in his yard in Denver May 17–21, 1962, and Mrs. R. M. Wilson (pers. comm.) recorded a high-plumaged male "singing with the sun shining on its gorgeous plumage" June 10, 1967 in her yard in Wheat Ridge (west Denver).

DICKCISSEL   *Spiza americana* (Gmelin). [604]

RECOGNITION.—Length 6–7 inches. *Male:* brown above, with back streaked; crown olive, cheeks and nape gray; superciliary, spot below eye, and under parts yellow; chin white; throat black; shoulders rufous. *Female:* like male, but paler; crown streaked; throat patch lacking; grayer below. *Young:* similar to female, but slightly streaked below. (Plate 112)

RANGE.—Breeds sporadically from eastern Montana, North Dakota, Minnesota, Michigan, Manitoba, Ontario, Massachusetts and New York south to Georgia and Oklahoma. Winters from Guatemala into South America.

Nebraska: migrant, and resident in east; Kansas: transient and resident, rare in the western part of the state; New Mexico: uncommon migrant, one collected from a flock of eleven in Grant Co. Sept. 8, 1964 (Auk, 82:650); Utah: five observed in Salt Lake City Oct. 1, 1959, and a specimen from Provo May 25, 1964 (Wilson Bull. 78:126); Wyoming: common summer resident in east, rare elsewhere.

COLORADO.—Irregularly common upon the eastern plains. Recorded nesting near Canyon City in 1890, west of Loveland in 1927, in Arapahoe Co. in 1948, near Colorado Springs in 1948, a pair near Golden July 30, 1959, and west of Denver August 15, 1959.

Early spring May 1 La Salle; fall Oct. 4 Gunnison Co.; winter December 1957 Boulder (banded by Mrs. John Hough).

EVENING GROSBEAK   *Hesperiphona vespertina brooksi* Grinnell. [514b]

RECOGNITION.—Length 7–8.5 inches. *Male:* forehead, scapulars, rump, and under parts olive-yellow; crown, wings, and tail black; neck and sides of head brown, lighter on back, large white wing patch. *Female:* gray above and yellow-gray below; wings and tail black; chin and spots on wings and tail white; bill green. *Young:* duller, but plumage pattern essentially that of adults; bill brown. (Plate 112)

RANGE.—The species breeds from British Columbia across a narrow belt of southern Canada to New Brunswick, south to Vermont and New York, and from California and Colorado to Arizona, and into the mountains of southeastern Mexico. This race nests and is resident from central British Columbia and Montana to Nevada, California, Utah, Arizona, and winters sporadically in lowlands of breeding range, south to southern California, and east to Texas.

Nebraska and Kansas: rare and irregular winter visitor; New Mexico: many records, resident and breeding; Utah: winter visitor, breeding rarely; Wyoming: resident and breeding.

COLORADO.—Usually uncommon resident, occasionally common locally, ranging from the plains to 10,000 feet, and nesting irregularly from near the foothills on the plains into the Transition Zone. Invasions of hundreds often occur in winter. A banded bird, one of a pair, penetrated the windshield of an airplane at an altitude of 12,500 feet over the Front Range of the Rockies about five miles south of Boulder March 18, 1964 (Bird-Banding 35:265).

PURPLE FINCH   *Carpodacus purpureus purpureus* (Gmelin). [517]

RECOGNITION.—Length 5–6 inches. *Male:* similar to male Cassin's Finch, but smaller; beak smaller and more curved; red tint and brown of back darker; under tail coverts white. *Female:* like female of Cassin's Finch, but smaller; back browner, superciliary line more pronounced. *Young:* similar to female. (Plate 112)

RANGE.—Breeds from northwestern British Columbia and Alberta across Canada to Newfoundland, south to New York, New Jersey, and West Virginia, west to Pennsylvania, Ohio, Michigan, Wisconsin, and North Dakota. Winters irregularly in, and north and south of breeding range.

Nebraska: rare migrant and winter visitor in east; Kansas: fairly common in winter in east.

COLORADO.—Straggler. A female (no. 2580) was collected at Denver Nov. 15, 1885; one was observed by Thompson Marsh southeast of Denver May 1, 1958 (C.B.N. 5:61), and one was recorded by George Shier at Golden on May 28, 1964 (12:20).

CASSIN'S FINCH   *Carpodacus cassinii* Baird. [518]

RECOGNITION.—Length 6–7 inches. *Male:* dark brown above, streaked with tan and tinged with red; crown crimson contrasting with brown neck, rump pink; pale pink below, blending to white on lower belly; under tail feathers streaked. *Female:* olive-gray, white below, entirely streaked with brown. *Young:* similar to female. (Plate 112)

RANGE.—Breeds from southern British Columbia, Alberta, Montana, Nevada, Utah, and Wyoming to Baja California and northern Arizona. Winters in lowlands of breeding range, south to the highlands of Mexico.

Nebraska and Kansas: rare migrant and winter visitor; New Mexico: summer resident, less common in winter; Utah: fairly common summer resident; Wyoming: common resident in summer, fewer in winter.

COLORADO.—Resident, breeding to 10,000 feet, ranging irregularly in winter over the entire state.

HOUSE FINCH   *Carpodacus mexicanus frontalis* (Say). [519]

RECOGNITION.—Length 5–5.75 inches. *Male:* gray-brown above, tinged with red; cheeks, throat, and rump pink to red; belly light, streaked with brown. *Female:* gray-brown above, faintly streaked; light below, streaked with brown. *Young:* like female but more streaked; buff on wing covert tips. (Plate 112)

RANGE.—The species breeds and is largely resident through much of the western half of the United States, and this race from British Columbia, Idaho, northern Wyoming, and western Nebraska south to Texas, northern Mexico, and Baja California.

Nebraska: common resident in Panhandle Region; Kansas: common in southwest in winter, status in summer uncertain; New Mexico: "abundant" resident; Utah: common summer resident in valleys, less numerous in winter; Wyoming: common resident.

COLORADO.—Common resident of the Upper Sonoran Zone into the foothills to 9000 feet, nest sites varying from low cactus and small conifers to high up in conifers.

PINE GROSBEAK   *Pinicola enucleator montana* Ridgway. [515a]

RECOGNITION.—Length 8–8.5 inches. *Male:* head, breast, and rump dark red; back and wings gray, tinged with red; belly gray; two white wing bars. *Female:* gray with head and rump tawny yellow; two white wing bars. *Young:* wing bars buffy; less yellow than female. (Plate 113)

RANGE.—The species breeds in the coniferous forests of the northern parts of both the Old and New Worlds, and this race is resident and breeding from British Columbia and Alberta south through the northern Cascade Range and Rocky Mountains from Oregon, Washington, Utah, eastern Arizona, and northern New Mexico.

Nebraska and Kansas: rare winter visitor; New Mexico: resident in northern mountains; Utah: uncommon resident in mountains; Wyoming: breeds in high mountains, and winter visitor at lower elevations.

COLORADO.—Fairly common resident of the coniferous forests of the Canadian Zone to timberline. Often common in winter in pinyons.

GRAY-CROWNED ROSY FINCH   *Leucosticte tephrocotis tephrocotis* (Swainson). [524]

RECOGNITION.—Length 6–7 inches. *Male:* plumage rich dark brown, wings and tail dusky; crown black, bordered by gray which is confined above the eye; belly, wings, and rump tinged with deep pink. *Female:* similar to male but duller and lighter. (Plate 113)

RANGE.—Breeds from northern Alaska, central Yukon, western Alberta and British Columbia to northwestern Montana. Winters from southern British Columbia, Alberta and Manitoba south to northern California and Nevada.

Nebraska: rare visitor in Panhandle Region; New Mexico: rare straggler; Utah: fairly common in winter; Wyoming: winter visitor, and breeder in Big Horn Mts.

COLORADO.—Common locally in winter in mixed flocks with Brown-capped and Black Rosy Finches in mountain parks, and often in towns, and occasionally to the base of the foothills.

Early fall Oct. 26 Pagoda, Routt Co. (no. 64405); late spring Apr. 11 Leadville (no. 1361).

Leucosticte tephrocotis littoralis Baird. [524a]

RECOGNITION.—Length 6–7 inches. *Male:* plumage rich dark brown; similar to *L.t. tephrocotis,* but black crown bordered by gray extending well *below the eyes. Female:* like male but paler. (Plate 113)

RANGE.—Breeds above timberline from central Alaska, southwestern Yukon, and northwestern British Columbia south through southeastern Alaska to the Cascade Mountains of Washington, Oregon, and northern California. Winters in the mountains from southern Alaska, British Columbia, Montana, and Nevada.

New Mexico: winter straggler; Utah: fairly common in winter; Wyoming: probably regular winter visitor.

COLORADO.—Common race wintering locally in mountain parks and elsewhere in mixed flocks as noted above.

BLACK ROSY FINCH   *Leucosticte atrata* Ridgway. [525]

RECOGNITION.—Length 5.5–6.5 inches. *Adult:* somewhat similar to Gray-crowned Rosy Finch, but brown plumage replaced by gray-black; wing edgings brighter pink; female less colorful. (Plate 113)

RANGE.—Breeds in mountains of southwestern Montana, central Idaho, Nevada, Utah, and Wyoming. Winters from central Idaho, Wyoming, southern Utah, Colorado, New Mexico, and northeastern California to northern Arizona.

New Mexico: uncommon winter visitor; Utah: breeds in Uinta, Wasatch, and La Sal Mountains, and fairly common in lowlands in winter; Wyoming: breeds in northwest mountains and winter visitor.

COLORADO.—Numerous locally in winter in mountain parks to Mesa Verde in flocks with other species of rosy finches.

BROWN-CAPPED ROSY FINCH   *Leucosticte australis* Ridgway. [526]

RECOGNITION.—Length 6–6.5 inches. *Male:* cinnamon brown; forehead black with gray-brown crown; wings and tail dusky; belly, rump, and edgings of tail and wings pink tinged. *Female:* gray-brown; pink markings paler. *Young:* gray-buff, pink lacking; wings and tail coverts edged with buff. (Plate 113)

RANGE.—Breeds above timberline in Colorado, in southeastern Wyoming, and northern New Mexico (Wheeler Peak). Winters at lower altitudes in breeding range.

New Mexico: resident in northern mountains (Wheeler Peak); Wyoming: breeding in Medicine Bow Range.

COLORADO.—Common resident and nesting species in high mountains, winters down to 8500 feet.

COMMON REDPOLL   *Acanthis flammea flammea* (Linnaeus). [528]

RECOGNITION.—Length 5–5.5 inches. *Male:* dark brown above, streaked with dusky; fore-crown crimson, chin black, throat, breast, and rump pink; belly and sides gray-white. *Female:* pink on throat and breast replaced by dusky streaked with brown. (Plate 114)

RANGE.—Breeds from northern Scandinavia, Russia, Siberia, and northern Europe, and western and central Alaska, over much of Canada, Labrador, and central British Columbia. Winters from Oregon to California, and from southern Canada into the northern United States, and in Europe and Asia.

Nebraska and Kansas: a rare and irregular straggler; Utah: very rare winter straggler (two specimens); Wyoming: irregular, but usually common in winter.

COLORADO.—Uncommon, irregular winter visitor from the eastern plains into the mountains.

Early fall Oct. 21 Crested Butte (Sclater, 1912); late spring Apr. 25 Fremont Co. (Sclater, 1912).

PINE SISKIN   *Spinus pinus pinus* (Wilson). [533]

RECOGNITION.—Length 4.5–5 inches. *Adult:* brown above, whitish below, entirely streaked with olive-brown; wing and tail markings of yellow, tail notched. *Young:* more yellow-brown; belly not streaked, wing spot brown. (Plate 114)

RANGE.—Breeds from southern Alaska and southern Yukon across Canada to Quebec, southern Labrador, and Newfoundland; in northern states from Wisconsin and Michigan east to New England, and south to North Carolina, Tennessee, Oklahoma, Utah, New Mexico, and southern California. Winters within the breeding range.

Nebraska: irregular migrant, winter visitor, and breeds locally; Kansas: common but irregular winter visitor (2 breeding records); New Mexico: fairly common in winter and spring (nesting Santa Fe June 3, 1920); Utah: common summer resident, less numerous in winter; Wyoming: common migrant and breeder in the mountains.

COLORADO.—Common resident, breeding from the plains into the mountains.

AMERICAN GOLDFINCH   *Spinus tristis tristis* (Linnaeus). [529]

RECOGNITION.—Length 4.5–5.5 inches. *Summer male:* plumage bright yellow; crown, wings, and tail black; wing bar, wing edgings, tail coverts, and tail patches white. *Winter male:* like summer female, but wings and tail darker. *Summer female:* olive-brown above, wings and tail dusky; pale yellow below; wing edgings and tail coverts whitish. *Winter female:* grayer above; wing and tail markings buffy. *Young:* like winter adult but darker. (Plate 114)

RANGE.—The species breeds from British Columbia across Canada to Nova Scotia, south to the Gulf coast states and Baja California; this race from Minnesota and central Ontario to Newfoundland, south to Oklahoma, Texas, Georgia, and North Carolina. Winters in numbers from breeding range south to Gulf coast.

Nebraska and Kansas: common resident in majority of counties; New Mexico: species formerly recorded from northwest but no recent records (Ligon, 1961); Utah: *S.t. pallidus* common summer resident in valleys, less numerous in winter; Wyoming: species common summer resident and migrant.

COLORADO.—Fairly common resident in eastern part of the state, wintering in flocks from the plains into the foothills.

Spinus tristis pallidus Mearns. [529a]

RECOGNITION.—Length 4.5–5.5 inches. *Adult:* similar to eastern goldfinch but slightly larger and paler; in winter with more white on wings and tail. *Young:* similar to the eastern form.

RANGE.—Breeds from southeastern British Columbia and southwestern Manitoba to Utah, Nevada, and Colorado. Winters south to Veracruz.

Nebraska: reported from northwestern part; New Mexico: records from northwest; Utah: common summer resident in valleys, less common in winter; Wyoming: probably occurs in west.

COLORADO.—This race, or intermediates, occurs throughout western counties, but records in literature are unreliable. There are six specimens from Colorado in the Museum collection, a female from Delta Co. Dec. 6, 1906, two males and two females collected by F. C. Lincoln in Paradox Valley in the southwestern corner of the state on May 8–9, 1915, and a male from Pitkin County May 6, 1939.

NESTING.—While *S.t. pallidus* or intermediate birds undoubtedly breed in western counties, we have one report only, a nest found by Natasha Boyd (letter), near New Castle, Garfield Co., in June 1959.

LESSER GOLDFINCH   *Spinus psaltria psaltria* (Say). [530]

RECOGNITION.—Length 4–4.5 inches. *Male:* upper parts black to green, ear coverts black; under parts yellow; wing spots and bases of outer tail feathers white. *Female:* olive-green above, with wings and tail dusky; white markings duller; green-yellow below. *Young:* female like adult but buffier; male often olive-green to black above, with crown black. (Plate 114)

RANGE.—The species breeds and is resident locally in the Lower Transition and Sonoran Zones of western United States, and this race from northern Colorado, Oklahoma, and north-central Texas to Mexico.

New Mexico: common summer resident; Utah: race *hesperophilus* common summer resident; Wyoming: casual migrant in south.

COLORADO.—Fairly common in summer from the edge of the foothills into the Transition Zone across the state and occurs occasionally at lower elevations in winter.

RED CROSSBILL   *Loxia curvirostra* Linnaeus.

RECOGNITION.—Length 5.5–6.75 inches. Adults with bills crossed, the tip of upper mandible extending beyond lower; small young with beaks uncrossed. *Male:* plumage dull red, brightest on rump; wings and tail dusky, mid-belly grayish. *Female:* plumage olive-yellow, brightest on rump; wings and tail dusky. *Young:* olive-gray streaked with dusky; male often with mixed patches of red, green, and yellow. (Plate 115)

RANGE.—The species ranges throughout much of the Northern Hemisphere—in the British Isles, Scandinavia, Russia, Siberia, northwest Africa, eastern Mediterranean islands, northern India, China, and Japan; Alaska, Canada, and irregularly in the mountains and lower elevations of the United States and Mexico.

Nebraska and Kansas: Irregular winter visitor as a species, four races listed in Nebraska and five from Kansas; New Mexico: uncommon species with three to four races; Utah: irregular, with four subspecies recorded "but little is known about the geographic variation of the breeding populations of Utah;" Wyoming: common resident as a species.

COLORADO.—Resident locally in small numbers each season, becoming an abundant nesting bird in favorable cone years in the ponderosa pines. Five races have been recorded from the state.

137

L.c. benti

Female on her nest April 20, 1948

Loxia curvirostra benti Griscom. [521e]

RECOGNITION.—Length 6–6.75; a bird with slightly smaller beak than the next race, *L.c. stricklandi*. *Adult male:* rosy-red with whitish belly; worn breeding plumage scarlet. *Adult female:* olive-yellow and lighter below. In worn plumage, the extremes of this race merge with others and are inseparable in size and coloration. *Small young:* uncrossed beaks; body plumage heavily streaked with dusky.

RANGE.—Breeding from the pine hills of southeastern Montana, eastern Wyoming, North and South Dakota, and the Transition and Canadian Zones of Colorado.

Nebraska: straggler; Kansas: most numerous of races occurring in state; Utah: breeds, population not typical; Wyoming: species common resident in mountains, but status of races undetermined.

COLORADO.—Resident; very numerous in good cone years. This is the most common of the crossbills of the Colorado Rockies and foothills, and the majority of sight records and references in the literature probably refer to this subspecies. The race cannot be satisfactorily identified by observations only. Breeds in favorable pine cone years.

Loxia curvirostra stricklandi Ridgway. [521a]

RECOGNITION.—This race is the largest of the New World crossbills. The birds have powerful beaks with exposed culmens 18–22.6 mm. in length and 10.8 to 12 mm. in depth. Males are deep scarlet and blood-red. Cannot be separated from *L.c. benti* in the field.

RANGE.—Resident from southern New Mexico, southeastern Arizona, and northern Baja California south through the tableland of Mexico. Wanders to Texas, California, and Nevada.

Kansas: rare straggler; New Mexico: numerous records; Utah: status uncertain, and reported from south-central part of the state; Wyoming: little information available on races.

COLORADO.—Rare straggler. A pair taken May 22, 1874 in El Paso Co., the male being in the Denver Museum (no. 25983). There are six other skins in the collection: three males (nos. 4294, 4296, and 4300) and a female (no. 4297) from near Boulder Feb. 20, 1915, a male (no. 7418) collected in Adams Co. Nov. 2, 1919, and a mounted male (no. 33834) taken in Jefferson Co. Nov. 14, 1965.

Loxia curvirostra minor (Brehm). [521]

RECOGNITION.—Medium-sized with a slender bill of medium length; culmen 15.5–17.5 mm. long and 9–10 mm. deep. *Adult male:* chiefly brick to dark coral-red, but few range into scarlet. *Female:* dull olive-yellowish; gray throat. *Young:* greenish body plumage heavily streaked with black; streaked plumage later replaced with rose in males, and yellowish in females.

RANGE.—Breeds and probably resident from Minnesota, Ontario, Quebec, New Brunswick, and Nova Scotia south irregularly into Wisconsin, Michigan, Massachusetts, New York, Maryland, West Virginia, North Carolina and Tennessee. Wanders widely, chiefly in winter, to Mackenzie, Saskatchewan, and south to Missouri, Georgia, and Florida.

Kansas: mentioned by Griscom (1937).

COLORADO.—Rare straggler. One record. A male in the U.S. Biological Survey collection taken at Limon, Lincoln Co., Nov. 28, 1914, was listed by Griscom (1937) and Bailey, Niedrach, and Baily (1953) as *Loxia c. neogaea* (Griscom), a race not recognized in the 1957 Check-list of North American Birds, and considered a synonym for *L.c. minor*.

Loxia curvirostra bendirei Ridgway. [521d]

RECOGNITION.—Similar to *L.c. minor*, but slightly larger, with longer wings and bill. Majority of males are bright scarlet instead of dull brick red. Cannot be separated from preceding or following in field identifications.

RANGE.—Resident from southern Yukon, British Columbia, south and east of the Cascade Mountains to Oregon, Washington, Idaho, Montana, and western Wyoming, and casually east and south through Colorado, New Mexico, and Arizona, and Trinity Mountain section of California. Wanders chiefly in winter, from southeastern Alaska to Arizona, Texas and Baja California.

Nebraska: irregular in winter; Kansas: uncommon, three listed by Griscom (1937); New Mexico: irregular (eight specimens listed by Griscom); Utah: casual straggler, possibly breeds; Wyoming: erratic but often common, and likely breeding in and adjacent to Yellowstone National Park.

COLORADO.—Rare straggler. There are ten specimens in the Museum collection, two from Denver, Jefferson, Lake, and Summit Counties, and one from Boulder and Douglas Counties.

Loxia curvirostra sitkensis Grinnell. [521c]

RECOGNITION.—Similar in color to *minor*, but smaller; wing of male 80.5–88.5 mm.; culmen 13.5–15.4 mm., and beak 8–8.8 mm. in depth.

RANGE.—This small form is the breeding bird of the Pacific Northwest coast district, from southern Alaska south to British Columbia and northwestern California. Wanders sporadically to Alberta, Wisconsin, Michigan, Ontario, Quebec, southern California, Arizona, Louisiana, South Carolina, Virginia, Pennsylvania, New York, and Massachusetts.

Nebraska: rare straggler, fourteen specimens listed by Griscom (1937); Kansas: irregular, two specimens reported by Griscom.

COLORADO.—Rare straggler. Two males (nos. 1632 and 1648) were collected near Breckenridge, Summit Co., in February 1878, and a female (no. 1649) on Mar. 20.

WHITE-WINGED CROSSBILL   *Loxia leucoptera leucoptera* Gmelin. [522]

RECOGNITION.—Length 6–6.75 inches. *Male:* plumage rose-red; wings and tail black; two *white wing bars. Female:* olive-green above, tinged with dusky; yellow-green below, rump yellow, wings and tail dusky; *white wing bars. Young:* like female but duller. (Plate 115)

RANGE.—Like the Red Crossbills, the species breeds in the northern parts of both the Old and New Worlds, and the race nests and is resident from tree limit in northwestern Alaska east to northern Quebec, Labrador, Nova Scotia, and New Brunswick to New Hampshire, New York, Vermont, Minnesota, Montana, and British Columbia. Wanders south to Oregon, Idaho, Nevada, Missouri, Indiana, Kentucky, Maryland, New Jersey, Virginia, and North Carolina.

Nebraska: rare; Kansas: rare (two specimens); New Mexico: one specimen from north of Clayton Nov. 4, 1954; Wyoming: rare winter visitor.

COLORADO.—Rare straggler. Only three specimens recorded, the first in San Juan Co., the second, a male (C.S.U. no. 5764) from Larimer Co. Aug. 14, 1908, and the third (no. 6585) from Boulder Co. May 17, 1917. Numerous observations have been listed in the literature through the years.

GREEN-TAILED TOWHEE   *Chlorura chlorura* (Audubon). [592.1]

RECOGNITION.—Length 6–7 inches. *Adult:* olive-green to gray above, wings and tail green-yellow; red-brown crown which can be erected into a crest; *throat* and mid-belly *white;* cheeks, breast, and sides gray. *Young:* brown above, tinged with green, streaked with dusky; dull white below, with breast and sides streaked; buffy wing bars. (Plate 116)

RANGE.—Breeds from central Oregon, Washington, Idaho, Nevada, Utah, and Montana to California, Arizona, and Texas. Winters from southern part of range into Mexico. Casual to Massachusetts, Virginia, South Carolina, and Louisiana. Winters from Texas, Arizona, and California into Mexico.

Nebraska: one banded at Stapleton in 1963; Kansas: fairly common in west, rare winter visitor in east; New Mexico: common migrant and regular breeder from 7000 to 9000 feet; Utah: common summer resident in mountains, transient in lowlands; Wyoming: common summer resident.

COLORADO.—Common migrant throughout the state, nesting on the ground or low in shrubs from lower edge of the foothills into the Transition Zone.

Early spring April 4 Colo. Spgs. (Sam Gadd); late fall Denver Nov. 24; winter Dec. 22 Jefferson Co.

RUFOUS-SIDED TOWHEE   *Pipilo erythrophthalmus montanus* Swarth. [588a]

RECOGNITION.—Length 7–8 inches. *Male:* head, breast, and upper parts black, with rump gray; many white markings in wings; tail corners white; sides, flanks, and under tail coverts rufous; belly white; iris red. *Female:* head and back lighter with brownish cast; back streaked. *Young:* brown above, buff below; back and under parts streaked; white spotting similar to adults. (Plate 116)

RANGE.—The species has a wide breeding range across southern Canada and throughout much of the United States south through Mexico into Guatemala. This western race nests from eastern California, southern and eastern Nevada east to Colorado, south to Arizona, west-central Texas, and into Mexico.

Nebraska and Kansas: species common migrant and breeding, this race transient in west; New Mexico, Utah, and Wyoming: common resident, breeder in oak thickets and shrubby hills.

COLORADO.—Common summer resident throughout the state in scrub oak habitat, and a few winter. Usually nests upon the ground at the base of scrub oaks, rose bushes or mountain mahogany.

Pipilo erythrophthalmus arcticus (Swainson). [588]

RECOGNITION.—Similar to *montanus*, but white wing markings more numerous, white tail corners more extensive; male with black back tinged with olive-gray; chestnut on flanks, and under tail coverts paler than in *montanus;* females with head and back light brown.

RANGE.—Breeds from central Alberta, central Saskatchewan, northern North Dakota, southeast of the Rockies to southeastern Wyoming, northeastern Colorado, and northern Nebraska. Winters Kansas and Colorado south into Mexico.

Nebraska: breeds locally; Kansas: occurs in winter; New Mexico: winter migrant; Utah: uncommon in winter.

COLORADO.—Probably a regular but uncommon winter visitor in the eastern part of the state. There are thirty-four skins in the Museum collection, identified as *P.e. arcticus* by Dr. Alden H. Miller;

Pipilo erythrophthalmus erythrophthalmus (Linnaeus). [587]

RECOGNITION.—Similar to preceding, but absence of white spots on wings distinguishes the eastern from the western races.

RANGE.—Breeds from southern Manitoba, northern Wisconsin, Michigan, southern Ontario, New York, and New England south to eastern Oklahoma, Arkansas, Georgia, South and North Carolina, and Virginia. Winters from Nebraska east to Massachusetts and south to the Gulf coast.

Nebraska: breeds locally in east, and a few winter; Kansas: transient and resident.

COLORADO.—Rare straggler. A specimen was secured (C.U. 6206) by Oakleigh Thorne, II, along Hillside Road, at Boulder on October 26, 1956 (Thorne, 1957).

BROWN TOWHEE   *Pipilo fuscus mesatus* Oberholser. [591i]

RECOGNITION.—Length 8–9 inches. *Adult:* Dull gray-brown above, crown pale rufous; throat buffy, edged with dark triangular spots; flanks and under tail coverts yellow-brown; belly gray-white. *Young:* Like adults, but breast and back streaked; lacks crown patch; wing band pale rufous. (Plate 116)

RANGE.—The species inhabits the dry semidesert areas from southwestern Arizona south through Baja California and from southeastern Colorado to Texas into Mexico. Twelve geographic races have been recognized, and *P.f. mesatus* has a restricted range, being a resident of southeastern Colorado, mainly south of the Arkansas River, northeastern New Mexico, and extreme northwestern Oklahoma.

COLORADO.—Fairly common resident of the cholla cactus and pinyon-juniper associations of the southeastern part of the state; uncommon north of Pueblo, El Paso, Fremont, and Boulder Counties.

MALE LARK BUNTING

Photograph by Patricia Bailey Witherspoon

LARK BUNTING   *Calamospiza melanocorys* Stejneger. [605]

RECOGNITION.—Length 6–7.5 inches. *Male:* in summer all black, with wing patch and edgings on wings, tail coverts, and outer tail feathers white. In winter, much like female, but chin black; black belly feathers hidden by whitish edgings. *Female:* gray-brown above and white below, streaked with dusky; wing patch buffy; superciliary line and edge of outer tail feathers white. *Young:* like female, but buffier above; narrower streaks below. (Plate 117)

RANGE.—Breeds from south-central Alberta, Saskatchewan, Manitoba, southeastern North Dakota, Minnesota, and Montana, and east of the Rockies to Oklahoma and northern Texas. Winters from California, Nevada, Louisiana, Arizona, and southern Texas into Mexico. Occasionally wanders eastward, and in the summer of 1962 our friend Raymond Middleton, an ardent bird bander, trapped one in his own yard in Norristown, Pa. (pers. comm.).

Nebraska and Kansas: common transient and summer resident in west; less numerous in east; New Mexico: summer resident and common migrant in spring and fall; Utah: uncommon transient; Wyoming: common summer resident.

COLORADO.—Summer resident, nesting on the eastern plains, and locally in mountain parks to 8000 feet throughout the state. This is the state bird of Colorado.

Early spring Apr. 19 Denver; late summer Oct., 1938 few at Strasburg (AMB); late fall Nov. 7 Saguache Co.; winter Dec. 25 Denver, and Feb. 12 Colo. Spgs. (Sam Gadd).

SAVANNAH SPARROW   *Passerculus sandwichensis nevadensis* Grinnell. [542]

RECOGNITION.—Length 4.5–5 inches. *Adult:* upper parts streaked with buff, tawny, and brown-black; crown dark with light median line, tail short and notched; white below with sides of throat, breast, sides, and flanks streaked with brown; *stripe over eye* and *bend of wing* pale *yellow. Young:* like adults, but breast more streaked. (Plate 118)

RANGE.—The species breeds from northern Alaska and Canada south into the northern states, and from California into Baja California. This race from British Columbia, Alberta, Saskatchewan, Manitoba, Oregon, eastern Washington, Montana, South Dakota, south to northern New Mexico and eastern California.

Nebraska: species common migrant and rare breeder locally (races represented include *oblitus, anthinus,* and *nevadensis*); Kansas: common transient and rare in winter (races *oblitus, nevadensis* and *savanna* recorded); New Mexico: *nevadensis* summer resident and common migrant; Utah: *nevadensis* fairly common summer resident, *alaudinus* rare straggler; Wyoming: common migrant and summer resident (no doubt several races in migration).

COLORADO.—Common summer resident of the plains in the eastern part of the state, nesting in moist areas upward into mountain parks to elevations of 9200 feet.

Early spring Mar. 23 Golden; late fall Nov. 11 Barr (no. 1780).

Passerculus sandwichensis anthinus Bonaparte. [542b]

RECOGNITION.—Length 4.5–5.15 inches. *Adult:* like *P.s. nevadensis,* but slightly larger, darker, and brown above. The two cannot be separated in the field.

RANGE.—Breeds in Alaska from Cape Prince of Wales north, and in Arctic Canada to Coronation Gulf, south to southwestern Alaska to British Columbia and east to the Yukon, Mackenzie, and northeastern Saskatchewan. Migrates through Colorado, New Mexico, Utah, and west-central states. Winters from California, Nevada, and Utah south into Mexico.

COLORADO.—Fairly common in migration upon the plains and in mountain parks in both spring and fall.

Passerculus sandwichensis rufofuscus Camras. [542g]

RECOGNITION.—Similar to *P.s. nevadensis,* but darker, richer rusty-brown above.

RANGE.—Breeds from South Park, Colorado, central Arizona, and north-central New Mexico south to central Chihuahua.

COLORADO.—Specimens, apparently breeding birds, taken in South Park in the summer of 1956 by A. R. Phillips (pers. comm.).

GRASSHOPPER SPARROW   *Ammodramus savannarum perpallidus* (Coues). [546a]

RECOGNITION.—Length 4.25–5 inches. *Adult:* striped above with black, and mottled with chestnut, gray, and buff; crown stripe buffy; *tail short* and notched; lores and bend of wing yellow; throat and belly white; breast, sides, and flanks ocher without streaks. *Young:* like adults, but paler, with clear breast streaks. (Plate 118)

RANGE.—Breeds from British Columbia, Alberta, and Saskatchewan to Ontario, south to Nevada, northern Utah to Oklahoma, central Texas, and southern California. Winters in southern part of breeding range into Mexico.

Nebraska and Kansas: common summer resident and migrant; New Mexico: uncommon summer resident and migrant; Utah: formerly summer resident, now rare migrant; Wyoming: uncommon summer resident in northeastern part of state.

COLORADO.—Irregularly common summer resident locally on the eastern plains; uncommon in western valleys.

Early spring Apr. 21 Larimer Co.; late fall Nov. 30 Georgetown.

BAIRD'S SPARROW   *Ammodramus bairdii* (Audubon). [545]

RECOGNITION.—Length 4.25–5.25 inches. *Adult:* head and neck buffy with yellow-brown *center* crown stripe; upper parts brown mottled with black and buff; breast finely streaked across with brown, sides and belly gray-white; tail with feathers pointed; long pipitlike hind claw. *Young:* darker above, with feather edgings buff. (Plate 118)

RANGE.—Breeds from southern Alberta, Saskatchewan, and Manitoba south to Montana, Minnesota, North Dakota, and South Dakota. Winters from southern New Mexico, central Texas, and southeastern Arizona into Mexico.

Nebraska and Kansas: uncommon migrant; New Mexico: fairly common migrant, ranging into the mountains; Utah: a few sight records; Wyoming: rare migrant in east.

COLORADO.—Regular but uncommon migrant and probably winter resident on the eastern plains.

Late spring May 20 Limon; early fall Aug. 23 El Paso Co.; winter Dec. 26 near Ft. Collins.

LE CONTE'S SPARROW   *Passerherbulus caudacutus* (Latham). [548]

RECOGNITION.—Length 4.5–5 inches. *Adult:* mottled brown above, with buff-brown nape band; *light buff crown stripe* between two black stripes; cheeks gray; light buffy eyeline; throat, breast, and sides buff-ocher; tail pointed. *Young:* buffy above, paler below, streaked throughout. (Plate 118)

RANGE.—Breeds locally from southern Mackenzie, Alberta, Saskatchewan, Manitoba, and northern Ontario to Montana, North and South Dakota, Minnesota, Wisconsin, Michigan, and Illinois. Winters from Missouri, Illinois, Kansas, Arkansas, and Tennessee south to Texas and Gulf coast states. Recorded west to Idaho and east to New York.

Nebraska: common but irregular migrant in east; Kansas: common transient and irregularly common winter resident; New Mexico: rare migrant and winter resident; Utah: one specimen from near Provo Dec. 24, 1927.

COLORADO.—Rare straggler, two specimens. The first was taken by Carter at Breckenridge Oct. 24, 1886, and the second, a skin in the Western State College Museum, was collected near Gunnison May 6, 1952. One was observed at Cherry Creek Res. May 10, 1967 (Hugh Kingery, pers. comm.).

SHARP-TAILED SPARROW   *Ammospiza caudacuta nelsoni* (Allen). [549.1]

RECOGNITION.—Length 5–6 inches. Upper parts olive-brown, broadly margined with white; the breast, sides, and throat "ochraceous-buff"; crown stripe, nape, and ear patch slate. (Plate 118)

RANGE.—The species occurs from southern Canada south in migration throughout much of the United States, and this race breeds locally from British Columbia, southern Mackenzie, Saskatchewan, Manitoba, Alberta, North and South Dakota, and northwestern Minnesota. Winters along the Gulf coast from Texas to Florida, and along the Atlantic coast from North Carolina south to Florida. In migration ranges northward to Maine.

Nebraska: rare transient; Kansas: rare migrant in east with specimens from Shawnee, Douglas, Woodson, and McPherson Counties.

COLORADO.—Straggler, one record, an immature male in the Western State College Museum taken by A. S. Hyde near Gunnison Oct. 23, 1952.

VESPER SPARROW   *Pooecetes gramineus confinis* Baird. [540a]

RECOGNITION.—Length 6–6.5 inches; brownish-gray above streaked with dusky; dull white below with breast and sides streaked; shoulder chestnut; edge of outer tail feathers white. (Plate 119)

RANGE.—Breeds from central and northeastern British Columbia, southwestern Mackenzie, central Manitoba, and western Ontario southward to eastern California, Nevada, New Mexico, and Arizona. Winters from southern California and Texas into Mexico.

Nebraska: locally a common breeder in the west; Kansas: probably uncommon summer resident in west. New Mexico, Utah, and Wyoming: common summer resident.

COLORADO.—Very common migrant and summer resident throughout state on plains and in foothills between 5000 and 9000 feet; ranges to above timberline after nesting season.

Early spring Feb. 26 Boulder; late fall Oct. 5 Boulder Co.; winter Jan. 28 (no. 23835) Deora, Baca Co.

LARK SPARROW   *Chondestes grammacus strigatus* Swainson. [552a]

RECOGNITION.—Length 5.5–6.5 inches; conspicuous *chestnut* and *black* and *white* head pattern, and a *rounded, white-tipped tail;* brownish-gray above streaked with dusky; median crown stripe, superciliary, and border of cheeks white; line through eye, throat stripe, and breast spot black; throat and under parts grayish-white. *Young:* buffy-brown above, streaked with dusky; breast streaked. The conspicuous head markings and fan-shaped *white-tipped tail are distinctive.* (Plate 119)

RANGE.—The species breeds across southern Canada south to Alabama, Louisiana, Texas, Arizona, and this race from British Columbia, Alberta, southern Saskatchewan, Manitoba, Oregon, Idaho, Utah, North Dakota, Arizona, and the Mexican tableland. Winters from California, Arizona, Texas, and Louisiana southwest into Mexico.

Nebraska, Kansas, Utah, and Wyoming: common summer resident.

COLORADO.—Common migrant and summer resident, nesting on the ground, usually, throughout the state from the plains into the mountains to 9000 feet.

Early spring Apr. 15 Denver (C.B.N. 12:20); late fall Oct. 1 Denver (H. Holt, pers. comm.).

RUFOUS-CROWNED SPARROW   *Aimophila ruficeps eremoeca* (Brown). [580b]

RECOGNITION.—Length 5–6 inches. *Adult:* crown rufous; back rufous streaked with gray; tail brown, throat white edged with dark brown; under parts white tinged with gray on breast, sides, and flanks. (Plate 118)

RANGE.—The species breeds in the southwest into Mexico and Baja California, and this race from southeastern Colorado, northern Oklahoma, New Mexico, and western Texas.

Kansas: two records, a male collected June 7, 1936 in Comanche Co., and one observed in Morton Co. May 21, 1950; New Mexico: widely distributed summer resident; Utah: wintering resident locally, and specimen collected (race *scotti*) in Zion Nat'l Park Nov. 5, 1963 (Condor, 67:447).

COLORADO.—Colorado references are scant but the birds occur rather commonly in the semidesert rocky butte formations of southeastern Colorado, with stragglers ranging along the foothills north to Platteville.

CASSIN'S SPARROW   *Aimophila cassinii* (Woodhouse). [578]

RECOGNITION.—Length 5–5.8 inches. *Adult:* upper parts tan-brown finely streaked with gray, crown appears uniform; under parts white, tinged with gray-brown on breast, sides, and flanks; tail rounded. (Plate 119)

RANGE.—Breeds from southwestern Kansas south to Oklahoma, and southwestern Texas into Mexico. Winters from Arizona and Texas into Mexico.

Kansas: common summer resident in southwest; New Mexico: widely distributed in warmer parts of the state.

COLORADO.—Fairly common resident in Baca and Prowers Counties, occurring regularly in summer, and nesting very irregularly northward to Adams and Morgan Counties. Male in courtship flight and song near Padroni, Logan Co. June 19, 1967 (Ron Lestina, pers. comm.).

BLACK-THROATED SPARROW   *Amphispiza bilineata deserticola* Ridgway. [573a]

RECOGNITION.—Length 4.75–5.5 inches. *Adult:* grayish-brown above, with crown gray, lores, throat, and chest black; superciliary and face lines white; under parts white; sides and flanks gray; outer tail feathers white. *Young:* paler above; lores brown; throat and breast white, streaked with brown. (Plate 119)

RANGE.—The species breeds in the deserts of the southwest into Mexico, and this subspecies from California, Utah, Wyoming, Nevada, and Colorado south to New Mexico, Arizona, and western Texas into Mexico. Winters from southern New Mexico and southeastern California into Mexico.

Kansas: one specimen collected in Finney Co. Nov. 25, 1952; New Mexico: common breeder, wintering in south; Utah: fairly common summer resident; Wyoming: rare in southern part of state.

COLORADO.—Uncommon summer resident of dry areas of the Upper Sonoran Zone throughout the southern half of the state. Reported nesting near Cañon City, Pueblo, and in Moffat Co.

SAGE SPARROW   *Amphispiza belli nevadensis* (Ridgway). [574.1]

RECOGNITION.—Length 6–6.25 inches. *Adult:* brown above with gray head; gray cheek outlined with white; eyering white, throat, and under parts white, with dark thin mark along throat; dark breast spot; sides and flanks streaked; tail edged with white. (Plate 119)

RANGE.—The species nests in western United States south into Baja California, and this race breeds east of the Cascade Range and the Sierra Nevada, and west of the Rocky Mountains from eastern Washington to southern Idaho, Nevada, southwestern Wyoming, Utah, northwestern New Mexico, and Arizona. Winters from southern part of breeding range to deserts of California, Arizona, New Mexico, and western Texas into Mexico.

Kansas: specimens and sight records from Morton and Seward Cos. in Nov. 1956 into Jan. 1957, winter resident in southwest; New Mexico: migrant and summer resident in northwest; Utah: summer resident in sage areas of north, winters in south; Wyoming: summer resident in southwest.

COLORADO.—Fairly common resident of the cholla cactus and pinyon-juniper associations of the southeastern part of the state; uncommon north of Pueblo, El Paso, and Fremont Counties, and casually to Boulder County.

Genus JUNCO

In the discussion of the juncos occurring in Colorado, as well as all other species, we have followed the nomenclature used in the fifth edition of the A.O.U. Check-list (1957) in which the White-winged Juncos, Slate-colored Juncos, Oregon Juncos, and Gray-headed Juncos are considered distinct species. It should be noted however, that Allan Phillips *et al.* (1964) in their excellent coverage of *The Birds of Arizona* have placed all the above as races of *Junco hyemalis* under the common name Brown-eyed Juncos.

144

WHITE-WINGED JUNCO   *Junco aikeni* Ridgway. [566]

RECOGNITION.—Length 6–6.5 inches. *Male:* light gray with white outer tail feathers and *two white wing bars.* *Female:* like male, but tinged with brown above, wing bars inconspicuous or lacking. *Young:* dark brown above, whitish below, and entirely streaked. The light slate coloration of adults and white wing bars are distinctive. (Plate 120)

RANGE.—Breeds from southeastern Montana and western South Dakota, south to northeastern Wyoming and northwestern Nebraska. Winters from the Black Hills to southern Colorado, Kansas, Oklahoma, New Mexico, and Arizona.

Nebraska: uncommon migrant and breeder in Panhandle Region; Kansas: fairly common transient and winter resident; New Mexico: uncommon winter resident; Wyoming: breeding in northeast.

COLORADO.—Common winter resident in the eastern half of the state.

Late spring Apr. 21 Jefferson Co. (no. 14171): summer June 26 Clear Creek Co. (10,000 feet), female (no. 9982) collected June 26, 1917; early fall Sept. 30 Platteville (C.B.N. 6:3).

SLATE-COLORED JUNCO   *Junco hyemalis hyemalis* (Linnaeus). [567]

RECOGNITION.—Length 5.5–6 inches. Plain slate-gray except for darker crown, white belly, and white outer tail feathers; female paler than male, young streaked and spotted except on white belly. Lack of wing bars and smaller size distinguish this from the White-winged Junco, while the gray sides and lack of a rufous saddle separate it from the other juncos of the state. (Plate 120)

RANGE.—The species occurs across the continent in the boreal forests during the nesting season, south to northern states and through the Appalachian Mountains to Georgia. This race breeds from western and northern Alaska and from British Columbia across Canada into Minnesota, Wisconsin, Michigan, Ohio, Pennsylvania, and intergrades with *J.h. carolinensis* in the Appalachians, New York, Connecticut, and Massachusetts. Winters from southeastern Alaska and southern Canada, chiefly east of the Rockies, to the Gulf coast.

Nebraska and Kansas: common winter visitor; New Mexico: casual in winter; Utah and Wyoming: uncommon winter resident.

COLORADO.—Fairly common in winter on eastern plains and low foothills; probably less numerous in the western part of the state.

Early fall Sept. 16 Weld Co. (no. 20542); late spring May 30 Estes Park (no. 22141).

Junco hyemalis cismontanus Dwight. [567k]

RECOGNITION.—Similar to *J.h. hyemalis,* but darker with ruddy from *J. oreganus* strain. Intergrades with *J.o. montanus* at western and southern borders of breeding range.

RANGE.—Breeds from south-central Yukon south to the interior of British Columbia and west-central Alberta. Winters from British Columbia and Minnesota south to Texas and Baja California.

Nebraska and Kansas: winter migrant; New Mexico: rare winter visitor; Utah: casual in winter; Wyoming: probably regular, but uncommon migrant and winter resident.

COLORADO.—Occurs more or less commonly along the eastern plains, and in western Colorado during the winter months. There are fourteen specimens in the Museum collection.

Early fall Nov. 25 Boulder (no. 13818); late spring Apr. 3 El Paso Co.

OREGON JUNCO   *Junco oreganus* (Townsend)

Oregon Juncos are very common in Colorado and may be observed throughout the winter months. The majority listed in Colorado Bird Notes under the species name could refer to any of the three races, *J.o. mearnsi, J.o. montanus* or *J.o. shufeldti,* the latter being less numerous than the others.

Junco oreganus mearnsi Ridgway. [567g]

RECOGNITION.—Length 5–6 inches. *Male:* head and breast slate gray; back dull brown; sides and flanks bright pinkish brown; belly white, outer tail feathers white. *Female:* head browner and plumage generally duller. The bright pink sides distinguish this bird from other subspecies. (Plate 120).

RANGE.—Breeds from southeastern Alberta and southwestern Saskatchewan south through central Montana to eastern Idaho and northern Wyoming. Winters through Wyoming, Utah, northwestern Nebraska, and Colorado to Arizona and Sonora, Mexico.

Nebraska, Kansas, and New Mexico: common winter visitor; Utah: summer resident in extreme north; Wyoming: breeds in the northwest mountains.

COLORADO.—Common winter resident throughout the state from the Upper Sonoran Zone into the mountains to 10,000 feet. Intergrades with *J.o. montanus.*

Early fall Sept. 9 Morgan Co. (no. 22277); late spring May 16 Denver (no. 13785).

Junco oreganus montanus Ridgway. [567f]

RECOGNITION.—Length 5–6 inches. Similar to *J.o. mearnsi*, but male with much darker head, ruddier back, and sides brownish. Field identifications separating *J.o. montanus* from the next race *J.o. shufeldti* are unsatisfactory; the two are much alike in color but this race, *montanus*, has slightly longer wings, males averaging longer than 76 mm. and females more than 72 mm.; the wings of *shufeldti* males average less than 77 mm. and females less than 73 mm. (Miller, 1941, p. 264). (Plate 120)

RANGE.—Breeds in mountains of Oregon, western Idaho, Montana, eastern Washington, and British Columbia. Winters from British Columbia and South Dakota south to Texas and into Mexico and Baja California.

Nebraska, Kansas, New Mexico, Utah, and Wyoming: regular and common winter visitor.

COLORADO.—Very common wintering junco throughout the state in the Upper Sonoran into the Transition Zone.

Early fall Sept. 14 Weld Co. (no. 23832); late spring May 9 Montrose Co. (no. 4487).

Junco oreganus shufeldti Coale. [567b]

RECOGNITION.—Length 5–6 inches. Similar to *J.o. montanus* but slightly smaller, with wings of males averaging less than 77 mm., and females less than 73.

RANGE.—Breeds from southwestern British Columbia south through western Washington and Oregon. Winters at lower altitudes in breeding range southward to central California, and eastward through Colorado, western Texas, and into Mexico.

New Mexico: migrant and winter visitor in south; Utah: rare transient and winter visitor; Wyoming: probably uncommon winter migrant.

COLORADO.—Casual migrant, the main route being west of the Rockies. There have been many records in the literature, but early identifications are not reliable.

Junco oreganus oreganus (Townsend). [567a]

RECOGNITION.—Length 5–6 inches; dark head with back and sides ruddy, and the head, sides, and back averaging darker than in other races.

RANGE.—Breeds in the coastal districts from southeastern Alaska to British Columbia. Winters southward into California and casually east to Nevada, and south to New Mexico and Arizona.

New Mexico: straggler at Fort Bayard in western part of state.

COLORADO.—Only one of this western race has been reported from Colorado, a male (no. 13813) taken along the Platte River near Denver on Oct. 16, 1885 by Horace G. Smith.

GRAY-HEADED JUNCO   *Junco caniceps caniceps* (Woodhouse). [570b]

RECOGNITION.—Length 5.5–6 inches. *Adult:* sexes colored much alike; slate-gray with back rufous and belly white; upper mandible flesh-colored; iris brown. *Young:* brown above, light below, and entirely streaked. The gray sides, brown eyes, and rufous back distinguish *caniceps* from other juncos. Interbreeds with races of Oregon Juncos where ranges overlap with consequent intermingling of colors. (Plate 120)

RANGE.—Breeds in the mountains of Colorado, New Mexico, Utah, Wyoming, Nevada, and eastern California. Winters at lower elevations, and south into Mexico.

Nebraska: uncommon in winter in western half; Kansas: sight record Dodge City, Jan. 13, 1962; New Mexico: abundant in mountains in summer, and at lower elevations in fall and winter; Utah: fairly common summer resident in mountains, a few in winter in valleys; Wyoming: common summer resident in southern half of the state.

COLORADO.—Common summer resident in the mountains and numerous in winter at lower elevations. Regular nester throughout the state from the foothills into the Hudsonian Zone, usually upon the ground.

TREE SPARROW   *Spizella arborea ochracea* Brewster. [559a]

RECOGNITION.—Length 5.5–6.5 inches; a rufous-crowned sparrow with a breast spot; buffy brown above; back streaked with black; two white wing bars; wings and tail dusky. (Plate 121)

RANGE.—The species breeds across the northern part of the continent south to Labrador and British Columbia, and this western race from northern Alaska, Yukon, and the Mackenzie Delta south to British Columbia. Migrates through western North America, wintering from British Columbia and South Dakota south to California and east to central Texas.

Nebraska and Kansas: common migrant and winter resident, *S.a. arborea* in east; New Mexico: uncommon winter resident; Utah: fairly common winter resident in valleys; Wyoming: common winter visitor.

COLORADO.—Common winter resident on eastern prairies into the foothills: less numerous in western counties. Early fall Oct. 6 Estes Park (C.B.N. 4:20); late spring May 21 Black Forest (8:40).

CHIPPING SPARROW   *Spizella passerina boreophila* Oberholser. [560b]

RECOGNITION.—Length 5–6 inches; a rufous-crowned sparrow without a breast spot. *Summer adult:* buffy or rusty brown above streaked with dusky; crown rufous and forehead black; superciliary, throat, and belly white; sides of head, breast, and rump gray; tail dusky. *Winter adult:* rufous crown obscured and colors duller. *Young:* crown streaked with rusty; under parts streaked. The rufous crown distinguishes it from the Clay-colored Sparrow, and the lack of a breast spot and inconspicuous white wing bars separate it from the Tree Sparrow. Immature Chipping, Clay-colored, and Brewer's Sparrows are practically impossible to separate in the field. (Plate 121)

RANGE.—The species breeds from central Alaska across Canada south to the Gulf coast, Texas, and into Mexico and Baja California. This race nests from east-central Alaska, Yukon, Mackenzie, Alberta, Saskatchewan, and Manitoba south through British Columbia and Idaho, east to North and South Dakota, and central Nebraska.

Nebraska: common migrant and locally common breeder (two races *S.p. passerina* and *S.p. boreophila*); Kansas: migrant and summer resident in east (*S.p. passerina*), less common in west (*S.p. boreophila*); New Mexico: very common breeder from 6000 to 8000 ft. (*S.p. arizonae?*); Utah: summer resident in north; Wyoming: common migrant and abundant breeder in the forests of the state.

COLORADO.—Common migrant and summer resident throughout the state, nesting in the Upper Sonoran Zone into the foothills to 8500 feet. A few occur in winter.

Spizella passerina arizonae Coues. [560a]

RECOGNITION.—Similar to *S.p. boreophila* but lighter, especially on the head, and sides of head and neck browner. The races can be identified only by comparison of specimens.

RANGE.—Breeds from Washington and Oregon south to California, to Baja California and Arizona into Mexico. Winters from central New Mexico, Texas, and Arizona to southern Mexico.

New Mexico: Summer and winter resident; Utah: common summer resident.

COLORADO.—Summer resident in La Plata County and possibly adjacent areas.

CLAY-COLORED SPARROW   *Spizella pallida* (Swainson). [561]

RECOGNITION.—Length 5–5.5 inches. Much like Chipping and Brewer's Sparrow. Differs from the former in having breast less gray; gray crown with light median stripe, brown *ear patch* with dark line above and below. (Plate 121)

RANGE.—Breeds from northeastern British Columbia, central southern Mackenzie, Saskatchewan, Manitoba, and Ontario south to Montana, Nebraska, Illinois, Michigan and northern Texas; winters from southern Texas into Mexico and Baja California, and casually to Guatemala.

Nebraska and Kansas: common migrant but no confirmation of breeding; New Mexico: common transient; Utah: one record Tooele Co. Sept. 21, 1934; Wyoming: common migrant in east.

COLORADO.—Common in migration in eastern counties, recorded very rarely in winter.

Early spring Mar. 29 Prowers Co. (no. 2550); late fall Oct. 21 Weldona; winter Jan. 3 Colo. Springs.

BREWER'S SPARROW   *Spizella breweri breweri* Cassin. [562]

RECOGNITION.—Length 5–5.5 inches. Much like Clay-colored Sparrow, but markings inconspicuous and streaks narrow, lacks definite cheek patch; streaked with gray and brown above. (Plate 121)

RANGE.—The northern race breeds from the southwestern Yukon, northwestern and central British Columbia and western Alberta, and this subspecies from southern British Columbia, Alberta, and Saskatchewan, south through Montana, Idaho, and South Dakota to Arizona and California. Winters from southern Nevada, Arizona, and Texas south into Mexico.

Nebraska: a common migrant, and uncommon breeder in Pine Ridge area; Kansas: common migrant in west; New Mexico: locally common breeding bird, with few in winter in south; Utah: common summer resident in sage brush areas; Wyoming: common summer resident.

COLORADO.—Common in summer on dry hillsides covered with mountain mahogany, or on sage flats of the western counties. A common nesting species on both sides of the Continental Divide, in sage, mountain mahogany, currant, or other low growth.

Early spring Apr. 24 Platteville (H. Holt, pers. comm.); late fall Oct. 25 Golden (C.B.N. 10:11).

FIELD SPARROW   *Spizella pusilla arenacea* Chadbourne. [563a]

RECOGNITION.—Length 5.5–6 inches; a small sparrow with two rufous crown stripes; rusty-brown above, streaked on back with dusky, cheeks and hind neck gray; under parts whitish, tinged with gray on sides; rump brownish-gray; two white wing bars; bill pinkish. The *reddish-pink bill* and tawny back serve to distinguish this bird from the Chipping, and the *gray cheeks* from the Clay-colored Sparrow. (Plate 121)

RANGE.—The eastern race breeds locally from Ontario and southwestern Quebec south to Gulf coast states and eastern Texas, and this subspecies from southeastern Montana and southwestern North Dakota to south-central Oklahoma. Winters from Kansas to Texas, Louisiana, and into northeastern Mexico.

Nebraska: a common migrant, and locally common breeder (races *S.p. pusilla* and *S.p. arenacea*); Kansas: common migrant and summer resident, occasional in winter, intergrading with *S.p. pusilla* in east; New Mexico: probably regular wintering bird. Two specimens, one taken in Lea Co., Dec. 23, 1961 and the other in Los Alamos Jan. 13, 1962 (Auk, 81:227).

COLORADO.—Uncommon summer resident on the eastern plains.

Early spring Mar. 29 Barr Lake; late fall Nov. 24 Weldona.

HARRIS' SPARROW *Zonotrichia querula* (Nuttall). [553]

RECOGNITION.—Length 7–7.5 inches. Top of head, breast patch, and lores black; bill pink; body grayish-brown streaked with black above; white below with sides streaked with darkish; two wing bars white. *Immature:* crown feathers edged with brown, the throat light, breast white streaked with black. (Plate 122)

RANGE.—Breeds locally from Mackenzie and southern Keewatin south to northeastern Saskatchewan and northern Manitoba, and casually east to northwestern Ontario. Winters from British Columbia east across northern states to Iowa, and south to Tennessee and Louisiana west to southern California.

Nebraska: a common migrant in east, and locally common in south in winter; Kansas: common transient and winter resident in east; New Mexico: migrant in east with records from Bitter Lake Refuge and Clayton area, and one collected by Ligon at Carlsbad Dec. 5, 1945; Utah: uncommon winter visitor in valley thickets throughout the state; Wyoming: uncommon transient and winter visitor.

COLORADO.—Uncommon but regular migrant and a few in winter from the Upper Sonoran into the Transition Zone.

Early fall Sept. 29 Weldona; late spring May 23 Colo. Spgs.

WHITE-CROWNED SPARROW *Zonotrichia leucophrys leucophrys* (Forster). [554]

RECOGNITION.—Length 6–7 inches. *Adult male:* crown stripes black and white; lores black; back streaked with brown, rump and tail clear brown; wings rusty, with two white bars; throat and belly white, sides buffy. *Female and young:* head stripes brownish. The black lores separate this bird from *Z.l. gambelii.* (Plate 122)

RANGE.—The species breeds from northern Alaska across Canada south to Newfoundland and in high country to central eastern California and Arizona. This race nests in eastern Canada east of Hudson and James Bays, Saskatchewan and Alberta, and on the tops of western mountains from Montana south to New Mexico, southern Utah, Nevada, and California. Winters in southern states to the Gulf, and Mexico.

Nebraska and Kansas: species common migrant and winter resident; New Mexico: common summer resident in northern mountains, and winters in low valleys; Utah: fairly common in summer in northern mountains, and rare in winter; Wyoming: common summer resident in mountains.

COLORADO.—Common transient on the plains and summer resident in high mountains; occasional in winter.

Zonotrichia leucophrys gambelii (Nuttall). [554a]

RECOGNITION.—Length 6–7 inches. Similar to *Z.l. leucophrys,* but white line above eye is continuous to the beak, instead of stopping over eye. (Plate 122)

RANGE.—Breeds from north-central Alaska and northern Yukon and east-central Mackenzie to southern Alaska, southern British Columbia, Alberta, Saskatchewan, and northern Manitoba. Intergrades with *leucophrys* from Jasper southward. Winters from British Columbia, Washington, Idaho, California, Utah, and Colorado to Mexico.

Nebraska: winter migrant; Kansas: winter resident, especially in the west; New Mexico: common winter resident; Utah: common winter visitor in lowlands; Wyoming: common migrant in winter.

COLORADO.—Common migrant and winter resident in the Upper Sonoran, ranging occasionally into the Canadian Zone.

Early fall Sept. 15 Barr (no. 22355); late spring May 29 Moffat Co. (no. 10858).

GOLDEN-CROWNED SPARROW *Zonotrichia atricapilla* (Gmelin). [557]

RECOGNITION.—Length 6–7 inches. A large sparrow; crown black with yellow median stripe at forehead and gray behind; cheeks, throat and breast gray, belly buffy white; sides brownish and white wing bars. *Young:* crown brown and median stripe brownish yellow. (Plate 122)

RANGE.—Breeds along western coastal Alaska (Cape Prince of Wales), central Yukon, and southeastern Alaska south along the Pacific coast to southern British Columbia, southwestern Alberta, and northern Washington. Winters from British Columbia, south casually to Baja California, and east to Colorado, New Mexico, and Arizona.

Nebraska: one record from Thomas Co.; New Mexico: rare winter migrant; Utah: one Zion Nat. Park Jan. 16, 1936, and one April 22, 1963 (A.F.N. 17: 423).

COLORADO.—An uncommon transient and winter visitor on both sides of the Continental Divide.

Early fall Aug. 30 Platteville (C.B.N. 8:12); late spring May 19 Colo. Spgs.

WHITE-THROATED SPARROW   *Zonotrichia albicollis* (Gmelin). [558]

RECOGNITION.—Length 6–7 inches. *Male:* rusty-brown above, streaked with dusky on back; crown stripes black and white; lores and edge of wing yellow; throat and belly white; breast and sides gray. *Female and young:* crown stripes tinged with brown. (Plate 122)

RANGE.—Breeds from southern Yukon, British Columbia, Alberta, Saskatchewan, central Mackenzie, Manitoba, Ontario, Quebec, and Labrador, south to West Virginia and west in northern states to North Dakota. Winters from California and the Mississippi Valley south to northern Mexico.

Nebraska: common migrant in east, uncommon in west; Kansas: common migrant and winter resident; New Mexico: uncommon, but probably regular in winter; Utah: uncommon winter visitor; Wyoming: regular but rather uncommon migrant and winter resident.

COLORADO.—An uncommon but regular winter resident in eastern counties. One was observed near Gunnison Nov. 22, 1952, and one collected Oct. 16, 1960 is in the Western State College Museum. Six noted Barr Lake on Spring Count May 22, 1965 (C.B.N. 13:31).

Early fall Sept. 18 Sedalia, banded by C. and M. Snyder (C.B.N. 12:51); late spring May 22 Barr Lake (above).

FOX SPARROW   *Passerella iliaca schistacea* Baird. [585c]

RECOGNITION.—Length 6.5–7.5 inches. Large sparrow, gray above, with streaked flanks, and breast with inverted V-striped spots; breast streakings gray-brown. (Plate 123)

RANGE.—The species breeds over much of Alaska and Canada south into the mountains of the northern states, and this race from southeastern British Columbia and southwestern Alberta south through the mountains from Oregon east to Nevada, Montana, Wyoming, and Colorado. Winters from California, Arizona, New Mexico, and Texas to Baja California.

Nebraska: status poorly known in west; New Mexico: occasional winter resident; Utah: transient (resident race *P.i. swarthi*); Wyoming: summer resident in western part of the state.

COLORADO.—An uncommon mountain resident, more numerous west of the Continental Divide, nesting low in thickets of moist Canadian Zone valleys. Two small young & egg in nest close to ground in willows along Rock Creek, Gore Range, June 21, 1964; two eggs in same area June 24, 1967 and third egg laid June 25 (H. Holt, pers. comm.).

Passerella iliaca zaboria Oberholser. [585p]

RECOGNITION.—Length 6.5–7.5 inches. *Adult:* shorter tailed than in *P.i. schistacea*, with brighter plumage; red-brown mixed with gray above; wings, rump, and tail bright red-brown; breast heavily streaked. *Young:* similar to adults but duller. (Plate 123)

RANGE.—Breeds from northeastern and interior of Alaska to Mackenzie and northern Manitoba south to British Columbia, Alberta, and Saskatchewan. Winters from eastern Kansas and Iowa south to the Gulf coast with stragglers ranging down the Great Plains to eastern Colorado and Arizona, and rarely westward to Washington and California.

Nebraska: species a rare migrant throughout the state; Kansas: species a fairly common migrant, sometimes wintering in the east.

COLORADO.—A rare straggler on the eastern slope. Two specimens have been collected, one near Denver (U.S.N.M. no. 12513) in Dec. 1884 by W. T. Strong, and a male (no. 6026) in Jefferson Co. Nov. 1, 1916 by R. J. Niedrach. An adult was trapped and banded 8 mi. W of Longmont Oct. 11, 1965 by Allegra Collister (pers. comm.).

LINCOLN'S SPARROW   *Melospiza lincolnii alticola* (Miller and McCabe). [583b]

RECOGNITION.—Length 5.5–6 inches. *Adult:* olive brown above streaked with dusky; crown red-brown with gray median stripe; sides of neck and superciliary grayish; buff breast band with fine streaking; belly whitish. *Young:* like adults, but markings less distinct. (Plate 123)

RANGE.—Breeds in the mountain areas of eastern Oregon, California east to Colorado and south to Arizona, Utah, and New Mexico. Winters south to Guatemala.

Nebraska and Kansas: probably a common migrant in west; New Mexico: breeding in northern mountains; Utah: uncommon summer resident in mountains, transient in valleys; Wyoming: common summer resident in mountains.

COLORADO.—Common spring and fall migrant upon the plains and in low valleys throughout the state, and a few winter; nests commonly in mountains in moist willow-grown boggy areas of the Transition and Canadian Zones.

This race, *alticola,* is recognized in the A.O.U. Check-list (1957) but Phillips *et al.* (1964) consider *alticola* to be a synonym of the nominate race *lincolnii.*

Melospiza lincolnii lincolnii (Audubon). [583]

RECOGNITION.—Similar to preceding race *M.l. alticola,* but wings average shorter with males having wing length under 64 mm., and females less than 60 mm.

RANGE.—Breeds from western and interior Alaska, central Yukon and across Canada to Newfoundland, south through interior British Columbia to the mountains of northern Washington, east in northern states to western New York. Winters southward into California and through the Mississippi Valley to southern states, to Baja California.

Nebraska and Kansas: common migrant, occasionally wintering; New Mexico: probably a regular migrant; Utah: uncommon transient; Wyoming: probably a common migrant in spring and fall.

COLORADO.—Migrant in spring and fall and likely winter resident.

SWAMP SPARROW   *Melospiza georgiana ericrypta* Oberholser. [584a]

RECOGNITION.—Length 5–5.5 inches. *Adult:* streaked with rusty-brown above, crown chestnut with faint buffy median stripe; throat dull white, breast gray with sides and flanks gray-brown; tail rusty. *Young:* chestnut crown lacking; breast faintly streaked. (Plate 123)

RANGE.—Breeds from southern Mackenzie, Saskatchewan, Manitoba, Ontario, Quebec, and Newfoundland south to northeastern British Columbia, Minnesota, and northeastern North Dakota. Winters south to the Gulf coast and Mexico, and casually from California, Montana, Nevada, Colorado, and Arizona.

Nebraska: a common migrant in east, and rare resident in west but status of races poorly known; Kansas: common migrant, uncommon in winter (both *M.g. georgiana* and *M.G. ericrypta*); New Mexico: uncommon winter visitor to Rio Grande and Pecos Valleys; Utah: casual, two specimens.

COLORADO.—Uncommon migrant and winter resident in eastern counties.

Early fall Aug. 22 Colo. Spgs.; late spring May 19 Crook.

SONG SPARROW   *Melospiza melodia montana* Henshaw. [581b]

RECOGNITION.—Length 5.5–6 inches. *Adult:* mottled above with rust-brown and gray, streaked with dark brown except on primaries and tail; crown with three broad gray stripes; buff-white stripe below cheek; under parts streaked with black-brown on dull white breast and white sides. *Young:* similar to adults, but browner and markings less distinct. (Plate 123)

RANGE.—The wide-ranging species breeds throughout much of North America and this race nests from northeastern Oregon to Idaho, Montana, Nevada, Utah, Colorado, south to eastern Arizona. Winters from Montana to Texas, southeastern California, and Mexico.

Nebraska and Kansas: migrant, three races recorded from both states and this subspecies probably a regular migrant in the west; New Mexico: breeding in northern mountains; Utah: summer resident, and numerous in winter in southwest; Wyoming: common resident along streams (type locality, Fort Bridger).

COLORADO.—Resident throughout the state, nesting in moist habitats of the Upper Sonoran and Transition Zones. Less common in winter.

Melospiza melodia merrilli Brewster. [581k]

RECOGNITION.—Length 5.5–6 inches. *Adult:* similar to *M.m. montana* but averages slightly larger, breast and flank markings wider and under parts red-brown instead of black-brown. Differs from *juddi* in larger size and markings below being more reddish.

RANGE.—Breeds from the southern interior of British Columbia, southwestern Alberta south to eastern Washington to northern Idaho and northwestern Montana. Winters from British Columbia and Montana south casually to Arizona.

New Mexico: rare transient; Utah: rare winter visitor; Wyoming: probably uncommon migrant.

COLORADO.—A fairly common winter resident.

Melospiza melodia juddi Bishop. [581j]

RECOGNITION.—Length 5.5–6 inches. *Adult:* quite similar to the *M.m. montana,* but feather edgings of upper parts less gray, giving rustier tone to the back; breast whiter.

RANGE.—Breeds from British Columbia, southern Mackenzie, northern Saskatchewan, Manitoba and Ontario, south through the plains of Alberta to Montana, North Dakota, and eastward. Winters from Montana, Minnesota, and southward to the Gulf coast and Arizona.

Nebraska and Kansas: transient and winter resident; New Mexico: likely an uncommon migrant; Utah: rare transient in east; Wyoming: probably fall and spring transient.

COLORADO.—Common winter resident on the eastern plains and less numerous in western counties.

McCOWN'S LONGSPUR   *Rhynchophanes mccownii* (Lawrence). [539]

RECOGNITION.—Length 5.5–6 inches. *Summer male:* crown and breast black, in sharp contrast with white superciliary and throat; back gray-brown streaked with black; wings gray-brown with red-brown shoulders, tail white, broadly tipped with black. *Winter male:* like female, but with reddish shoulder patches. *Female:* gray-brown above, back streaked with dusky, cheeks and foreneck buffy; chin and belly white. *Young:* dusky above; white below, with breast buff and faintly streaked. (Plate 124)

RANGE.—Breeds from southern Alberta, Saskatchewan, Manitoba, and North Dakota south to Wyoming, northeastern Colorado, and northwestern Nebraska. Winters from Colorado and Kansas to New Mexico, Texas, Arizona, and into Mexico.

Nebraska: breeds in northwest and common migrant, uncommon in winter; Kansas: common migrant and winter resident, rare in east; New Mexico: common winter resident of the eastern and southern plains; Utah: one sight record; Wyoming: common migrant and breeder in eastern part of state.

COLORADO.—Fairly common on plains in migration and nesting in northeastern counties, wintering casually. Forty-one banded in summer of 1966 (A. Collister, pers. comm.).

LAPLAND LONGSPUR   *Calcarius lapponicus alascensis* Ridgway. [536a]

RECOGNITION.—Length 6–7 inches. *Summer male:* head, neck, and breast black; nape chestnut; belly white; buffy line back of eye; back streaked with gray-brown; wings and tail gray-brown with web of outer tail feathers white. *Winter male:* black and chestnut colors restricted. *Female:* plumage yellow-brown streaked with dusky except for white on throat, tail, and belly. *Young:* streaked above with brown and dusky; wings and tail brown; buffy below, with throat, breast, and sides streaked. (Plate 124)

RANGE.—The species breeds from northern Alaska across Canada, Greenland, northern Scandinavia, and Siberia, and this race from northwestern Alaska and northern Yukon, to northwestern Mackenzie. Winters from British Columbia, Montana, and Nebraska south to Texas and Arizona.

Nebraska and Kansas: common migrant and wintering species; New Mexico: recorded in A.O.U. Check-list from Picacho; Utah: casual, several specimen records; Wyoming: common migrant and winter resident in east.

COLORADO.—Irregular and sometimes common winter visitor on the eastern plains, rarely into mountain parks.

Late spring Apr. 1 Weldona; early fall Sept. 18 Longmont.

Calcarius lapponicus lapponicus (Linnaeus). [536]

RECOGNITION.—Very similar to *C.l. alascensis* but darker above, especially in winter plumage, with summer adults having broader streaks of black and ochraceous on back. Wings darker.

RANGE.—Breeds from northern Ontario, Quebec, and Labrador, southern Greenland, Norway, Sweden, and eastern Siberia. Winters from England, northern Europe, and eastern Siberia to France, Italy, and southern Russia, and in much of eastern United States, west to Minnesota, eastern Colorado, and south to northeastern Texas.

COLORADO.—Probably of regular occurrence in eastern counties. There are two specimens in the Museum collection from Barr Lake, a male (no. 1742) Dec. 28, 1909, and a female (no. 8554) Jan. 30, 1938.

* SMITH'S LONGSPUR   *Calcarius pictus* (Swainson). [537]

RECOGNITION.—Length 6.5 inches. Buffy below, outer tail feathers white; *spring male* with white cheek spot lined with black.

RANGE.—Breeds in northern Alaska, Yukon, and Mackenzie south to Keewatin, Manitoba, and Ontario. Winters from Kansas and central Iowa to Oklahoma, Texas, and Louisiana.

Nebraska: rare migrant; Kansas: fairly common migrant and winter resident in western counties, rare in east.

COLORADO.—A rare visitor. Recorded at Bonny Res. Apr. 29 and 30, 1966 by Marie and George Shier and Nancy Hurley (A.F.N. 20:524).

151

Photographs from movie frame by authors

CHESTNUT-COLLARED LONGSPUR
The male was solicitous in caring for the small young

CHESTNUT-COLLARED LONGSPUR   *Calcarius ornatus* (Townsend). [538]

RECOGNITION.—Length 5.5–6.5 inches. *Summer male:* crown and belly black; nape chestnut; dull brown above, streaked with black; outer tail feathers conspicuously white in flight, with black tips on central portion. *Winter male:* black and chestnut colors obscured by brown feather tips. *Female and young:* plumage gray-brown, streaked above with dusky, and indistinct below. (Plate 124)

RANGE.—Breeds from southern Alberta, southern Saskatchewan, and Manitoba, to Wyoming, Colorado, Nebraska, and western Minnesota. Winters from Nebraska and Colorado south to Louisiana and Texas into Mexico.

Nebraska: common migrant, summer resident in Panhandle, and an uncommon winter resident in west; Kansas: common transient and winter resident in west; New Mexico: rather uncommon transient and winter resident; Utah: casual, one record specimen; Wyoming: common summer resident in eastern counties.

COLORADO.—Nests locally in Weld Co., and winters in small numbers upon the eastern prairies.

SNOW BUNTING   *Plectrophenax nivalis nivalis* (Linnaeus). [534]

RECOGNITION.—Length 6.5–7.5 inches. *Male:* white except for black primaries, scapulars, mid-back, and middle tail feathers; in winter with a buffy or rusty wash on upper parts, cheeks, and breast. *Female:* primaries and middle tail feathers dusky brown; in winter with rusty wash on upper parts and sides. *Young:* gray above and dull white below; wings and tail dark brown with little white. (Plate 124)

RANGE.—Breeds from Alaska across Canada to Greenland, Sweden, Finland, Spitsbergen, and northwestern Russia, south to northern Quebec, Southampton Island, and Hudson and James Bays. Winters from southern and western Alaska across southern Canada south to northern states.

Nebraska: very irregular visitor; Kansas: very rare, one taken Cheyenne Bottoms in Dec. 1965 (D. F. Parmelee, pers. comm.); Utah: uncommon in winter in north; Wyoming: uncommon winter visitor.

COLORADO.—Rare winter visitor. Although these beautiful little sparrows have been mentioned by various authors, actual observations in Colorado have been few.

Early winter Dec. 24 Denver; late spring Apr. 18 Berthoud Pass.

ABBREVIATIONS

Specimens listed without initials (example, no. 10) refer to skins in the Denver Museum of Natural History except where a reference indicates otherwise; (C.C. no. 10) to the collections of the Colorado College Museum in Colorado Springs, the majority of the specimens now being in the University of Colorado Museum; (C.U. no. 10) to the University of Colorado at Boulder; (C.S.C. no. 10) to Colorado State College at Greeley, formerly the State Teachers College; (C.S.U. no. 10) to the Colorado State University at Fort Collins, formerly Colorado A. & M. College; and (C. no. 10) to the Edwin Carter collection.

Abbreviations are:

A. F. N.	Audubon Field Notes
AMB	Alfred M. Bailey
A.O.U.	American Ornithologists' Union
A. & W.	Aiken and Warren
B. & N.	Bailey and Niedrach
C.B.N.	Colorado Bird Notes; C.B.N. usually used once under each species and only volume and pages in following references, e.g. (9:13).
C.C.	Colorado College (Colorado Springs)
C.F.O.	Colorado Field Ornithologist
C.S.C.	Colorado State College (Greeley)
C.S.U.	Colorado State University (Fort Collins)
C.U.	University of Colorado (Boulder)
D.F.O.	Denver Field Ornithologists (also monthly report of field observations)
H. & R.	Hersey and Rockwell
M.H.D.C.	Mile High Duck Club (Adams Co.)
N. & R.	Niedrach and Rockwell
pers. comm.	personal communication
RJN	Robert J. Niedrach
R.Mt.N.P.	Rocky Mountain National Park

BIBLIOGRAPHY

AIKEN, CHARLES EDWARD HOWARD.

1872. See Holden, C. H., Jr.
1873a. A glimpse at Colorado and its birds. American Naturalist, 7:13–16.
1873b. A new species of sparrow. *Ibid.*, 7:236–237.
1875a. The nidification of the blue crow and of the gray-headed snowbird. American Sportsman, 5:370.
1875b. See Henshaw, Henry Wetherby.
1900. Seven new birds for Colorado. Auk, 17:298–299.
1927. Three records for Colorado. Auk, 44:432.
1928a. Notes on the golden eagle (*Aquila chrysaetos*) in Colorado. Auk, 45:373–374.
1928b. Roadrunner first discovered by Lieut. Zebulon Pike. Auk, 45:375.
1941. From Colorado Springs to Horse Creek in 1878 (edited by Edward R. Warren). Auk, 58:70–73.

AIKEN, CHARLES EDWARD HOWARD, and EDWARD R. WARREN.

1914. The birds of El Paso County, Colorado. Colorado College Science Series, 12:455–603.

ALDRICH, JOHN W.

1951. A review of the races of the Traill's flycatcher. Wilson Bull., 63:192–197.

ALEXANDER, GORDON.

1935. An influx of the dickcissels into central Colorado. Condor, 37:38.
1936. Eastern summer tanager in Colorado. Auk, 53:452.
1937a. Least tern in Colorado. Auk, 54:390–391.
1937b. The birds of Boulder County, Colorado. Univ. of Colorado Studies, 24:79–105.
1938. Observations on hybrid flickers in Colorado. Jour. of Colorado-Wyoming Acad. of Science, 2:27–29.
1941. Scarlet tanager at Boulder, Colorado. Condor, 43:158.
1944. Unusual records from Boulder County, Colorado. Condor, 46:36.
1945. Natural hybrids between *Dendroica coronata* and *D. auduboni*. Auk, 62:623–626.

AMERICAN ORNITHOLOGISTS' UNION.

1957. Check-list of North American birds. Fifth edition, The Lord Baltimore Press, Baltimore, Maryland. 691 pp.

BAILEY, ALFRED M.

1919. Observations on the water birds of Louisiana. Natural History, 19:44–72.
1925. Segregation of the sexes in the sage hen. Condor, 27:172–173.
1926a. Notes on Colorado shore birds. Condor, 28:46–47.
1926b. The ivory gull in Colorado. Condor, 28:182–183.
1927. Notes on the birds of southeastern Alaska. Auk, 44:1–23, 184–205, 351–367.
1928. A study of the snowy herons of the United States. Auk, 45:430–440.
1930a. The upland plover. Natural History, 30:177–181.
1930b. The piper of the dunes. *Ibid.*, 30:627–634.
1931. Sac-a-plomb. *Ibid.*, 31:417–423.
1935. Kok-ar-ow. Bird Lore, 37:13–16.
1938a. Eastern warbling vireo in Colorado. Wilson Bull., 50:57.
1938b. The golden eagle in Colorado. Rocky Mt. Sportsman, 1(1):7.
1939a. Snowy plover from Colorado. Condor, 41:127 (with R. J. N.).
1939b. Ivory-billed woodpecker's beak in an Indian grave in Colorado. Condor, 41:164.
1942. The black pigeon hawk in Colorado. Condor, 44:37.
1943. The birds of Cape Prince of Wales. Proc. Colorado (Denver) Mus. Nat. Hist., 18(1), 112 pp.
1944. History of mourning dove's nest. Wilson Bull., 56:171–172.
1945. Rivoli's hummingbird (*Eugenes fulgens*) in Colorado. Auk, 62:630–631.
1946. High country of Colorado. National Geographic Magazine, 89:43–72.
1947a. Black and mottled ducks in Colorado. Condor, 49:209.
1947b. Western palm warbler in Colorado. Wilson Bull., 59:173.
1948. Birds of Arctic Alaska. Colorado (Denver) Mus. Nat. Hist., Popular Series 8, 317 pp.
1949. Hybrid of snow and Canada goose. Auk, 66:197.
1957. Hudsonian godwit in Colorado. Wilson Bull., 69:112.
1960. Rivoli's hummingbird in Colorado. Auk, 77:345–346.

BAILEY, ALFRED M., and FRED G. BRANDENBURG.

1940. The snowy plover in Colorado. Condor, 42:128.
1941. Colorado nesting records. Condor, 43:73–74.

BAILEY, ALFRED M., and F. R. DICKINSON.

1932. The woodcock. Natural History, 32:273–279.
1933. Camera hunting in the haunts of the golden eagle. *Ibid.*, 33:257–270.

BAILEY, ALFRED M., and FREDERICK C. LINCOLN.

1954. The yellow-billed loon (*Gavia adamsi*) in Colorado. Auk, 71:203.

BAILEY, ALFRED M., and ROBERT J. NIEDRACH.

1926. The Franklin's gull in Colorado. Condor, 28:44–45.
1931. American egret in Colorado. Condor, 33:250.
1932. Domain of the camp robber. American Forests, 38:492.
1933a. The mountain plovers of the prairies. Natural History, 33:75–80.
1933b. The avo-chic. *Ibid.*, 33:209–217.
1933c. The prairie falcon. American Forests, 39:356–358.
1934. Photographing the western horned owl. *Ibid.*, 40:18–20.
1936. Community nesting of western robins and house finches. Condor, 38:214.
1937a. Trailing birds of prey. American Forests, 43:218–220, 251.
1937b. Five species new to Colorado. Condor, 39:132–133.
1937c. Notes on Colorado birds. Auk, 54:524–527.
1938a. A day with a nesting goshawk. Nature Magazine, 31:38–40.
1938b. Brewster's egret nesting in Colorado. Condor, 40:44–45.
1938c. Western grebe in Colorado. Auk, 55:119.
1938d. Nesting of Virginia's warbler. Auk, 55:176–178.
1938e. Notes on Colorado geese. Auk, 55:519–520.
1938f. Nelson's downy woodpecker from Colorado. Auk, 55:672–673.
1938g. Rose-breasted grosbeak in Colorado. Auk, 55:676.
1938h. The chestnut-collared longspur in Colorado. Wilson Bull., 50:243–246.
1938i. The red phalarope and ruddy turnstone in Colorado. Condor, 40:227.
1939a. Notes on jaegers and gulls of Colorado. Auk, 56:79–81.
1939b. Eastern hermit thrush in Colorado. Condor, 41:123.
1939c. Snowy plover from Colorado. Condor, 41:127.
1939d. Filming the golden eagle. American Forests, 45:446–449, 476–477.
1939e. Ivory-billed woodpecker's beak in an Indian grave in Colorado. Condor, 41:165.
1939f. Piping plover from Colorado. Condor, 41:216.
1939g. Fan and bubble dance. Rocky Mt. Sportsman, 2(5):8–11, 30–31.
1944. Spring in the high marsh. Bird-Lore, 46:71–75.

1946.   Duck hawk nesting in Colorado. Auk, 63:253.
1965.   Birds of Colorado. Denver Museum of Nat. Hist., 2 vol., 124 color
                plates, 400 photographs, 895 pp.

BAILEY, ALFRED M., ROBERT J. NIEDRACH, and A. LANG BAILY.
1953.   The red crossbills of Colorado. Denver Mus. Nat. Hist., Museum Pictorial 9, 63 pp.

BAILEY, FLORENCE MERRIAM.
1905a.   Scaled partridge at Pueblo. Condor, 7:112.
1905b.   Notes from northern New Mexico. Auk, 22:316–318.
1928.   Birds of New Mexico. New Mexico Dept. of Game and Fish, Judd and Detweiler Press, Inc., Wash-
                ington, D. C. 807 pp.

BAILY, A. LANG.
1950.   See Knorr, Owen A.
1953a.   Eastern race of yellow-bellied sapsucker in Colorado. Condor, 55:219.
1953b.   See Bailey, Alfred M., *et al.*
1954.   Indigo bunting nesting in Colorado. Auk, 71:330.

BAILY, A. LANG, and ROBERT P. FOX.
1953.   Notes on warblers in Colorado. Wilson Bull., 65:47.

BEHLE, WILLIAM H.
1942.   Distribution and variation of the horned larks (*Otocoris alpestris*) of western North America. Univ.
                of California Publ. in Zool., 46:205–316.
1944.   Check-list of the birds of Utah. Condor, 46:67–87.

BEISE, CHARLES J.
1943.   Piedra turkeys. Nature Magazine, 36:523–526.

BERGTOLD, WILLIAM HARRY.
1904.   White-winged scoter in Colorado. Auk, 21:78.
1907.   The house finch from an office window. Bird-Lore, 9:61–64.
1909a.   Mexican goldfinch in Colorado. Auk, 26:79.
1909b.   Albino robins. Auk, 26:196–198.
1910.   Barn owl in Colorado. Auk, 27:207.
1911.   The western evening grosbeak in Denver, Colorado. Auk, 28:369
1913a.   A study of the house finch. Auk, 30:40–73.
1913b.   White pelican in Colorado. Auk, 30:430.
1913c.   Roadrunner in Colorado. Auk, 30:434.
1914a.   Franklin's grouse in Colorado. Auk, 31:246.
1914b.   Magnolia warbler in Colorado. Auk, 31:253.
1914c.   Canadian warbler in Colorado. Auk, 31:253.
1914d.   Chestnut-collared longspur in Colorado. Auk, 31:541.
1914e.   Yellow-crowned night heron in Colorado. Auk, 31:535.
1915a.   The yellow-crowned heron in Colorado—a correction. Auk, 32:97.
1915b.   Black-throated blue warbler in Colorado. Auk, 32:498.
1915c.   The indigo bunting in Colorado. Auk, 32:498.
1915d.   The camp-bird. Bird-Lore, 17:454.
1916a.   The Calaveras warbler in Colorado. Auk, 33:325.
1916b.   Cassin's sparrow in Colorado. Auk, 33:435.
1917a.   An early Colorado record of the white-tailed ptarmigan. Auk, 34:334.
1917b.   The slate-colored junco in Colorado. Auk, 34:480.
1917c.   Notes from field and study. Bird-Lore, 19:340.
1917d.   The birds of Denver. Wilson Bull., 29:113–129.
1918.   The harpy eagle in Colorado. Auk, 35:77–78.
1919a.   The crow in Colorado. Auk, 36:198–205.
1919b.   The season. Bird-Lore, 21:54, 116, 252, 313, 369.
1920a.   The crow of Colorado. Auk, 37:134.
1920b.   Clark's crow in Denver. Auk, 37:297.
1920c.   The season. Bird-Lore, 22:52, 108, 170, 231, 295, 330, 360.
1921a.   The English sparrow (*Passer domesticus*) and the motor vehicle. Auk, 38:244–250.
1921b.   The season. Bird-Lore, 23:38, 96, 147, 207, 312.
1921c.   Denver birds. Wilson Bull., 33:102–103.
1922a.   The Lapland longspur in Colorado. Auk, 39:419.
1922b.   The season. Bird-Lore, 24:48, 160, 224, 286, 354.
1923a.   Another Calaveras warbler in Colorado. Auk, 40:334.
1923b.   The season. Bird-Lore, 25:52, 135, 199, 265, 329, 405.
1924a.   Colorado Anatidae. Auk, 41:72–89.

1924b.   The Colorado crow. Auk, 41:158.
1924c.   The black duck in Colorado. Auk, 41:338.
1924d.   Blackpoll warbler in Denver. Auk, 41:485.
1924e.   A summer occurrence of the Bohemian waxwing in Colorado. Auk, 41:614.
1924f.   The season. Bird-Lore, 26:61, 127, 274, 342.
1925.   The season. Bird-Lore, 27:18, 121, 193, 268, 344, 413.
1926a.   Colorado ducks. Auk, 43:231.
1926b.   Harris' sparrow in Colorado. Auk, 43:245.
1926c.   Passerine birds eating trout fry. Auk, 43:558.
1926d.   Bobolinks in Colorado. Bird-Lore, 28:396–397.
1926e.   About the western house finch. Bird-Lore, 28:197.
1926f.   The season. Bird-Lore, 28:143, 215, 284, 350, 410.
1927a.   The Colorado sparrow hawks. Auk, 44:28–37.
1927b.   A house finch infected by fly larvae. Auk, 44:106–107.
1927c.   The cardinal in Colorado. Auk, 44:108.
1927d.   The dickcissel in Colorado. Auk, 44:109–110.
1927e.   The rusty blackbird in Colorado. Auk, 44:253.
1927f.   In re of a Colorado collector. Auk, 44:266.
1927g.   Denver birds. Auk, 44:432–433.
1927h.   The season. Bird-Lore, 29:60–62.
1928a.   A guide to the birds of Colorado. Smith-Brooks Printing Co., Denver. 207 pp.
1928b.   More Colorado ducks. Auk, 45:170–176.
1928c.   The season. Bird-Lore, 30:20, 134, 204, 278, 344, 407.
1929a.   Harris' sparrow in Denver. Auk, 46:119.
1929b.   Another cardinal in Colorado. Auk, 46:550.
1929c.   The season. Bird-Lore, 31:18, 130, 206, 279, 348, 414
1930a.   The blue grosbeak in Colorado. Auk, 47:421.
1930b.   Snow buntings in Colorado. Auk, 47:421.
1930c.   Mourning dove behavior. Bird-Lore, 32:335–337.
1930d.   The season. Bird-Lore, 32:16, 143, 214, 288, 364, 437.
1931a.   Bohemian waxwings in Colorado. Auk, 48:432–434.
1931b.   The season. Bird-Lore, 33:19, 134, 201, 273, 338, 413.
1932a.   Bohemian waxwings in Colorado, 1931–32. Condor, 34:229–230.
1932b.   The American eider in Colorado. Auk, 49:346.
1932c.   The season. Bird-Lore, 34:18, 147, 213, 278, 346, 405.
1933a.   The Bohemian waxwing. Bird-Lore, 35:3–5.
1933b.   The season. Bird-Lore, 35:109, 164, 216, 227, 384.
1934.   The season. Bird-Lore, 36:118, 186, 249, 314, 376.
1935.   The season. Bird-Lore, 37:145, 228, 294.

BERTHOUD, EDWARD L.
1877.   *Melopelia leucoptera* in Colorado. Bull. Nuttall Ornith. Club, 2:83.
1887.   Birds, their geological history, migration and uses. Transcript Press, Golden, Colorado. 22 pp.

BETTS, NORMAN deWITT.
1910.   Notes from Boulder, Colorado. Auk, 27:218–219.
1911.   Notes from Boulder County, Colorado. Auk, 28:118.
1912.   Notes from Boulder County, Colorado. Auk, 29:399–400.
1913.   Birds of Boulder County, Colorado. Univ. of Colorado Studies, 10:177–232.

BRADBURY, WILLIAM C.
1915.   Notes on the nesting of the white-tailed ptarmigan in Colorado. Condor, 17:214–222.
1917a.   Notes on the black-crowned night heron near Denver. Condor, 19:142–143.
1917b.   Notes on the nesting habits of the Clarke nutcracker in Colorado. Condor, 19:149–155.
1918a.   Notes on the nesting habits of the white-throated swift in Colorado. Condor, 20:103–110.
1918b.   Notes on the nesting of the mountain plover. Condor, 20:157–163.
1918c.   Nesting of the Rocky Mountain jay. Condor, 20:197–208.
1919.   Nesting notes on the Rocky Mountain creeper. Condor, 21:49–52.
1924.   Nesting habits of the ptarmigan. Bull., Colorado Fish and Game Protective Assoc., 4(3):6.

BRANDENBURG, FREDERICK G.
1939.   Breaking into the private life of the golden eagle. Rocky Mt. Sportsman, 3:8–10, 44.
1940.   See Bailey, Alfred M.
1941.   See Bailey, Alfred M.

BURNETT, L. E.
1904.   Whip-poor-will (*Antrostomus vociferus*), a new bird for Colorado. Auk, 21:278–279.

BURNETT, WILLIAM L.
1896.   Nest of the dusky grouse. Nidologist, 3:64.

1900a.   Unique nesting site of Say's phoebe. Condor, 2:89.
1900b.   The indigo bunting in Colorado. Condor, 2:90.
1901.   Alma's thrush in Colorado. Condor, 3:114.
1902.   The rose-breasted grosbeak in Colorado. Condor, 4:94.
1903.   The Rocky Mountain screech owl in Larimer County, Colorado. Condor, 5:156.
1908.   Another cañon wren record for Colorado. Auk, 25:87.
1915.   Notes on some birds of Spring Canyon, Colorado. Condor, 17:148–151.
1916.   Two trumpeter swan records for Colorado. Auk, 33:198.
1921.   A new bird for Larimer County, Colorado. Condor, 23:167.
1922.   A December record for the sage thrasher in Colorado. Condor, 24:63.
1924.   Colorado bird notes. Auk, 41:618.

CARY, MERRITT.

1909.   New records and important range extensions of Colorado birds. Auk, 26:180–185, 312.
1911.   A biological survey of Colorado. North American Fauna 33, U. S. Dept. of Agric., Bur. of Biol. Survey, 256 pp.

COLLISTER, ALLEGRA E.

1954.   Hudsonian curlew and knot in Colorado. Wilson Bull., 66:273.
1963.   Operation recovery in Colorado. Western Bird Bander, 38:30–34.
1965.   A list of birds of Rocky Mountain National Park. Rocky Mt. Nature Assoc., Estes Park, Colorado. 16 pp.

COOKE, WELLS WOODBRIDGE.

1894.   Ten new birds for Colorado. Auk, 11:182–183.
1895.   The summer range of Colorado birds. Auk, 12:150–155.
1897a.   The birds of Colorado. State Agric. College (Colorado State Univ.), Bull. 37, (Tech. Series 2), Smith-Brooks Printing Co., Denver. 144 pp.
1897b.   The scarlet ibis in Colorado. Auk, 14:316.
1897c.   Bendire's thrasher in Colorado. Osprey, 2:7.
1897d.   A new bird for Colorado. Oregon Naturalist, 4:65.
1898a.   Further notes on the birds of Colorado: an appendix to Bull. 37. State Agric. College (Colorado State Univ.), Agric. Exp. Sta., Fort Collins, Bull. 44, (Tech. Series 4), pp. 147–176; Smith-Brooks Printing Co., Denver.
1898b.   A new bird for Colorado (*Ammodramus lecontei*). Osprey, 3:13.
1898c.   The scarlet ibis—a correction. Auk, 15:183.
1899.   More new birds for Colorado. Auk, 16:187–188.
1900.   The birds of Colorado: a second appendix to Bull. 37. Agric. College of Colorado (Colorado State Univ.), Bull. 56, (Tech. Series 5), published by Agric. Exp. Sta., Fort Collins, pp. 179–239.
1909a.   Some new birds for Colorado. Auk, 26:314.
1909b.   The birds of Colorado—third supplement. Auk, 26:400–422.
1912.   The present status of the Colorado check-list of birds. Condor, 14:147–153.
1913.   The wild turkeys of Colorado. Condor, 15:104–105.

DILLE, FRED M.

1885.   Nesting of *Archibuteo ferrugineus*. Young Oologist, pp. 44–45.
1886a.   Colorado birds: the black-billed magpie. Sunny South Oologist, 1:7–8.
1886b.   Egg collecting in Colorado. *Ibid.*, 1:15.
1886c.   Colorado birds: lark bunting and mountain plover. *Ibid.*, 1:29.
1887.   A week's trip after hawk's eggs in Colorado. Ornith. and Ool., 12:97–100.
1888.   Nesting of the black-billed magpie. *Ibid.*, 13:23–24.
1894.   Home life of the mountain bluebird. Nidologist, 2:36.
1900a.   The club collection of birds. Condor, 2:69.
1900b.   Nesting of the pine siskin at Denver, Colo. Condor, 2:73.
1900c.   Nesting of the eastern bluebird at Denver, Colorado. Condor, 2:88.
1902.   Western blue grosbeak in northern Colorado. Condor, 4:94.
1903a.   Nesting dates for birds in the Denver district, Colorado. Condor, 5:73–74.
1903b.   Concerning spotted eggs of the lark bunting. Condor, 5:79.
1904a.   Eggs of flammulated screech owl and western evening grosbeak, taken in Estes Park, Colorado. Condor, 6:50.
1904b.   A sage sparrow in Boulder County, Colorado. Condor, 6:79.

DREW, FRANK M.

1881a.   Field notes on the birds of San Juan County, Colorado. Bull. Nuttall Ornith. Club., 6:85–91, 138–143.
1881b.   Song of the white-bellied swallow (*Iridoprocne bicolor*). *Ibid.*, 6:115.
1881c.   The golden crested wren breeding in the Colorado Valley. *Ibid.*, 6:244.
1881d.   *Lobipes hyperboreus* at 9500 feet. *Ibid.*, 6:249.

1882.   Notes on the plumage of *Nephoecetes niger borealis. Ibid.,* 7:182–183.
1884.   Notes on *Lagopus leucurus.* Auk, 1:392–393.
1885.   On the vertical range of birds in Colorado. Auk, 2:11–18.

EDGERTON, HAROLD E., ROBERT J. NIEDRACH, and WALKER VAN RIPER.
1951.   Freezing the flight of hummingbirds. National Geographic Magazine, 100:245–261.

FELGER, ALVA HOWARD.
1901.   The Mexican cormorant in Colorado. Auk, 18:189.
1902.   Colorado bird notes. Auk, 19:294.
1903a. The wood ibis again in Colorado. Auk, 20:65.
1903b. Birds killed by hailstones. Auk, 20:70.
1903c. Hybrid duck—mallard *(Anas boschas)* + pintail *(Dafila acuta).* Auk, 20:303–304.
1905.   Two records for Colorado. Auk, 22:421.
1907a. Ross's snow goose in Colorado. Auk, 24:211–212.
1907b. The prothonotary warbler in Colorado. Auk, 24:342.
1907c. A new record for Colorado. Condor, 9:110.
1909a. Colorado notes. Auk, 26:85–86.
1909b. Wild turkey *(Meleagris gallopavo).* Auk, 26:191.
1909c. Annotated list of the water birds of Weld, Morgan, and Adams Counties, Colorado, south to the first sectional line below the fortieth parallel. Auk, 26:272–291.
1910a. Colorado notes. Auk, 27:89.
1910b. Status of the black duck *(Anas rubripes)* in Colorado. Auk, 27:451–452.
1910c. Birds and mammals of northwestern Colorado. Univ. of Colorado Studies, 7:132–146.
1917.   Blue jay in Jefferson County, Colorado. Auk, 34:209–210.
1919.   Blue jay again in Jefferson County, Colorado. Auk, 36:422.

FIGGINS, JESSE DADE.
1913.   The status of the Gambel quail in Colorado. Condor, 15:158.
1914.   The fallacy of the tendency toward ultraminute distinctions. Auk, 31:62–69.
1917.   Winter visitors to City Park, Denver, Colorado. Bird-Lore, 19:305–309.
1920.   The status of the subspecific races of *Branta canadensis.* Auk, 37:94–102.
1926.   William C. Bradbury. Condor, 28:74–76.
1930.   Proposals relative to certain subspecific groups of *Carpodacus mexicanus.* Proc. Colorado (Denver) Mus. Nat. Hist., 9:1–3.

GADD, SAMUEL W.
1941a. Starlings in central Colorado. Wilson Bull., 53:46.
1941b. Range of the Texas woodpecker in Colorado. Condor, 43:201.
1942.   Spotted owl nesting in Colorado. Condor, 44:35.

GRISCOM, LUDLOW.
1937.   A monographic study of the red crossbill. Proc. Boston Soc. Nat. Hist., 41:77–210.
1938.   See Peters, James Lee.

HENDEE, RUSSELL W.
1929.   Notes on birds observed in Moffat County, Colorado. Condor, 31:24–32.

HENDERSON, JUNIUS.
1901.   The western grosbeak in Colorado. Wilson Bull., 13:45–46.
1902.   Boulder, Colorado, birds increasing. Wilson Bull., 14:74.
1903a. Mountain bluebird increasing in Boulder, Colo. Wilson Bull., 15:74–75.
1903b. Preliminary list of birds of Boulder County, Colorado. Univ. of Colorado Studies, 1:233–237.
1904a. Additional list of Boulder County birds, with comments thereon. *Ibid.,* 2:107–112.
1904b. The bobolink in Colorado. Auk, 21:486.
1904c. Notes from Boulder, Colorado. Wilson Bull., 16:27.
1904d. Bobolinks increasing at Boulder, Colorado. Wilson Bull., 16:92.
1905a. The blue jay at Yuma, Colorado. Auk, 22:82.
1905b. Colorado notes. Auk, 22:421–422.
1906.   With the birds in northeastern Colorado. Wilson Bull., 18:105–110.
1907a. Nesting of crossbills in Colorado. Auk, 24:440–442.
1907b. Destruction of herons by a hailstorm. Condor, 9:162.
1907c. Colorado notes. Condor, 9:198.
1907d. An early Colorado naturalist—Denis Gale. Univ. of Colorado Studies, 5:25–34.
1908.   The American dipper in Colorado. Bird-Lore, 10:1–7.
1909.   An annotated list of the birds of Boulder County, Colorado. Univ. of Colorado Studies, 6:219–242.
1912.   A history of the birds of Colorado: in part, a review of Sclater's, 1912, publication. Auk, 29:277–278; Condor, 15:8, 47, 159.
1916a. House finch or linnet? Condor, 18:30.

1916b. Marbled godwit in Colorado. Condor, 18:35.
1916c. A populous shore. Condor, 18:100–110.
1917. The Bohemian waxwing in Colorado. Condor, 19:141.
1920a. Migrations of the pinyon jay in Colorado. Condor, 22:36.
1920b. Further Colorado notes. Condor, 22:42–43, 75.
1922. The black vulture in Colorado. Condor, 24:26.
1924. Status of the black and mottled ducks in Colorado. Auk, 41:471.
1925a. Some Colorado and Wyoming records of the varied thrush and the rusty blackbird. Condor, 27:74–76.
1925b. Bobolink in Colorado. Auk, 42:135–136.
1927. The blue jay at Boulder, Colorado. Condor, 29:80.

HENRY, T. C.
1855. Notes derived from observations made on the birds of New Mexico during the years 1853 and 1854. Proc. Acad. Nat. Science, Philadelphia, 7:306–317.

HERSEY, LUMAN JOEL.
1911. Some new birds for Colorado. Auk, 28:490.
1912a. Two new birds for Colorado. Condor, 14:108.
1912b. A bird new to Colorado. Condor, 14:154.
1913. Gambel quail (*Lophortyx gambeli*) in Colorado. Condor, 15:93–94.

HERSEY, LUMAN JOEL, and ROBERT B. ROCKWELL.
1907. A new breeding bird for Colorado: the Cassin sparrow (*Peucaea cassini*) nesting near Denver. Condor, 9:191–194.
1909. An annotated list of the birds of the Barr Lake district, Adams County, Colorado. Condor, 11:109–122.

HURLBUTT, CATHERINE A.
1929. A resident of the snow-caps. Bird Lore, 31:259–260.
1930. Two more nocturnal singers. Bird-Lore, 32:130–131.
1932. At home with the camp robber. Bird-Lore, 34:383–385.

HYDE, A. SYDNEY.
1951. White-faced glossy ibis and long-billed curlew in western Colorado. Condor, 53:98–99.
1953. Unusual records from western Colorado. Condor, 55:216.
1958. Sharp-tailed sparrow and grasshopper sparrow in Gunnison County, Colorado. Condor, 60:68.

IMLER, RALPH H.
1939. The starling in Colorado and western Kansas. Wilson Bull., 51:46.

JEWETT, STANLEY G.
1942. An unrecorded Eskimo curlew from Colorado. Condor, 44:74.

JOHNSTON, RICHARD F.
1960. Directory to the bird-life of Kansas. Univ. of Kansas Publ., Mus. of Nat. Hist. Misc. Publ., 23:1–69.
1964. The breeding birds of Kansas. Univ. of Kansas Publ., Mus. of Nat. Hist., 12:575–655.

KALMBACH, EDWIN R.
1942. Whooping cranes in eastern Colorado. Auk, 59:307.

KLEINSCHNITZ, FERD C.
1937. Field manual of birds of the Rocky Mountain National Park. Published by the author, Denver. 60 pp.

KNORR, OWEN A.
1957. Communal roosting of the pygmy nuthatch. Condor, 59:398.
1958. Nesting of the chimney swift in Colorado. Wilson Bull., 70:97.
1959a. First Carolina wren taken in Colorado. Auk, 76:95.
1959b. The birds of El Paso County, Colorado. Univ. of Colorado Studies, Series in Biology 5, 48 pp.
1961. The geographical and ecological distribution of the black swift in Colorado. Wilson Bull., 73:155–170.
1962. Black swift breeds in Utah. Condor, 64:79.

KNORR, OWEN A., and A. LANG BAILY.
1950. First breeding record of black swift, *Nephoecetes n. borealis*, in Colorado. Auk, 67:516.

LIGON, J. STOKLEY.
1961. New Mexico birds. Univ. of New Mexico Press, Albuquerque. 360 pp.

LINCOLN, FREDERICK C.

1912.   Notes on the dickcissel in Colorado. Auk, 29:544–545.
1913a.   The alder flycatcher in Colorado. Auk, 30:112.
1913b.   The slate-colored fox sparrow breeding in Colorado. Auk, 30:113–114.
1914a.   Two species new to Colorado. Auk, 31:256.
1914b.   The pelican in Colorado. City of Denver, 3:10–11.
1915a.   Description of a new bobwhite from Colorado. Proc. Biol. Soc. of Washington, 28:103.
1915b.   The birds of Yuma County, Colorado. Proc. Colorado (Denver) Mus. Nat. Hist., 1, 14 pp.
1916.   The discovery of the nest and eggs of *Leucosticte australis*. Auk, 33:41–42.
1917a.   Bohemian waxwing (*Bombycilla garrula*) in Colorado. Auk, 34:341.
1917b.   A review of the genus *Pedioecetes* in Colorado. Proc. Biol. Soc. of Washington, 30:83–86.
1918a.   The harpy eagle in Colorado. Auk, 35:78–79.
1918b.   Notes on some species new to the Colorado list of birds. Auk, 35:236–237.
1918c.   A strange case of hybridism. Wilson Bull., 30:1–2.
1919.   Additional notes and records from Colorado. Condor, 21:237–238.
1920a.   Birds of the Clear Creek district, Colorado. Auk, 37:60–77.
1920b.   The status of Harlan's hawk in Colorado. Auk, 37:130–131.
1920c.   *Zonotrichia albicollis* again in Colorado. Auk, 37:300.
1920d.   The least tern in Colorado—a correction. Wilson Bull., 32:65.
1927.   A note on the longevity of the pintail. Condor, 29:15.
1929.   In memoriam—Edwin Carter. Condor, 31:196–200.
1932.   A longevity record for the Hutchins' goose. Bird-Banding, 3:114.
1939.   The migration of American birds. Doubleday, Doran and Co., Inc., New York. 189 pp.
1950.   Migration of birds. U. S. Dept. of Int., Fish and Wildlife Service Circ. 16, 102 pp.
1952a.   An early specimen of the eastern fox sparrow from Colorado. Condor, 54:319–320.
1952b.   Migration of birds. Doubleday and Co., Garden City, New York. 102 pp.
1954.   See Bailey, Alfred M.

LODGE, FRED S.

1930.   Note on the woodcock carrying young. Program of Activities, Chicago Acad. of Sciences, 1:9–10.

LOWE, WILLOUGHBY P.

1892.   Some spring arrivals at Pueblo County, Colorado. Ornith. and Ool., 17:101.
1894a.   A list of the birds of the Wet Mountains, Huerfano County, Colorado. Auk, 11:266–270.
1894b.   The scarlet ibis (*Guara rubra*) in Colorado. Auk, 11:324.
1895a.   Arrival of the English sparrow at Pueblo, Colo. Nidologist, 2:99.
1895b.   Low nesting sites of *Bubo*. *Ibid*., 2:169.
1895c.   Notes from the field. *Ibid*., 2:169.
1895d.   An albino pallid horned lark. *Ibid*., 2:170.
1895e.   An addition to the birds of Colorado. Auk, 12:298.
1897.   A young ferruginous rough-leg. Nidologist, 4:69–70.
1901.   Bird notes from Pueblo County, Colorado. Auk, 18:276.
1914.   Phoebe (*Sayornis phoebe*) in Colorado. Auk, 31:102.
1917.   Remarks on Colorado birds. Auk, 34:453–455.

MARKMAN, HARVEY C.

1907.   Scientific expedition to northeastern Colorado: Zoology—account of species seen, with distribution. Univ. of Colorado Studies, 4:153–158.

MARSH, THOMPSON G.

1927.   Rusty blackbird again in Colorado. Auk, 44:567.
1929.   Blue jay in Denver, Colorado. Auk, 46:389.
1931a.   A history of the first records of all the birds reported to have been seen within the present boundaries of the state of Colorado prior to settlement. Master's thesis, Univ. of Denver. (Copy in library of Denver Mus. of Nat. Hist.)
1931b.   The chimney swift in Colorado. Auk. 48:427–428.
1942.   Black-billed cuckoo in Colorado. Auk, 59:111.

MURPHY, JOHN A., JR.

1951.   The nesting of the black swift. Natural History, 60:446–449.

NEFF, JOHNSON A., and ROBERT J. NIEDRACH.

1946.   Nesting of the band-tailed pigeon in Colorado. Condor, 48:72–74.

NIEDRACH, ROBERT J.

1923.   Two interesting additions to the known avifauna of Colorado. Condor, 25:182.
1924.   The white-necked raven nesting in eastern Colorado. Condor, 26:105.

NIEDRACH, ROBERT J., and ROBERT B. ROCKWELL.

1939.   The birds of Denver and Mountain Parks. Colorado (Denver) Mus. Nat. Hist. Popular Series 5. 195 pp.

1959.   [Same title]. 2nd printing includes supplement adding species recorded in the Denver area since first printing. Denver Mus. Nat. Hist., Popular Series 5, 203 pp.

PACKARD, FRED MALLERY.

1939.   Northern sage sparrow on the east slope of the Rockies in Colorado. Auk, 56:481–482.

1943a.   Predation upon Wilson's phalarope by Treganza's heron. Auk, 60:97.

1943b.   Second record of the wood thrush in Colorado, with other observations. Auk, 60:107–108.

1945a.   On "*Hylocichla guttata oromela.*" Auk, 62:345.

1945b.   The birds of Rocky Mountain National Park, Colorado. Auk, 62:371–394.

1945c.   Possible intergrades between the Myrtle and Audubon's warblers. Auk, 62:623.

1946a.   Some observations of birds eating salt. Auk, 63:89.

1946b.   Midsummer wandering of certain Rocky Mountain birds. Auk, 63:152–158.

1950.   The birds of Rocky Mountain National Park. Rocky Mt. Nature Assoc., Estes Park, Colorado. 81 pp.

PETERSON, ROGER TORY.

1942.   Life zones, biomes, or life forms. Audubon Magazine, 44:21–30.

1961a.   Bird's-eye view. *Ibid.*, 63:72–73.

1961b.   A field guide to western birds. Houghton Mifflin Co., Boston. 366 pp.

1963.   The birds. Life Nature Library, Time, Inc., New York. 192 pp.

PHILLIPS, ALLAN R., and JOE MARSHALL, and GALE MONSON.

1964.   The birds of Arizona. Univ. of Arizona Press, Tucson. 212 pp.

RAPP, WILLIAM F., JR., JANET L. C. RAPP, HENRY E. BAUMGARTEN, and R. ALLYN MOSER.

1958.   Revised check-list of Nebraska birds. Occas. Papers, Nebraska Ornith. Union, 5:1–45.

ROCKWELL, ROBERT B.

1907a.   The Woodhouse jay in western Colorado. Condor, 9:81–84.

1907b.   Some Colorado notes on the Rocky Mountain screech owl. Condor, 9:140–145.

1907c.   See Hersey, Luman Joel.

1908a.   Nesting of the western horned owl in Colorado. Condor, 1908, 86; 10:14–17.

1908b.   The red-winged blackbirds of Colorado. Condor, 10:93.

1908c.   An annotated list of the birds of Mesa County, Colorado. Condor, 10:152–180.

1908d.   A one-legged red-winged blackbird. Condor, 10:182.

1908e.   Note on South Platte River [following George Richard's article on nuthatch]. Condor, 10:195–196.

1908f.   A striking example of protective coloration. Condor, 10:207–208.

1909a.   The history of Colorado ornithology. Condor, 11:24–34, 69.

1909b.   The use of magpies' nests by other birds. Condor, 11:90–92.

1910a.   An albino magpie. Condor, 12:45.

1910b.   Some Colorado night heron notes. Condor, 12:113–121.

1910c.   Nesting of the gray-headed junco. Condor, 12:164–165.

1910d.   Nesting notes on the American eared grebe and pied-billed grebe. Condor, 12:188–193.

1911a.   Notes on the nesting of the Forster and black terns in Colorado. Condor, 13:57–63.

1911b.   Nesting notes on the ducks of the Barr Lake region, Colorado. Condor, 13:121–128.

1911c.   [Same title]: part 2. Condor, 13:186–195.

1912.   Notes on the wading birds of the Barr Lake region, Colorado. Condor, 14:117–131.

1920.   Owls. Trail and Timberline, no. 27 (Dec.):2–7.

1939a.   The starling in Colorado. Wilson Bull., 51:46.

1939b.   See Niedrach, Robert J.

1959.   See Niedrach, Robert J.

ROCKWELL, ROBERT B., and CLARK BLICKENSDERFER.

1921.   Glimpses of the home life of the saw-whet owl. Natural History, 21:626–635.

1932.   Colorado's avian host. Nature Magazine, pp. 284–322.

ROCKWELL, ROBERT B., and ALEXANDER WETMORE.

1914.   A list of birds from the vicinity of Golden, Colorado. Auk, 31:309–333.

RYDER, RONALD A.

1950.   New breeding records for Colorado. Condor, 52:133–134.

1951.   Waterfowl production in the San Luis Valley, Colorado. (Unpublished Master's thesis, Colorado A. and M. College [Colorado State Univ.], Fort Collins.) 166 pp.

1952b.   Bird notes from southern Colorado. Condor, 54:317–318.

1955a.	Long gone goslings. Colorado Conservation, 4:16–17.
1955b.	A preliminary analysis of waterfowl recoveries in Colorado with notes on trapping and banding. Completion report, Federal Aid Project W-37-R-8, game bird surveys, Colorado Game and Fish Dept. 72 pp.
1960.	The grouse of Colorado. Colorado Outdoors, Dept. of Game and Fish, 9:1–7.
1963.	Mottled duck and knot in Colorado. Condor, 65:333.
1964.	California gulls nesting in Colorado. Condor, 66:440.

SCLATER, WILLIAM HENRY.
1908.	The winter birds of Colorado. Ibis, 9th series, 2:443–450.
1912.	A history of the birds of Colorado. Witherby and Co., London. 576 pp.

SCOTT, JOHN W.
1942.	Mating behavior of the sage grouse. Auk, 59:447–498.

SCOTT, W. E. D.
1878a.	Birds about Denver (Col.). The Country [New York paper], 2:136.
1878b.	A mountain drive [birds in the foothills near Denver]. Ibid., 2:152, 168.
1879.	Notes on birds observed at Twin Lakes, Lake County, Colorado. Bull. Nuttall Ornith. Club, 4:90–96.

SELANDER, ROBERT K.
1954.	A systematic review of the booming nighthawks of western North America. Condor, 56:57–82.

SHICKLEY, GAIL.
1960.	Rivoli's hummingbird in Colorado. Colorado Bird Notes, 8:25–26.

SMITH, HORACE GARDNER.
1884a.	History of a magpie. Ornith. and Ool., 9:76.
1884b.	The shore lark (Eremophila cornuta). Ibid., 9:95.
1884c.	Notes from Denver, Colorado. Ibid., 9:120–121.
1885.	Cassin's purple finch (Carpodacus cassini). Ibid., 10:90.
1886a.	Some additions to the avifauna of Colorado. Auk, 3:284–286.
1886b.	Colorado bird notes. Random Notes on Natural History, 3:13, 17, 25, 66.
1888.	Food of the great northern shrike. Ornith. and Ool., 13:163–164.
1893a.	Another Megascops flammeolus for Colorado. Auk, 10:364.
1893b.	City birds of Denver, Colorado. Science, 22:244.
1895.	Some birds new to Colorado—with notes on others of little known distribution in the state. Nidologist, 3:48–49.
1896.	[Same title]. Ibid., 3:65, 76.
1902.	Another scarlet tanager for Colorado. Auk, 19:290.
1903.	Bell's vireo (Vireo bellii) in Colorado. Auk, 20:438.
1905.	The blue jay and other eastern birds at Wray, Yuma County, Colorado. Auk, 22:81–82.
1908.	Random notes on the distribution of some Colorado birds, with additions to the state avifauna. Auk, 25:184–191.
1910.	Two avian stragglers within the state of Colorado. Condor, 12:133.

SMITH, WILLIAM G.
1886a.	Winter birds in Larimer County, Colorado. Random Notes on Natural History, 3:13.
1886b.	Nest of rock wren. Ibid., 3:17.
1886c.	Nest and eggs of Myadestes townsendii (Townsend flycatcher). Ibid., 3:25.
1886d.	Notes from Colorado [mountain-tit]. Ibid., 3:66–67.
1887.	Hybrid ducks. Ornith. and Ool., 12:169.
1888a.	Nesting of Audubon's warbler. Ibid., 13:114–115.
1888b.	Nesting of the ruddy duck. Ibid., 13:132.
1888c.	Nesting of the water ouzel. Ibid., 13:149.
1888d.	Breeding habits of the mountain plover. Ibid., 13:187–188.
1889a.	Nesting of the cinnamon teal. Ibid., 14:77.
1889b.	Nesting of the pied-billed grebe. Ibid., 14:138–139.
1889c.	Brief notes [Sabine's gull]. Ibid., 14:176.
1890.	Nesting of the eared grebe. Ibid., 15:141.
1891.	Nesting of the flammulated screech owl. Ibid., 16:27.

STABLER, ROBERT M.
1957.	Three uncommon birds from El Paso Co., Colorado: red-bellied woodpecker, wood thrush, black and white warbler. Journ. Colo.-Wyo. Acad. of Sci., 4(9):52.
1959.	Nesting of the blue grosbeak in Colorado. Condor, 61:46–48.
1960.	The whistling swan in El Paso Co., Colorado. Journ. Colo.-Wyo. Acad. of Sci., 5(1):51.

THATCHER, DONALD M.
    1954.   Carolina wren at Palmer Lake. Colorado Bird Notes, 2(1):7.
    1963.   The Sprague's pipit in Colorado. *Ibid.,* 10:44.

THORNE, OAKLEIGH, II.
    1957.   Rufous-sided towhee in Colorado. Condor, 59:340.

TORDOFF, HARRISON B.
    1956.   Check-list of the birds of Kansas. Univ. of Kansas Publ., Mus. of Nat. Hist., Lawrence, 8:307–359.

WARREN, EDWARD R.
    1900.   Photographing ptarmigan. Bird-Lore, 2:169–174.
    1902.   Whiskey John in Colorado. Bird-Lore, 4:186–188.
    1903.   A nest of the western horned owl. Wilson Bull., 15:87–91.
    1904a.   A sandhill crane's nest. Condor, 6:39–40.
    1904b.   Horned larks in Colorado Springs, Colorado. Bird-Lore, 6:6.
    1905.   Cassin's sparrow in Colorado. Auk, 22:417.
    1906a.   A collecting trip to southeastern Colorado. Condor, 8:18–24.
    1906b.   *Contopus virens* in Colorado. Condor, 8:130.
    1907a.   A hummingbird that wanted light. Bird-Lore, 9:81.
    1907b.   Photographing magpies. Condor, 9:5–9.
    1907c.   An interesting occurrence of the canyon wren. Condor, 9:111.
    1908.   Northwestern Colorado bird notes. Condor, 10:18–26.
    1909a.   Notes on the birds of southwestern Montrose County, Colorado. Condor, 11:11–17.
    1909b.   Concerning *Thryomanes bewicki cryptus* in Colorado. Auk, 26:311–312.
    1909c.   Some interesting Colorado records. Condor, 11:33.
    1910a.   Some central Colorado bird notes. Condor. 12:23–39.
    1910b.   Bird notes from Salida, Chaffee County, Colorado. Auk, 27:142–151.
    1911.   Some Colorado horned owl notes. Condor, 13:153–156.
    1912a.   Some north-central Colorado bird notes. Condor, 14:81–104.
    1912b.   The magpies of Culebra Creek. Bird-Lore, 14:329–333.
    1913a.   Swallows and bedbugs. Condor, 15:14–16.
    1913b.   Notes on some Mesa County, Colorado, birds. Condor, 15:110–111.
    1914.   See Aiken, Charles Edward Howard.
    1915.   Some Park County, Colorado, bird notes. Condor, 17:90–95.
    1916a.   Notes on the birds of the Elk Mountain region, Gunnison County, Colorado. Auk, 33:292–317.
    1916b.   The birds of Monument Valley Park, Colorado Springs, Colorado. Bird-Lore, 18:217–228.
    1919a.   Bird notes of a stormy May in Colorado Springs. Condor, 21:62–65.
    1919b.   Notes on albino robins. Bird-Lore, 21:246.
    1923a.   Concerning the Cassiar junco. Condor, 25:27–28.
    1923b.   Some robins and their nests. Bird-Lore, 25:108–110.
    1926.   Misapplied perseverance. Condor, 28:270.
    1927.   Three records from Colorado. Auk, 44:432.
    1928.   Additional notes on the birds of the Elk Mountain region, Colorado. Auk, 45:106–108.
    1936.   Charles Edward Howard Aiken. Condor, 38:234–238.
    1941.   [Edited Charles E. H. Aiken's notes] From Colorado Springs to Horse Creek in 1878. Auk, 58:70–73; Condor, 34:43.

WITHERSPOON, PATRICIA BAILEY.
    1953.   Home life of the house finches. Nature Magazine, 46:262–264.
    1957.   Shorebird of the prairie. Natural History, 66:384–386.
    1958.   At home with the killdeer. Frontiers, 22:74–75.
    1962.   Wanderers of the North. Pacific Discovery, 15:2–7.

ZIMMERMAN, JOHN L.
    1964.   First specimen of cattle egret for Kansas. Kansas Ornith. Soc. Bull., 15:20.

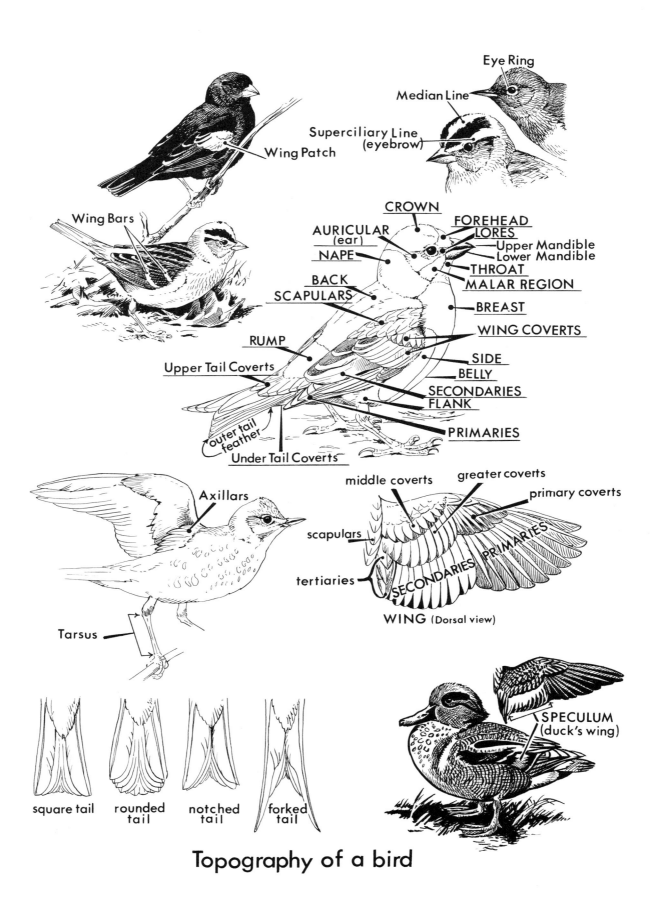

Eye Ring

Median Line

Superciliary Line
(eyebrow)

Wing Patch

Wing Bars

CROWN

FOREHEAD
LORES
Upper Mandible
Lower Mandible

AURICULAR
(ear)

NAPE

THROAT
MALAR REGION

BACK

BREAST

SCAPULARS

WING COVERTS

RUMP

SIDE
BELLY

Upper Tail Coverts

SECONDARIES
FLANK

PRIMARIES

outer tail
feather

Under Tail Coverts

Axillars

middle coverts   greater coverts

primary coverts

scapulars

SECONDARIES   PRIMARIES

tertiaries

WING (Dorsal view)

Tarsus

SPECULUM
(duck's wing)

square tail   rounded   notched   forked
                tail   tail   tail

Topography of a bird

INDEX

Color Plates

of

COLORADO BIRDS

John Crosby

RED-THROATED LOON *(winter and spring)*

ARCTIC LOON *(spring and winter)*

COMMON LOON *(winter and spring)*

YELLOW-BILLED LOON *(spring adult)*

Plate 1

PIED-BILLED GREBE
Podilymbus podiceps podiceps
Length 12–15 inches
A common summer resident and breeding bird
in Colorado marshes

(immature and adult)

HORNED GREBE
Podiceps auritus cornutus
Length 12–15 inches
A regular spring and fall migrant upon the lakes
and reservoirs of the eastern part of the state

(spring and winter plumage)

EARED GREBE
Podiceps caspicus californicus
Length 12–15 inches
A common spring and fall migrant and occasional
nesting diver on lakes and reservoirs with a stable
water level

(winter and spring plumage)

(Plate 2 by John A. Crosby)

PIED-BILLED GREBE (immature and adult)

HORNED GREBE (spring and winter)

EARED GREBE (winter and spring)

Plate 2

RED-NECKED GREBE
Podiceps grisegena holbollii
Length 19–22 inches
An uncommon migrant in spring and fall

(winter and spring plumage)

WESTERN GREBE
Aechmophorus occidentalis
Length 24–29 inches
A spring and fall migrant, and summer resident,
breeding regularly, and a few remaining in win-
ter as long as the reservoirs are free of ice

(spring plumage)

RED-NECKED GREBE *(winter and spring)*

WESTERN GREBE *(spring plumage)*

Plate 3

REDDISH EGRET
Dichromanassa rufescens rufescens
Length 27–32 inches
One specimen record
(white and dark phases in spring)

BROWN PELICAN
Pelecanus occidentalis carolinensis
Length 48–56 inches
One specimen record
(spring plumage)

WHITE PELICAN
Pelecanus erythrorhynchos
Length 52–65 inches
A common summer resident upon lakes and reservoirs, and recorded nesting on Riverside Reservoir in 1962
(spring plumage)

OLIVACEOUS CORMORANT
Phalacrocorax olivaceus mexicanus
Length 23–28 inches
One specimen record
(spring plumage)

(Plate 4 by Donald L. Malick)

BROWN PELICAN
WHITE PELICAN
OLIVACEOUS CORMORANT

REDDISH EGRET (white and dark phase)

ANHINGA
Anhinga anhinga leucogaster
Length 32–36 inches
A rare straggler in Colorado with two specimens
recorded
(female and male in spring plumage)

DOUBLE-CRESTED CORMORANT
Phalacrocorax auritus auritus
Length 30–34 inches
A common summer resident, nesting in colonies
in cottonwoods along the shores of lakes and
reservoirs of eastern Colorado
(flying immature and spring adult in water)

(Plate 5 by John A. Crosby)

ANHINGA *(female and male)*

Plate 5

DOUBLE-CRESTED CORMORANT *(flying immature)*

GREAT BLUE HERON
Ardea herodias treganzai

Length 42–50 inches

A common summer resident throughout the state, nesting in colonies in wooded areas adjacent to lakes and reservoirs. A few remain throughout the winter

(adult spring plumage)

SNOWY EGRET
Leucophoyx thula brewsteri

Length 22–27 inches

A regular but not common summer resident nesting in willows and low cottonwoods, often associated with Great Blue Herons

(spring plumage)

COMMON EGRET
Casmerodius albus egretta

Length 38–42 inches

An irregular summer visitor

(spring plumage)

(Plate 6 by John A. Crosby)

GREAT BLUE HERON

SNOWY EGRET   COMMON EGRET

Plate 6

GREEN HERON
Butorides virescens virescens
Length 17–20 inches
A regular but uncommon summer visitor

(flying adult in spring)

BLACK-CROWNED NIGHT HERON
Nycticorax nycticorax hoactli
Length 23–26 inches
A common summer resident nesting locally in colonies in trees along reservoirs and streams throughout the state

(immature above, adult near center)

YELLOW-CROWNED NIGHT HERON
Nyctanassa violacea violacea
Length 22–28 inches
A rare straggler from southern breeding areas

(adult in spring plumage)

LITTLE BLUE HERON
Florida caerulea caerulea
Length 22–28 inches
A rare summer visitor

(white immature at left and adult below)

(Plate 7 by John A. Crosby)

Plate 7

GREEN HERON

BLACK-CROWNED NIGHT HERON
(immature above, adult center)

LITTLE BLUE HERON
(immature left, adult below)

YELLOW-CROWNED NIGHT HERON

AMERICAN BITTERN
Botaurus lentiginosus
Length 24–34 inches
An inconspicuous marsh-dweller, common in summer, rare in winter

LEAST BITTERN
Ixobrychus exilis exilis
Length 12–14 inches
An uncommon summer resident in marsh areas

(immature at left, adult male at right; females have plain brown backs)

(Plate 8 by John A. Crosby)

AMERICAN BITTERN

LEAST BITTERN
(immature at left, adult male at right)

Plate 8

ROSEATE SPOONBILL
Ajaia ajaja
Length 30–35 inches
There are several observations of this rare bird
from Colorado

WHITE IBIS
Eudocimus albus
Length 21–27 inches
A rare straggler

WOOD IBIS
Mycteria americana
Length 35–46 inches
A rare straggler, but there are at least seven re-
ports of its occurrence

WHITE-FACED IBIS
Plegadis chihi
Length 20–26 inches
A regular summer visitor to the eastern plains

GLOSSY IBIS
Plegadis falcinellus falcinellus
Length 20–26 inches
A rare straggler

(Plate 9 by John A. Crosby)

Plate 9

WHITE IBIS   ROSEATE SPOONBILL

WHITE-FACED IBIS   WOOD IBIS

GLOSSY IBIS

TRUMPETER SWAN
Olor buccinator

Length 60–65 inches

For many years this beautiful swan was on verge of extinction, but thanks to wise conservation practices it has become fairly numerous. Colorado is east of the normal range and there is only one known specimen from the state

WHISTLING SWAN
Olor columbianus

Length 48–56 inches

This Far North breeding bird has increased in numbers and is a very common migrant in many areas throughout much of the country. It occurs rather regularly on reservoirs of eastern Colorado during migration, and a few remain in winter

(Plate 10 by F. L. Jaques)

TRUMPETER SWAN

WHISTLING SWAN

Plate 10

CANADA GOOSE
Branta canadensis parvipes

Length 25–30 inches

Canada Geese have been divided into numerous geographic races and five have been recorded from Colorado. This intermediate subspecies, often known as the Lesser Canada occurs in large flocks in winter upon the eastern reservoirs, especially in Kiowa, Bent, and Baca Counties

WHITE-FRONTED GOOSE
Anser albifrons frontalis

Length 27–30 inches

The species is nearly circumpolar in distribution during the breeding season, and this race nests in western and northern Alaska east to Mackenzie and northeastern Keewatin. It winters chiefly west of the Mississippi south into Mexico. An uncommon migrant through Colorado, but a few usually are recorded each season. Sometimes called Speckled-bellied Brant

CANADA GOOSE
Branta canadensis moffitti

Length 27–30 inches

This race formerly nested commonly west of the Continental Divide, but now breeding areas have been restricted. Numbers still occur along the Yampa and Green Rivers. The largest of the species, weighing from twelve to eighteen pounds, *B.c. maxima*, long thought to be extinct, nests on lakes and reservoirs near Denver and Longmont, and several hundred winter in City Park, Denver, and adjacent protected places

(Plate 11 by T. M. Shortt)

CANADA GOOSE *(B.c. parvipes)*

WHITE-FRONTED GOOSE

CANADA GOOSE *(B.c. moffitti)*

Plate 11

BLUE GOOSE
Chen caerulescens
Length 24–30 inches

Breeds on Southhampton and Baffin Islands, and south of Eskimo Point, Northwest Territories, and migrates chiefly through the Mississippi Valley to and from the main wintering areas along the Louisiana Gulf coast, where flocks of thousands occur in winter. A rare bird in Colorado, with a few records only

(immature above and adult below)

SNOW GOOSE
Chen hyperborea hyperborea
Length 24–30 inches

These conspicuous birds appear during migration and winter in small numbers rather regularly. They breed in the Far North, and winter chiefly in British Columbia, Washington and California, and along the Gulf coast from western Louisiana and Texas into Mexico

(adult and immature)

ROSS' GOOSE
Chen rossii
Length 20–26 inches

The remote breeding area of this small goose was unknown until 1940, when birds were discovered along a tributary of the Perry River, fifty miles north of the Arctic Circle in northern Canada. Three Colorado specimens have been taken of this rare bird, and several others have been observed in the state. The main wintering ground is in California

(adult and immature)

(Plate 12 by Owen J. Gromme)

BLUE GOOSE *(immature above)*

SNOW GOOSE *(adult and immature)*

ROSS' GOOSE *(adult and immature)*

Plate 12

MEXICAN DUCK
Anas diazi novimexicana
Length 21–22 inches

Very rare ducks in their natural habitat and only stragglers in Colorado, with three specimens collected. They resemble dark female Mallards and could be confused with Mottled Ducks. The white lines, one in front and one back of the wing speculum, serve to separate them from Mottled and Black Ducks

(adult male but sexes much alike)

MOTTLED DUCK
Anas fulvigula maculosa
Length 20–21 inches

Much like the Mexican Duck but has only *one white wing line* instead of two. This is a bird of the coastal savannahs of Louisiana and Texas but a few occasionally wander beyond their normal range and two specimens have been taken in Colorado. The plumage of this species so resembles immatures of the Mallard that only discerning hunters would likely observe the difference

(adult male)

BLACK DUCK
Anas rubripes
Length 21–25 inches

Like the above, this species is a straggler in the state, but occurs more commonly. It is considerably darker than the Mottled Duck—both of which have the single white lines below the wing speculum. This is one of the favorite game birds of the east

(adult male)

MALLARD
Anas platyrhynchos platyrhynchos
Length 21–27 inches

The "green head" and his brownish mate are the most numerous of all Colorado waterfowl. They nest in numbers in San Luis Valley, North Park and along the reservoirs of the eastern prairies, and thousands of northern breeding birds spend the winter on the larger waterways. The female mallard, with her two white wing bars, could be confused with the slightly darker, and very rare Mexican Duck

(adult female and male)

(Plate 13 by T. M. Shortt)

MEXICAN DUCK

MOTTLED DUCK

BLACK DUCK

MALLARD *(female and male)*

Plate 13

PINTAIL

Anas acuta

Length 25–30 inches

A wide-ranging species which breeds in both the Old and New Worlds and winters in southern Europe, Asia and into Africa, and locally from Alaska throughout much of the United States south into South America. One of the popular game birds of Colorado which nests rather commonly on eastern prairies, in San Luis Valley and North Park

(female above, male below)

GADWALL

Anas strepera

Length 19–21 inches

Like the Mallards and Pintails, these ducks occur irregularly throughout the Northern Hemisphere in the Old and New Worlds. Although common birds in the state, comparatively few nests have been found — the majority breeding on the western slope, in San Luis Valley and in North Park

(female above at left, male at right)

(Plate 14 by T. M. Shortt)

PINTAIL *(female above)*

GADWALL *(female above and left)*

Plate 14

GREEN-WINGED TEAL
Anas carolinensis
Length 12.5–15 inches

Common migrant, a few remain in summer and nest from the plains into mountain parks, especially in San Luis Valley and North Park, and occasionally to 10,000 feet. The fall migration into Colorado is usually about mid-October when bands of swift-flying birds appear over the lakes and reservoirs throughout the state. They are favorite game birds but due to selective shooting — the taking of larger species — these teal still are numerous

(top left full eclipse male, top right partial eclipse male, adult female and male)

BLUE-WINGED TEAL
Anas discors discors
Length 14.5–16 inches

The beautiful Blue-wings are common nesting ducks on the ponds and reservoirs of the eastern plains. Many breed in San Luis Valley and North Park, but the females are so similar to Cinnamon Teal that they and their young cannot be identified in field observations. Both species migrate early in the fall, usually before the hunting season, and consequently their numbers have not been reduced as have some of the later migrants

(eclipse male above, adult female and male)

CINNAMON TEAL
Anas cyanoptera septentrionalium
Length 15–17 inches

The colorful males are conspicuous upon the smaller ponds and reservoirs of the state in early spring as they carry on their courtship antics before the little brown females. It is impossible to distinguish between broods of this teal and the Blue-winged for the females of the two species look alike, and the males do not attend their mates after the eggs are hatched

(top sub-adult male, full eclipse male, adult female and male)

(Plate 15 by Peter Scott)

GREEN-WINGED TEAL

CINNAMON TEAL

BLUE-WINGED TEAL

WOOD DUCK
Aix sponsa
Length 17–20 inches

Wood Ducks, considered by many to be the most beautiful of North American waterfowl, are uncommon birds in Colorado. A few occur each winter near Denver, and elsewhere on the eastern prairies, and a female with her brood was observed in Dolores Co. June 2, 1952, as the young left the nesting cavity in a dead aspen

(female, male, and eclipse male)

SHOVELER
Spatula clypeata
Length 17–20 inches

A common summer resident with many nesting in North Park. Paired birds may be seen on all marshy areas of the eastern counties but few nests have been found. Many remain in winter, as long as open water prevails, and they are especially conspicuous in City Park, Denver, where they become so tame they take food provided by interested visitors. The broad bill with its fringed edges is ideally adapted for surface feeding

(eclipse male above, adult female and male)

AMERICAN WIDGEON
Mareca americana
Length 18–22 inches

Numerous in migration, with many remaining in San Luis Valley and North Park to breed. Banding returns indicate young raised in the latter area winter chiefly from New Mexico into Mexico. One hundred or more usually remain in City Park, Denver, through mild winters where pairs working together indicate they remain mated after the breeding season, or acquire new mates long before spring migration

(adult male and female)

(Plate 16 by Peter Scott)

WOOD DUCK *(female, male and eclipse male)*

SHOVELER *(eclipse male above, adult female and male)*

AMERICAN WIDGEON *(adult male and female)*

Plate 16

CANVASBACK
Aythya valisineria
Length 20–24 inches

An uncommon migrant and summer resident on both sides of the Continental Divide. Formerly abundant throughout its range, its numbers have dwindled alarmingly in recent years

(female and male)

REDHEAD
Aythya americana
Length 17–22 inches

Fairly common migrant throughout the state, breeding regularly in suitable marshy cover of the eastern prairies and of the mountain parks

(female and male)

RUDDY DUCK
Oxyura jamaicensis rubida
Length 14–16 inches

A common migrant, and fairly numerous resident throughout the state, nesting regularly in tules and cattails. Males often accompany the females and young

Note: Ruddy Duck caption on opposite page should read
(adult winter male, adult male and female)

(Plate 17 by H. Albert Hochbaum)

CANVASBACK *(female and male)*
REDHEAD *(female and male)*
RUDDY DUCK *(female, male and immature)*

Plate 17

DOWNY YOUNG WATERFOWL

MALLARD

GADWALL

GREEN-WINGED TEAL

BLUE-WINGED TEAL

CINNAMON TEAL

AMERICAN WIDGEON

SHOVELER

WOOD DUCK

CANADA GOOSE

PINTAIL

(Plate 18 by H. Albert Hochbaum)

H. Albert Hochbaum

MALLARD
BLUE-WINGED TEAL
SHOVELER

CANADA GOOSE

CINNAMON TEAL

WOOD DUCK

GADWALL
GREEN-WINGED TEAL
AMERICAN WIDGEON

PINTAIL

Plate 18

DOWNY YOUNG WATERFOWL

CANVASBACK

REDHEAD

LESSER SCAUP   RING-NECKED DUCK

BUFFLEHEAD

RUDDY DUCK

AMERICAN GOLDENEYE

HARLEQUIN DUCK

COMMON MERGANSER

(Plate 19 by H. Albert Hochbaum)

REDHEAD
LESSER SCAUP
BUFFLEHEAD
HARLEQUIN DUCK

CANVASBACK
RING-NECKED DUCK
RUDDY DUCK
AMERICAN GOLDENEYE
COMMON MERGANSER

Plate 19

H.Albert Hochbaum

GREATER SCAUP
Aythya marila nearctica

Length 16–21 inches

The species is distributed throughout much of the Northern Hemisphere and this race nests in northern Alaska and Canada south to Canadian border states. Rare migrant in Colorado

(female and male)

LESSER SCAUP
Aythya affinis

Length 15–18 inches

A common spring and fall migrant upon the waterways of the state, with a few remaining in summer and in mild winters

(female and male)

RING-NECKED DUCK
Aythya collaris

Length 15–18 inches

A regular but rather uncommon migrant throughout the state, with a small nesting population in the southwest and in North Park

(female and male)

(Plate 20 by Angus H. Shortt)

GREATER SCAUP

LESSER SCAUP

RING-NECKED DUCK

Plate 20

OLDSQUAW
Clangula hyemalis
Length: male 20–23 inches, female 16–18 inches

These far northern breeding birds appear irregularly upon the larger lakes and reservoirs of the state. They have musical "a-nuk, a-nuk" notes characteristic of the species

(female and male)

BARROW'S GOLDENEYE
Bucephala islandica
Length 16.5–21 inches

The males have white crescent-shaped cheek patches while the Common Goldeneye has rounded spots. The females of the two species cannot be identified in the field, except by the company they keep. A rare but regular migrant in eastern counties, which formerly nested along mountain streams

BUFFLEHEAD
Bucephala albeola
Length 13–15 inches

A rather common late fall migrant and winter resident upon the waterways of the state. The beautiful little ducks, either in flight or resting upon the water, look like miniatures of the goldeneyes

(male and female)

COMMON GOLDENEYE
Bucephala clangula americana
Length 16–21 inches

Common in late fall, winter, and early spring upon the large reservoirs of eastern Colorado, and along the mountain streams of the west. Sometimes known as the "Whistler" because of the musical sound made by fast-moving wings

(Plate 21 by Dexter F. Landau)

OLDSQUAW *(female and male)*
BUFFLEHEAD *(male and female)*
BARROW'S GOLDENEYE *(male and female)*
COMMON GOLDENEYE *(male)*

Plate 21

COMMON EIDER
Somateria mollissima dresseri
Length 23–26 inches
A rare straggler to eastern Colorado which has been recorded two times

(male with female below)

HARLEQUIN DUCK
Histrionicus histrionicus
Length 15.5–20 inches
A very rare wanderer into the state. Carter collected several specimens, two of which are in the Museum collection

(male with female below)

SURF SCOTER
Melanitta perspicillata
Length 18–21 inches
An uncommon winter visitor on the large reservoirs of eastern Colorado. There are nine specimens in the Museum collection

(male and female)

COMMON SCOTER
Oidemia nigra americana
Length 17–21 inches
There are only four reports of this northern sea duck from the state, the most recent a specimen from near Ft. Collins November 24, 1960

(male with female above)

WHITE-WINGED SCOTER
Melanitta deglandi deglandi
Length 19–23 inches
An uncommon winter visitor which has been recorded in the state on numerous occasions. There are nine specimens in the Museum collection. The color illustrations should have been slightly larger, in comparison with the other scoters

(female and male)

(Plate 22 by Dexter F. Landau)

COMMON EIDER *(female below male)*   HARLEQUIN DUCK *(female below)*

SURF SCOTER *(male and female)*   COMMON SCOTER *(female above)*

WHITE-WINGED SCOTER *(female and male)*

COMMON MERGANSER
Mergus merganser americanus

Length 21–27 inches

This, the largest and most common of the mergansers, is a regular winter visitor on the reservoirs and rivers of the state. A few nest regularly in La Plata Co., and probably in North Park

(female and male)

RED-BREASTED MERGANSER
Mergus serrator serrator

Length 20–25 inches

A hardy species widely distributed in both the Old and New Worlds. It is an uncommon winter visitor in eastern Colorado. The females are very similar to those of the Common Merganser

(male and female)

HOODED MERGANSER
Lophodytes cucullatus

Length 16–19 inches

An uncommon but regular visitor to the waterways of the state. The conspicuous white head patch of the male is an excellent field mark

(female and male)

(Plate 23 by Angus H. Shortt)

Plate 23

COMMON MERGANSER *(female and male)*
RED-BREASTED MERGANSER *(male and female)*
HOODED MERGANSER *(female and male)*

TURKEY VULTURE
Cathartes aura teter

Length 26–32 inches

Fairly common birds in the southern half of the state, and recorded regularly in the north. Conspicuous as they ride the air currents on widespread wings

CARACARA
Caracara cheriway audubonii

Length 20–25 inches

A southern vulture-like bird which has been recorded once in the state, near Glenwood Springs

BLACK VULTURE
Coragyps atratus

Length 23–27 inches

Two were seen in flight by a competent observer near Pueblo May 27, 1953. They were far from their normal range

(Plate 24 by Earl L. Poole)

TURKEY VULTURE

CARACARA

BLACK VULTURE

Plate 24

E.L.Poole

SWALLOW-TAILED KITE
Elanoides forficatus forficatus
Length 19–25 inches
Recorded on several occasions and three reported collected

MISSISSIPPI KITE
Ictinia misisippiensis
Length 14–16 inches
A rare straggler

(Plate 25 by Earl L. Poole)

E.L.Poole

GOSHAWK
Accipiter gentilis atricapillus
Length 20–28 inches
A resident in the mountains, ranging down to the plains in winter

SHARP-SHINNED HAWK
Accipiter striatus velox
Length 10–14 inches
Uncommon resident in lower mountains, and regular in winter upon the plains

(Note square tail)

COOPER'S HAWK
Accipiter cooperii
Length 14–20 inches
Resident from lower mountains into higher, and on plains in winter

(Note rounded tail, immature in flight)

(Plate 26 by Earl L. Poole)

GOSHAWK *(spring plumage)*

SHARP-SHINNED HAWK
(adult and flying immature below)

COOPER'S HAWK *(adult and flying immature above)*

Plate 26

E.L.Poole

RED-TAILED HAWK

Buteo jamaicensis kriderii

Length 19–22 inches

A light phase of Red-tailed Hawk which occurs rarely in Colorado, formerly known as Krider's Hawk

HARLAN'S HAWK

Buteo harlani

Length 19–25 inches

A dark hawk, variable in color, closely related, and possibly a race of the Red-tailed Hawk. Rare in Colorado

RED-TAILED HAWK

Buteo jamaicensis calurus

Length 20–25 inches

A common migrant, and resident from the plains into the mountains. Six races are recognized in the A.O.U. Check-list, and two are listed from Colorado

(immature and medium-dark phase adult)

(Plate 27 by Earl L. Poole)

RED-TAILED HAWK   HARLAN'S HAWK

Plate 27

Buteo jamaicensis kriderii

RED-TAILED HAWK
(immature at left, adult at right)

SWAINSON'S HAWK
Buteo swainsoni
Length 19–22 inches
A common resident and migrant on the plains into the foothills. There are dark and intermediate color phases. Migrates into southern South America

(typical adult and immature)

RED-SHOULDERED HAWK
Buteo lineatus lineatus
Length 18–22 inches
This common bird of the east is a very rare straggler into Colorado

(adult and immature)

BROAD-WINGED HAWK
Buteo platypterus platypterus
Length 13–18 inches
An uncommon, but probably a regular visitor east of the foothills

(adult and immature)

(Plate 28 by Earl L. Poole)

SWAINSON'S HAWK *(adult and immature)*

RED-SHOULDERED HAWK
(adult and immature)

BROAD-WINGED HAWK
(adult and immature)

Plate 28

FERRUGINOUS HAWK
Buteo regalis
Length 22–25 inches

Formerly common, but less so of recent years, from the plains into the low mountains of Colorado. They nest in trees and on steep cliffs

(typical adult and dark phase)

ROUGH-LEGGED HAWK
Buteo lagopus s. johannis
Length 20–24 inches

A winter resident throughout the state from low elevations into the mountains. Formerly numerous, they have become less common with the destruction of prairie dogs

(typical adult and dark phase)

E.L.Poole.

FERRUGINOUS HAWK *(typical adult plumage and dark phase)*

ROUGH-LEGGED HAWK *(typical adult and dark phase)*

Plate 29

GOLDEN EAGLE
Aquila chrysaetos canadensis

Length 30–42 inches

Formerly common nesting birds on steep escarpments of the plains and mountains, and in ponderosa pines, but less numerous due to constant persecution. Immatures have basal two-thirds of tail white. Protected by Federal law

(adult and immature)

BALD EAGLE
Haliaeetus leucocephalus alascanus

Length 34–44 inches

A regular winter visitor and uncommon in summer. In early fall there is a migration of Bald Eagles from the north and some remain around reservoirs and rivers to feed upon fish and carrion. Formerly more numerous and now protected by Federal law

(immature and adult)

(Plate 30 by Earl L. Poole)

GOLDEN EAGLE *(adult and immature)*

BALD EAGLE *(immature and adult)*

Plate 30

OSPREY
Pandion haliaetus carolinensis

Length 21–24 inches

An uncommon straggler and summer resident from the plains in Colorado into the lower mountains. They feed primarily upon fish and often are called Fish Hawks

(typical adult plumage)

MARSH HAWK
Circus cyaneus hudsonius

Length 17–22 inches

A common species, nesting on the ground in moist or marshy swales, and ranging upward over the high mountains in late summer

(adult female and male)

(Plate 31 by Earl L. Poole)

OSPREY

MARSH HAWK *(female and male)*

Plate 31

PRAIRIE FALCON
Falco mexicanus
Length 18–20 inches
A fairly common resident, nesting on ledges of prairie escarpments of eastern Colorado and less numerous west of the Continental Divide

(adult plumage)

PEREGRINE FALCON
Falco peregrinus anatum
Length 15–22 inches
A regular migrant and an uncommon summer resident in Colorado, nesting rather rarely on precipitous ledges. The species is nearly cosmopolitan and is one of the favored birds used in falconry

(adult plumage)

(Plate 32 by Earl L. Poole)

PRAIRIE FALCON

PEREGRINE FALCON

Plate 32

PIGEON HAWK
Falco columbarius
Length 10–13 inches

The species ranges the northern parts of both the New and Old Worlds. Six races are recognized in North America and three have been recorded in Colorado. Both *F.c. richardsonii* and *F.c. bendirei* occur regularly in migration, and there is one record specimen of *F.c. suckleyi*

SPARROW HAWK
Falco sparverius sparverius
Length 9–12 inches

The species ranges from northern Alaska to southern South America. This race nests locally from Alaska and northern Canada south throughout much of the United States. The nests are placed in cavities in trees, in arroyo banks, in cliffs, or in crannies of buildings

(adult male and female)

(Plate 33 by Earl L. Poole)

PIGEON HAWK
(*Falco c. bendirei; Falco c. richardsonii; Falco c. suckleyi*)

SPARROW HAWK
(*adult male and female*)

Plate 33

E.L.Poole

BLUE GROUSE
Dendragapus obscurus obscurus
Length 16–23 inches

The species ranges in timbered mountainous regions from southeastern Alaska, southern Yukon, and southwestern Mackenzie and Alberta south to Arizona and California. Eight local races are recognized, and the Colorado form *D.o. obscurus* is resident in the forests from 7,000 to 10,000 feet. The males have far-reaching ventriloquistic booming notes

(adult female and male)

(Plate 34 by Owen J. Gromme)

Plate 34

BLUE GROUSE
(adult female and male)

SPRUCE GROUSE
Canachites canadensis franklinii

Length 14–17 inches

This is a wide ranging species of the evergreen forests from central Alaska south to Oregon, Idaho, Montana, Wyoming, Minnesota east to New England states. The race is listed from Colorado on the basis of a specimen shot at Palmer Lake in September 1896 and reported by W. H. Bergtold (Auk, 31: 246)

(adult male and female)

RUFFED GROUSE
Bonasa umbellus incana

Length 15–19 inches

A widely distributed species in the forested areas from central Alaska across Canada to northern United States and south in eastern mountains to northern Georgia. This race probably was never numerous in Colorado, but there are several authentic records

(adult female and male)

SPRUCE GROUSE *(adult male and female)*

RUFFED GROUSE *(adult female and male)*

WHITE-TAILED PTARMIGAN
Lagopus leucurus altipetens

Length 12–13 inches

Ptarmigan are true grouse which occupy the northern part of the Northern Hemisphere, or high mountains to the southward where alpine conditions exist. Four species are recognized and three occur in North America. The White-tailed have the southernmost extension of their range above timberline in Colorado and northern New Mexico; they are protectively colored, their plumage changing from the inconspicuous browns and whites of summer to mottled white and brown in the fall—and pure white in winter. The nests are upon the ground and the females are tame, depending upon their concealing markings for protection

(Plate 36 by Dexter F. Landau)

WHITE-TAILED PTARMIGAN
(top: male and female in spring; center:
male in fall; below: adults in winter white)

Plate 36

LESSER PRAIRIE CHICKEN
Tympanuchus pallidicinctus
Length 16–18 inches

Once fairly numerous on the grasslands of south-eastern Colorado and neighboring states, this small grouse has become rare over much of its former range. A few areas still remain in Baca County where the males gather each spring to perform for prospective mates

SHARP-TAILED GROUSE
Pedioecetes phasianellus jamesi
Length 15–19 inches

GREATER PRAIRIE CHICKEN
Tympanuchus cupido pinnatus
Length 17–19 inches

Both the Greater Prairie Chicken and the Sharp-tailed Grouse were abundant when white men arrived on the scene, but much of the natural grassland habitat has been destroyed and both species have diminished in numbers

Six races of Sharp-tailed Grouse are recognized and the form *P.p. jamesi* is resident from Alberta south to Colorado on the plains, and *P.p. columbianus* is fairly numerous in shrubby habitat, west of the Continental Divide

Three races of this prairie chicken are recognized —the eastern form long-known as the Heath Hen is extinct, and the southern *T.c. attwateri* of Texas and Louisiana has become rare. The subspecies *pinnatus* still ranges widely in small numbers from southern central Canada south in the Mississippi Valley, west to eastern Colorado

(Plate 37 by Owen J. Gromme)

LESSER PRAIRIE CHICKEN

SHARP-TAILED GROUSE   GREATER PRAIRIE CHICKEN
(strutting male with purple neck sac)   *(strutting male with orange neck sac)*

Plate 37

SAGE GROUSE
Centrocercus urophasianus urophasianus
Length 22–30 inches

Sage Grouse, the "Cocks of the Plains," were once resident in sage-grown habitats from southern British Columbia south to eastern California, and east through southern Canada and northern states to North Dakota and Nebraska, and south to the Oklahoma Panhandle. Now their numbers have greatly diminished because of shooting and destruction of habitat. Many still occur in western Colorado, where the males assemble each spring upon strutting grounds, and perform for the benefit of prospective mates

Plate 38

SAGE GROUSE
(males above in strutting postures, and females below)

SCALED QUAIL
Callipepla squamata pallida
Length 10–12 inches

The species ranges the dry open areas from south-western Kansas, Colorado, New Mexico and western Oklahoma south into Mexico. This race of "Cotton Top" is fairly numerous on the open slopes and in the dry canyons of southeastern Colorado

GAMBEL'S QUAIL
Lophortyx gambelii sanus
Length 10–12 inches

This beautiful species is resident over much of the semi-desert areas of the southwest into Baja California, and the race occurs locally in west-central Colorado. The species differs from the California Quail in having a conspicuous black patch on the light belly while the latter has feathers of the belly lined with dark

BOBWHITE
Colinus virginianus taylori
Length 9–11 inches

The species occurs in Wyoming east to southern Ontario and Maine south through eastern Colorado and western Texas to Florida, and from Arizona into Mexico. This western race was once common in eastern Colorado, but now ranges locally in small flocks. Bobwhites are favorite game birds of sportsmen

(Plate 39 by Owen J. Gromme)

SCALED QUAIL *(male right)*

GAMBEL'S QUAIL *(male right)*

BOBWHITE *(male left)*

Plate 39

CALIFORNIA QUAIL
Lophortyx californicus californicus
Length 10–12 inches

A common bird of western states. The species, introduced into Colorado, occurs locally in Larimer and Weld Counties

RED-LEGGED PARTRIDGE
Alectoris rufa hispanica
Length 12–14 inches

A few were introduced in 1955 and some young were hatched. Whether the "plant" was successful remains in doubt. Plate does not show the conspicuous red eye ring so characteristic of the species

CHUKAR
Alectoris graeca
Length 12–14 inches

This hardy species of the Old World has been successfully introduced into Colorado and other western states. Numerous broods of young have been raised in Delta, Montrose, and other counties and hunting was allowed in 1962

GRAY PARTRIDGE
Perdix perdix perdix
Length 12–14 inches

The Gray or Hungarian Partridge has been introduced widely in Canada and the United States. Numerous birds have been "planted" in Colorado, but all attempts met with poor success

RING-NECKED PHEASANT
Phasianus colchicus
Length 22–36 inches

This native of Asia has been successfully introduced into many sections of the United States, and it occurs locally in Colorado on the plains and in the valleys throughout the state

(Plate 40 by Dexter F. Landau)

Plate 40

CALIFORNIA QUAIL *(female above)*   RED-LEGGED PARTRIDGE

CHUKAR

GRAY PARTRIDGE   RING-NECKED PHEASANT

WILD TURKEY
Meleagris gallopavo merriami
Length 36–50 inches

The Wild Turkey was a wide-ranging bird over much of the eastern and southern half of the United States into the wooded mountains of Mexico. The species was introduced into Europe from Mexico by the Spaniards, and was reintroduced into the United States as a domesticated bird. This, the largest of the four races, occurs locally in ponderosa pine and shrub oak country of southwestern Colorado south to Arizona and Texas. It was domesticated by the Cliff Dwellers of Mesa Verde, apparently more for ceremonial feathers than for food. Many individuals have rumps more conspicuously white than shown on the color plate

(Plate 41 by Owen J. Gromme)

Plate 41

WILD TURKEY

WHOOPING CRANE
Grus americana
Length 50–56 inches

Once breeding in great numbers from the marshes of Louisiana northward into Canadian Provinces, these white cranes, the most conspicuous of all North American birds, are nearing extinction. Of the great numbers that once migrated up the Mississippi Valley, only about thirty-five wild birds and a few in captivity remained in 1963. They breed beyond the agricultural belt in Canada and winter on the Aransas National Wildlife Refuge in Texas

SANDHILL CRANE
Grus canadensis canadensis
Grus canadensis tabida
Length 40–48 inches

The large, gray, Sandhill Crane *(Grus. c. tabida)*, has a local breeding range from western southern Canada south in northern United States and east to Michigan and Ohio. It has become very rare in many areas, but nests locally in small numbers in isolated or protected marshy habitats. Formerly a regular breeder in western Colorado, there are few records of recent nesting. Two adults shown in flight

The smaller race, *G.c. canadensis*, often called the Little Brown Crane, with a Far North breeding range from Siberia, northern Alaska, and across Canada to Southhampton Island, has held its own because of the remoteness of nesting areas — and thousands migrate regularly throughout Colorado in both spring and fall

(Plate 42 by Roger Tory Peterson)

WHOOPING CRANE

SANDHILL CRANE
(*Grus c. tabida*)

SANDHILL CRANE
(*Grus c. canadensis*)

Plate 42

YELLOW RAIL
Coturnicops noveboracensis noveboracensis
Length 6–8 inches

Breeds locally in central eastern Colorado, across southern Canada from Manitoba and Mackenzie to New Brunswick, and in northern states from Minnesota to Maine. Winters locally along the Gulf coast, and from Oregon through California. A small, inconspicuous, secretive bird which has been recorded rarely from Nebraska and Kansas, and there is but one specimen from Colorado

BLACK RAIL
Laterallus jamaicensis jamaicensis
Length 5–6 inches

The smallest of North American rails, which, as a species, breeds locally from California south to Baja California, and from the Mississippi Valley eastward to New England states, and southward to the Gulf coast. The species is uncommon in Nebraska and Kansas, but was recorded nesting in the latter state in June 1963. It is only a straggler in Colorado. Males and females of all rails are colored much alike

SORA
Porzana carolina
Length 8–10 inches

A locally common summer resident in Colorado, this medium-sized rail breeds in suitable cover of the prairie marshes, and uncommonly into the mountains. They are short-billed birds, easily distinguished from the Virginia Rails which have long, slender beaks. Rails are elusive and difficult to flush, and they usually attempt to escape by running rather than flying

VIRGINIA RAIL
Rallus limicola limicola
Length 8–11 inches

Like the Sora, these elusive rails occur commonly in the tule and cattail-grown marshes throughout the state, where their harsh voices often betray their presence, even though the birds remain hidden. All rails, when disturbed, rise awkwardly from cover and have a labored flight — and they usually drop quickly into cover

(Plate 43 by Donald L. Malick)

YELLOW RAIL

SORA

BLACK RAIL

VIRGINIA RAIL

PURPLE GALLINULE
Porphyrula martinica
Length 12–14 inches

This common bird, the most beautiful of the rail family in this country, dwells in southern marshes, and is a mere straggler into Colorado. One specimen, now in the Museum, was taken near Florence, Fremont County, June 17, 1911

(males and females differ little in color)

COMMON GALLINULE
Gallinula chloropus cachinnans
Length 12–14 inches

The species is wide ranging over much of the Old and New Worlds, and this race breeds locally in the majority of southern states. Has wandered casually into Colorado, where it has been observed on three occasions

(plumage of males and females much alike in color)

AMERICAN COOT
Fulica americana americana
Length 13–16 inches

Coots are very abundant water birds, their range, like that of Gallinules as a species, extending throughout much of the world.

American Coots, often called Mud Hens, nest from southern Canada south throughout much of the United States. They build their bulky nests in dense growths of cattails and tules, and both adults incubate and care for the young. Very common in Colorado

(sexes much alike in color)

(Plate 44 by Donald L. Malick)

PURPLE GALLINULE

COMMON GALLINULE

AMERICAN COOT

Plate 44

SNOWY PLOVER
Charadrius alexandrinus nivosus
Length 6–7.5 inches

This species is wide-ranging throughout much of the world. The Snowy Plover differs from the Piping Plover in having the neck band reduced to side patches and having black legs

(adult and immature)

PIPING PLOVER
Charadrius melodus circumcinctus
Length 6–7.5 inches

Differs from the above in being slightly darker, has yellow legs, and yellow beak with black tip. Black collar extends over back. Rare in Colorado

(adult and immature)

SEMIPALMATED PLOVER
Charadrius semipalmatus
Length 6.5–7.5 inches

A regular spring and fall migrant through Colorado in small numbers. Nests from British Columbia and Labrador north. Dark breast band sometimes broken in front. White spot on forehead between dark feathers; legs orange yellow

(immature above)

(Plate 45 by Walter J. Breckenridge)

SNOWY PLOVER *(adult and immature)*

PIPING PLOVER *(adult and immature)*

SEMIPALMATED PLOVER *(immature above)*

KILLDEER
Charadrius vociferus vociferus

Length 9.5–11 inches

Breeds from Alaska across Canada and south throughout much of the United States. A common bird in Colorado, often wintering in numbers

(adult, eggs and downy young)

AMERICAN GOLDEN PLOVER
Pluvialis dominica dominica

Length 10–11 inches

Nests in Arctic Alaska and Canada, and migrates to South America. An uncommon spring and fall migrant

(immature and adult male)

BLACK-BELLIED PLOVER
Squatarola squatarola

Length 11–13.5 inches

Breeds on the Arctic tundras of Russia, Siberia, Alaska, and Canada, and migrates regularly through Colorado

(sexes much alike)

(Plate 46 by Walter J. Breckenridge)

BRECKENRIDGE

KILLDEER *(adult, eggs and downy young)*

AMERICAN GOLDEN PLOVER *(immature and adult male)*

BLACK-BELLIED PLOVER *(adult and flying immature)*

Plate 46

RUDDY TURNSTONE
Arenaria interpres morinella
Length 8.5–10 inches
The species breeds in high latitudes of both the New and Old Worlds. A rare migrant through Colorado

(adult male and immature)

SANDERLING
Crocethia alba
Length 7–8.5 inches
A regular spring and fall migrant along the reservoirs of eastern Colorado. Breeds in Arctic areas of both the Old and New Worlds

(adult male and immature)

KNOT
Calidris canutus rufa
Length 10–11 inches
Migrates along both coasts of the United States and breeds in Arctic Alaska, Canada, and Siberia. Rare straggler in Colorado

(adult male and immature)

(Plate 47 by Walter J. Breckenridge)

RUDDY TURNSTONE *(adult male and immature)*

SANDERLING *(adult male and immature)*

KNOT *(adult male and immature)*

Plate 47

SPOTTED SANDPIPER
Actitis macularia
Length 7–8 inches
A common summer resident from the plains to over 10,000 feet in the mountains

(adult and immature)

COMMON SNIPE
Capella gallinago delicata
Length 10–11 inches
The species breeds in both the New and Old Worlds. This race is a common migrant and winter resident in Colorado and nests regularly in moist locations

(sexes alike)

AMERICAN WOODCOCK
Philohela minor
Length 10–12 inches
An inhabitant of moist woodlands of central and eastern states. This inconspicuous bird is a casual migrant in Colorado

(sexes alike)

(Plate 48 by Walter J. Breckenridge)

COMMON SNIPE

SPOTTED SANDPIPER (*adult and immature*)

AMERICAN WOODCOCK

ESKIMO CURLEW
Numenius borealis

Length 12–14.5 inches

Only a few of the species exist today, but two were observed in Texas in 1962. Specimens were collected near Denver in 1882

LONG-BILLED CURLEW
Numenius americanus americanus

Length 20–26 inches

A regular migrant along the reservoirs of the eastern part of the state, and a summer resident and regular breeder in southeastern counties

WHIMBREL
Numenius phaeopus hudsonicus

Length 16–18 inches

The species is represented throughout much of the world and this race, a common bird through the interior states in migration, has been recorded rarely in Colorado

(Plate 49 by John A. Crosby)

ESKIMO CURLEW

Plate 49

LONG-BILLED CURLEW (*also flying*)

WHIMBREL

MOUNTAIN PLOVER
Eupoda montana
Length 8–9 inches

This is a bird of the high prairies which has become comparatively rare of recent years due to the destruction of its natural short grass and cactus habitat

WILLET
Catoptrophorus semipalmatus inornatus
Length 14–16.5 inches

A wide-ranging species, breeding from the Gulf coast northward along both coasts to Nova Scotia, southern Canadian Provinces, and Oregon. Uncommon migrant and summer resident in Colorado

UPLAND PLOVER
Bartramia longicauda
Length 11–13 inches

A rather uncommon migrant and summer resident of the grasslands of the eastern part of the state

BUFF-BREASTED SANDPIPER
Tryngites subruficollis
Length 7–9 inches

Breeds locally from northern Alaska across Arctic Canada and migrates through the Mississippi Valley. Rarely recorded in Colorado

(Plate 50 by Walter J. Breckenridge)

DENVER MUSEUM OF NATURAL HISTORY

MOUNTAIN PLOVER

WILLET

UPLAND PLOVER

BUFF-BREASTED SANDPIPER

Plate 50

STILT SANDPIPER
Micropalama himantopus

Length 7–9 inches

A rather common but irregular migrant through-out much of the state. Often flocks of adults with distinct brood patches appear early in the sum-mer — possibly birds which had poor nesting success on their northern breeding grounds

(immature and adult)

SOLITARY SANDPIPER
Tringa solitaria cinnamomea

Length 7–9 inches

A well-named, inconspicuous shore bird, usually seen alone or in pairs. Regular but uncommon migrant, and non-breeding summer resident

LESSER YELLOWLEGS
Totanus flavipes

Length 10–11 inches

A common migrant and occasionally non-breed-ing summer resident along the reservoirs of the Upper Sonoran Zone

GREATER YELLOWLEGS
Totanus melanoleucus

Length 12–15 inches

An irregular and rather uncommon migrant, oc-curring casually in summer on both sides of the Continental Divide

(Plate 51 by Walter J. Breckenridge)

STILT SANDPIPER *(immature and adult)*　　SOLITARY SANDPIPER

LESSER YELLOWLEGS　　GREATER YELLOWLEGS

WHITE-RUMPED SANDPIPER
Erolia fuscicollis
Length 7–8 inches

Regular in spring and summer, occasionally in flocks. White-rumps conspicuous when birds are in flight

DUNLIN
Erolia alpina pacifica
Length 7–8 inches

Conspicuous and easily identified in high plumage. The immatures and birds in winter dress may be recognized by the slightly curved beak, and their habit of feeding with beak thrust sharply downward. Uncommon in Colorado

(adult and immature in winter)

PECTORAL SANDPIPER
Erolia melanotos
Length 8–9.5 inches

Slightly larger than Baird's and White-rumped Sandpipers, and has streaked breast sharply defined from white underparts; greenish legs. Regular, but uncommon in the state

BAIRD'S SANDPIPER
Erolia bairdii
Length 7–8 inches

Back feathers edged with white giving a scaly appearance; legs black. Very common migrant and occasional non-nesting summer resident along reservoirs

(Plate 52 by John A. Crosby)

Crosby

DUNLIN
(adult and immature in winter)

WHITE-RUMPED SANDPIPER
(also in flight)

Plate 52

PECTORAL SANDPIPER

BAIRD'S SANDPIPER

LEAST SANDPIPER
Erolia minutilla

Length 5–7 inches

All three of the small "peeps" on this page are common in migration and occasionally as non-breeding summer residents. They are difficult to separate in the field but the Least has yellowish to greenish legs and a very slender bill. The Semipalmated is grayer and has black legs, and a shorter, heavier bill, while the Western Sandpiper has a longer, thicker bill, slightly decurved, and the spring plumage is bright rusty above. Legs black. All three in immature dress are grayish and difficult to identify.

(spring and winter)

WESTERN SANDPIPER
Ereunetes mauri

Length 6–7 inches

Slightly longer, heavier beak at base, plumage rustier, legs black

(spring, winter above)

SEMIPALMATED SANDPIPER
Ereunetes pusillus

Length 6–7 inches

Short rather stubby beaks; legs black and plumage grayer. Toes semiwebbed

(spring and winter)

(Plate 53 by Walter J. Breckenridge)

LEAST SANDPIPER *(spring and winter adults)*

SEMIPALMATED SANDPIPER
(spring and winter adults)

WESTERN SANDPIPER
(winter adult above, spring adult below)

Plate 53

MARBLED GODWIT
Limosa fedoa
Length 16–20 inches

A large, long-legged shore bird with a slightly upturned beak and brown plumage, which nests in Alberta, Saskatchewan, and Manitoba south into Montana, North and South Dakota, and Minnesota. Occurs regularly in eastern Colorado, and rather uncommonly in bordering states in spring and fall along reservoir shores

(spring plumage)

LONG-BILLED DOWITCHER
Limnodromus scolopaceus
Length 11–12 inches

Breeds in the north from Siberia and Alaska across Canada, and migrates regularly through Colorado and neighboring states in both spring and fall. Dowitcher females usually have longer beaks than males. Occasionally numerous on the eastern prairie ponds in summer, possibly birds that had failed in their nesting

(winter and breeding plumage)

HUDSONIAN GODWIT
Limosa haemastica
Length 14–17 inches

Averages slightly smaller than the Marbled Godwit and has a more northerly breeding range extending locally from the mouth of the Mackenzie River to Manitoba. The white base of the black tail is very conspicuous when bird is in flight. Migrates through Great Plains but is a straggler only in Colorado. Uncommon migrant in Nebraska and Kansas

(winter and breeding plumage)

(Plate 54 by Walter J. Breckenridge)

Plate 54

LONG-BILLED DOWITCHER
(winter and breeding plumage)

MARBLED GODWIT
(spring plumage)

HUDSONIAN GODWIT
(winter and breeding plumage)

BLACK-NECKED STILT
Himantopus mexicanus

Length 13–16 inches

Two species of stilts are recognized, the American bird with a range from Oregon and southern Saskatchewan, south locally into South America, and a widespread species of several races which occurs from Asia south into Africa, from Borneo to Australia and New Zealand, and a subspecies recognized from the Hawaiian Island. All have the characteristic long legs which have given them the common name *Stilt*. This species is a comparatively rare summer resident in Colorado, and no nests have been found in recent years

(males: females similar except backs grayish brown)

AMERICAN AVOCET
Recurvirostra americana

Length 15–18.5 inches

Avocets are found throughout much of the world. Four species have been described and the American bird, with a range from southern Saskatchewan, Manitoba, and Alberta south locally through western states, is one of the most conspicuous shore birds. They are communal nesters in that many pairs will build on small islands or along the shores of reservoirs, where their protectively colored eggs are placed in scantily lined depressions. Avocets are among the most beautiful, conspicuous, and noisy breeding wading birds of Colorado

(sexes colored much alike)

(Plate 55 by Roger Tory Peterson)

BLACK-NECKED STILT
AMERICAN AVOCET

RED PHALAROPE
Phalaropus fulicarius

Length 7–9 inches

Nests on northern tundras of both the Old and New Worlds and winters off the coasts of South America and Africa to New Zealand. The females of all phalaropes are more colorful than the males. The species is a mere straggler in Colorado and neighboring states

(female and male)

WILSON'S PHALAROPE
Steganopus tricolor

Length 8–10 inches

A common breeding species in short grass, moist areas adjacent to lakes and reservoirs of the state. The males, as is true with all phalaropes, incubate and care for the young. Groups of adults and young often are seen in summer swimming and twirling in shallow waters of prairie ponds as they gather food from the surface

(female and male)

NORTHERN PHALAROPE
Lobipes lobatus

Length 6.5–8 inches

These phalaropes, like the Red, are more at home over the oceans than inland. They also occur in both the Old and New Worlds, nesting in northern areas and migrating south of the equator to spend the winter in the Southern Hemisphere. Common in migration through Colorado

(male and female)

(Plate 56 by Walter J. Breckenridge)

BRECKENRIDGE

WILSON'S PHALAROPE
(female and male)

RED PHALAROPE
(female and male)

NORTHERN PHALAROPE
(male and female)

POMARINE JAEGER
Stercorarius pomarinus
Length 21–24 inches

Jaegers are slim-winged, swift-flying sea birds with strong beaks. This and the Parasitic have color phases of plumage ranging from light to dark and both are circumpolar in distribution. All three species are predators upon other birds; they are rare stragglers in Colorado, and this large form is the most easily identified

LONG-TAILED JAEGER
Stercorarius longicaudus
Length 20–23 inches

A very slender, light-colored jaeger with long central tail feathers. The adults do not seem to have a dark phase, but the immatures do. One specimen recorded from the state. Sight identifications of this and the Parasitic are questionable

PARASITIC JAEGER
Stercorarius parasiticus
Length 18–21 inches

Smaller than the Pomarine Jaeger and differs from the Long-tailed in having shorter central tail feathers and being a slightly stockier bird. Three specimens of this northern nesting species have been reported from Colorado

(light phase above, dark phase below)

ANCIENT MURRELET
Synthliboramphus antiquum
Length 9–11 inches

This species, a sea bird on northern islands of the Asiatic and American coasts, is a rare straggler, the single specimen taken in Boulder County being the only representative of the Family ALCIDAE from the state

(Plate 57 by Wayne Trimm)

Plate 57

POMARINE JAEGER

LONG-TAILED JAEGER

ANCIENT MURRELET

PARASITIC JAEGER *(light phase above)*
(dark phase below)

ICELAND GULL
Larus glaucoides kumlieni
Length 23–24 inches

The species breeds in northeastern North America, Iceland, and Greenland, and winters south along the Labrador coast to New York — and casually inland to the Great Lakes. It is a rare straggler westward, with an occurrence in Nebraska in 1907, and a specimen from Colorado in 1938

(adult above, immature below)

WESTERN GULL
Larus occidentalis
Length 24–26 inches

These dark-backed gulls are common birds along the Pacific coast from Washington to Baja California. Apparently they prefer salt water to fresh for only two of the species have been recorded from far inland, one from Colorado (race undetermined) and one from Illinois *(L.o. wymani)*

(immature and adult)

IVORY GULL
Pagophila eburnea
Length 16–19 inches

Breeds on remote Arctic islands from Baffin Island, Greenland, and Franz Joseph Land, and winters casually south to New Jersey and Great Britain in the east, and south through Bering Strait into Bering Sea, and rarely to British Columbia in the west. Stragglers have been recorded inland in Manitoba, Ontario, Wisconsin, and Colorado

(immature above, adult below)

BLACK-LEGGED KITTIWAKE
Rissa tridactyla tridactyla
Length 16–18 inches

A common, gentle, cliff-nesting species of the northern parts of both the New and Old Worlds. The eastern race wanders widely in migration south in Europe to Germany and Switzerland, and in North America in migration south to New York, and has been reported from Montana, Utah, Wyoming, New Mexico, Arizona, and Kansas. Several observations and one specimen from Colorado

(immature left, adult right)

(Plate 58 by Arthur Singer)

WESTERN GULL
(immature and adult)

ICELAND GULL
(adult, immature below)

IVORY GULL
(adult, immature above)

BLACK-LEGGED KITTIWAKE *(immature and adult)*

Plate 58

HERRING GULL
Larus argentatus smithsonianus
Length 22–26 inches

A common species of both the New and Old Worlds. Usually uncommon winter resident in Colorado, but occasionally numerous. Adults pearl gray above with *pinkish* or flesh-colored legs, and primaries black with white spots. The smaller race *(L.a. thayeri)* occurs rarely in the state

(adult, second winter immature at left)

GLAUCOUS GULL
Larus hyperboreus barrovianus
Length 26–32 inches

A common light-winged species of the Far North, which is generally similar in color to the smaller Iceland Gull. Wanders south in winter to Colorado, Utah, Wyoming, Nebraska, and Kansas. Immatures light brownish with no black on wings

(adult in spring plumage)

RING-BILLED GULL
Larus delawarensis
Length 18–20 inches

Very common gulls which breed locally across southern Canada and in northern states, and occur regularly in summer. Nonbreeding birds remain in the state in summer, and often are numerous in winter. Beak with black ring, legs greenish-yellow

(adult, immature at top of plate)

CALIFORNIA GULL
Larus californicus
Length 20–24 inches

Smaller than the Herring Gull, gray wings slightly darker, black wing tips with more white at end, and legs *greenish* instead of flesh-colored. Breeds commonly in Utah, and is a regular summer visitor to Colorado, nesting on a small island of Riverside Reservoir

(Plate 59 by Wayne Trimm)

Plate 59

HERRING GULL
(adult, second year immature at left)

GLAUCOUS GULL   RING-BILLED GULL *(immature top bird)*

CALIFORNIA GULL

LAUGHING GULL
Larus atricilla
Length 15–17 inches

Four species of dark-headed gulls (in summer plumage) have been recorded from Colorado. Heads are whitish in winter. This bird, with dark wings and wing tips, is larger than the others, and is a rare straggler to the state

(adult, flying immature above at right)

BONAPARTE'S GULL
Larus philadelphia
Length 12–14 inches

Outer primaries conspicuously white with front edge and tips black; legs and feet orange red. Breeds in Alaska and Canada, and is a regular spring and fall migrant in small numbers through Colorado

(spring adult)

FRANKLIN'S GULL
Larus pipixcan
Length 13–16 inches

Nests in southern Canada and northern states, and occurs on eastern prairies of Colorado in great numbers in late summer. Adults have incomplete eyerings, slaty wings edged and tipped with white with narrow subterminal black band, and the bills and feet are dark red

(adult, first winter immature above at left)

SABINE'S GULL
Xema sabini sabini
Length 13–14 inches

Small black-headed gull and the only one with a forked tail. Outer primaries black, tipped with white, and has conspicuous white patch separating gray of wings; beak black with yellowish tip, legs black. Uncommon fall migrant in Colorado

(spring adult)

(Plate 60 by Wayne Trimm)

LAUGHING GULL *(immature above)*

Plate 60

FRANKLIN'S GULL
(adult, immature above)

BONAPARTE'S GULL

SABINE'S GULL

BLACK TERN
Chlidonias niger surinamensis
Length 9–10 inches
A common bird locally, breeding in northern states into southern Canada. Only a few Colorado nesting reports

(adult, immature at lower right)

COMMON TERN
Sterna hirundo hirundo
Length 14–16 inches
Has bill red at base instead of orange, as in *S. forsteri*. Outer web of outer tail feather darker than inside. A cosmopolitan species which occurs uncommonly in Colorado

ARCTIC TERN
Sterna paradisaea
Length 14–17 inches
A northern breeding species which migrates in our winter into the Southern Hemisphere. A rare bird in Colorado. The dark gray breast and *red bill* separate the species from the Common and Forster's Terns

LEAST TERN
Sterna albifrons athalassos
Length 9–10 inches
A common species locally in temperate and warm parts of the world, and in much of the United States. This race of the interior occurs rarely in Colorado. Characterized by small size, yellow legs, and yellow bill tipped with black

FORSTER'S TERN
Sterna forsteri
Length 14–16 inches
Has outer web of outer tail feathers whiter than inner. A common summer resident of the eastern plains, and less numerous in the west

(Plate 61 by Wayne Trimm)

COMMON TERN   BLACK TERN *(adult, and immature)*

LEAST TERN   ARCTIC TERN

FORSTER'S TERN

Plate 61

BAND-TAILED PIGEON
Columba fasciata fasciata
Length 15–16 inches

The large Band-tailed Pigeons have a wide breeding range which extends southward from British Columbia to California, and the southwestern states into Mexico and Central America. They occur locally in summer throughout the Transition and lower Canadian Zones of the southern half of Colorado, northward to Rocky Mountain National Park, their numbers in a given season probably fluctuating according to the abundance of acorns available as food. Although undoubtedly breeding in Colorado regularly, few nests have been found in recent years — two of which were in lodgepole pines in the Rampart Range at an elevation of over 9000 feet. The nests were flimsy structures; one discovered August 22, 1945, contained a day-old squab, and another, located August 31, had a young about twenty days old. Probably the nesting season extends from mid-July into September. Flocks of adults and young band together in the early fall, and the majority migrate southward by late October

(Plate 62 by Donald L. Malick)

BAND-TAILED PIGEON

MOURNING DOVE
Zenaidura macroura marginella
Length 11–13 inches

A very common species in summer from Alaska and southern Canada south into Mexico. This race occurs in the western half of the country, and is especially numerous in Colorado, where it ranges from low elevations into the foothills to 7000 feet. A large percentage nests upon the ground, pairs often raising three or more broods each season. These fast-flying birds are considered as game in many states — unfortunately, the open season starting while young are unfledged. The majority migrate southward, but a few occur during the winter months

GROUND DOVE
Columbigallina passerina pallescens
Length 6.25–7.25 inches

A species, appropriately named because of its terrestrial habits, which ranges northward to southern New Mexico, Kansas, and Colorado. The occurrence of this colorful but inconspicuous small dove in the latter two states is based on sight records

WHITE-WINGED DOVE
Zenaida asiatica mearnsi
Length 11–12.5 inches

These common doves of the Southwest are mere stragglers northward into Colorado and Wyoming. The conspicuous white wing patches and the rounded tail distinguish this bird from the slender Mourning Dove — which lacks white on wings and has a pointed tail. Both species are considered game birds

(Plate 63 by Donald L. Malick)

Plate 63

MOURNING DOVE   GROUND DOVE

WHITE-WINGED DOVE

BLACK-BILLED CUCKOO
Coccyzus erythropthalmus
Length 11–13 inches

An inconspicuous bird, which breeds from south-central Canada to Quebec and southward to Wyoming, Colorado, Nebraska, and Kansas to Georgia. The black bill and small white edgings on tail feathers are distinguishing characters. It is an uncommon summer resident in Colorado, Nebraska, and Kansas, and more numerous in Wyoming

YELLOW-BILLED CUCKOO
Coccyzus americanus americanus
Length 11–13 inches

The "Rain Crow," so called because it seems more vocal on wet days, as a species is widely distributed from southern Canada south through the United States into Mexico, wintering into South America. It is a secretive, uncommon summer resident below 7000 feet throughout the deciduous wooded areas of Colorado and neighboring states. The nests, so fragile the pale blue eggs often are visible from underneath, are placed on low shrubbery. The yellow lower mandible and the large white tail spots are good field marks

ROADRUNNER
Geococcyx californianus
Length 19–25 inches

This well-known ground cuckoo of the dry country of the Southwest is resident in small numbers in the southern part of Colorado, Kansas, New Mexico, and Utah. The bulky nests are built in cacti or in low shrubs, and the birds are carnivorous, feeding upon insects, small birds, mammals, amphibians, and reptiles. The common name of the species is an appropriate one, for often the birds may be seen running along the desert trails and roadways

(Plate 64 by Orville O. Rice)

Plate 64

BLACK-BILLED CUCKOO

YELLOW-BILLED CUCKOO

ROADRUNNER

FLAMMULATED OWL
Otus flammeolus flammeolus
Length 6–7 inches

Appears much like a miniature Screech Owl, but the ear tufts are very short, and the eyes are dark instead of yellow. An uncommon bird of the forested mountains of the Transition and Canadian Zones of Colorado. Nests at high altitudes in tree cavities, usually in the Canadian Zone. Only one Colorado breeding record during the last sixty years

PYGMY OWL
Glaucidium gnoma californicum
Length 6.5–7.5 inches

A small owl with yellow eyes, and no ear tufts. An uncommon resident of the forested mountain slopes throughout the state, the majority occurring above 9000 feet. These little owls are pugnacious and are active during daylight hours; they are fearless and readily attack birds of large size

BOREAL OWL
Aegolius funereus richardsoni
Length 9–12 inches

Medium-sized, yellow-eyed, brown owl without ear tufts. A species of the northern forests which wanders casually southward into Colorado. The stragglers recorded in winter possibly were forced below their normal range by failure of food supply

SCREECH OWL
Otus asio
Length 8–10 inches

The species is resident locally from southeastern Alaska across southern Canada south into Mexico. Eighteen races are recognized in the Checklist, three of which occur in Colorado All are uncommon. O.a. maxwelliae is a large light-colored bird, O.a. aikeni is smaller and darker, and there is one record of the red phase of O.a. naevius. All are inconspicuous, night-flying birds, the preferred habitats of maxwelliae and aikeni being in tangled thickets bordering the wooded shores of streams of the Upper Sonoran Zone and the adjacent foothills

SAW-WHET OWL
Aegolius acadicus acadicus
Length 7–8.5 inches

This little bird, named because of its distinctive "Saw-whet" calls, appears as a small version of the Boreal Owl. It is an uncommon resident from the prairies into the lower mountains, with its center of population being in the Transition into the lower Canadian Zones. Like the other small owls, this species nests in cavities of trees, often in holes abandoned by flickers

(Plate 65 by Donald L. Malick)

Plate 65

FLAMMULATED OWL

PYGMY OWL

BOREAL OWL

SCREECH OWL

SAW-WHET OWL

GREAT HORNED OWL
Bubo virginianus
Length 19–25 inches

Great Horned Owls, as a species, range widely from the limit of trees in Arctic Alaska and Canada south to the Straits of Magellan. Ten races are included in the A.O.U. Check-list, and numerous others have been described from Mexico southward. Four subspecies have been recorded from Colorado. B.v. occidentalis is the resident form, and the three others are winter migrants or stragglers into the state

BURROWING OWL
Speotyto cunicularia hypugaea
Length 9–11 inches

Formerly a very common summer resident throughout Colorado and neighboring states in prairie dog "towns." This beneficial little daylight owl, which feeds primarily upon grasshoppers and other insects during the breeding season, has declined in numbers with the destruction of prairie dogs. Nests may be in burrows dug by the owls or in abandoned homes of the mammals with which they associate in summer

BARN OWL
Tyto alba pratincola
Length 15–20 inches

A cosmopolitan species found on all continents. An uncommon but regular summer resident in Colorado, with a few wintering. Nests in buildings, in cavities on cliffs or arroyo banks, or in holes in trees. Like other owls, these capable birds feed primarily upon small mammals, have a keen sense of hearing, and are able to locate prey in absolute darkness

SNOWY OWL
Nyctea scandiaca
Length 21–27 inches

These large white owls are birds of the northern tundras of both the New and Old Worlds. They migrate southward into northern states on occasions of shortage of lemmings or other small mammals which probably are their main source of food. Snowy Owls have been recorded irregularly through the years in Colorado and adjacent areas

(Plate 66 by Wayne Trimm)

Plate 66

GREAT HORNED OWL

BURROWING OWL   BARN OWL

SNOWY OWL

LONG-EARED OWL
Asio otus wilsonianus
Length 13–16 inches

A medium-sized owl which occurs regularly along the wooded areas of the eastern prairies into the foothills to an elevation of 7000 feet, and in the same type of habitat on the western slope. As with all other hawks and owls, their numbers have declined steadily as the human population has increased. Nesting sites in eastern Colorado are usually on old platforms of magpies and hawks

BARRED OWL
Strix varia varia
Length 19–24 inches

The range of this eastern "hoot owl" extends westward into Colorado, where it is uncommon. A variety of nest sites are used, but the preferred locations are in hollows of trees, where pairs may nest annually as long as they are undisturbed. Several owls observed adjacent to the eastern foothills, and listed in the literature as this species, probably were Spotted Owls

SPOTTED OWL
Strix occidentalis lucida
Length 16–18 inches

This large, inconspicuous owl of the West, which is resident locally from British Columbia southward into Mexico, east to Colorado and Texas, closely resembles the Barred Owl. It is a bird of coniferous forests and canyon country, nesting in crannies of cliffs, in tree cavities, or old platforms which previously had been used by other species of birds—especially hawks and magpies

SHORT-EARED OWL
Asio flammeus flammeus
Length 14–17 inches

An uncommon resident throughout the state, nesting locally upon the ground in moist areas. The Short-eared population increases greatly when migrants appear from the north to winter along the weed-grown borders of marshes adjacent to lakes and reservoirs. Often birds may be seen in the late evening, as they fly low, scanning terrain in search of rodents and other small mammals

(Plate 67 by Donald L. Malick)

Plate 67

LONG-EARED OWL

BARRED OWL

SPOTTED OWL

SHORT-EARED OWL

LESSER NIGHTHAWK
Chordeiles acutipennis texensis
Length 8.2–9.3 inches

This small nighthawk of the Southwest ranges northward to southern Colorado. Although there are few records, the bird probably occurs regularly within the state. Specimens taken in Las Animas and El Paso Counties in June and August may indicate breeding in these areas. The white wing band is nearer the wing tip than in the Common Nighthawks

COMMON NIGHTHAWK
Chordeiles minor
Length 8.5–10 inches

Eight geographic races of this species are listed in the A.O.U. Check-list, five of which have been recorded from Colorado. They are so similar in appearance that specimens are necessary to make proper identifications. Often during migration dozens of birds may be seen flying over the wooded areas of towns and cities as the birds catch insects. The males have spectacular diving flights which result in making "booming" sounds

POOR-WILL
Phalaenoptilus nuttallii nuttallii
Length 7–8.5 inches

Poor-wills are smaller than nighthawks and differ from the latter in having rounded instead of forked tails, and no white on the wings. They occur throughout the state from the foothill areas at an elevation of 6000 feet upwards into the Transition Zone to 8000 feet. Their nests and two white eggs are placed upon the ground, as are those of the Common and Lesser Nighthawks and the Whip-poor-wills

WHIP-POOR-WILL
Caprimulgus vociferus vociferus
Length 9–10 inches

These are common and well-known birds of the eastern half of the country, their "whip-poor-will" calls being familiar night sounds throughout the summer months. Like other members of the family, they are concealingly marked, blending perfectly with their surroundings. Although locally common in neighboring states to the eastward, they apparently are mere stragglers in Colorado

(Plate 68 by Donald L. Malick)

Plate 68

LESSER NIGHTHAWK

POOR-WILL   COMMON NIGHTHAWK

WHIP-POOR-WILL

CHIMNEY SWIFT
Chaetura pelagica
Length 5–5.5 inches

A very common species of the eastern half of the country, breeding from southern Canada to Florida and the Gulf coast. As their name implies, the birds nest in chimneys. In migration, swarms of thousands often swirl into chimneys to spend the night. Uncommon in Colorado but numbers have been observed in Boulder and Denver

BLACK SWIFT
Cypseloides niger borealis
Length 7–7.5 inches

Breeds along sea cliffs in California, and in the mountains of the West from southeastern Alaska, British Columbia, and Montana to an elevation of over 10,000 feet in Colorado. The isolated colonies are small and the nests, scattered along precipitous cliffs, usually are associated with waterfalls

WHITE-THROATED SWIFT
Aeronautes saxatalis sclateri
Length 6–7 inches

A common nesting species locally from British Columbia to Alberta, south into the mountains of Central America. Nests are usually built in crannies of almost inaccessible cliffs; two especially spectacular Colorado sites are in Red Rocks Park near Denver and in the Garden of the Gods at Colorado Springs

(Plate 69 by Donald L. Malick)

Plate 69

CHIMNEY SWIFT

BLACK SWIFT   WHITE-THROATED SWIFT

CALLIOPE HUMMINGBIRD
Stellula calliope
Length 3–3.5 inches

A western species which ranges eastward to Nebraska and Kansas, and is a regular summer resident in Colorado, New Mexico, Utah, and Wyoming. The conspicuous iridescent gorget rays serve as excellent field marks. Hummingbird females incubate the eggs and care for the young

(male left)

RUFOUS HUMMINGBIRD
Selasphorus rufus
Length 3.2–3.6 inches

One of the most beautiful of the small hummingbirds. They migrate regularly from their northern breeding grounds through the foothills and mountains of Wyoming, Utah, Colorado, and New Mexico, during July and August, and are conspicuous wherever bottles of sweetened water have been placed for their benefit. Being pugnacious, they drive larger hummers away from feeding stations

(male above)

RIVOLI'S HUMMINGBIRD
Eugenes fulgens aureoviridis
Length 4.5–5 inches

A conspicuous hummingbird which ranges from its normal habitat in the mountains of Arizona and northern Mexico northward into Colorado. It has been observed in Jackson, Boulder, and Gunnison Counties, and at the Long's Peak Campgrounds near Rocky Mountain National Park throughout summer months

(male left)

BLACK-CHINNED HUMMINGBIRD
Archilochus alexandri
Length 3.40–3.75 inches

An inconspicuous hummer which breeds from southwestern British Columbia and northwestern Montana south in central Idaho, and is a summer resident of the low valleys of Utah, New Mexico, and of the west and southwestern portions of Colorado. It is a bird of the pinyon-juniper and sage associations, rather than of mountainous terrain, and often in late summer may be seen securing nectar and insects from thistle blossoms

(male below)

BROAD-TAILED HUMMINGBIRD
Selasphorus platycercus platycercus
Length 4–4.5 inches

This is the common species of the Rocky Mountain region, west to the mountains of east-central California. In Colorado it nests from the plains upward, the center of abundance being in the Transition Zone, but breeds regularly to over 10,-000 feet. Females often return to identical nesting places of the year before

(male below)

(Plate 70 by Donald L. Malick)

Plate 70

CALLIOPE HUMMINGBIRD

RIVOLI'S HUMMINGBIRD

RUFOUS HUMMINGBIRD

BLACK-CHINNED HUMMINGBIRD

BROAD-TAILED HUMMINGBIRD

BELTED KINGFISHER
Megaceryle alcyon alcyon
Length 11–14 inches

The species breeds from Alaska across southern Canada south to the Gulf coast, and to Baja California, and this race ranges from the Rockies over the eastern half of the continent. These noisy, picturesque birds are fairly common residents along the waterways of Colorado and neighboring states

(female above)

YELLOW-SHAFTED FLICKER
Colaptes auratus luteus
Length 12–14 inches

The species breeds from the limit of trees in central Alaska to Labrador, and in the eastern half of the United States. They are common summer residents of Nebraska and Kansas, and range westward into Colorado where the majority of birds with yellow shafts probably are hybrids. Both adults have red on nape, and male has *black* malar stripe

(female above)

RED-SHAFTED FLICKER
Colaptes cafer collaris
Length 12–14 inches

This flicker, as a species, occupies the western half of the country from southern Alaska, Alberta, Saskatchewan, and North Dakota southward along the Great Plains, and in western states into Mexico. It is a common resident of Colorado from the prairies into the mountains, and many migrate upward to near timberline after the breeding season. Hybridizes freely with the Yellow-shafted Flicker where the ranges of the two species meet. No red on nape, and male has *red* malar stripe

(female at right)

(Plate 71 by Wayne Trimm)

Plate 71

BELTED KINGFISHER
(female above)

YELLOW-SHAFTED FLICKER
(female above)

RED-SHAFTED FLICKER
(female at right)

YELLOW-BELLIED SAPSUCKER
Sphyrapicus varius
Length 8–9 inches

This mountain race is a common bird of the coniferous forests of Colorado, New Mexico, Utah,
and Wyoming, while the eastern subspecies
(*S.v. varius*) occurs uncommonly in western Nebraska, Kansas, and on the adjacent prairies of
Colorado. The males are similar in color, and
both have red crowns bordered at back with a
black stripe. The western bird, however, has a
red band across the back of the head below the
black border — hence the former common name
— Red-naped Sapsucker. The eastern females
have *white throats*, and *S.v. nuchalis* has *red
throat* with *white chin*

*(adult male of S.v. nuchalis upper left, and immature
male below; male of S.v. varius at right)*

WILLIAMSON'S SAPSUCKER
Sphyrapicus thyroideus nataliae
Length 9–9.5 inches

A common bird of the mountains of the West.
In Colorado, this race is partial to the ponderosa
pine belt, the nesting holes usually are drilled
into the living trees, and both adults share the
task of feeding the young. The entrances to the
nests are on the southern side of trees where they
are warmed by the sun. The females are so unlike the males in color that originally the two
were described as separate species

(female and male)

RED-BELLIED WOODPECKER
Centurus carolinus zebra
Length 9–10 inches

This colorful species ranges widely over much of
the eastern half of the United States. It occurs
commonly in eastern Nebraska and Kansas, and
is an uncommon resident along the wooded
watercourses of the eastern plains of Colorado.
The birds are so inconspicuous they easily could
be overlooked, but they advertise their presence
with harsh calls. The female is similar to the
male in color, except it has a gray forecrown

(adult male, female above)

RED-HEADED WOODPECKER
Melanerpes erythrocephalus caurinus
Length 8.5–10 inches

These brightly colored woodpeckers are common
locally in Nebraska and Kansas, and in Colorado
on the plains into the low foothills. They have an
unfortunate habit of alighting on highways to
feed upon insects, and many are killed by fast-
moving motor cars. Their nests are drilled in
cottonwoods, willows, and occasionally in tele-
phone poles

(immature and adult)

(Plate 72 by Donald L. Malick)

YELLOW-BELLIED SAPSUCKER
*(adult male nuchalis above, immature male
below; adult male varius right)*

RED-BELLIED WOODPECKER
(adult male, female above)

WILLIAMSON'S SAPSUCKER
(female and male)

RED-HEADED WOODPECKER
(immature left, adult right)

Plate 72

LEWIS' WOODPECKER
Asyndesmus lewis
Length 10–11.5 inches

The range of this species extends from South Dakota, Nebraska, Kansas, and New Mexico westward to California and British Columbia. It is rather common locally in Colorado along the cottonwood draws of the eastern plains to the foothills, and less common in similar habitat in western counties. Slow of flight, the birds are sometimes called the Crow Woodpeckers. They prefer stands of dead timber but drill their nesting cavities in live trees as well

NORTHERN THREE-TOED WOODPECKER
Picoïdes tridactylus dorsalis
Length 8.5 to 9.5 inches

These high altitude birds are dark above and have a general resemblance to the Hairy Woodpeckers, but the males have yellow caps in contrast to the red markings of the Hairy Woodpeckers. They are uncommon birds of the coniferous forests of the higher Rockies of New Mexico, Utah, and Wyoming, and rarely are observed below 8000 feet

PILEATED WOODPECKER
Dryocopus pileatus picinus
Length 16–19 inches

A resident in forests from southern Mackenzie across Canada to Nova Scotia, south to California, Texas, the Gulf coast, and Florida, the species is rare in Colorado and neighboring states. These woodpeckers are the largest of their family in the United States except the nearly extinct Ivory-billed. They are noisy, and when pounding upon a tree may be heard for a considerable distance. Armed with strong beaks, they are able to reduce a partially decayed log to chips in a very short time

(female at right)

(Plate 73 by Donald L. Malick)

Plate 73

LEWIS' WOODPECKER
(adult male)

NORTHERN THREE-TOED WOODPECKER
(adult male)

PILEATED WOODPECKER
(female at right)

HAIRY WOODPECKER
Dendrocopos villosus
Length 8.5–10.5 inches

Twelve races are recognized in the A.O.U. Checklist, and three occur in Colorado. The subspecies (D.v. villosus), with conspicuously spotted wings, at left, shown small because of distance, is the common form of the eastern states west to Kansas and Nebraska. It is the same size as the mountain race (D.v. monticola) which has almost unmarked wings. The latter is fairly common in the mountains of Colorado, New Mexico, Utah, and Wyoming in summer, and winters at lower elevations. A northern race with conspicuously white spotted wings ranges southward to Nebraska and Colorado in winter

(male with red markings on head)

LADDER-BACKED WOODPECKER
Dendrocopos scalaris symplectus
Length 7–8 inches

These active little woodpeckers, residents of the semi-desert areas of the Southwest, are colored to match their sunlight and shadow habitat, the black and white bars of the back often serving as a perfect camouflage. They are uncommon in southeastern Colorado in the dry juniper-pinyon country, and are residents of southwest Kansas, New Mexico, and Utah

(male with red cap)

DOWNY WOODPECKER
Dendrocopos pubescens
Length 6-8 inches

Three races occur in Colorado. They are nearly the same size, but the eastern form (D.p. medianus) with white spotted wings, is shown smaller in the illustration, because of the perspective. The common mountain birds (D.p. leucurus) have less white on their wings. They nest among the aspens and ponderosa pines throughout Colorado and neighboring mountain states from 6000 to 9000 feet, and their habits are generally similar to those of their larger relatives, the Hairy Woodpeckers. The northern breeding form (D.p. nelsoni), which is whiter below, has white wing spots, and less dark barring on the tail than leucurus, ranges into Colorado in winter

(males with red on heads)

(Plate 74 by Donald L. Malick)

Plate 74

HAIRY WOODPECKER
*(mountain race in center, female at right; at left the eastern
form made small because of distance. Both races are the same size)*

DOWNY WOODPECKER
*(eastern race with spotted wings above,
mountain form below; males with red head markings)*

LADDER-BACKED WOODPECKER
(female and male)

GREAT CRESTED FLYCATCHER
Myiarchus crinitus boreus
Length 8–9 inches

Nests commonly from the eastern half of southern Canada south to Georgia, Louisiana, and Texas; it is a common summer resident of Nebraska and Kansas, and is a straggler in eastern Colorado, probably breeding in the Bonny Reservoir area of Yuma County. They are hole nesting birds, and some adorn their nests with shed snake skins

ASH-THROATED FLYCATCHER
Myiarchus cinerascens cinerascens
Length 7.5–8.5 inches

Rather silent flycatchers, the Ash-throated are smaller and have whiter throats than the Great Crested. These are birds of the dry canyon country from Oregon and Washington to Colorado, and south to Texas into Mexico. Nests regularly in natural cavities and old woodpecker holes in southern counties of Colorado, New Mexico, and Utah southward

OLIVACEOUS FLYCATCHER
Myiarchus tuberculifer olivascens
Length 6.5–7 inches

This flycatcher of the dry Mexican border country and southward ranges rarely northward into New Mexico, and one specimen was taken in southern Colorado

EASTERN PHOEBE
Sayornis phoebe
Length 6.5–7 inches

This phoebe breeds from British Columbia across southern Canada, south to Texas, Alabama, and South Carolina, and vest to Nebraska, Kansas, and Oklahoma, and has been recorded as a casual visitor in Wyoming and Utah. A summer resident in eastern Colorado, and nesting in Baca County

SAY'S PHOEBE
Sayornis saya saya
Length 7.5–8 inches

Breeds commonly from British Columbia to Manitoba south to Texas, and southern California into Mexico. A common migrant from Nebraska and Kansas westward, they are birds of open spaces, building in a variety of sites, under bridges, in old buildings, or along arroyo banks

(Plate 75 by Donald L. Malick)

Plate 75

GREAT CRESTED FLYCATCHER

ASH-THROATED FLYCATCHER

OLIVACEOUS FLYCATCHER

EASTERN PHOEBE

SAY'S PHOEBE

SCISSOR-TAILED FLYCATCHER
Muscivora forficata

Length 10.5–14.5 inches

This species, the most spectacular of the fly-catchers of our central-southern states, has a comparatively limited breeding range which extends from Colorado, Nebraska, and Kansas to Louisiana and Texas. It has been described by Florence Merriam Bailey as "an astonishing creature with glistening black, white, and salmon plumage and white forked tail twice its length . . . known as the Texas Bird of Paradise." It is a noisy, pugnacious bird perfectly willing to give chase to others of its kind, or any species coming close to a nest site — including birds of prey from the size of Sparrow Hawks to Golden Eagles. The Scissor-tail has no fear of passing motor cars, and as a consequence, often nests at low elevations along highways. The center of abundance of the species is in Texas, with the breeding range extending northward to southeastern Colorado, southern Nebraska, and Kansas

(sexes colored much alike)

(Plate 76 by Donald L. Malick)

Plate 76

SCISSOR-TAILED FLYCATCHER

CASSIN'S KINGBIRD
Tyrannus vociferans vociferans

The members of this genus are well-named *tyrannus*, for all are aggressive and readily attack much larger species which may invade their nesting territory. Cassin's Kingbirds are similar to the Western, but they are darker above and their tails are tipped with whitish, and the outer tail feathers are edged with dusky rather than conspicuous white. Their breeding range extends from Montana and Wyoming to Nebraska and Kansas south to Arizona, and from central California into Mexico

WESTERN KINGBIRD
Tyrannus verticalis

These noisy birds are the most conspicuous of the kingbird tribe in Colorado and neighboring states. They are abundant and well-known locally over much of the western half of the continent, from southern Manitoba to British Columbia and south to west-central Texas and northern Mexico. In Colorado, all three species of kingbirds seem to occupy similar types of country, and choose nest sites which are alike. Cassin's possibly may prefer higher elevations, but both Western and Cassin's have been recorded on the plains — nesting harmoniously in the same cottonwoods

EASTERN KINGBIRD
Tyrannus tyrannus

The common name Tyrant Flycatcher would seem more appropriate for this bird than Eastern, for the species ranges completely across the continent from British Columbia to Newfoundland, and occurs in many western states. Like the other kingbirds, they are pugnacious toward birds of prey, and are intolerant of small species in their nesting territories. Strangely, however, nests of both Western and Eastern Kingbirds often will be in close proximity, and life goes on with only occasional protests

(Plate 77 by Donald L. Malick)

Plate 77

CASSIN'S KINGBIRD

WESTERN KINGBIRD

EASTERN KINGBIRD

Nine species of the genus *Empidonax* are included in the A.O.U. Check-list of North American birds, and six have been recorded from Colorado and the majority of neighboring states. They are all small flycatchers so similar in size, coloring, and habits that they are difficult to identify in the field, and only an optimist would make the attempt. Students familiar with the various species, however, have learned to separate them by their voices, or chosen habitat during the breeding season. Often it is difficult to identify birds in the hand. All are olive-gray or green with more or less brownish above the grayish-white below; eyering whitish. Slightly larger is the pewee, belonging to the genus *Contopus*.

1. **WESTERN WOOD PEWEE**
Contopus sordidulus veliei
Length 6–6.5 inches

Larger than flycatchers of the genus *Empidonax*. Has two whitish wing bars, *no white eyering*, underparts light olive-gray with distinctive lighter line down center of breast and lower mandible yellowish. The Eastern Wood Pewee is similar, but darker

2. **HAMMOND'S FLYCATCHER**
Empidonax hammondii
Length 5.5–5.75 inches

4. **GRAY FLYCATCHER**
Empidonax wrightii
Length 5.25–5.75 inches

3. **TRAILL'S FLYCATCHER**
Empidonax traillii
Length 5.5–6.5 inches

5. **LEAST FLYCATCHER**
Empidonax minimus
Length 5–5.5 inches

Traill's Flycatcher has a rounded tail while all others of the genus are notched. The light lower mandible differs from that of the other *Empidonax* except *E. wrightii*. The Least Flycatcher is smaller, grayer above, white below, and both mandibles are dark

6. **DUSKY FLYCATCHER**
Empidonax oberholseri
Length 5.5–6 inches

These three species are generally similar, nos. 2 and 6 being practically indistinguishable in the field. Each is found in a different habitat; no. 2 frequents Engelmann spruce forests, no. 6 likes the open parks and brushy hillsides, no. 4, the Gray Flycatcher, is a bird of the pinyon-juniper mesa country

7. **WESTERN FLYCATCHER**
Empidonax difficilis hellmayri
Length 5.5–6 inches

Common bird of the Colorado mountains, the only one of the genus with yellowish throat instead of white

9. (male) **VERMILION FLYCATCHER**
10. (Female) *Pyrocephalus rubinus flammeus*
Length 5.5–6.5 inches

The male is the most brilliant of the flycatchers of the Southwest. The species breeds over much of the Lower Sonoran desert country, being especially conspicuous along watercourses. Individuals often wander far north of their breeding range — to Canada, northeastern states, and at least five have been observed in Colorado in the last twelve years (1952-1964)

8. **OLIVE-SIDED FLYCATCHER**
Nuttallornis borealis
Length 7–8 inches

A rather stout, large headed, dark olive bird, grayish above, with *dark chest patches* and whitish line down abdomen. Conspicuous yellowish-white feathers on flank. Bird of the coniferous forests in Colorado which sings from the tops of the highest trees

(Plate 78 by Donald L. Malick)

1. WESTERN WOOD PEWEE   2. HAMMOND'S FLYCATCHER

3. TRAILL'S FLYCATCHER   4. GRAY FLYCATCHER   5. LEAST FLYCATCHER

7. WESTERN FLYCATCHER   6. DUSKY FLYCATCHER

10. (female),   9. (male) VERMILION FLYCATCHER   8. OLIVE-SIDED FLYCATCHER

PURPLE MARTIN
Progne subis subis
Length 7–8.5 inches

A well-known bird with a wide breeding range locally, from British Columbia south to the Mexican border; across southern Canada to New Brunswick, in northern states to Florida, Texas, and Arizona. An uncommon summer resident in Colorado with majority of records from western counties

(female above)

TREE SWALLOW
Iridoprocne bicolor
Length 5–6 inches

Breeds locally throughout much of North America from the northern limit of trees in north-central Alaska and Canada, south into southern California, New England states, and casually to Louisiana and Mississippi. Rather uncommon breeding bird in the mountainous portions of Colorado, where the nests are built in natural cavities or old woodpecker holes

VIOLET-GREEN SWALLOW
Tachycineta thalassina lepida
Length 5–5.5 inches

A common bird in hills and mountains from Alaska and British Columbia east to South Dakota, and south into Mexico. The conspicuous greenish back and white rump patches are good field marks to separate this species from the Tree Swallow. Nests regularly to timberline in Colorado, and in the Transition Zone and higher in neighboring states

HORNED LARK
Eremophila alpestris
Length 6.5–8 inches

A species which is widespread throughout the Northern Hemisphere in both the New and Old Worlds. Many geographic races have been described — twenty-one are listed from North America — and the breeding bird of Colorado (E.a. leucolaema) is abundant upon the prairies, and nests regularly in the grasslands of mountain parks, and above timberline in the Arctic-Alpine Zone

(adult female at left)

(Plate 79 by Donald L. Malick)

DENVER MUSEUM OF NATURAL HISTORY

PURPLE MARTIN
(female above)

TREE SWALLOW

VIOLET-GREEN SWALLOW

HORNED LARK
(female at left)

Plate 79

BANK SWALLOW
Riparia riparia riparia
Length 4.75–5.25 inches

The species occurs in the Old World from the British Isles, northern Scandinavia, Russia, and Siberia, south to Japan, India, Iraq, and northern Africa. This race breeds in North America from north-central Alaska across Canada, and south through Virginia to Alabama, Texas, and southern California. Common summer resident locally in Colorado from the plains into the lower foothills, and in neighboring states in suitable habitat, nesting in holes in banks

CLIFF SWALLOW
Petrochelidon pyrrhonota pyrrhonota
Length 5–6 inches

A common species locally, breeding from central Alaska cross Canada to Nova Scotia south to northern Gulf coast states, Texas, Arizona, and Baja California. A colonial bird, often with hundreds of domed mud nests on sides of buildings, under bridges, or along cliffs. *Brownish rump; white forehead* conspicuous

BARN SWALLOW
Hirundo rustica erythrogaster
Length 6–7.5 inches

Occurs over a great part of the Northern Hemisphere, in the Old World from the Faeroes, Scandinavia, Russia, and Siberia to China, India, Asia Minor, and Africa. This race breeds from Alaska across southern Canada into northern Mexico. It is common upon the plains into the mountains of Colorado, and a summer resident in neighboring states, the open mud nests usually being placed under bridges and culverts, or on beams of buildings

ROUGH-WINGED SWALLOW
Stelgidopteryx ruficollis serripennis
Length 5–5.5 inches

This brownish swallow has a wide range from southern Canada throughout much of the United States, into South America. It is a common summer resident and breeder in Colorado and adjacent states, but usually only a few dwell in a given colony. It is duskier below than is the Bank Swallow, with which it often associates along steep banks and arroyos

(Plate 80 by Orville O. Rice)

BANK SWALLOW   CLIFF SWALLOW

BARN SWALLOW   ROUGH-WINGED SWALLOW

BLUE JAY
Cyanocitta cristata
Length 11–12 inches

This common jay of the eastern half of the continent breeds from Wyoming, the Dakotas, and central Saskatchewan to Newfoundland, and south to Gulf coast states from Florida to Texas. The race cyanotephra is resident from southeastern Wyoming, Kansas, and Oklahoma to Texas. It is fairly common in Colorado along wooded stream bottoms of the eastern plains to the foothills, and has been recorded regularly from El Paso to Weld County

SCRUB JAY
Aphelocoma coerulescens woodhouseii
Length 11–13 inches

The rather secretive Scrub Jay is resident from Washington and Oregon east to Wyoming, and south through California and Texas into Mexico. As a result of the isolation of breeding communities, geographic differences have evolved, and thirteen races are recognized in the A.O.U. Checklist. The subspecies woodhouseii is a common form throughout Colorado, where it is usually associated with scrub oak and pinyon pine

STELLER'S JAY
Cyanocitta stelleri macrolopha
Length 12–13.5 inches

The species ranges locally from South Dakota, Nebraska, Kansas, and Texas westward, and from southeastern Alaska through California and Mexico to El Salvador and southern Nicaragua. Thirteen races are recognized and macrolopha, formerly known by the common name Long-crested Jay, is the common form in Colorado, where the center of abundance is in the Transition Zone, especially in association with the ponderosa pine

GRAY JAY
Perisoreus canadensis capitalis
Length 10.5–13 inches

A common species of the northern forests from north-central Alaska across Canada, and south into northern states, and in the mountains of northern California and South Dakota to central Arizona. This race is a common mountain form in Colorado from timberline through the Canadian Zone, especially in the Engelmann spruce forests. It is an uncommon visitor in Nebraska, but is resident in Wyoming, Utah, and northern New Mexico

(Plate 81 by Charles L. Ripper)

Plate 81

BLUE JAY   SCRUB JAY

STELLER'S JAY   GRAY JAY

COMMON CROW
Corvus brachyrhynchos brachyrhynchos
Length 17–20 inches

The species ranges throughout much of the United States, and this race from the Atlantic coast westward to Alberta, Montana, Wyoming, and Arizona to the Gulf of Mexico. It is common locally in Kansas, Nebraska, Colorado, and New Mexico, and uncommon in Utah and Wyoming. Ranges in the mountain states from plains and valleys into the foothills

WHITE-NECKED RAVEN
Corvus cryptoleucus
Length 19–21 inches

Resident from Nebraska, Kansas, New Mexico, and Arizona into Mexico. This small raven was formerly numerous over the Great Plains to the foothills, probably reaching its maximum during the years that bison were being slaughtered by the thousands. The species is uncommon in Nebraska, fairly common in summer in western Kansas, and in the dry unforested regions of New Mexico, uncommon in Wyoming, and in Colorado occurs locally in Kiowa and adjacent counties

COMMON RAVEN
Corvus corax sinuatus
Length 21–26 inches

Ravens, as a species, range throughout much of the Eastern Hemisphere from the British Isles, northern Scandinavia, northern Russia and Siberia, south to northwestern Africa, and southern Asia east to Japan; and in the New World from Alaska and Canada south to Georgia and Baja California. There are no recent records from Nebraska and Kansas but ravens are still fairly numerous in New Mexico, Utah, and Wyoming, and in the mountains and in western counties of Colorado, where they nest on inaccessible ledges

(Plate 82 by E. R. Kalmbach)

COMMON CROW

WHITE-NECKED RAVEN

COMMON RAVEN

Plate 82

CLARK'S NUTCRACKER
Nucifraga columbiana
Length 12–13 inches

Resident in mountainous areas of the West, from Wyoming, Colorado, New Mexico, and Arizona to British Columbia, California, and northern Baja California. Common locally in the mountains of Colorado, New Mexico, Utah, and Wyoming, and nests from pinyon-pine associations into the Canadian Zone. Occurs as an irregular visitor out on the Great Plains into Nebraska and Kansas. Nests early in the year, often when snows are deep over the highest forested slopes

BLACK-BILLED MAGPIE
Pica pica hudsonia
Length 17–21 inches

The species ranges in the Old World from the British Isles, Scandinavia, northern Europe, Russia, and Siberia to China, Japan, Asia Minor, and northwestern Africa; in the New World in the western half of the continent from Manitoba, South Dakota, Kansas, Nebraska, and Texas. A very common and conspicuous bird in Colorado and neighboring states, the nests being substantial domed structures with small entrances giving access to the mud-plastered cup

PINYON JAY
Gymnorhinus cyanocephalus
Length 10–11.5 inches

Common resident locally from Arizona, western Oklahoma, and South Dakota to Oregon, eastern California and Baja California. It breeds in the Panhandle of Nebraska, is an irregular visitor in western Kansas, and a fairly common summer resident in Colorado, New Mexico, Utah, and Wyoming, chiefly in pinyon-juniper associations, but wanders widely in straggling flocks after breeding season

(Plate 83 by Donald L. Malick)

Plate 83

CLARK'S NUTCRACKER

BLACK-BILLED MAGPIE

PINYON JAY

MOUNTAIN CHICKADEE
Parus gambeli gambeli

Length 5–5.5 inches

Slightly larger than the Black-capped, has a *white line* over the eye, and under parts usually grayer. This species is a common mountain bird from southwestern Texas, New Mexico, and Colorado to British Columbia south to northern Baja California. Chickadees of this race are common throughout the higher coniferous-clad slopes of Colorado and adjacent states, where, like others of the species, they nest in natural crannies in trees, or in old homes of woodpeckers

BLACK-CAPPED CHICKADEE
Parus atricapillus septentrionalis

Length 4.75–5.5 inches

The species has a wide range from central Alaska across Canada, and in the northern tier of states from North Carolina to the Rocky Mountain region and California. This race is resident from the Yukon, British Columbia east to South Dakota, Colorado, and Kansas, and winters south to Texas. In Colorado they occur from the plains along the wooded watercourses into the foothills. The subspecies *garrinus* is found in western counties, and in neighboring states

COMMON BUSHTIT
Psaltriparus minimus plumbeus

Length 4–4.5 inches

The little bushtits, as a species, are associates of the Plain Titmouse, being partial, in Colorado, to the dry hillsides and canyons of the pinyon-juniper areas of southern and western counties. Their beautiful, long pendant nests, with small openings on the side, are nicely woven from plant fibers, with mosses, lichens, and spider webs incorporated in the structure. Often the nests are only six to eight feet from the ground. The bushtits tend to wander after the nesting season, and many have been recorded in winter as far north as Boulder and Larimer Counties

PLAIN TITMOUSE
Parus inornatus ridgwayi

Length 5–5.5 inches

This inconspicuously marked bird is an active resident of the lower hill and canyon country of the West, usually, in Colorado, being associated with pinyon-junipers in the Upper Sonoran Zone. Apparently resident birds are confined to limited territories for ten races have evolved, with two or more often occurring in the same state. The titmouse nests in cavities in trees, and occasional incubating or brooding birds are so tame they refuse to leave their eggs or young, and if forcibly removed, will promptly return to their duties

(Plate 84 by Donald L. Malick)

Plate 84

MOUNTAIN CHICKADEE   BLACK-CAPPED CHICKADEE

COMMON BUSHTIT   PLAIN TITMOUSE

WHITE-BREASTED NUTHATCH
Sitta carolinensis nelsoni
Length 5–6 inches

This common species ranges throughout much of North America from southern British Columbia across Canada to Nova Scotia and south into Mexico. Eight races are recognized in the Checklist, and the form *nelsoni* is resident in the Rocky Mountain region, casually into western Nebraska and Kansas. In Colorado it nests from wooded stream beds on the plains into the mountains, with its center of abundance in the ponderosa pine belt

RED-BREASTED NUTHATCH
Sitta canadensis
Length 4–4.5 inches

The active little Red-breasted Nuthatch is a Canadian Zone species which ranges widely from southeastern Alaska across Canada, and throughout higher elevations southward locally into Mexico, and at lower elevations in winter. It is a winter visitor in Nebraska and Kansas, and an uncommon resident in Colorado mountains to timberline in summer, and on the plains in winter

PYGMY NUTHATCH
Sitta pygmaea melanotis
Length 4–4.5 inches

This well-known species of the wooded sections of the Transition Zone of the western part of the country ranges from mountainous areas of British Columbia to Baja California eastward to Pine Ridge country of Nebraska and south to the highlands of Mexico. It is a very common summer resident in the Transition Zone of Colorado, associated with ponderosa pines, and numerous in wooded areas of the plains in winter

BROWN CREEPER
Certhia familiaris montana
Length 5–5.5 inches

The members of the Creeper family occur throughout much of the Northern Hemisphere south to Africa and Australia. The species is circumpolar in distribution, in the Old World ranging south to northern Spain and eastward across Asia to China, Korea, and Japan. It is widespread in the New World from southeastern Alaska across Canada southward over much of the United States during breeding season, wintering at lower elevations in its nesting range. This race in Colorado is a resident of the coniferous forests; breeding from 8000 feet to timberline

(Plate 85 by A. H. Short)

Plate 85

WHITE-BREASTED NUTHATCH   RED-BREASTED NUTHATCH

PYGMY NUTHATCH   BROWN CREEPER

HOUSE WREN
Troglodytes aedon parkmanii
Length 4.5–5 inches

Wrens are found throughout much of the world. There are approximately sixty species, small birds with short wings, and the majority dwell in rather heavy cover. The House Wren is a well-known species which occurs over much of southern Canada south through the United States. This western race breeds commonly from British Columbia east to Ontario, and south to Baja California

BEWICK'S WREN
Thryomanes bewickii eremophilus
Length 5–5.5 inches

These wrens, as a species, occur over much of the United States, and this race is resident throughout areas of the West from Wyoming, New Mexico, and Arizona to California. In Colorado it is a resident of the pinyon-juniper country of the southern and western counties, nesting in natural cavities, especially in pinyons. Stragglers often range northward in winter along the eastern slope, and individuals have been observed in Boulder and Morgan Counties

WINTER WREN
Troglodytes troglodytes pacificus
Length 4–4.5 inches

The species ranges throughout the Northern Hemisphere in both the New and Old Worlds, and this western race breeds from Alaska to central California east to western Montana. It is an uncommon winter visitor in Nebraska, Kansas, Colorado and other adjacent states. Tiny sprites, usually keeping low in dense cover, they are difficult to observe, and may easily escape detection

CAROLINA WREN
Thryothorus ludovicianus ludovicianus
Length 5.5–6 inches

A common resident of southern states, this large, colorful wren ranges northward locally to Nebraska and Kansas eastward to southern Ontario and Massachusetts. It is a rare straggler in Colorado and New Mexico. Like the little Winter Wren, these birds are partial to dense shrubbery where they can move secretively. Often they would pass unnoticed except for their musical voices

DIPPER
Cinclus mexicanus unicolor
Length 7–8 inches

Dippers occur in Europe, Asia, and in the New World. This species ranges from the Aleutian Islands and north-central Alaska south through the mountainous regions of the western part of the United States through the highlands of Mexico to Panama. It is a common bird in Colorado, New Mexico, Utah, and Wyoming along swift-flowing streams, and nests regularly, the domed nests of moss being placed along canyon walls. Although the feet are not webbed, the Dippers are excellent divers, even in fast water, where they secure aquatic insects and fish. They drop to lower elevations during winter, wherever there is open water along the mountain streams

(Plate 86 by Donald L. Malick)

HOUSE WREN

BEWICK'S WREN

WINTER WREN

CAROLINA WREN

DIPPER

LONG-BILLED MARSH WREN
Telmatodytes palustris plesius
Length 4.5–5.5 inches

A common wide-ranging species over much of North America from British Columbia across Canada south to Florida, the Gulf coast, and Baja California. This race breeds locally over much of western United States. It is a winter resident on eastern plains of Colorado and breeds commonly in the San Luis Lakes marshes of Saguache County

SHORT-BILLED MARSH WREN
Cistothorus platensis stellaris
Length 4–4.5 inches

Species ranges across Canada and through much of the United States, south through Mexico, Central America, and South America to Tierra del Fuego. This race, which breeds in the northern states of the eastern half of the country and winters to the Gulf coast and into Mexico, is a mere straggler in Colorado

CANYON WREN
Salpinctes mexicanus conspersus
Length 5–5.5 inches

The species, well-named because of its choice of habitat, is a western bird which dwells in rugged terrain of the lower hills from British Columbia to South Dakota, south to southern Mexico, and Baja California. It is a fairly common resident in Colorado, New Mexico, and Utah, advertising its presence by characteristic loud, clear songs

ROCK WREN
Salpinctes obsoletus obsoletus
Length 5–6 inches

The Rock Wren is another of the western species which ranges widely from southern prairies of Canada east to North Dakota and south through the Mexican highlands and on offshore islands. Six races of the species are recognized, and this form is resident from Nebraska, Kansas, Wyoming, New Mexico, and Utah. In Colorado it is a common migrant on the plains, nesting along rocky escarpments of the foothills to above timberline

(Plate 87 by Walter J. Breckenridge)

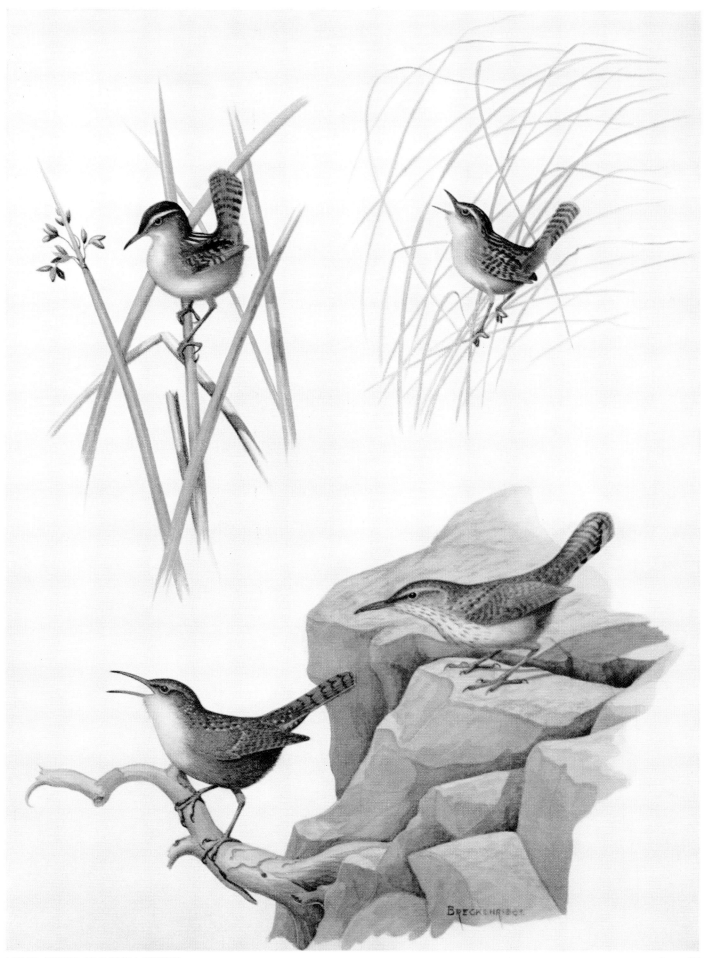

LONG-BILLED MARSH WREN   SHORT-BILLED MARSH WREN

CANYON WREN   ROCK WREN

MOCKINGBIRD
Mimus polyglottos leucopterus
Length 9.5–11 inches

These common birds, excellent mimics of other species, are resident locally throughout much of the United States, and their range extends northward into southern Canada from British Columbia to Nova Scotia. They occur throughout southern Colorado, but are uncommon in the northern part of the state. Intergradation with birds of the eastern subspecies occurs on the plains areas from Nebraska, Kansas, Oklahoma, and central Texas

CATBIRD
Dumetella carolinensis
Length 8–9 inches

These rather secretive birds are fairly common summer residents throughout their range, breeding from British Columbia across southern Canada, and from Washington and eastern Oregon to north-central Utah, Wyoming, New Mexico, Arizona, and throughout eastern states. They are fairly common summer residents in Colorado from the plains into the foothills, and although beautiful songsters, they also have harsh discordant notes — especially a cat-like "me-ou"

(Plate 88 by Orville O. Rice)

Plate 88

MOCKINGBIRD

CATBIRD

BENDIRE'S THRASHER
Toxostoma bendirei

Length 9–10.5 inches

Three species of thrashers of the Southwest have been recorded from Colorado, and one Bendire's Thrasher, which ranges from Nevada and southeastern California into Arizona and Mexico, was collected in El Paso County on May 8, 1882

CURVE-BILLED THRASHER
Toxostoma curvirostre celsum

Length 9.5–11 inches

A southwest species of the semidesert country which ranges from southern New Mexico and western Oklahoma southward into Texas. Individuals have wandered north occasionally to Nebraska, and there is one specimen from Prowers County, Colorado, which was collected March 25, 1951

SAGE THRASHER
Oreoscoptes montanus

Length 8–9 inches

This small gray-brown thrasher is a transient in Nebraska and Kansas, and a common summer resident of Colorado, New Mexico, Utah, and Wyoming in association with sage habitats. Often they are seen along highways, resting upon fence posts, during spring migration

BROWN THRASHER
Toxostoma rufum longicauda

Length 10–11.5 inches

Colorful, rufous-red thrashers, well-known throughout much of southern Canada and eastern United States west to the Rocky Mountains. They are common in Kansas, Nebraska, Wyoming, and Colorado, occasionally occurring in winter, and are beautiful songsters as well as mimics of other species. The sturdy nests usually are placed at low elevations in thick cover

LONG-BILLED THRASHER
Toxostoma longirostre sennetti

Length 10.5–12 inches

A species of the Mexican border country which is very similar to the Brown Thrasher, but is less reddish and has a longer bill. Like the Bendire's and Curve-billed Thrashers, they are birds of semidesert regions. One of this species, a female, was collected at Barr Lake in May 1906

(Plate 89 by Donald L. Malick)

Plate 89

BENDIRE'S THRASHER
CURVE-BILLED THRASHER   SAGE THRASHER
BROWN THRASHER
LONG-BILLED THRASHER

WOOD THRUSH
Hylocichla mustelina
Length 7.5–8.5 inches

This common bird of the east, from southern Canada to the Gulf coast, has extended its range westward to the Great Plains. It is a summer resident in Kansas and Nebraska, and a casual visitor in Wyoming and Colorado

VARIED THRUSH
Ixoreus naevius meruloides
Length 9–10 inches

There are reports of this thrush, which dwells in the forests of the northwest, from Utah, Wyoming, Nebraska, Kansas, and New Mexico. Numerous birds have been observed in Colorado in late fall, winter, and early spring in Denver, Boulder, and Ft. Collins

ROBIN
Turdus migratorius propinquus
Length 9.5–11 inches

The Robin, as a species, occurs over much of North America, breeding from southern states northward to the limit of trees, and from the plains to timberline in mountainous areas. This western race occurs in Nebraska and Kansas, and is the common breeding form in Colorado, where, in the fall, flocks of grayish Robins, possibly another subspecies, appear in migration. Many remain on southern mountain hillsides during the winter months

(Plate 90 by W. C. Dilger)

Plate 90

WOOD THRUSH

VARIED THRUSH *(female rear)*

ROBIN *(female rear)*

WHEATEAR
Oenanthe oenanthe oenanthe
Length 5.5–6 inches

The species is circumpolar in distribution, breeding in northern Alaska, Canada, northern Europe, and Asia, south to Portugal, France, Italy, Greece, Asia Minor, and Iran. Stragglers have wandered southward in the United States to New York, Pennsylvania, Louisiana, and Colorado

(adult male left, female right)

HERMIT THRUSH
Hylocichla guttata auduboni
Length 7–8 inches

Eight geographic races of this common species are recognized, some being of very local distribution, breeding populations occurring from Alaska across Canada southward into northern states and mountainous areas. Several races migrate through the Rockies and neighboring areas, and *auduboni* is the nesting form of Colorado

VEERY
Hylocichla fuscescens salicicola
Length 6.5–7.5 inches

The secretive Veery, as a species, is a rather uncommon migrant through Nebraska, Kansas, and New Mexico, and is an uncommon summer resident in Utah, Wyoming, and Colorado. It is a bird partial to moist areas, particularly willow-grown streams, where the tangled vegetation affords protective cover

SWAINSON'S THRUSH
Hylocichla ustulata almae
Length 6.5–7.5 inches

A very common migrant, as a species, throughout much of the United States and Canada, wintering from southern Mexico to Peru, Brazil, Paraguay, and Argentina. This race breeds in the mountains of Colorado and Utah northwest into British Columbia and Alaska

GRAY-CHEEKED THRUSH
Hylocichla minima minima
Length 7–8 inches

Migrates in the Mississippi Valley westward to Nebraska and Kansas, and probably irregularly through eastern Colorado and Wyoming, breeding in eastern Siberia, northern Alaska, and Canada. Winters from southern Mexico and islands of the Caribbean into northern South America

(Plate 91 by Donald L. Malick)

WHEATEAR *(male left, female right)*

VEERY

HERMIT THRUSH

GRAY-CHEEKED THRUSH

SWAINSON'S THRUSH

MOUNTAIN BLUEBIRD
Sialia currucoides
Length 6.5–7.5 inches

Breeds commonly in holes of trees throughout much of the west northward into Alaska and Canada, and in Colorado from the foothills into the mountains to about 9000 feet, and less commonly to timberline. Nests in western Nebraska, and winters commonly in Kansas

(male above, female at nesting hole)

EASTERN BLUEBIRD
Sialia sialis sialis
Length 6.5–7.5 inches

A wide-ranging species over much of the eastern half of the continent, breeding from southern Canada south to Gulf states and west to Colorado where it is a regular summer resident along the wooded stream bottoms of eastern counties to the foothills

WESTERN BLUEBIRD
Sialia mexicana bairdi
Length 6.5–7 inches

Fairly common summer resident and breeder in the Transition Zone, from Nevada, Utah, and Colorado south through the mountains of Arizona and Texas into northern Mexico. Nests commonly in the ponderosa pine belt of Colorado

TOWNSEND'S SOLITAIRE
Myadestes townsendi townsendi
Length 8–9.5 inches

Breeds from Alaska and the southern Yukon south through Canada and in western states to California, Utah, and Wyoming, to northeastern Arizona. A common summer resident of Colorado from the lower mountains to above timberline. Bulky nests are placed in cavities of banks, under rocks, or in exposed roots of overturned trees. In winter numbers migrate to the prairies and eastward into Nebraska and Kansas. Buffy wing patches and white edging of tail feathers show to advantage when the bird is in flight

(Plate 92 by W. C. Dilger)

Plate 92

MOUNTAIN BLUEBIRD (male above)

EASTERN BLUEBIRD (male)

WESTERN BLUEBIRD (male)

TOWNSEND'S SOLITAIRE

RUBY-CROWNED KINGLET
Regulus calendula cineraceus

Length 3.4–5 inches

A wide-ranging species, breeding from Alaska across Canada south into northern states, and mountains of California through the Rocky Mountains — this race nesting commonly in the coniferous forests of Utah, New Mexico, and Colorado

(female above)

GOLDEN-CROWNED KINGLET
Regulus satrapa amoenus

Length 3.5–4 inches

These small birds, like their relatives the Ruby-crowned, are common birds from Alaska eastward, and south into mountainous areas. Four races are recognized, this form breeding from Alaska to southern California, Nevada, Utah, and Colorado

(female above)

BLUE-GRAY GNATCATCHER
Polioptila caerulea amoenissima

Length 4–5 inches

A common bird over much of the United States as a species. This race is partial to pinyon-juniper country, breeding from California, Nevada, Utah, Wyoming, Nebraska, and Kansas south into Mexico. A fairly common summer resident of southern and western counties of Colorado

WATER PIPIT
Anthus spinoletta alticola

Length 6–7 inches

The species breeds in high latitudes or altitudes irregularly in both the New and Old Worlds. Four races occur in North America and this form nests on the alpine tundra of the high mountains of Wyoming, Utah, Colorado, and New Mexico

SPRAGUE'S PIPIT
Anthus spragueii

Length 6.7–7 inches

Ranges in summer from Alberta, Saskatchewan, and Manitoba south into Montana, North Dakota, and Minnesota, and winters in southern states into Mexico. A regular migrant over the Great Plains and a casual straggler in New Mexico, Colorado, and Wyoming

(Plate 93 by Donald L. Malick)

Plate 93

RUBY-CROWNED KINGLET *(female above)*

GOLDEN-CROWNED KINGLET *(female above)*

BLUE-GRAY GNATCATCHER

WATER PIPIT

SPRAGUE'S PIPIT

BOHEMIAN WAXWING
Bombycilla garrulus pallidiceps
Length 7.5–8.5 inches

Occurs throughout the northern parts of both the New and Old Worlds. In North America breeds from Alaska and Canada south to Washington, Idaho, and Montana. An irregularly abundant winter visitor in Colorado from the foothills to lower elevations, often occurring in large flocks. Yellow and white on wings and chestnut under tail feathers are good field marks

CEDAR WAXWING
Bombycilla cedrorum
Length 6.5–7.5 inches

Breeds from Alaska across Canada and south throughout much of the United States to California, northern Alabama, and northern Georgia. An uncommon and irregular summer resident in Colorado, occasionally numerous in winter from the lower mountains to the plains. Both species of waxwings feed upon fruit and berries

LOGGERHEAD SHRIKE
Lanius ludovicianus excubitorides
Length 8.5–10 inches

The species occurs over much of the continent from southern Canada into Mexico. Common summer resident upon the plains to the foothills. They are birds of the open country but their nests are usually well concealed in tangled vegetation of willows, hedgerows, or conifers

NORTHERN SHRIKE
Lanius excubitor invictus
Length 9–10.5 inches

Species occurs in the Old World from Scandinavia, Russia, Siberia, India, Arabia, and Africa, and in North America breeds in northern Alaska and Canada. Regular winter visitor throughout lower elevations of Colorado. Usually seen singly, and preys upon other birds and small mammals, but a large per cent of food consists of insects

(Plate 94 by D. M. Henry)

D.M. HENRY.

BOHEMIAN WAXWING

CEDAR WAXWING

LOGGERHEAD SHRIKE

NORTHERN SHRIKE

BELL'S VIREO
Vireo bellii bellii
Length 4.5–5 inches

An inconspicuous species which has an extensive breeding range locally in suitable wooded habitat from Illinois west to California and south into Mexico. It is fairly common in Colorado, Nebraska, and Kansas

WARBLING VIREO
Vireo gilvus swainsonii
Length 4.5–5.5 inches

The species breeds over much of North America from southern Canada nearly to the Gulf coast. This western race is most numerous in the Transition Zone, from British Columbia and Alberta south to the mountains of Texas, Arizona, and California

STARLING
Sturnus vulgaris vulgaris
Length 7.5–8.5 inches

This Old World bird, introduced into North America in 1890, found conditions suitable for its ways of life, and now ranges from southern Newfoundland westward across Canada to British Columbia and south throughout the United States to the Gulf coast and northeastern Mexico. Usually the first records of birds in a given area have been in winter; a few remained to nest, and now the Starling, in many parts of the country, is more numerous than the colonial nesting blackbirds. Because of their aggressiveness, they compete with native birds for nesting holes

(immature above, winter left, summer adult right)

(Plate 95 by Donald L. Malick)

Plate 95

BELL'S VIREO

WARBLING VIREO

STARLING
(Immature above, winter adult left, summer right)

GRAY VIREO
Vireo vicinior
Length 5–5.75 inches

Although there are few records of this inconspicuous vireo from the state, it undoubtedly ranges regularly through the pinyon-juniper habitats of southern and western counties

(vireo males and females are colored much alike)

SOLITARY VIREO
Vireo solitarius plumbeus
Length 5.6 inches

A very common and tame species in the scrub oak-ponderosa pine associations of Colorado during the breeding season. The males have the delightful habit of singing on the nest as they share the responsibility of incubation

PHILADELPHIA VIREO
Vireo philadelphicus
Length 4.5–5.25 inches

A species which migrates chiefly through the Mississippi River basin westward to Kansas and Nebraska, which has been observed several times in Colorado. Because of the similarity of this small vireo to the larger Red-eyed, it easily could be overlooked

YELLOW-THROATED VIREO
Vireo flavifrons
Length 5.50–6 inches

This colorful and easily identified vireo of eastern states is an uncommon summer resident of Nebraska and Kansas, and a rare straggler in eastern counties of Colorado, from where there have been several reports by qualified observers

RED-EYED VIREO
Vireo olivaceus
Length 5.5–6.5 inches

A fairly common summer resident in Colorado locally from the low deciduous forests to the wooded foothills. Breeds along prairie streams, in parks of towns and cities, and in the scrub oaks to the edge of the Transition Zone

(Plate 96 by Donald L. Malick)

Plate 96

GRAY VIREO

SOLITARY VIREO

PHILADELPHIA VIREO

YELLOW-THROATED VIREO

RED-EYED VIREO

BLACK-AND-WHITE WARBLER
Mniotilta varia

Length 4.75–5.5 inches

Regular but uncommon migrant and occasional winter resident on the plains — usually observed singly, or in pairs, working up and down tree trunks, creeper fashion, where they are well camouflaged as they search for insects

(female above)

PAINTED REDSTART
Setophaga picta

Length 5–5.5 inches

This colorful species, which breeds in southwestern New Mexico, was recorded by qualified observers in El Paso Co., Colorado, on October 25 and November 8, 1958

(sexes colored much alike)

PROTHONOTARY WARBLER
Protonotaria citrea

Length 5.25–5.75 inches

A common bird of eastern states. Individuals of the species have wandered widely; they are rare in Colorado, but specimens have been taken in Arizona, Nevada and California

(female above)

SWAINSON'S WARBLER
Limnothlypis swainsonii

Length 5–5.5 inches

An inconspicuous inhabitant of moist lowlands, from Oklahoma eastward to West Virginia, and south to Gulf coast states. One specimen was collected in Prowers Co., Colorado, on May 12, 1913

(sexes colored much alike)

(Plate 97 by Donald L. Malick)

BLACK-AND-WHITE WARBLER *(female above)*

PROTHONOTARY WARBLER
(female above)

PAINTED REDSTART

SWAINSON'S WARBLER

Plate 97

GOLDEN-WINGED WARBLER
Vermivora chrysoptera
Length 4.5–5 inches

A beautiful warbler of eastern states which breeds over a wide range from southern Manitoba and Ontario south to the hill country of northern Georgia. It has been observed rarely in Nebraska, Kansas and eastern Colorado

(female lower right)

TENNESSEE WARBLER
Vermivora peregrina
Length 4.5–5 inches

Breeds from Wisconsin to New York and northward across Canada to British Columbia, the Yukon and central Mackenzie and occurs in eastern Colorado regularly as a spring and fall migrant. There are a few records for the western slope

(female at right)

ORANGE-CROWNED WARBLER
Vermivora celata orestera
Length 4.5–5 inches

An inconspicuous warbler, olive green above, which occurs commonly in Colorado during migration, and a few probably remain in the mountains to nest. The race *V.c. celata*, which is very similar but less yellowish below than *V.c. orestera*, also is a regular migrant, but is less common

(female above at right)

WORM-EATING WARBLER
Helmitheros vermivorus
Length 5–6 inches

There have been three reports from Colorado of this illusive dweller of moist bottomlands of the Mississippi Valley and eastern states, south to Georgia and Louisiana. One was found dead at Durango October 20, 1960

(sexes colored much alike)

(Plate 98 by Richard A. Parks)

Plate 98

GOLDEN-WINGED WARBLER *(female below at right)*
TENNESSEE WARBLER *(male and female)*
ORANGE-CROWNED WARBLER *(female above at right)*
WORM-EATING WARBLER

PARULA WARBLER
Parula americana
Length 4–4.5 inches

There are numerous Colorado records of this rather rare straggler. It has an eastern breeding range from southern Canada south to the Gulf coast, the nests being concealed in the trailing strands of tree lichens in the east, and in "Spanish moss" in the south

(male above)

LUCY'S WARBLER
Vermivora luciae
Length 4–4.5 inches

An inconspicuous, active little warbler of the mesquite country of southwestern states from southern Nevada and Utah south into Mexico. The chestnut-colored rump is a good field mark

(female above)

NASHVILLE WARBLER
Vermivora ruficapilla ridgwayi
Length 4.5–5 inches

Probably a regular but uncommon spring and fall migrant throughout the state. The species breeds from northern Utah west to California, and in view of the several summer observations in Colorado, it is possible a few may nest in the state

(female below)

VIRGINIA'S WARBLER
Vermivora virginiae
Length 4.5–5 inches

A common bird of the scrub oak — ponderosa pine associations of the Colorado foothills, the nests being placed on the ground under shrubs where they are well sheltered by growing vegetation

(female below)

(Plate 99 by Richard A. Parks)

Richard A. Parks

Plate 99

PARULA WARBLER *(female below)*

LUCY'S WARBLER *(female above)*

NASHVILLE WARBLER *(female below)*

VIRGINIA'S WARBLER *(female below)*

MAGNOLIA WARBLER
Dendroica magnolia

Length 4.5–5 inches

This colorful warbler, a common bird in eastern states, is a straggler over the eastern plains to the base of the foothills. The majority occur in spring but a few have been recorded in fall and early winter

(female at right)

MYRTLE WARBLER
Dendroica coronata coronata

Length 5–6 inches

A very common spring and fall transient east of the Continental Divide, and less numerous to the west. Very similar to Audubon's Warbler except for its conspicuous white throat instead of yellow as in *auduboni*

(female above)

AUDUBON'S WARBLER
Dendroica auduboni memorabilis

Length 5–6 inches

Common in spring and fall upon the plains, breeding from the Transition Zone to timberline. The yellow throat is a good field mark separating Audubon's from the white-throated Myrtle Warbler. Many intergrades, with white and yellow feathers on the throat, have been recorded

(female at left)

YELLOW WARBLER
Dendroica petechia aestiva

Length 4.5–5.25 inches

The most conspicuous of Colorado warblers, nesting commonly along the wooded valleys of the Upper Sonoran Zone, and in the parks of cities and towns throughout the state

(female at right)

(Plate 100 by Al Kreml)

Plate 100

MAGNOLIA WARBLER *(male and female)*

MYRTLE WARBLER *(female above)*

AUDUBON'S WARBLER *(female and male)*

YELLOW WARBLER *(male and female)*

CAPE MAY WARBLER
Dendroica tigrina

Length 5–5.5 inches

A mere straggler into eastern Colorado. Listed from the state on basis of one reported by skilled observers at Boulder May 20, 1953

(female below)

BLACK-THROATED BLUE WARBLER
Dendroica caerulescens caerulescens

Length 5–5.5 inches

A casual visitor to the foothills with several specimens collected and numerous observations of this eastern bird

(female below)

TOWNSEND'S WARBLER
Dendroica townsendi

Length 4.5–5 inches

A regular spring and fall migrant throughout the state from the plains into the Canadian Zone. Less common in spring

(female at right below)

BLACK-THROATED GREEN WARBLER
Dendroica virens virens

Length 4.5–5 inches

This eastern warbler is a straggler only in the state. Three specimens have been taken and there are several observations

(female below)

BLACK-THROATED GRAY WARBLER
Dendroica nigrescens

Length 4.5–5 inches

A fairly common summer resident in the pinyon-juniper associations of the southern and western counties with occasional individuals straggling northward

(female above)

(Plate 101 by Richard A. Parks)

CAPE MAY WARBLER (female below)

BLACK-THROATED BLUE WARBLER (female below)

TOWNSEND'S WARBLER (female right)

BLACK-THROATED GREEN WARBLER (female below)   BLACK-THROATED GRAY WARBLER (female above)

BLACKBURNIAN WARBLER
Dendroica fusca
Length 5–5.5 inches

An uncommon straggler over the eastern prairies
with six reports by qualified observers since 1955

(male and female)

YELLOW-THROATED WARBLER
Dendroica dominica albilora
Length 5–5.5 inches

Another straggler to Colorado, far from its normal
habitat. A dead bird was found at Loveland in
July 1956, one was observed in Chaffee County
June 2, 1957 and one at Golden May 6, 1961

(sexes colored much alike)

GRACE'S WARBLER
Dendroica graciae graciae
Length 4.5–5 inches

An uncommon warbler of the southwestern counties, which occasionally has been recorded northwest to Loveland and Rocky Mountain National
Park

(sexes colored much alike)

CERULEAN WARBLER
Dendroica cerulea
Length 4.5–5 inches

A rare straggler in Colorado. One observed in
Denver May 17, 1873, a specimen was collected
in Douglas Co. September 20, 1936, and one was
seen in City Park, Denver, May 13, 1959

(female and male)

CHESTNUT-SIDED WARBLER
Dendroica pensylvanica
Length 4.5–5.25 inches

These colorful warblers occasionally wander into
eastern Colorado to the base of the foothills but
there are no fall records. A specimen was collected near Barr Lake May 16, 1933

(female and male)

(Plate 102 by Richard A. Parks)

BLACKBURNIAN WARBLER *(female right)*

YELLOW-THROATED WARBLER *(adult male)*　　　　GRACE'S WARBLER *(adult male)*

CERULEAN WARBLER *(female left)*

CHESTNUT-SIDED WARBLER *(female left)*

Plate 102

BLACKPOLL WARBLER
Dendroica striata

Length 5–5.5 inches

An early spring migrant along the wooded watercourses of the prairie, often occurring before the willows and cottonwoods are tinged with green

(female and male)

BAY-BREASTED WARBLER
Dendroica castanea

Length 5–6 inches

This beautiful well-marked warbler has been reported five times by qualified observers. It is a straggler only from its eastern range

(male and female)

PALM WARBLER
Dendroica palmarum palmarum

Length 4.5–5.5 inches

An uncommon migrant which has been recorded in May, June, November and December. A specimen was collected near Limon May 13, 1947

(sexes colored much alike)

OVENBIRD
Seiurus aurocapillus cinereus

Length 5.5–6 inches

Warblers of this Rocky Mountain race are fairly numerous on the plains in migration, and as a summer resident in the foothills of El Paso and Douglas Counties where singing males often reveal the general location of nest sites

(sexes colored much alike)

NORTHERN WATERTHRUSH
Seiurus noveboracensis notabilis

Length 5.5–6 inches

Migrates regularly throughout the state in both spring and fall, usually individuals keeping to heavy cover in moist places along wooded stream bottoms. Breeds from northern states into Canada and Alaska

(sexes colored much alike)

(Plate 103 by Richard A. Parks)

Plate 103

BLACKPOLL WARBLER *(female and male)*
BAY-BREASTED WARBLER *(male and female)*
PALM WARBLER *(adult male)*
OVENBIRD *(adult male)*
NORTHERN WATERTHRUSH *(adult male)*

YELLOW-BREASTED CHAT
Icteria virens auricollis
Length 6.5–7.5 inches

The secretive chats are summer residents throughout the state in areas of low shrubs below 7000
feet. The males sing from perches elevated above
the surrounding vegetation during the courtship
period. Sexes similar in color

YELLOWTHROAT
Geothlypis trichas occidentalis
Length 4.5–5.5 inches

Yellowthroats are birds of moist sloughs and cattail marshes. They are common summer residents
throughout the state in their preferred habitat

(male above)

MacGILLIVRAY'S WARBLER
Oporornis tolmiei monticola
Length 5–5.5 inches

Common migrant and summer resident, usually
associated with low growth. The majority of recorded Colorado nests have been close to the
ground in gooseberry bushes. Male differs from
male of Connecticut Warbler in having a broken
white eyering, and the lores and breast of this
species have black feathering

(female and male)

CONNECTICUT WARBLER
Oporornis agilis
Length 5.5–6 inches

An eastern warbler which wanders rarely to Colorado. The male has a gray head resembling the
female MacGillivray's, with which it easily could
be confused, except the white eyering of this
species is complete, and is broken in MacGillivray's; the males do not have the black throat
feathers of the latter

(male and female)

(Plate 104 by Richard A. Parks)

YELLOW-BREASTED CHAT

YELLOWTHROAT *(female below)*
MacGILLIVRAY'S WARBLER *(female and male)*
CONNECTICUT WARBLER *(male and female)*

Plate 104

Richard A. Parks

AMERICAN REDSTART
Setophaga ruticilla tricolora

Length 5–5.5 inches

These colorful warblers are regular spring and early fall migrants throughout the state in the Upper Sonoran Zone, and a few have been recorded in the mountains. Has nested near Loveland, Longmont and Boulder

(female above)

HOODED WARBLER
Wilsonia citrina

Length 5–5.75 inches

A rare straggler into eastern Colorado. The handsome males are easily identified but the inconspicuous females could be overlooked. Four reports from the state and one specimen collected

(female and male)

CANADA WARBLER
Wilsonia canadensis

Length 5–5.75 inches

An eastern species which occasionally wanders into the borders of Colorado. Two specimens have been collected and there are several sight records, the latest June 13, 1960 at 8600 feet in Boulder County

(female above)

WILSON'S WARBLER
Wilsonia pusilla pileolata

Length 4.5–5 inches

A very numerous migrant in spring and fall throughout the state; nests commonly at high elevations of the Canadian Zone in willow thickets of boggy areas

(female below)

(Plate 105 by Richard A. Parks)

Plate 105

AMERICAN REDSTART *(female above)*

HOODED WARBLER *(female and male)*

CANADA WARBLER *(female above)*

WILSON'S WARBLER *(female below)*

RED-WINGED BLACKBIRD
Agelaius phoeniceus fortis
Length 8–9.5 inches

Conspicuous colonial nesting species throughout marsh areas of the Upper Sonoran and Transition Zones. The males arrive on their former nesting territories early in the spring, each aggressively defending its territory against invasion by other males of the species. This race is a common breeding bird of the state

(male above, female below)

BOBOLINK
Dolichonyx oryzivorus
Length 6.5–7.5 inches

Occurs irregularly throughout the state in open fields from the Upper Sonoran into the mountains to over 10,000 feet. Prefers cultivated lands for nest sites, and has been recorded breeding at Meeker, Gunnison and Boulder

(male above, female below)

YELLOW-HEADED BLACKBIRD
Xanthocephalus xanthocephalus
Length 9.5–11 inches

The Yellow-heads are the showiest of the marsh dwellers of Colorado — nesting in colonies — often in the same cattail marshes with the Red-winged, but the breeding groups usually separated. The males balance on the tips of tules or rushes, swinging in the wind, as with open beak and throat feathers ruffled they give their raspingly nonmusical notes

(male above, female below)

WESTERN MEADOWLARK
Sturnella neglecta
Length 8–10 inches

One of the most common and beautiful birds of the roadsides, the open prairies and mountain parks. The golden yellow breasts, the white tail feathers conspicuous when the birds are in flight and the melodious songs are excellent field identification characters. Many remain throughout mild winters

(sexes colored much alike)

(Plate 106 by Wayne Trimm)

Plate 106

BOBOLINK *(female below)*

WESTERN MEADOWLARK

RED-WINGED BLACKBIRD *(female below)*

YELLOW-HEADED BLACKBIRD *(female below)*

BALTIMORE ORIOLE
Icterus galbula
Length 7–8 inches

This common bird of the east has extended its range westward into Colorado where the species intergrades regularly with Bullock's Orioles. Uncommon except in Yuma and Prowers Counties

(female and male)

ORCHARD ORIOLE
Icterus spurius
Length 6–7 inches

These rather inconspicuous little orioles are numerous in eastern counties where they nest high in deciduous trees, in contrast to the low sites often chosen in southern states. They are non-aggressive and the males are tolerant of other males around their nests

(female below)

BULLOCK'S ORIOLE
Icterus bullockii
Length 7–8 inches

An abundant colorful species throughout the state from the plains into the foothills. Their characteristic pendant nests are usually placed at the tips of deciduous trees, and the singing males advertise the general nest sites

(female below)

(Plate 107 by D. M. Henry)

Plate 107

BALTIMORE ORIOLE *(female and male)*

ORCHARD ORIOLE *(female below)*

BULLOCK'S ORIOLE *(female below)*

BREWER'S BLACKBIRD
Euphagus cyanocephalus
Length 8.5–10 inches

Very common summer resident throughout the state, nesting in a variety of locations — on the ground, in bushes, deciduous trees and evergreens. They are extremely pugnacious and make themselves unpopular during the breeding season by dive-bombing any moving creature in the vicinity — be he man or beast. Often assemble in large bands in fall

(male and female)

BROWN-HEADED COWBIRD
Molothrus ater artemisiae
Length 6–8 inches

An abundant resident in summer throughout the state in the Upper Sonoran Zone to 7000 feet. This efficient parasite lays its eggs in the nests of other birds and practically all the small species of the state are imposed upon. Vireos and warblers are good hosts and usually their own young are crowded out by the larger baby cowbirds

(female and male)

COMMON GRACKLE
Quiscalus quiscula versicolor
Length 11–13.5 inches

The large showy grackles with V-shaped tails nest locally in small communities from eastern counties to the foothills. They are trim, stately, gregarious birds with glossy plumage, and often they occur in flocks of fifty or more as they search for insects in parks and upon the lawns of cities and towns

(female and male)

RUSTY BLACKBIRD
Euphagus carolinus carolinus
Length 8.5–9.5 inches

These northern nesting blackbirds are irregular and uncommon migrants and winter residents throughout the state. Rarely have they been observed in flocks in Colorado, usually only one, two or three being together. Because of their similarity to the Brewer's they easily could be misidentified

(winter male, female and male)

(Plate 108 by Dexter F. Landau)

Plate 108

BROWN-HEADED COWBIRD *(female and male)*

BREWER'S BLACKBIRD

COMMON GRACKLE *(female and male)*

RUSTY BLACKBIRD *(winter male, female and male)*

WESTERN TANAGER
Piranga ludoviciana
Length 6–7.5 inches

These colorful tanagers are among the most conspicuous of spring migrants throughout the state. They nest commonly from pinyon-juniper associations into the Transition Zone — on horizontal branches of scrub oaks and ponderosa pines. The females are so modestly dressed they are difficult to see, their olive-green plumage matching the surrounding vegetation

(male and female)

SCARLET TANAGER
Piranga olivacea
Length 6.5–7.5 inches

The brilliantly dressed Scarlet Tanagers have been recorded on numerous occasions from the prairie counties of eastern Colorado to Rocky Mountain National Park — usually just single birds. They are fairly common birds of eastern states, and the song of the male "is a loud, cheery, rhythmical carol, suggesting the song of the Robin"

(female and male)

SUMMER TANAGER
Piranga rubra
Length 6.5–7.75 inches

Common to the east and south of Colorado, only occasional birds of this species have wandered into the state. Four specimens have been collected; there have been several observations, and one was banded at Longmont May 20, 1961

(female above)

HEPATIC TANAGER
Piranga flava
Length 7–7.80 inches

This bird of the Southwest is included in the list of Colorado birds on the basis of an observation at Boulder May 15, 1956 by three qualified ornithologists. The normal range of the species is in the Transition Zone of New Mexico, Arizona and western Texas south into the mountains of Mexico

(female above)

(Plate 109 by Donald L. Malick)

SCARLET TANAGER *(female above)*

WESTERN TANAGER *(male and female)*

HEPATIC TANAGER *(female above)*

SUMMER TANAGER *(female above)*

CARDINAL
Richmondena cardinalis cardinalis
Length 7.5–9 inches

Cardinals as a species occur over much of the United States, and the clear songs of the males in late winter are reminders that spring cannot be far away. There are seven races, six with very limited ranges, but *cardinalis* is common and is extending its range over much of the eastern half of the continent. It is uncommon in western Nebraska and Kansas, and a rare resident in Colorado east of the foothills

BLACK-HEADED GROSBEAK
Pheucticus melanocephalus melanocephalus
Length 6.5–7.75 inches

A wide-ranging bird from the prairies into the mountains, the Black-headed is the common grosbeak in the state. It arrives early upon the plains along the wooded water courses and nests regularly in the parks of cities and towns throughout the state. Possibly the center of abundance would be in the lower Transition Zone where scrub oaks offer attractive sites. Both adults share the task of incubation and care of the young. A common species in states bordering Colorado

BLUE GROSBEAK
Guiraca caerulea interfusa
Length 6–7.5 inches

Colorado and neighboring states are blessed with a variety of beautiful grosbeaks and their relatives. The male Blue Grosbeaks in spring plumage are among the most colorful of the sparrow tribe. Although uncommon summer residents in Colorado, there have been many observations and numerous references to nesting — usually in weed patches or other areas of low growth — and often in *Rhus trilobata*

ROSE-BREASTED GROSBEAK
Pheucticus ludovicianus
Length 6.5–7 inches

Common locally in Nebraska and Kansas, and a straggler in New Mexico, Utah, and Wyoming. These colorful grosbeaks have been observed on numerous occasions in eastern Colorado; a few have been recorded close to the foothills, and at least two in Rocky Mountain National Park, and a male at Walden in North Park. The majority observed in the state have been males — possibly because they are more conspicuous than their drab-colored mates. Although no nests have been found in Colorado, adults have been observed feeding young

(Plate 110 by Charles L. Ripper)

Charles L. Ripper

CARDINAL *(female left)*

BLACK-HEADED GROSBEAK *(female below)*

BLUE GROSBEAK *(female below)*

ROSE-BREASTED GROSBEAK *(female below)*

PAINTED BUNTING
Passerina ciris pallidior
Length 5–5.5 inches

This southern "feathered jewel" is a mere straggler in the state. A specimen was collected in Mesa Verde National Park August 29, 1938; one was observed near Westcliffe, Custer County, in June 1958; and A. M. Bailey caught a beautiful male in a mist net and banded it, at his home in Denver on May 17, 1962. The bird remained at the feeder through May 21, and was checked on the Spring Count May 20. One recorded from Nebraska, and a summer resident in Kansas and New Mexico

LAZULI BUNTING
Passerina amoena
Length 5–5.5 inches

These buntings are among the most beautiful of the smaller members of the sparrow tribe. They are common birds of Nebraska, Kansas, and Rocky Mountain states. In Colorado they are numerous where the plains merge with the foothills at the lower edge of the Transition Zone; and on the western slope, near Gothic, they have been observed to 9500 feet. Nests regularly in low shrubs, and often parasitized by cowbirds

INDIGO BUNTING
Passerina cyanea
Length 5–5.75 inches

A summer resident in Nebraska and Kansas, and casual in New Mexico, Utah, and Wyoming. Although an uncommon bird on the eastern plains of Colorado to the foothills, there have been many observations of these buntings. The many recorded in the ten years since 1953 would tend to indicate the species is extending its range, but the apparent increase probably reflects a greater number of observers. The first nest was found near Morrison August 8, 1953 and several others have been recorded. This species hybridizes regularly with the Lazuli Bunting

(Plate 111 by D. M. Henry)

PAINTED BUNTING *(female above)*

LAZULI BUNTING *(female below)*

INDIGO BUNTING *(female left)*

CASSIN'S FINCH
Carpodacus cassinii
Length 6–7 inches

A summer resident of Colorado mountains from the foothills into the Canadian Zone, and often wintering commonly on the plains. The nests usually are placed on horizontal branches of coniferous trees, but strangely, comparatively few breeding records have been published. This bird is larger and more brightly colored than the Purple Finch

PURPLE FINCH
Carpodacus purpureus purpureus
Length 5–6 inches

This common finch of the east wanders westward to Nebraska and Kansas, and is known from Colorado on the basis of a specimen collected in Denver November 15, 1885. It is so similar to the House Finch that field identification would be very difficult

EVENING GROSBEAK
Hesperiphona vespertina brooksi
Length 7–8.5 inches

Irregular winter resident, often common with occasional nesting in the ponderosa pines of the Transition Zone. On occasion exceedingly numerous in winter in the towns and cities of the plains, and valleys of western counties, with many staying through the summer months. Photographs of adults and their young were secured in Denver in 1963

HOUSE FINCH
Carpodacus mexicanus frontalis
Length 5–5.75 inches

The House Finch as a species occurs over much of western states from Kansas and Nebraska south into Mexico. It is a very common resident in Colorado from the Upper Sonoran into the Transition Zone, nesting in cane cactus on desert flats, in cottonwoods, under bridges, and small ornamental spruces are favored sites in towns and villages

DICKCISSEL
Spiza americana
Length 6–7 inches

An erratic summer resident from eastern counties to the foothills — sometimes numerous and other years not present. Has been recorded nesting at Cañon City, Colorado Springs, Arapahoe County, Golden, and Loveland. Its preferred habitat is partially open grasslands especially adjacent to small meandering streams with weed-lined fence rows

(Plate 112 by Charles L. Ripper)

CASSIN'S FINCH *(female below)*

PURPLE FINCH *(female left)*

EVENING GROSBEAK *(female right)*

HOUSE FINCH *(female above)*

DICKCISSEL *(female below)*

BROWN-CAPPED ROSY FINCH
Leucosticte australis
Length 6–6.5 inches

While this species breeds in Wyoming, it could be considered Colorado's own high altitude bird. It is resident in the high mountains, nesting along cliffs to timberline, and wintering commonly in mountain parks south to the northern mountains of New Mexico. Its center of abundance is in Colorado

GRAY-CROWNED ROSY FINCH
Leucosticte tephrocotis
Length 6–7 inches

Two races, *tephrocotis* and *littoralis*, winter commonly in Rocky Mountain states, the latter being the less common in Colorado. These Rosy Finches occur in mixed flocks in high parks and towns of the western part of the state, and less commonly east of the Continental Divide. Both subspecies are shown on the opposite plate with *littoralis* the upper figure

BLACK ROSY FINCH
Leucosticte atrata
Length 5.5–6.5 inches

A high altitude species which breeds locally in Montana, Idaho, Nevada, Utah, and Wyoming. It winters uncommonly in New Mexico but occurs regularly in flocks with other species during winter in Colorado mountain parks south to Mesa Verde

PINE GROSBEAK
Pinicola enucleator montana
Length 8–8.5 inches

A wide-ranging species of the northern coniferous forests of both the Old and New Worlds. This race ranges casually into Kansas and Nebraska, is resident in New Mexico, Arizona, Utah, and Colorado, and is fairly common in the high mountains of Colorado, where nests have been found from 9000 feet to timberline

(Plate 113 by Donald L. Malick)

BROWN-CAPPED ROSY FINCH

GRAY-CROWNED ROSY FINCH
(race littoralis above, tephrocotis below)

BLACK ROSY FINCH

PINE GROSBEAK *(female below)*

LESSER GOLDFINCH
Spinus psaltria psaltria

Length 4–4.5 inches

A bird of semi-open woodlands of Colorado, especially where the Upper Sonoran merges with the Transition Zone. Scrub oaks and ponderosa pines in the foothills, or trees of towns and cities are favored nesting places. Because of their protective coloration, they are apt to be overlooked, but the musical voices of the males often reveal their presence

AMERICAN GOLDFINCH
Spinus tristis tristis

Length 4.5–5.5 inches

The goldfinches nest later than the majority of the sparrow tribe, and in the east preferred sites are in thistles. Willows and cottonwoods along stream beds, and ash and elm trees in parks are used in Colorado. Although the birds are fairly common, few nests have been recorded. This race occurs on the eastern plains, and western birds tend toward the light-colored *pallidus*

PINE SISKIN
Spinus pinus pinus

Length 4.5–5 inches

A common bird throughout the state from the plains into the Transition and Lower Canadian Zones, with the center of abundance in the ponderosa pine belt. They occur erratically, nesting commonly in deciduous trees or evergreens one year, but absent in following seasons. They have a jerky flight and the flash of yellow in the wings and tail is a good field mark

(sexes colored much alike)

COMMON REDPOLL
Acanthis flammea flammea

Length 5–5.5 inches

Although occasionally numerous, these brightly colored little finches are exceedingly erratic in their visits to Colorado. They have been recorded over much of the state from the plains into the mountains to 10,000 feet. The species breeds in the northern parts of both the Old and New Worlds, and the periodic winter invasions far to the southward may indicate severe weather conditions or failure of food supply in the north

(Plate 114 by Donald L. Malick)

LESSER GOLDFINCH *(female below)*

AMERICAN GOLDFINCH *(female below)*
(Winter male below female)

PINE SISKIN

COMMON REDPOLL *(female below)*

WHITE-WINGED CROSSBILL
Loxia leucoptera leucoptera
Length 6–6.75 inches

A northern nesting species of the coniferous forests of both the New and Old Worlds, this race is resident in Alaska and across Canada, and in northern states. It is a rare straggler to Colorado with comparatively few records through the years. Crossbills have the habit of feeding on cones high in the trees, making identification difficult, so it is possible this species occurs more regularly than believed. All crossbills are erratic and make journeys beyond their normal range, such invasions usually coinciding with favorable cone crops

RED CROSSBILL
Loxia curvirostra
Length 5.5–6.75 inches

Red Crossbills, as a species, also occur throughout much of the mountainous areas of the Northern Hemisphere in both Old and New Worlds. Eight races from North America are recognized and five have been recorded from Colorado. Crossbills are erratic — abundant during favorable pine cone years, with comparatively few at other times. Many nested near Denver in ponderosa pines during the winter and early spring of 1947-1948 and from January to June 1952. The common nesting form of Colorado is *Loxia c. benti,* and the color plate shows adults and a male below at the left in transition plumage.

Plate 115

WHITE-WINGED CROSSBILL *(female left)*
RED CROSSBILL *(female above)*
(male in transition plumage at left)

GREEN-TAILED TOWHEE
Chlorura chlorura

Length 6–7 inches

Ranges westward from Nebraska and Kansas, breeding commonly in the Transition Zone of northern mountains south to Arizona. A rather secretive bird, it nests close to the ground in low bushes, and seeks to escape observation by running, rather than flying

BROWN TOWHEE
Pipilo fuscus mesatus

Length 8–9 inches

These large, inconspicuous towhees are dwellers of the arid regions of southwestern states, and this race has a breeding range restricted, for the most part, to southeastern Colorado into adjacent areas of Oklahoma and New Mexico. In Colorado, nests have been found in junipers and in clumps of clematis

RUFOUS-SIDED TOWHEE
Pipilo erythrophthalmus montanus

Length 7–8 inches

The species breeds across southern Canada south through the United States into Mexico. Three of the numerous races have been recorded in Colorado, the common form *montanus* nesting westward to California and southward. Nests upon the ground or in low bushes, and males in spring have prominent song perches. A common summer resident in scrub oaks near Denver

(Plate 116 by Donald L. Malick)

GREEN-TAILED TOWHEE

BROWN TOWHEE

RUFOUS-SIDED TOWHEE *(female below)*

STATE BIRD OF COLORADO
The
LARK BUNTING
Calamospiza melanocorys
Length 6–7.5 inches

This conspicuous bunting has an extensive breeding range from Alberta, Saskatchewan and Manitoba, south into Montana, Wyoming, Minnesota, and North Dakota, to Oklahoma and New Mexico. It is a common bird of eastern Colorado. Considerable controversy was aroused when the Lark Bunting was named the *State Bird* by the Colorado Legislature in 1931, for many bird enthusiasts preferred a year-around resident, such as the Mountain Bluebird. The latter lives in the rugged, wooded terrain for which Colorado is famous — it is a beautiful colorful species at home against a backdrop of towering peaks, while the bunting is a mere migrant and summer resident upon the rolling plains. True, the black males with their white-patched wings are spectacular in their spring courtship performances, as they rise higher and higher into the blue of the prairie skies, singing as they circle, and descend with wings held V-shaped, to alight on favorite song perches. The nests are upon the ground and incubation of the five or more pale blue eggs often is shared by the inconspicuously striped female and her mate

(Plate 117 by Don R. Eckelberry)

Plate 117

LARK BUNTING
(female and male)

BAIRD'S SPARROW
Ammodramus bairdii
Length 4.25–5.25 inches

Breeds locally in Alberta, Saskatchewan, and Manitoba south into northern states, and migrates through eastern Colorado, Nebraska, Kansas, New Mexico, Utah, and Wyoming. An inconspicuous bird difficult to identify

LE CONTE'S SPARROW
Passerherbulus caudacutus
Length 4.5–5 inches

Nests in south-central Canada and adjoining northern states, and migrates along the Mississippi Valley and the Great Plains through Nebraska and Kansas. A rare straggler in Colorado, New Mexico, and Utah

SAVANNAH SPARROW
Passerculus sandwichensis nevadensis
Length 4.5–5 inches

A breeding species across Alaska and Canada south locally to Guatemala. Three races have been recorded from Colorado, and *nevadensis*, the common nesting form, ranges from South Dakota, Nebraska, and Arizona westward to British Columbia and California. Occurs throughout the state in moist meadows to an elevation of 9200 feet

GRASSHOPPER SPARROW
Ammodramus savannarum perpallidus
Length 4.25–5 inches

Widely distributed as a species from across southern Canada south to Panama and Ecuador. This race breeds from Ontario, Nebraska, Kansas, Oklahoma, and Texas west to British Columbia and California. Nests irregularly upon the eastern plains of Colorado

SHARP-TAILED SPARROW
Ammospiza caudacuta nelsoni
Length 5–6 inches

The species nests across southern Canada and from Quebec to North Carolina. This race occurs in marshes from British Columbia to Manitoba into Minnesota and South Dakota. It is a rare straggler in Nebraska, Kansas, and Colorado

RUFOUS-CROWNED SPARROW
Aimophila ruficeps eremoeca
Length 5–6 inches

A species of the semi-dry southwestern states into Mexico. Occurs in Baca County, Colorado, and neighboring areas along yucca- and shrub-grown rocky flats and arroyos

(Plate 118 by Donald L. Malick)

DENVER MUSEUM OF NATURAL HISTORY

Plate 118

BAIRD'S SPARROW   GRASSHOPPER SPARROW
LE CONTE'S SPARROW SHARP-TAILED SPARROW
SAVANNAH SPARROW RUFOUS-CROWNED SPARROW

BLACK-THROATED SPARROW
Amphispiza bilineata deserticola

Length 4.75–5.5 inches

Ranges, as a species, through the deserts of southwestern states into Mexico. This race breeds from California east to New Mexico; it is an uncommon summer resident in the semiarid portions of Colorado. Occasional stragglers travel northward as far as Denver and Grand Junction. Preferred nesting sites of the species are in cane cacti

SAGE SPARROW
Amphispiza belli nevadensis

Length 6–6.25 inches

The favored habitat of this sparrow is on the rolling sage-covered plains of western United States southward into Baja California. It is a common bird west of the Continental Divide in Colorado, and individuals occasionally wander to the eastern slope

CASSIN'S SPARROW
Aimophila cassinii

Length 5–5.8 inches

A bird of the lower Great Plains from Kansas, Oklahoma, and New Mexico southward into Mexico. It is a fairly common nesting species of the dry southeastern counties of Colorado which seems to be extending its range northward, for numerous individuals have been seen in recent years near Weldona and Fort Morgan

LARK SPARROW
Chondestes grammacus strigatus

Length 5.5–6.5 inches

Very common, with a wide breeding range across southern Canada south through the United States into Mexico. This race occurs from western Nebraska, Kansas, and New Mexico to California. In Colorado the nests, from the plains into the foothills, are placed upon the ground, usually at the base of shrubs or near flowering plants. The rounded, white-tipped tails, conspicuous in flight, are excellent field marks

VESPER SPARROW
Pooecetes gramineus confinis

Length 6–6.5 inches

An abundant sparrow, as a species, across Canada and northern states during the nesting season. Breeds in Colorado from low elevations into the foothills; nests upon the ground and assembles in flocks after breeding season, usually being conspicuous along highways, the white outer tail feathers showing when the birds are in flight

(Plate 119 by R. M. Mengel)

BLACK-THROATED SPARROW

SAGE SPARROW   CASSIN'S SPARROW

LARK SPARROW   VESPER SPARROW

(sexes of each species colored much alike)

OREGON JUNCO
Junco oreganus
Length 5–6 inches

Eight races have been recognized, four of which have been recorded from Colorado during migration and winter. They are so similar it is difficult, or impossible, to separate satisfactorily the forms in the field. Possibly the most common in this and neighboring states is *J.o. mearnsi* with its light gray head and pink sides; *J.o. montanus* also a very common bird, differs from *mearnsi* in having a darker head, while the *J.o. shufeldti,* colored like *montanus* but slightly smaller occurs casually, for it has a more westerly distribution. It has been suggested that the *oreganus* Juncos and others now considered as species should be considered as races of *Junco hyemalis*

GRAY-HEADED JUNCO
Junco caniceps caniceps
Length 5.5–6 inches

A common nesting species of the Upper Transition and Canadian Zones mountainous areas of western states, wintering at lower elevations within the breeding areas. Numerous nests, containing four to five eggs, nicely concealed in vegetation, have been found west of Denver at 10,000 feet or higher, with one located above timberline. A juvenile is shown at left

SLATE-COLORED JUNCO
Junco hyemalis hyemalis
Length 5.5–6 inches

A common winter resident of Kansas, Nebraska, and Colorado, and less numerous in New Mexico, Utah, and Wyoming. The species breeds in the boreal forests of Alaska and Canada south into eastern mountains, and winters south of the nesting range, chiefly east of the Rockies to the Gulf coast into Mexico. Three races are recognized

WHITE-WINGED JUNCO
Junco aikeni
Length 6–6.5 inches

This large, light-colored junco, with a limited breeding range in Montana, Wyoming, South Dakota, and Nebraska, is a winter resident in Colorado from the plains into the mountains, its center of abundance being along warm hillsides of the Transition Zone

(Plate 120 by Donald L. Malick)

OREGON JUNCO
(male J.o. montanus, female below)   *(male J.o. mearnsi)*
SLATE-COLORED JUNCO   GRAY-HEADED JUNCO *(juvenile at left)*
WHITE-WINGED JUNCO

CHIPPING SPARROW
Spizella passerina boreophila
Length 5–6 inches

Very common species from Canada south throughout the United States into Central America. This is a northern breeding race, ranging from the Yukon and British Columbia east to the Dakotas and Nebraska. It nests commonly in Colorado from the plains of the east and valleys of the west into the Transition Zone. The conspicuous rufous crown, the gray unmarked breast and line over eye, and white throat and wing bars are excellent field marks

TREE SPARROW
Spizella arborea ochracea
Length 5.5–6.5 inches

Nests in Alaska and Canada and winters into the United States south to California, Arizona, and Texas. In Colorado a common winter resident at low elevations into the foothills. Has rufous crown and white wing bars but is distinguished from the Chipping Sparrow by being slightly larger, by lack of white line over eye and white throat, and has a conspicuous dark spot on gray breast

FIELD SPARROW
Spizella pusilla arenacea
Length 5.5–6 inches

Occurs from Montana east to Quebec and south to the Gulf coast. This subspecies has a comparatively limited breeding range from Montana to North Dakota south to Kansas and Oklahoma. An uncommon summer resident on the eastern plains of Colorado

BREWER'S SPARROW
Spizella breweri breweri
Length 5–5.5 inches

Ranges in summer from British Columbia and Alberta to Saskatchewan, and North and South Dakota south to Arizona and California. A very common summer resident throughout Colorado in sage, mountain mahogany, currant, or other low growth. Differs from the Clay-colored Sparrow in having fine head streaks and lacking definite cheek patch

CLAY-COLORED SPARROW
Spizella pallida
Length 5–5.5 inches

Breeds across Canada and locally in many northern states. A common migrant in eastern counties of Colorado, and in Nebraska and Kansas, but no breeding records. This species averages smaller than the Chipping Sparrow, the plain breast is less gray, and there is a conspicuous cheek patch with dark lines above and below

(Plate 121 by Donald L. Malick)

CHIPPING SPARROW

TREE SPARROW

FIELD SPARROW

BREWER'S SPARROW

CLAY-COLORED SPARROW

WHITE-THROATED SPARROW
Zonotrichia albicollis

Length 6–7 inches

Breeds from North Dakota to West Virginia and northward through Canada to the Yukon and Mackenzie. Occurs regularly in migration in Nebraska, Kansas, Wyoming, and New Mexico, wintering from California, Colorado, and Kansas east to New York, and eastern Canada south to the Gulf coast into Mexico

GOLDEN-CROWNED SPARROW
Zonotrichia atricapilla

Length 6–7 inches

Ranges in summer from northwestern Alaska south to British Columbia, Alberta, and Washington. Considered an uncommon or rare winter visitor in Colorado, probably on both sides of the Continental Divide, but immatures and adults in winter dress would be hard to recognize when associated with other members of the genus. Three specimens have been taken in the state, and there are several observations. The species occurs as stragglers in Nebraska, New Mexico, and Utah

WHITE-CROWNED SPARROW
Zonotrichia leucophrys

Length 6–7 inches

Common nesting species of Colorado at high altitudes. The immatures with buff lines through the eyes and the males with the white lines are the migrant *Z.l. gambelii* from the northwestern half of the continent, while the adult shown on the plate with the black lores (*Z.l. leucophrys*) breeds in the eastern half of Canada, southern Alberta and Saskatchewan, and on mountain summits of western states, from 9000 feet to above timberline

HARRIS' SPARROW
Zonotrichia querula

Length 7–7.5 inches

These Canadian nesting sparrows occur irregularly on the eastern plains of Colorado as migrants and uncommon winter residents. Their large size and dark head markings serve to distinguish them from the more common White-crowned Sparrows with which they usually associate in scattered flocks. They are migrants and winter residents in Nebraska, Kansas, New Mexico, and Utah

(Plate 122 by Donald L. Malick)

Plate 122

WHITE-THROATED SPARROW *(immature left)*

GOLDEN-CROWNED SPARROW *(immature left)*

WHITE-CROWNED SPARROW
(immature above; gambelii middle; leucophrys below)

HARRIS' SPARROW *(female left)*

SWAMP SPARROW
Melospiza georgiana ericrypta
Length 5–5.5 inches

Inconspicuous in their brushy or moist habitat. Swamp Sparrows migrate regularly down the eastern plains of Colorado and adjoining states, the comparatively few records being due to scarcity of observers rather than birds. Three races are recognized, and this subspecies has a more northerly distribution in summer than the others

SONG SPARROW
Melospiza melodia
Length 5.5–6 inches

Like the Fox Sparrow, these birds break into many geographic races (thirty-one subspecies given in the Check-list), of which at least three have been reported from this and neighboring states. The common nesting form of Colorado (*M.m. montana*) breeds along moist wooded banks of the Upper Sonoran Zone into the Transition Zone to an altitude of over 7000 feet

LINCOLN'S SPARROW
Melospiza lincolnii alticola
Length 5.5–6 inches

Two of the three races of the Lincoln's Sparrow have been recorded from Colorado. *M.l. lincolnii*, which breeds in Alaska and Canada, apparently occurs in Nebraska, Wyoming, Colorado, and New Mexico as a migrant, and *M.l. alticola* is the breeding form of many mountainous areas of the west. The two races cannot be separated in field observations

FOX SPARROW
Passerella iliaca
Length 6.5–7.5 inches

The species ranges throughout North America. Eighteen races are recognized in the Check-list, two of which have been recorded from Colorado, *P.i. zaboria* shown above, and *P.i. schistacea* below, formerly known as the Slate-colored Fox Sparrow, which is the common nesting form of Wyoming and Colorado. The eastern race has a brighter plumage than the grayer mountain form

(Plate 123 by Donald L. Malick)

SWAMP SPARROW *(immature below)*

LINCOLN'S SPARROW

SONG SPARROW

FOX SPARROW
(race zaboria above, schistacea below)

CHESTNUT-COLLARED LONGSPUR
Calcarius ornatus
Length 5.5–6.5 inches

Breeds in southern Canada on the plains of Alberta, Saskatchewan, and Manitoba south to Wyoming, Colorado, Nebraska, and Minnesota, and is a common migrant in Nebraska and Kansas. Nests in northeastern Colorado in a limited area in Weld County adjacent to the Wyoming-Colorado state line

McCOWN'S LONGSPUR
Rhynchophanes mccownii
Length 5.5–6 inches

A plains bird with a comparatively restricted breeding range from Alberta, Saskatchewan, and Manitoba south to Wyoming, Colorado, North Dakota, and Nebraska. It is a common form of the northeastern prairies of Colorado during summer, and a few winter

LAPLAND LONGSPUR
Calcarius lapponicus alascensis
Length 6–7 inches

A common but irregular local wintering species in Wyoming, Colorado, Nebraska, and Kansas, this far north summer resident is uncommon in New Mexico and Utah. They appear on their fall migration in October, and may be abundant until early March. This race is paler than *lapponicus* which breeds in eastern Canada and in high latitudes of the Old World

SNOW BUNTING
Plectrophenax nivalis nivalis
Length 6.5–7.5 inches

An uncommon migrant and winter resident in Colorado and adjacent states. This cosmopolitan species, which breeds abundantly at high latitudes of both the New and Old Worlds, probably nests farther north than any other passerine species

(Plate 124 by Donald L. Malick)

CHESTNUT-COLLARED LONGSPUR *(female below)* McCOWN'S LONGSPUR *(female below)*

LAPLAND LONGSPUR *(winter left)*

SNOW BUNTING *(female left)*